The spoken word

MANCHESTER
UNIVERSITY PRESS

Politics, culture and society in early modern Britain

General Editors
PROFESSOR ANN HUGHES
DR ANTHONY MILTON
PROFESSOR PETER LAKE

This important series publishes monographs that take a fresh and challenging look at the interactions between politics, culture and society in Britain between 1500 and the mid-eighteenth century. It counteracts the fragmentation of current historiography through encouraging a variety of approaches which attempt to redefine the political, social and cultural worlds, and to explore their interconnection in a flexible and creative fashion. All the volumes in the series question and transcend traditional interdisciplinary boundaries, such as those between political history and literary studies, social history and divinity, urban history and anthropology. They thus contribute to a broader understanding of crucial developments in early modern Britain.

Already published in the series

Leicester and the Court: essays on Elizabethan politics SIMON ADAMS

Ambition and failure in Stuart England: the career of John, first Viscount Scudamore IAN ATHERTON

The idea of property in seventeenth-century England: tithes and the individual LAURA BRACE

Betting on lives: the culture of life insurance in England, 1695–1775 GEOFFREY CLARK

Home divisions: aristocracy, the state and provincial conflict THOMAS COGSWELL

A religion of the Word: the defence of the reformation in the reign of Edward VI CATHARINE DAVIES

Cromwell's major-generals: godly government during the English Revolution CHRISTOPHER DURSTON

Urbane and rustic England: cultural ties and social spheres in the provinces, 1660–1750 CARL B. ESTABROOK

The English sermon revised: religion, literature and history, 1600–1750 LORI ANNE FERRELL *and* PETER MCCULLOUGH (*eds*)

Londinopolis: essays in the cultural and social history of early modern London PAUL GRIFFITHS *and* MARK JENNER (*eds*)

Inventing a republic: the political culture of the English Commonwealth, 1649–1653 SEAN KELSEY

The boxmaker's revenge: 'orthodoxy', 'heterodoxy' and the politics of the parish in early Stuart London PETER LAKE

Theatre and empire: Great Britain on the London stages under James VI and I TRISTAN MARSHALL

Courtship and constraint: rethinking the making of marriage in Tudor England DIANA O'HARA

Communities in early modern England: networks, place, rhetoric ALEXANDRA SHEPARD *and* PHILIP WITHINGTON

Aspects of English Protestantism, c. 1530–1700 NICHOLAS TYACKE

Political passions: gender, the family and political argument in England, 1680–1714 RACHEL WEIL

The spoken word

Oral culture in Britain 1500–1850

edited by
Adam Fox and Daniel Woolf

Manchester
University Press

Manchester and New York

distributed exclusively in the USA by Palgrave

Published by Manchester University Press
Oxford Road, Manchester M13 9NR, UK
and Room 400, 175 Fifth Avenue, New York, NY 10010, USA
www.manchesteruniversitypress.co.uk

Distributed exclusively in the USA by
Palgrave, 175 Fifth Avenue, New York,
NY 10010, USA

Distributed exclusively in Canada by
UBC Press, University of British Columbia, 2029 West Mall,
Vancouver, BC, Canada V6T 1Z2

British Library Cataloguing-in-Publication Data
A catalogue record for this book is available from the British Library

Library of Congress Cataloging-in-Publication Data applied for

ISBN 0 7190 5746 9 *hardback*
0 7190 5747 7 *paperback*

First published 2002

10 09 08 07 06 05 04 03 02 10 9 8 7 6 5 4 3 2 1

Typeset in Scala with Pastonchi display
by Carnegie Publishing, Lancaster
Printed in Great Britain
by Bookcraft (Bath) Ltd, Midsomer Norton

Contents

Preface and acknowledgments

THE ORIGINS of this volume lie in the desire of the editors, both historians of England with an interest in the oral culture of the early modern era, to situate their subject in a wider British context. This is in keeping with a major thrust of British historiography in the last decade and a half, which has increasingly stressed the importance of taking Scotland, Wales and Ireland into account. We reached the decision early on that Scotland and Wales alone would provide sufficient material for an already lengthy volume, but there is no question that Irish material could usefully have been brought to bear here, and at least one contributor, Martin MacGregor, treats it in passing below. We have likewise taken a long, rather than a short, view of the appropriate time period for discussion; although many of the essays rest squarely in the sixteenth and seventeenth centuries, others range earlier and later, in one case as far as the early twentieth century.

Further contexts for the book are provided by a number of other historiographical problems, not least the relations between literacy and orality, and between speech, writing and print; and those between elite and popular culture. There has been a tendency, until recently, to regard these as exclusive categories, if not poles; the essays that follow both individually and collectively emphasize the complexities of these relationships.

As noted in the Introduction, below, this book on aspects of the spoken word in Britain has been written by two editors and seven other contributors, geographically even further removed than the Scottish Highlands were from Wales or London. We are most grateful to our contributors, and to Manchester University Press, for making efficient use of email for the exchange of texts. We are similarly grateful to our contributors for their patience with our queries, and for their willingness to undertake revisions to their individual pieces in order to render them more coherent with the themes of the book as a whole. We received helpful comments from the series editors and from an anonymous referee on an early version of the manuscript; these have assisted immeasurably in revision. We would also like to acknowledge the advice and suggestions at various stages of Tim Stretton, Mark Stoyle and Ian Dyck, each of whom has expertise in related areas.

Notes on contributors

BOB BUSHAWAY's doctoral thesis at the University of Southampton was published as *By Rite: Custom, Ceremony and Community in England 1700–1880* in 1982. He has written and broadcast on aspects of English rural culture in the eighteenth and nineteenth centuries and, more recently, on the social history of the First World War. He is the Director of Research and Enterprise Services at the University of Birmingham.

ADAM FOX is Lecturer in Economic and Social History at the University of Edinburgh. He has published *Oral and Literate Culture in England 1500–1700* (Oxford, 2000), articles in *Past and Present* and other journals, and a co-edited volume, *The Experience of Authority in Early Modern England* (Basingstoke and New York, 1996).

MARTIN MACGREGOR is Lecturer in Scottish History at the University of Glasgow. Recent publications include 'Church and Culture in the Late Medieval Highlands', in *The Church in the Highlands*, ed. J. Kirk (Edinburgh, 1998), 1–36, and '"Surely One of the Greatest Poems Ever Made in Britain": the Lament for Griogair Ruadh MacGregor of Glen Strae and its Historical Background', in E. J. Cowan and D. Gifford (eds), *The Polar Twins* (Edinburgh, 2000), 114–53.

DONALD E. MEEK recently returned to the University of Edinburgh as Professor of Scottish and Gaelic Studies, having previously held the Chair of Celtic at the University of Aberdeen. A native of Tiree in the Inner Hebrides, he writes extensively on many aspects of Gaelic literature and language, medieval and modern. He has a particular interest in the relationship between Christianity and Gaelic culture in the Scottish Highlands and Islands. His most recent book is *The Quest for Celtic Christianity* (Edinburgh, 2000).

NICHOLAS HUDSON is Professor of English at the University of British Columbia, Vancouver, and has published *Samuel Johnson and Eighteenth-century Thought* (Oxford, 1988), *Writing and European Thought, 1660–1830* (Cambridge, 1994) along with many essays on literature, linguistics, and intellectual history from the Renaissance to romanticism.

RICHARD SUGGETT read anthropology at the Universities of Durham and Oxford and has been a University of Wales Research Fellow and Tutor at Coleg Harlech. He is currently an Investigator at the Royal Commission on the Ancient and Historical Monuments of Wales and has research interests in popular culture and the social history of housing. He has published on witchcraft, festivals and the social history of language in early modern Wales. Architectural publications include a study of John Nash (1996) and the forthcoming *Houses and History in the Welsh Marches* (2003).

ALEXANDRA WALSHAM is Senior Lecturer in History at the University of Exeter. Her research interests focus upon the religious and cultural impact of the Reformation in England. As well as a number of essays and articles, she has published *Church Papists: Catholicism, Conformity and Confessional Polemic in Early Modern England* (Woodbridge, 1993) and *Providence in Early Modern England* (Oxford, 1999), which won the Longman–History Today Book of the Year Prize 2000.

ERYN M. WHITE is Lecturer in Welsh History in the Department of History and Welsh History at University of Wales, Aberystwyth. She has published on religion, women and education in eighteenth-century Wales and contributed substantially to the University of Wales Centre for Advanced Welsh and Celtic Studies' project on the social history of the Welsh Language.

DANIEL WOOLF is Professor of History and Dean of the Faculty of Arts at the University of Alberta in Edmondton, Canada. He is the author *The Idea of History in Early Stuart England* (Toronto, 1990) and *Reading History in Early Modern England* (Cambridge, 2000), as well as of many essays on early modern historical thought and writing. He has also edited the two-volume *Global Encyclopedia of Historical Writing* (New York, 1998).

Chapter 1

Introduction

Adam Fox and Daniel Woolf

AS WE ENTER the sixth millennium of recorded civilization, human beings have developed a superabundance of ways of communicating with each other. Some, such as writing, are several millennia old. Most have a much more recent vintage. Printing, the mechanical means whereby written symbols are reproduced in multiple identical copies, is barely five centuries old, despite some medieval and traditional Chinese precursors. The telegraph, invented in the nineteenth century, first allowed humans to communicate with others at a considerable distance. Radio, at the start of the last century, extended that technical immediacy by allowing the human voice to be carried, wireless, across great distances. Television and film reinserted the represented physical presence of the speaking human, and their modern successors, the live videophone and videoconference, have facilitated meetings of individuals as far apart as Canada and Australia. More mundane instruments, unheard of twenty years ago, now fill our personal informational universes: cell phones that allow us to converse at a distance but no longer tied to a fixed instrument in our homes or offices; and pocket organizers that 'beam' information to each other. Above all, email has become a matter of routine for hundreds of thousands of users. (It is worth remarking that the present book – perhaps ironically given its subject – has been co-edited by two historians who at the time it went to press had not, in fact, ever met face to face, and that virtually all of their interaction, including exchanges of the text of this introduction, occurred through email and the occasional phone call.)

In the light of all this, it is easy to overlook the fundamental importance of speech, the oldest form of intelligent communication, and of its reception-end counterpart, hearing. Although modern social theorists decry the disintegration of society, or of the family, and have argued that we are becoming atomized individuals without enduring social bonds, there is plenty of evidence to the contrary. Conversation, the subject of analysis by social scientists,[1] is now much less formal than it was a hundred or even fifty years ago, and somewhat less subject to class boundaries. It is also considerably less structured by formal education and manuals for aristocratic and gentle behaviour than was the case for our more remote, early modern, ancestors.[2] We speak freely with our co-workers, our families, our friends, and to the dozens of people with whom we interact, however casually, over the course of our lives. Our topics range from the weather to politics, work priorities, gossip, our own personal lives, religion, entertainment and even once taboo subjects such as sex. The electronic and mechanical implements that we have devised to allow us to project our verbalized thoughts at others not physically in view have aided this activity, but not replaced it. One can imagine a fictional 'Y2K' situation in which all electronic forms of communication ceased to function. This would limit the choice of persons with whom we could speak to those in proximate view, but it would not affect our choice of topics or our ability to conceive of an idea and then express it.

It is not a coincidence that the twentieth century, which witnessed remarkable changes in the modes of communication, was also the century that developed theories and models for explaining how it works. These have taken a number of forms, across a number of disciplines, several of which have approached communication principally through the theoretical, philosophical, and empirical study of language. Analytical philosophy, beginning with Frege, Russell and Wittgenstein, first developed a modern logic for the representation and linguistic denotation of 'ideas', thereby setting off a 'linguistic turn' decades before that phrase became associated with deconstruction and postmodernism. Less than a century later, philosophy of language remains a vitally important if difficult branch of the discipline and has helped to spawn newer areas of study such as cognitive science.[3] Linguistics proper, which has historical origins in the study of family relationships among words, through comparative philology, has borrowed from the philosophers of language and also from psychology and anthropology. This may be seen, for instance, in the work of the American linguists Edward Sapir and Benjamin Lee Whorf, whose 'linguistic determinism' postulated that human thought was invariably constrained by the cultural categories available in a particular language.[4] In its structuralist form, descending from Saussure via Jakobson, Lévi-Strauss and literary structuralism, linguistics examines the relations not only of words, but also of grammatical structures. Noam Chomsky has famously posited an innate human ability to create a 'generative grammar' (cohering to a 'universal grammar') of which any given individual will be unaware but which enables his or her native-language fluency. A widely read recent adaptation of Chomsky's views by Steven Pinker, a cognitive scientist, has gone so far as to postulate a 'language instinct'.[5] From a different perspective, semiotics, the study of sign systems or modes of signification, has for many years ranged beyond language proper and into the analysis of ritual and popular culture. It now routinely examines non-verbal ways of communicating such as dress, gesture, visual art, and performance.[6]

It would seem that the more means we have developed to communicate with one another, the greater our urge 'as reflective, not merely communicative, animals' to understand how and why such communications take place. Perhaps the most ambitious and inclusive discipline is a comparatively new one, the sometimes amorphous but immensely popular field of 'communication studies'.[7] The Canadian historian Harold Innis (1894–1952), for instance, saw communications technology as the key to understanding world history. Innis linked different communicative processes and media (which included transportation networks) to social evolution, and in particular to the development of political régimes. Perhaps his most interesting insight was to point to the inherent 'bias' in any communications system toward either time or space. Thus, stone tablets and hieroglyphs had an inherent temporal bias, since they could endure many generations, even millennia. They were, however, not easily transportable and therefore poorly disposed spatially, which made them good instruments of central record-keeping but not well-suited for governing geographically large territories. In contrast, papyrus and paper had (and have) a spatial bias. Lightweight, they are easily transportable over great distances, but their very lightness makes them temporally ephemeral.[8]

Innis's views, like those of his younger and more famous contemporary Marshall McLuhan (to whom we will return), rely on an evolutionary model of technological progress that envisions communicative change as not simply forward-moving, but also constitutive of other types of change, social, political, economic, and even cognitive. In one form or another, this perspective has until relatively recently underpinned most accounts of media transformation in various historical periods. Thus for Innis communications advances 'caused' (in the sense of providing the necessary and sufficient conditions for) most significant political changes, though the direction of these developments was neither invariably clear nor unambiguously progressive. The advent of papyrus, for example, had a democratizing effect on knowledge in ancient Egypt by spreading information afar and beyond a priestly class. Much later, a further technological advance, the printing press, became (Innis here quotes G. M. Trevelyan) 'a battering-ram to bring abbeys and castles crashing to the ground'. Innis's work was filled with unresolved contradictions and puzzles such as this: at the same period that print was supposedly engineering the downfall of monastic and aristocratic medieval power, Innis suggested, Tudor censorship also restricted its use. This tension in turn facilitated a widespread contemporary interest in drama 'and the flowering of the oral tradition in the plays of Shakespeare'.[9]

ORALITY AND LITERACY

Within the broader study of communications, the relationship of the spoken word to other media has always been complex and problematic. As argued in Michael Hobart and Zachary Schiffman's recent survey, *Information Ages*, what we say has never been divorceable from the means by which we say it, or from the forms within which we give it expression, though the medium is not (*pace* McLuhan) equivalent to the message.[10] Plato, in the fourth century BC, recognized the impact of the Greek alphabet and of writing. He warned of the corrosive effect that the commitment of thought to inscriptions would have on face-to-face communication, and particularly on memory, thitherto the basic means of recording something said and replicating it for others not present at the original conversation. Nearly two millennia later Renaissance thinkers such as Erasmus, though they made great use of print, expressed similar concerns.[11] Rousseau, building on two centuries of European encounters with largely non-literate New World peoples, romanticized oral culture in his *Essay on the Origin of Language*, becoming perhaps the first to conceive of the oral–literate transition as an intellectual and cultural problem. This so-called 'privileging' of orality as a more natural and primary human form of communication has been a recurrent theme in Western thought, as one of its most famous critics, Jacques Derrida, pointed out many years ago.[12] There is little doubt that the ability to write and read opens communicative worlds for individuals and that it makes reliance on memory for some, though not all, tasks redundant. With each new innovation in human communications, there have been those who have regretted the passing, perceived or real, of old ways, and those who have anticipated social consequences, for good or ill.

The consideration of writing and its relations with speech present one set of problems for all periods prior to the late fifteenth century. These are by now relatively well defined, and some remarkably subtle work has been done in recent years on medieval communication. Brian Stock's important investigation of the creation of literary communities in the High Middle Ages is one example and Michael Clanchy's erudite study of the transition in post-Conquest England 'from memory to written record' another.[13] From the mid-fifteenth century, however, the issues take on a different level of complexity principally owing to the introduction of another variable in the form of a new medium: mass-producible typographic print. Early modern Europe faced a communications change that was arguably as revolutionary as the one that we have lived through in very recent years.

The impact of movable type on early modern culture has been much debated. Two scholars writing principally in the 1950s and 1960s, Marshall McLuhan and his one-time graduate student Walter J. Ong, SJ argued in different ways that the press fundamentally changed the ways in which humans communicated, and each tended to decry the results. McLuhan made the press, along with later electronic media, especially television (he did not live into the age of the Internet), the twin foci of an elliptical critique of modern culture. His work, written in a deliberately idiosyncratic and often impenetrable 'mosaic' style that has irritated many of his readers, has nevertheless exercised a continued influence on modern communications research.

McLuhan's own reputation has ebbed and flowed since the 1960s, and he is alternatively revered as a prophet of the Information Age, and even of postmodernism, or decried as superfluous manufacturer of 'self-destructing clichés'.[14] Ong, in contrast, has retained a higher credibility, principally owing to his impressive credentials as a historical scholar and the relative clarity of his thought. Ong began with a specific period, the late sixteenth century, and a particular genre. He examined the impact of printed logic textbooks, especially those of the French pedagogue Petrus Ramus, in support of a broader argument. That argument may be summarized thus: that during the later Renaissance knowledge first became cognitively 'spatialized' (Innis's earlier view on the geographically spatial bias in paper is not intended here), and conceived of as something primarily to be found 'contained' in the physical location of a book, rather than communicated dialogically. Ong's analysis of the flood of Ramist books on logic and rhetoric (the first major reform to Aristotelian systems in nearly two millennia) suggested that they considerably simplified the teaching of those subjects, virtually reducing rhetoric to a subcategory of logic. This was not necessarily to the gain of either discipline, or of their subsequent generations of students.[15] The re-orientation to spatialized knowledge diminished the age-old primacy of the human voice, 'the primordial medium of communication, the basis of all dialogue'.[16] A corollary of Ong's specific conclusion about Ramism, still cast in a McLuhanesque mould, was another, more wide-ranging, thesis: that Western culture had fundamentally shifted at the Renaissance from a primarily auditory perceptual and cognitive mode to a primarily visual one, 'and that the vehicle for this shift was the invention of printing'.[17] The interactions between the spoken and the not merely written but printed word are a major connecting theme of several of the chapters below.

Less speculative treatments than Ong's or McLuhan's abound.[18] Indeed, it is fair to say that since the Second World War, considerations of the impact of print in particular have tended to dominate treatments of communications change in past times, especially in the first two centuries or so of printing's history. (The parallel but not identical relationship between speech and writing has been given comparatively less attention, and is often subsumed.) Innis himself had already made print the *terminus ad quem* of his *Empire and Communications* in 1950, and general studies by S. H. Steinberg and by Lucien Febvre and Henri-Jean Martin followed within a decade.[19] For the past twenty years, however, much of the discussion has occurred in the spreading wake of Elizabeth Eisenstein's major study, *The Printing Press as an Agent of Change*.[20] This has sometimes been criticized for overemphasizing both the impact of the press and the objectivity or fixity of the 'print culture' it is supposed to have created.[21] Nevertheless, Eisenstein's book has had the merit of reviving discussion of issues such as the past relations of speech, writing and print during a modern cultural moment of even more profound significance for early twenty-first-century humans. According to Eisenstein, the impact of print can be measured in a variety of ways, not least in its enabling of the Reformation. Luther's revolt was more successful than that of previous, medieval, heretics because he was literally able to get The Word out, in the form of his German Bible and of hundreds of polemical and pastoral tracts. Protestant countries moved from a religion based on ritual and auditory communication with the divine through a priest, to one based on private study and devotion focused on a personal experience of the Gospel.[22] In the two centuries thereafter, print's influence spread further, creating the international learned community that was able to share experimental and mathematical knowledge (in addition to more conventional textual scholarship). It thereby facilitated the second great intellectual phenomenon of the post-Renaissance era, the Scientific Revolution.

The study of the impact of print has been renewed with vigour since Eisenstein's book first appeared.[23] During this time, the subject has to a considerable degree converged with the related histories of the book, of libraries, of reading, and of popular mentalities.[24] Select older treatments such as that by Febvre and Martin have become available in translation, along with the more recent work of Roger Chartier, the best-known of the current generation of French scholars. Chartier, like the late Robert Mandrou, has also been interested in the profound influence of printing on popular culture, as a written world associated with the literate elite collided with the oral and mnemonic world of the vast majority of the population who could neither read nor write.[25] British and North American scholars have also addressed these matters, and while the impact of print is conceded to have been immense, it has also been qualified in some important respects. In particular, the notion of a print culture that overwhelmed and eventually eradicated the oral ritualistic culture of the masses has been fairly convincingly undermined as far too simplistic. The spread of print was neither rapid, nor universal, outside of major commercial and political centres. Indeed, it did not completely 'supplant' writing as the vehicle of choice for elite literary communication, since 'scribal publication' retained a high social status among the affluent and the educated throughout the sixteenth and seventeenth centuries.[26] Even after the Copyright Act of 1710, Margaret Ezell has suggested, script remained 'a competitive mode of transmitting and reading'.[27] Both writing and print also retained some of the dialogic quality of speech in the sense that texts in both forms were routinely annotated and revised by readers.[28]

How many people were reading, and in what ways, has in itself proved very difficult to assess with much precision. European literacy was indeed increasing (much more rapidly in the seventeenth and eighteenth centuries than in the sixteenth), but both the rate of that change and what exactly was changing remain obscure, a problem to which we shall return in greater detail below. For now it is sufficient to note that the once-accepted measure of literacy, ability to sign one's name, is no longer regarded as a reliable index of reading ability, much less of full literacy; conversely, those who could not write at all were sometimes able to read.[29] The reformers who sought to spread Protestant piety and doctrine, though they stressed the virtues of education as an aid to spirituality, nonetheless recognized that the vast majority of the population that they needed to win over was illiterate in whole or part, and they quite reasonably compensated for this in various ways. Use of vivid pictorial images by reformers, ably demonstrated by the late Robert Scribner for Germany, and more recently by Tessa Watt, Margaret Spufford, Margaret Aston, Ian Green and others for the English Reformation, enabled the evangelical message to penetrate even the humblest households. Shared reading, in familial or devotional settings, provided the means to use the spoken word to bring the otherwise inaccessible printed page to the attention of those who could not read it on their own.[30] Even among those who could read with facility there are important distinctions to be made. There were those, for instance, who could read one style of typeface more easily than another.[31] A significant subset of the fully literate was 'unlettered' in the classical sense of being unable to read Latin (much less other languages.) This too is an important division in an era when literary writing was both highly allusive and often linguistically hybrid, English texts still including extensive passages and quotations in Latin and other languages.

It is not very helpful to cling firmly to the technological progressivism of the Innis–McLuhan school, for three reasons. The first is that the cognitive superiority or even modernity of one medium (writing) relative to others (such as speech) has not been satisfactorily established in any cross-cultural context, a point made most sharply by Ruth Finnegan.[32] Secondly, the tripartite relationship between speech, writing and print over the long early modern period from 1500 to 1850 – in technological terms, the age of the hand-operated press – is different from the equivalent relationship since then. (This in turn has now been further complicated by very recent developments such as the Internet, cellular phones and satellite television.) Thirdly, and perhaps most important, this same relationship can be shown to have altered and evolved dynamically at various times, in different regions, and within quite distinct social contexts – even within the era covered by the present book.

We should not, therefore, spend much more effort in re-'proving' (or even reproving) the notion of a grand cultural shift – whether conceived of as progress or decline scarcely matters – from 'spoken/auditory' to 'written/ visual'. Rather, we need to attend more closely to the ways in which writing or printing, either separately or in combination, can be said to have modified, marginalized or reinforced different aspects of oral culture. This process was not one-way, since the spoken word itself continued to inform and shape what was put into script or print. Ong himself acknowledged this in postulating a kind of 'secondary orality' detectable in literate societies, and he identified a good example of this in the form of an 'oral residue' in Tudor prose.[33] Above all, though there were unquestionably arenas of conflict between spoken and written, such as the law and custom, these are not usefully generalized into a polarized relationship which sees orality and literacy as Manichaean opposites. As Finnegan has aptly remarked, 'orality' and 'literacy' are not two separate and independent things. Nor (to put it more concretely) are oral and written modes two mutually exclusive and opposed processes for representing and communicating information.[34] Harvey J. Graff has similarly warned that 'the oral and the literate, like the written and the printed, need not be opposed as simple choices'.[35] We are much better off conceiving of overlapping spheres of the oral and the literate, within which many of a culture's communicative activities occur in different ways depending upon a variety of factors such as time, location, purpose, and the identity and status of the communicators. This is a less orderly and simple model, but it permits us to recognize differences between the forms of communication without losing sight of their similarities, their connections, or their historical mutability.[36] Within the period covered by this book, the spoken and the written or printed interacted in a complex and often circular fashion. This is not to argue that oral culture was utterly immune to the effects of writing and print, which would be foolish, or that some aspects of it were not seriously altered, marginalized or even eliminated. It is simply to acknowledge that instances of this were particular, rather than general, and that other aspects of orality adapted to a more literate environment and even thrived on writing and print, which were in turn affected in style and content by speech. In other words, the ever-increasing presence of the written or the printed word in early modern Britain cannot be assumed to have occurred invariably at the expense of or in opposition to the spoken word.

RE-CAPTURING ORAL CULTURE

The modern study of oral culture has developed quite independently of the study of print culture, but the collision of the spoken and the graphic (whether alphabetical or iconographic) in the sixteenth and seventeenth centuries has marked out some lines of mutual influence and of tension. As noted above, there has been a tendency since Plato to valorize the oral as more immediate and personal than the written, at the same time that the more 'modern' character of written communication is conceded. (The result has sometimes been a kind of 'world-we-have-lost' nostalgia for an imagined pure orality, supposedly shared by past times and by more recent primitive societies.) Social anthropologists, Claude Lévi-Strauss in particular, have demonstrated how aspects of culture, especially myth, are transmitted in predominantly oral 'traditional' societies.[37] Among the best-known studies, that of Milman Parry and Albert Lord of the poetic recitations of Slavic guslars cast new light on a much older problem, the oral composition of the Homeric poems, to which they exhibited some similarities.[38] The implications of this for ancient literacy were more fully worked out by Eric Havelock in his classic *Preface to Plato*, which examined the transition from orality to literacy in ancient Athens.[39] There are differences in the various treatments, but a common presumption is that literacy so fundamentally restructures human thought as to fossilize even an orally based subculture, turning the traditional songs of Lord's guslars, for example, away from a performative and creative process into a more straightforwardly text-emulating and recitative one.[40]

Historians have approached the problem of orality from a slightly different angle. We are naturally inclined to favour the document, even while recognizing that it, too, is incomplete, partial and selective.[41] Given this long-standing preference, we have to face the inescapable fact that societies without writing (or non-literate segments of the population within partially literate societies) do not by definition generate written records that can provide local evidence of that culture's past life, including its communicative aspects. How then to verify historical information derived from the traditions preserved by such a society? Africanists such as Jan Vansina and David Henige have addressed such issues directly, working out the structure and typology of oral traditions and offering methods by which external evidence (colonial records, or the written records of neighbouring and more highly literate indigenous societies) can be used to verify such fundamental historical details as chronology and genealogy. At the same time, they have also been careful to admit some of the problems with using oral traditions as a source equivalent to a written document (which leaves aside the issue of the degree to which documents themselves are inherently more trustworthy). These problems include 'telescoping', or the reduction/conflation of generations to fit a preconceived time scheme; the jettisoning of unwanted or undesirable forebears, and of those for whom no present trace of influence continues to exist in the present; and, of most significance for the present book, the idea of 'feedback'. This last phenomenon occurs when an oral culture comes into contact with a written one, and apparently pure mnemonic recitations are tainted with the written records generated by an alien, often colonizing, society. Vansina's and Henige's studies, among others, have also demolished nineteenth-century romantic notions of the superiority and inherent reliability of the oral tradition (the conceptual background for which is captured in Nicholas Hudson's essay in Chapter 8 of this volume) while nevertheless preserving the essence of the position that it is a usable and critically testable type of source.[42] Others have been less cautious. The fate of the African-American popular novelist and journalist Alex Haley stands as a permanent warning against uncritical acceptance of tradition as if it were a literal and verbatim genealogical and historical record – a written record minus the writing. Haley's *Roots,* a mid-1970s' bestseller and television series, appears to have rested on an enthusiastic search for his ancestral origins, sufficiently well advertised in advance that he was able to hear what he wished to hear from a well-prepared Gambian story-teller.[43]

Much additional scholarly work has appeared in the past thirty years on various forms of African oral literature and on its griots, or traditional performers.[44] Finnegan in particular has drawn a distinction between traditional (trans-generational) oral literature and that which is non-traditional. She makes the point that there are many examples of cultures with precisely memorized oral literature, composed by one group (for instance medieval Irish poets or French troubadours) and recited by another. In contrast, oral traditional literature rarely passes down verbatim over several generations, as if it were simply a memorized historical record repeated *viva voce* from the aged to the young. Nor, she suggests, does it arise from a 'people' as a generalized voice of the volk. Rather, it generally consists of a central story or message sequentially improvised upon by a series of individual performers, often in response to time-specific social situations, and highly dependent on the performer's choice of language, use of intonation and gesture – some of these, indeed, features that cannot be adequately captured in a transcribed version.[45]

The sorts of problems that the Africanists have identified can guide, *mutatis mutandis,* our treatment of other cultures. Early modern European countries were communicatively hybrid, with widely varying levels of literacy, and geographically uneven penetration by the written or printed word. We as their modern historians are highly dependent on written sources in our efforts to gain access to oral culture. Further problems arise. These written sources have nearly always been bequeathed us by privileged observers who were themselves geographically external to the oral culture on which they were reporting – antiquaries and travel writers for instance. Even more frequently, they stood 'above' that culture, socially and intellectually, however interested and sympathetic they may have been (and in many cases they were not). Yet these written testimonies are often our only means to recapture traditions, riddles, rituals and proverbs which may or may not have been purely oral in their own time, but which have now disappeared or been altered beyond recognition. The authors of another recent work on orality, who range all the way from Homer to African-American rap artists, invite their reader to step 'through the medium of print' into the 'oral world' (the singular is significant) of 'Homer, the rapper, the orators of Madagascar and Samoa, the story-tellers of Africa and the Caribbean and many, many more'.[46] The notion that all these cultures constitute a single 'oral world' is itself troublesome. So is the suggestion that we can gain direct entry to such a world through literary and archival sources. In fact, the oral worlds of the past, like other locations in that 'foreign country' and perhaps even more so, cannot be entered, at least not directly. We cannot, to paraphrase Ranke, restore their reality *wie es eigentlich gewesen*. We can, however, study the traces of that reality, the reflected remnants of those worlds, through other means, and even empathetically imagine how those worlds functioned, so long as we also recognize the indirect nature of our evidence.

ORAL CULTURE, ORAL COMMUNICATION AND ORAL TRADITION

The present volume investigates the nature of oral culture in Britain between the early sixteenth and mid-nineteenth centuries. The authors recognize that the singular 'culture' is indeed a construct, and that it is probably more accurate to talk of distinct oral cultures, not least because some very different regions and linguistic environments are involved. Nevertheless, we hope to point to some common features that justify the theoretical use of the singular, with the caution that it is virtually never monolithic in practice.

Of what does an oral culture consist? Jack Goody has recently defined it as 'a culture without writing'. Within an early modern British setting this definition is too exclusionary given the increasing number of ways in which speech and writing could come into contact, ways which increased as we move ahead within the period. But Goody immediately points out that writing does not supplant oral communication; instead it provides it with another channel, 'substituting for the oral only in certain contexts but at the same time developing new ones'.[47] It is perhaps best not to define oral culture as an identifiable social unit (that is, as an oral society). Used in that sense, Britain more realistically consisted of a number of subcultures since at no time in the early modern period was an entire region of Britain, of any significant size, utterly untouched by writing, except perhaps in the most remote and outlying regions of the Scottish Highlands and Western Isles. We prefer to define oral culture as a collection of communicative habits and practices, premissed on primarily face-to-face *viva voce* communication, and occurring within a variety of contexts. These habits and practices were more or less capable of adapting to encounters with the written or printed word.

In the case of early modern Britain, they were lived through in different ways, at different times, in different parts of the land. They were unquestionably subject to social differentiation. But if 'literate' can no longer be taken as a synonym for elite (or even educated), then 'oral' is emphatically not coterminous with popular or marginal. Speech figured in every human being's life, from kings and archbishops down to minstrels and vagrants, and for every human being it was the most routine and commonplace, as well as most powerful, instrument of communication. To be sure, certain aspects of speech were increasingly seen by the educated as inappropriate, inelegant, or rude. But others ran with great freedom between speech and writing, writing and print, print and speech, as well as up and down social strata. Nor was the appropriation of oral elements of culture unidirectional. Universityeducated figures such as James Howell could collect popular proverbs into printed editions,[48] or into private commonplace books. Conversely, literate culture frequently doubled back into speech: the origins of many Tudor popular tales about the past can be found in late medieval literary sources, while biblical episodes repeated through Scripture-based sermons exemplify the appropriation by oral culture of a literary form.

It may be helpful at this point to differentiate clearly between oral 'culture', the more general term, and other phrases, such as 'oral tradition' and 'oral communication', which are associated with but not equivalent to that culture. All of these represent a quality that can be called 'orality', in the sense that the spoken word features prominently and even dominantly. But there are distinctions to be drawn. Oral culture we have already here defined, in a sense, as the aggregate of those things which are communicated orally in a specific social, linguistic and geographic setting, together with the vocal means by which they are communicated. Oral communication is thus one aspect of an oral culture, that which involves the method of transmission. Simply put, it is a specific act, occurring within a social setting (whether predominantly illiterate, overwhelmingly literate, or hybrid). That act routinely occurs in the form of a verbal exchange between individuals, or between individuals and groups, relying principally on the human voice. (The 'principally' is important since oral communication could and did frequently occur around or with the help of written and printed aids, for instance in the preaching of sermons from notes, or in the kind of reading aloud described below in Chapter 4.) Oral Tradition in the singular, the subject of several of the essays herein, is in turn a subspecies of oral communication – the means by which a primarily or exclusively oral story, song, or saying is transmitted from one generation to the next. At the same time, one may also speak of oral traditions in the plural, which are properly considered as the narratable individual stories, songs, sayings which are to be so transmitted via 'Tradition'. A particular story about a local monument and its origins thus makes up a 'tradition' which is orally *communicated* among contemporaries but also orally *transmitted*, via Tradition (the trans-generational vehicle) to listeners yet unborn.[49]

The authors of the essays in this book use all of these terms at different points. All are part of oral culture, along with many other elements that are in other ways 'traditional' (that is, not written down but repeated across many generations) such as local ritual and custom as described below in Bob Bushaway's essay (Chapter 9). During this period oral tradition remained a vehicle of the utmost importance in the transmission of received wisdom, the creation of cultural capital and the dissemination of knowledge. But other, non-traditional forms of oral communication were equally important. This was an environment in which the ability to read was partially and unevenly dispersed throughout society, the ability to write even more circumscribed, and the capacity to print what one had written still slow and expensive. The spoken word necessarily remained the first and in many cases the only means by which the vast majority of people at all social levels exchanged ideas and acquired information.

VERNACULAR CULTURES

Oral cultures are by their very nature highly variegated. The myriad diverse communities which made up England, Scotland and Wales each supported their own quite particular vernacular repertoires which served to divide up all three countries into a series of palpably distinct cultural environments and, in each case, to cut across any sense of common national identity. Linguistically there was a high degree of variety not only between the constituent parts of the British Isles but also within them. In these, as in all other societies, the very forms of the spoken word, the vocabularies and phraseologies in which ideas were expressed, provide the most immediate and graphical insight into the mental world of their diverse inhabitants.[50]

In Scotland, the English language was already long established in the Lowlands by the sixteenth century, although many people spoke Scots, or 'Scottis', a strain which would have been unintelligible to most people south of the Tweed. Meanwhile, Gaelic, or 'Erse', continued to thrive in the Highlands and Islands, while traces of it lingered in Lowland Aberdeenshire and endured in Galloway into the seventeenth century. Communities which straddled the Highland line became bilingual or were even rent in two on linguistic grounds. James IV (1488–1513) is said to have claimed that the inhabitants of Nairn were thus divided by mutual incomprehension; almost three centuries later it would be here that Boswell and Johnson first heard the Gaelic language on their travels through Scotland. In 1655 Thomas Tucker could report from Inverness, not far away, that the town was split between Gaelic speakers and English 'such that one halfe of the people understand not one another'. Similarly, when the English antiquary, Thomas Kirke, encountered the folk of border regions between Highland and Lowlands in the 1670s he found them to 'speak both' languages but to be 'so currish, that if a stranger enquire the way in English, they will certainly answer in Erst, and find no other language than what is inforc'd from them with a cudgel'. A century later Thomas Pennant found that of the ten parishes in Caithness 'only the four that lie s[outh] e[ast] speak Erse; all the others speak English'.[51]

Nor were these Gaelic, Scots and English regions by any means monolithic in the variety of the tongue which they spoke. At the end of the seventeenth century, the Reverend James Kirkwood, a native of Dunbar in East Lothian, observed of the Lowlands that 'every countrey has its own accent and mode of speech; by which ordinarly they know one an other'. As for the Highlanders, they too had many and various dialects of Gaelic which instantly identified the origin of their speakers and abruptly made them unintelligible to others. As Kirkwood put it: 'Of their language there are several dialects, which make them to one another partly unintelligible, partly ridiculous. The purest dialect is thought to be in Cantyre, Argyle and the Western Isles. Where they confine with the Lowlands they speak most corrupt. They can discern the countrey one is of by his dialect'.[52]

In Wales the Welsh language was the sole tongue of the vast majority of the people throughout this period and beyond. Following the Henrician legislation of 1536–43 which secured political union with England, English became the normal medium of administration and law throughout the principality, a process traced by Richard Suggett and Eryn White in Chapter 2. But although the imported language was quickly adopted by the anglicizing Welsh gentry and made some progress among the mercantile and professional classes in those border regions with strong economic links to England, it achieved few inroads elsewhere. Only in south Pembrokeshire, the Gower peninsula and the Vale of Glamorgan, where English had been planted well before this period, was there any element of linguistic and cultural divide. At the end of Elizabeth's reign, George Owen could report from Pembrokeshire that 'half the shire is mere English, both in speech and manners', while 'the other half speaks the Welsh tongue'. This 'diversity of speech breeds some inconveniences', he admitted, 'so that often times is found at the assizes that in a jury of twelve men there will be one half that cannot understand the other's words ...'. Elsewhere, however, monoglot Welsh speakers were in the overwhelming majority. In 1700, 90 per cent of Welsh people spoke only their mother tongue and the figure was still as high as 70 per cent in 1800. The nature of that Welsh also varied enormously across the country, however. The almanac writer and bookseller, Thomas Jones, could declare in the late seventeenth century that there was a closer affinity between Welsh and Hebrew than there was between the Welsh spoken in Gwynedd and that in south Wales. Meanwhile it was a lament from the sixteenth century onwards that encroaching English influence in the Welsh border regions was hybridizing the speech of local people.[53]

On the English side of the border some of the same influences were felt. Bilingual Welsh and English speakers could be found sprinkled throughout the western regions of abutting counties. 'About the beginning of Queen Elizabeth's time', reflected John Aubrey in the later seventeenth century, 'Welsh was spoken in Hereford and I believe 100 years before that as far as the Severn.' In the 1690s the great Celtic scholar, Edward Lhwyd, intended to visit all those parishes 'in Shropshire and Herefordshire where the [Welsh] language and ancient names of places are still retained'. At the same time, the yeoman Richard Gough knew several neighbours in Myddle who 'could speake neither good Welsh nor good English'. Further south, in Cornwall, meanwhile, the Cornish language stubbornly remained alive among an ever dwindling minority, although by the end of the sixteenth century the local antiquary Richard Carew was already reporting that English had driven it to 'the vtter-most skirts of the shire. Most of the inhabitants can no word of Cornish; but very few are ignorant of the English ...'. Aubrey later thought that in Cornwall, as in south Wales, English 'weares out more and more ... especially since the civill warres', but he had still heard of 'a woman towards the farther end of Cornwall that could speak no English'.[54]

Throughout the rest of England a more or less common literary language had developed during the fifteenth century, while something like a standard spoken vernacular seems to have been emerging simultaneously, at least among some sections of society. Nevertheless, pronounced regional and local differences in speech would prove enduring, and marked variations in vocabulary and pronunciation created a patchwork of often quite small and highly distinct 'speech communities' across the nation. The size of such communities was estimated in 1551 by the orthoepist John Hart who reported that if people 'heare their neyghbour borne of their next citie, or d[w]elling not past one or two dais [j]orney from theim, speaking some other word then is (in that place) emongest theim used, yt so litell contenteth their eare, that ... they seem the stranger were therfore worthie to be derided, and skorned'. When the pronunciation of English was investigated more systematically in the nineteenth century it was discovered that England and Lowland Scotland could be divided into forty-two dialect districts, twenty one of which could further be divided into varieties and eight of these into subvarieties.[55]

It is scarcely legitimate to think in terms of a national spoken tongue in any one of Scotland, Wales or England in the early modern period, therefore, still less of a vernacular common to Britain as a whole. Even within the ostensibly homogeneous linguistic zone of England, communication could be a real problem between natives of different regions and localities. Daniel Defoe formed the judgement, as he toured the country at the beginning of the eighteenth century, that the dialects of the common people were as distinct as the patois spoken in provincial France. Two generations later the agricultural writer William Marshall was to find the observation no less valid.[56]

The linguistic variety within Britain was only the most fundamental and powerful expression of the richly variegated oral traditions which existed both between and within the many regional zones of England, Wales and Scotland. In addition, every speech community also contained its own distinctive repertoire of sayings and phrases, of stories and songs, myths and legends, which contributed to its parochial mentality and fabricated its distinct identity. In the case of proverbs, for example, 'it is well known', wrote one commentator about 1640, 'that everie nation hath the[ir] own proverbs and proverbiall speeches, yea everie shire or part of a nation hath some proverbiall speeches, which others hath not'.[57] Such expressions of the local vernacular culture were rarely recorded in detail: rather, they were the intellectual inheritance of generations of people who never wrote down their thoughts or expressions for posterity nor were such things usually deemed worthy of transcription by others. But like the language itself, these traditions formed a fundamental part of the perceptions and consciousness of their speakers. They were the cultural building blocks through which the sense of belonging to a particular locality or 'country' was fashioned and sustained.[58]

These distinctive 'countries', or agrarian *pays*, which disaggregated Britain's regions were as crucial in the construction of cultural identity as they were in the determination of economic organization and social structure. Many such geographical areas could be located, some of them retaining elements of particularity to this day. One such was the district of Hallamshire, around Sheffield, where in the early nineteenth century Joseph Hunter thought that 'rustic and mechanic' people were still speaking the language of Shakespeare and Jonson.[59] Distinctive countries were equally constituted of Redesdale and North Tynedale in the western highlands of Northumberland, the Wealden areas of Kent and east Sussex, or the cloth districts of the Stour valley along the Essex–Suffolk border, among myriad others.[60] Or consider the vale of Berkeley in Gloucestershire. In 1639 the estate steward, John Smyth of Nibley, penned a description of this clearly demarcated agrarian *pays*, bounded by solid natural barriers in the form of the River Severn to the west and the Cotswold edge to the east, and tributaries of the Severn marking the border with Somerset to the south and the vale of Gloucester to the north. What defined the area and its people most readily and most graphically was their particular vernacular culture, their 'certaine words, proverbs and phrases of speach' which they believed 'to bee not only native but confined the soile bounds and territory thereof; which if found in the mouthes of any forraigners, wee deeme them as leapt over our wall, or as strayed from their proper pasture and dwellinge place'.[61]

Another vivid example of such a 'country', defined not only in terms of topography and economy, but also by ways of life and modes of expression, was the north-east of Scotland. This was a distinctive border region on the cusp of Highlands and Lowlands, bounded by the sea to the north and east, by the Grampian mountains to the south and the Cairngorms to the west. This geographical isolation created a distinct cultural environment and bred a particular character among the inhabitants; it also nurtured and preserved a quite unique set of oral traditions over many centuries. The people spoke a dialect known locally as 'the Doric', a form of Scots–English elaborated by borrowings from Gaelic as well as the Scandinavian and other northern European languages, reflecting the nature of the region's contact with outsiders over centuries. Until the Victorian period, literacy levels in the region were very low and it produced little in the way of imaginative prose or written lyric poetry. But it fostered instead a rich tradition of folklore and folktale, of proverbial wisdom and vernacular forms, and above all it afforded the principal fount of Scottish balladry.[62]

In the early eighteenth century Anne Farquharson lived in the pastoral countryside of Braemar in Aberdeenshire. There she was said to have 'spent her days ... among flocks and herds at Allan-a-quoich' and thanks to 'a tenacious memory' she learned and 'retained all the songs she had heard the nurses and old women sing in that neighbourhood'. Later she moved to Old Aberdeen and there in the early 1750s she passed on 'her songs and tales of chivalry and love' to her young niece, Anna Gordon. Anna probably learned these ballads before she could read and write and even when, much later in life, she came to set them down, she did so 'entirely from recollection', for, she confessed, 'I never saw one of them in print or manuscript; but I learned them all when a child, by hearing them sung by ... Mrs Farquharson, by my own mother, and an old maid-servant that had long been in the family'. In total, Anna Gordon, or Mrs Brown as she became, wrote out thirty-three ballad stories in a variety of versions before her death in 1810 and they were later to provide some of the finest examples in Child's *English and Scottish Popular Ballads* (1882–98).[63]

Mrs Brown exemplified and bore witness to the important role played by women in the transmission of so much oral tradition. Within the home 'nurses and old women' were responsible for the dissemination of stories and songs, nursery rhymes and word games which could bear little or no relation to the world of literature and print. Children learned these things by heart and transmitted them, in turn, without reference to text. When elements of nursery lore began to be enshrined in print in the eighteenth century they represented the first full recordings of rhymes and tales which, thanks to occasional references to them much earlier, are known to have been circulating by word of mouth for centuries before. In the later seventeenth century, John Aubrey was to reflect back on his childhood in rural Wiltshire during the reign of Charles I in which the narratives and superstitions of his own nurse together with those of the other women of the neighbourhood had exercised such a formative influence upon him. 'When I was child (and so before the civill warres)', he remembered, 'the fashion was for old women and mayds to tell fabulous stories nightimes of sprights, and walking ghosts &c'. It was also common for the 'maydes to sitt-up late by the fire [and] tell old romantique stories of the old time', for in those days, 'the old ignorant times, before woomen were readers, the history was handed downe from mother to daughter'.[64]

Aubrey's nurse, Katherine Bushell, knew the history of England from the Norman Conquest down to her own day in the form of ballads and she, like Mrs Brown much later, testifies to the importance of song as a source of both edification and entertainment in all these cultures. Indeed, scarcely any aspect of work or leisure, it seems, went unaccompanied by a tune and each nation had its distinctive inheritance in this as in other contexts. 'The vulgar sort of people in Wales have a humour of singing extempore upon occasion', observed one seventeenth-century commentator, noticing how in one place 'the woemen that were washing at the river fell all a singing in Welsh'. Equally, it was said of the Scottish Highlanders at the same time that 'their women are good at vocal music; and inventing of songs'. Edward Lhwyd divided these into 'rowing songs for sea' which they called *iorraim*; any 'raucous song' or *crònan*; 'a melodious cheefull song' or *luinneag*; and 'any grave serious song', *amhran*. In England, no less, it was normal for women to sing as they sat and sewed, for men to sustain their ploughing with a tune, or for 'manual labourers and mechanicall artificers of all sorts' to 'keepe such a chaunting and singing in their shoppes'.[65]

An important element within this repertoire of popular song was that which related stories about the past. Accounts of the great deeds of former kings and national heroes, yarns of the miracles performed by saints and magicians, myths about the giants and devils whose extraordinary deeds helped to explain so much of the physical landscape in which people lived, all provided significant components of these varied oral cultures.[66] Thus, at the beginning of the seventeenth century the people of north Wales were reported to climb their hilltops on Sundays and listen to

> theire harpers and crowthers singe them songs of the dooings of theire ancestors ... and then they ripp upp theire petigres at lenght howe eche of them is discended from those theire ould princes. Here alsoe they spende theire time in hearinge some part of the lives of ... the intended prophets and saincts of that cuntrie.

Equally, in the 1560s the Scottish Highland bards were said to 'maintain and improve' old 'tales composed about ... the sons of Milesius and about the heroes and Fionn mac Cumhaill and his warriors'. At the end of the seventeenth century, it was claimed of the Highland people in general that they sing verses 'containing for the most part praises of valiant men, and there is almost no other argument of which their rhimes are composed'. In the north of England, it was later remembered, 'the winter evenings were often spent in listning to the traditionary tales and songs, relating to men who had been eminent for their prowess and bravery in the border wars'.[67]

THE SCRIBAL TRADITION

The importance of the spoken word in fashioning the mental world of most of the partially literate populations of England, Scotland and Wales in this period can scarcely be doubted. These references to the performances of bards, however, draw attention to the fact that much of the repertoire of story and song, phrase and fable, which was passed on one to another by word of mouth was by no means the pure water of unmediated oral tradition. A large part, indeed perhaps the majority, of the material which came to infuse the common stock was the product, at one remove or another, of a long heritage which derived from the highly learned and literate traditions of bardic and monastic culture. Wales and Scotland had supported since the early Middle Ages elite orders of hereditary bardic families whose written compositions in verse had enshrined the early histories and legends of these countries, setting on foot stories and songs which passed from their texts into the fireside narratives of the people and provided such a stimulus to local folklore.[68]

In 1693 Dr James Garden, Professor of Theology at King's College, Aberdeen, penned an account of the bards of the *Gàidhealtachd*, or Gaelic Scotland. His source was 'a gentleman's son in Strathspey' who was able to offer an account of them 'as they are at present in these parts, and such as they were within the memory of my informer's father (who is an aged man of ninetie seaven years)'. He described the skilled poets, or *phili*, who 'frequent onlie the company of persons of qualitie and each of them has some particular person whom he owns his master'.

> These bards in former times used to travel in companies, sometimes 40, 50, 60 persons between men, wives and childrene, and they were thus ranked. The first were termed *philies*, i.e. poets, and they were divided thus – some made panagyricks onlie, others made onlie satyrs. The second degree consisted of those called *skealichin* or *sheanachin*, i.e. narrators of antiquitie and old historie, especialie geneoligies of great persons and families, *skealich* or *sheanachi* properlie signifieing ane historian. The third order contained [those] named *kreahkirin*, i.e. such as could discourse on anie short or transient subject, told newes and such modern things, *kreahkish* properlie signifieing anie discourse. And the fourth consisted of those named *kheahkirin*, i.e. such as proponed enigmaes and othere difficult questions, *kheahkir* intimating one that delights to invade others with subtilities and ambiguous questions.[69]

In addition to these highly skilled literati, of course, were many common minstrels and harpers, whom Garden branded the 'inferior sort, otherwise called beggers', and who make 'few or no verses or rhymes of their own, but onlie makes use of such as hath been composed by others'. But such popular performers, whose fortunes in sixteenth-century Wales are described by Richard Suggett in Chapter 5, played a crucial role as cultural mediators, serving to disseminate the remnants of high bardic production among a wider audience.[70]

Thus, in the Highlands and Islands of Scotland, for example, the people told many stories of Fionn mac Cumhaill and his exploits in which common narrative threads would be woven into the texture of a particular landscape and rendered meaningful to people by being endowed with specific local associations. The origin of these traditions was, however, highly literary, deriving from the eleventh-century Fionn cycle of Irish tales in which this hero was famed for his deeds as the leader of the band of elite fighting men, the Fianna. The ubiquity of his legend in the north and the Western Isles of Scotland is testimony, therefore, to their cultural contact with Ireland and the literary exchanges in Classical Common Gaelic between them over many centuries. From such sources tales of Fionn found their way into local tradition, so that by the seventeenth century it could be reported that on high hills throughout the Highlands were 'vestiges of great bulwarks of very big dry stones, so big as four oxen can not draw. These they say, were the habitation of giants who were the attendants of Fin Mac Cûil ...'. Thus the legendary warrior, like so many heroes of popular tradition in this period, had gained, by his allegedly prodigious strength and gargantuan feats, the reputation of being a giant. Of the three cairns on the coast of the Isle of Skye the local people were said to 'have a tradition that upon these stones a big cauldron was set for boiling Fin-Mac-Coul's meat'. On the west coast of the Isle of Arran could be seen a huge cave in which it was affirmed the 'great giant' had lodged during his mighty battle there, and the stone circle on the moor to the east of Druim-cruey 'was made by the giant Fin-Ma-Coul, and that to the single stone, Bran, Fin-Ma-Coul's hunting-dog, was usually tied'.[71]

Perhaps the most ubiquitous figure in the popular traditions of England, Scotland and Wales by the early modern period was King Arthur. Here too, of course, local folklore represented the assimilation and translation into parochial settings of the products of a long learned and literary tradition. It had been some of the great monastic chronicles, most especially Geoffrey of Monmouth's *Historia Regum Britanniae*, written in the 1130s, which had contributed significantly to the propagation of the Arthurian myth across Britain. In addition to these chronicles, a variety of manuscripts preserved fragments of the ancient bardic tradition of story and song, such as the Black Book of Carmarthen, a manuscript of *c.* 1200 containing poems in which reference is made to the mystery of Arthur's burial place. Among the three manuscript collections of prose romances now known collectively as the *Mabinogion* is preserved *Culhwch ac Olwen*, probably written about 1100 and thus one of the earliest tales about Arthur in Welsh.[72]

With Malory's *Le Morte D'Arthur* (printed in 1485) the legend came to receive even more elaborate literary treatment and, recycled thereafter in poetry, prose and song, no less than in ritual, pageantry and drama, it became in its many forms a staple of the developing mass media. All of these sources provided the narrative framework both to reinforce and to invent the stories and songs of local tradition by which communities nationwide claimed for themselves some association with the great king. In the mid-sixteenth century the Welsh historian Sir John Price could endorse Geoffrey of Monmouth's fabulous account of Arthur by pointing as corroborative evidence to the great number of places and landmarks throughout Wales which bore his name.[73] Among innumerable such was the hill in south Brecknockshire 'proportionate to the dimensions of that great and mighty person', known as 'Arthur's chair', or the huge boulder called 'Arthur's stone' in south-west Glamorgan. There was 'Arthur's gate' at Montgomery and 'Arthur's hill' near Brecon; at Caerleon in Monmouthshire were inscriptions which told that this had once been the hero's home; while on top of Mount Snowdon lay the pile of stones marking the spot where, as Geoffrey had stated, he slew the giant Ritho.[74]

LITERACY AND PRINT

By the early modern period, therefore, many of the inherited forms of oral culture in the various parts of Britain were already the distillation of a long series of interactions between the spoken and the written word. The majority of people had always received a large part of their knowledge, entertainment and edification through listening to narratives and songs, anecdotes and sayings, which were either imbibed unconsciously or else learned off by heart without reference to text. But some form of scribal influence often played a part in their preservation and propagation at one level or another. In the early modern centuries, moreover, this reciprocal relationship between the oral and textual realms was to develop more rapidly and dynamically than ever before. The reasons for this were many and varied, but they included the advent of printing which enormously increased the quantity and distribution of texts from the late fifteenth century; the continued and steady circulation of written works in manuscript; and the significant expansion across the country and down through society of the ability to read.

Throughout England, many parts of Wales and much of the Lowlands of Scotland, the centuries after the Reformation witnessed sustained if uneven growth in the varied skills of reading and writing. Detailed calculations of 'literacy' levels have been made based upon the percentage of people who could sign their name on a document as opposed merely to making a mark.[75] As suggested above, these probably represent quite serious underestimates of the ability to read since all the evidence points to a diffusion of basic reading capability well beyond the capacity to wield a pen. Thus, although in England, as a national aggregate, only 10 per cent of women and 30 per cent of men could sign their names in 1640, and only 25 per cent of women and 45 per cent of men could accomplish this by the mid-eighteenth century, it is likely a majority of the adult population could read print to some degree by the latter date.[76] Behind these crude nationwide percentages, however, could lie a significant amount of social and regional variation. The gentry were universally able to sign their names by 1600, while among the professions there was near complete literacy by the same date. Craftsmen, artisans and yeomen were always likely to be more literate than husbandmen and labourers. Urban areas tended to be more literate than rural: the spectacular example was London which was home to perhaps one tenth of England's population by the mid-seventeenth century at which time some 67 per cent of its inhabitants could sign their names.[77]

These advances in reading ability were paralleled by a huge expansion in the number of printed books over the course of the early modern period. Thus, around forty-six titles were published in England in the year 1500; by 1530, this figure had risen to 214; 259 works were printed in 1600, and 577 in 1640. Given print runs of about 1,500 copies per title, it has been estimated that there were, on average, around 300,000 volumes published every year between 1576 and 1640. At the same time cheap and ephemeral prints were being produced in enormous quantities for a mass market. The four decades between 1560 and 1600 probably witnessed some four million broadside ballads printed in England. The 1620s saw the advent of the newsbook and the 'small book', or 'chapbook' as it was later known, which sold unbound for a few pence and carried a similar range of material. By the 1660s chapbooks were probably selling in numbers of about 400,000 per year, a quantity matched by that of printed almanacs.[78]

When control of the press lapsed in the middle decades of the seventeenth century some years saw up to 2,000 titles appearing. The suspension of censorship in the 1640s and 1650s also allowed newsbooks to proliferate: in 1644 a dozen were appearing in London every week selling anything between 200 and 1,000 copies each. By 1695 the licensing of the press, re-established with only partial success after the Restoration, lapsed altogether and with this presses spread beyond the capitals and university towns. Daily newspapers began to proliferate with a total of 130 newspaper titles established in England between 1700 and 1760.[79] In parallel with this, periodical and magazine publications became an established part of both metropolitan and provincial culture and the publication and distribution of all manner of books continued to increase inordinately during the eighteenth century.[80] At the same time, moreover, the period witnessed new developments such as the serialization of otherwise expensive titles in order to make them affordable to the middling sort of reader, and the expansion of public and circulating libraries in England, Scotland and Wales.[81] Popular formats, well-established over the previous two centuries, such as broadside ballads, chapbooks and almanacs were endlessly reprinted and recycled.[82]

The social and geographical penetration of such material was extensive and its contents clearly fed into oral communication, structuring its form and determining its contents. Cheap print was sold in the shops of stationers in provincial towns from the early sixteenth century onwards and was dispersed around the country, in urban and rural areas alike, by an increasing network of chapmen and pedlars. One of the many cultural consequences of the dissemination of common literary forms in standard written English was to further the progress of anglicization in Wales. During the seventeenth century English books were sold by mercers in Welsh market centres and these may have included broadside ballads, as may the packs of the pedlars, one hundred of them licensed in 1698, who retailed their goods throughout the Welsh countryside. It is tempting to wonder whether the 'poor pedlar ... that had ballads and some good books' who, around 1630, came to the door of Richard Baxter's father in the little village of Eaton Constantine, just south-east of Shrewsbury, was on his way into Wales.[83]

As Eryn White has shown elsewhere, there were at the same time significant advances in the provision of education in Wales. This cause was given an enormous boost by the Act for the Better Preaching and Propagation of the Gospel in Wales which the Puritan regime passed in 1650. It provided for the foundation of elementary schools out of sequestrated Church funds in its mission to instill Protestantism in the native population and it succeeded in establishing sixty-three elementary schools in Welsh towns. Thereafter the major initiatives were the work of philanthropic organizations and individuals: the Welsh Trust (1674–81), the Society for the Promotion of Christian Knowledge (1699–1737), the Circulating Schools of Griffith Jones (1731–79) and the Sunday schools of Thomas Charles from 1785. Their combined success in bringing basic literacy and numeracy to the Welsh population seems to have been considerable, an achievement enormously aided by the decision in the second quarter of the eighteenth century to teach reading in Welsh, the single tongue of the overwhelming majority.[84]

The impact of these developments is evident in the steady increase in the number of books published in Welsh during the course of this period. The first book to emerge from the London press in the language was Sir John Prys's *Yn y Lhyvyr Hwnn* (1546) [translates as 'In This Book']; the New Testament in the vernacular appeared in 1567, the work of William Salesbury with the help of Bishop Richard Davies and Thomas Huet; and in 1588 Bishop William Morgan produced the great literary monument of early modern Wales in his translation of the complete Bible, a text which was to exercise a profound influence on the written language into the twentieth century. Whereas the period of over a century between 1546 and 1660 saw only around 108 separate titles issued in the native tongue, the forty years between 1660 and 1699 witnessed the publication of 112. Thereafter, there were 614 Welsh books printed between 1700 and 1749, and fully 1,907 in the second half of the eighteenth century. This steadily rising output benefited greatly from the general development of the provincial press following the lapse of the Licensing Act in 1695, and Shrewsbury, Trefhedyn and Carmarthen were to emerge as centres of the trade thereafter.[85]

In the Lowlands of Scotland, meanwhile, literacy levels exhibited similar trends. In 1650 an aggregate of around 75 per cent of Lowlanders were unable to write their names, but considerable improvement over the course of the following century meant that 'illiteracy' on this measure had fallen to perhaps 35 per cent among adult males by 1760. Here, as elsewhere, women consistently lagged behind men, however, and rural dwellers always betrayed less signing ability than urban. In the mid-seventeenth century, for example, evidence suggests that 68 per cent of residents in the capital city, Edinburgh, could write their names, as against a mere 24 per cent of the inhabitants of the parish of Newbattle out in rural Midlothian. Predictably enough, familiarity with the pen also varied markedly with social status. Figures calculated for Edinburgh and Glasgow over the whole period from 1650 to 1760 indicate that while those of gentle and professional status were 'literate' in terms of their ability to sign, craft and tradespeople were on average about 90 per cent so capable, and servants only about 63 per cent. At the same time, the literacy levels for these same occupational and social groups in rural society were far lower at 95, 61 and 33 per cent respectively. The appetite for reading material was satisfied in part by books and pamphlets produced in Edinburgh which, after the setting up of its licensed press in 1507, became the centre of a native book trade. Output from the Edinburgh printers, augmented by that from the smaller operations in Aberdeen and Glasgow, began to increase significantly from the 1670s and thereafter grew rapidly throughout the eighteenth century.[86]

In the Scottish Highlands, by contrast, there persisted throughout this period and beyond an oral culture much less influenced by the written word. The ability to read and write Gaelic remained the preserve of a few literati and although a variety of manuscript works both in poetry and prose were written in this tongue over the course of the early modern centuries, one category of which is given detailed treatment in Martin MacGregor's essay (Chapter 7), it was barely a language of print. During the late 1680s and early 1690s, the efforts of Robert Boyle, aided by James Kirkwood and Robert

Kirk, had succeeded in transcribing into Latin type the Irish Gaelic Bible translated by James Ussher in 1603, and had disseminated it with limited success across the Highlands. But even this did not represent the current spoken tongue of the people. The first printed book in Scottish Gaelic had been John Carswell's translation of the *Book of Common Order*, the 'Foirm na n-Urrnuidheadh', published in Edinburgh in 1567. An edition of the Psalms in the language was printed in 1690 but the first New Testament thus rendered did not appear until 1767 and a complete version of the Bible had to wait until the beginning of the nineteenth century, as Donald Meek explains below. Indeed, there were no more than seventy titles sent to the press in the Scottish Gaelic language before 1800.[87] In the 1770s, Dr Johnson articulated the common, although erroneous, belief about Scottish Gaelic when he dismissed it as 'the rude speech of a barbarous people', for reason

> that the Earse never was a written language; that there is not in the world an Earse manuscript a hundred years old; and that the sounds of the Highlanders were never expressed by letters, till some little books of piety were translated, and a metrical version of the Psalms was made by the Synod of Argyle. Whoever therefore now writes in this language, spells according to his own perception of the sound, and his own idea of the power of the letters. The Welsh and the Irish are cultivated tongues. The Welsh, two hundred years ago, insulted their English neighbours for the instability of their orthography; while the Earse merely floated in the breath of the people, and could therefore receive little improvement.[88]

It is hardly surprising therefore that there should have been high degrees of illiteracy among Gaelic speakers. The attempt to reform the 'heathenism' of the Highlands through a process of education which had begun with James VI and I's edict of 1616 was always partial in its reach and limited in its success. In addition to the problems of the lack of an educated ministry and the truncated efforts to found parochial schools, the texts of instruction were all in English, meaning that, as Johnson realized, those children who did receive instruction learned to 'read a language which they may never use or understand'. Predictably enough, therefore, the *Statistical Account* of the Isle of Harris in the 1790s revealed that of the 2,536 inhabitants, only 108 could read or write and that these inabilities were particularly acute among the Gaelic-speaking population. Another survey undertaken in the first decades of the nineteenth century found that 86 per cent of the 22,501 people living in seven West Highland parishes could read neither Gaelic nor English. This literacy divide added a further dimension to the linguistic, cultural and socio-economic factors which partitioned Highland regions from Lowland within Scotland. Based on the evidence of ability to write a signature, it has been calculated that by the mid-eighteenth century adult males in the Highlands were 20–30 per cent less 'literate' than those in the Lowlands.[89]

The experience of the Highlands notwithstanding, the significant developments, both in the expansion of reading ability and in the mass production of cheap printed matter, were to have enormous influence on the cultures of most parts of Britain during the early modern period. On the one hand, elements from oral tradition were taken up by the new medium of print and disseminated over a much wider area than ever before; on the other hand, new material from print fed into oral circulation, greatly expanding the repertoire of the spoken word and enriching its contents. Many instances of the reciprocal borrowings of oral, scribal and print culture could be cited which demonstrate the way in which the written word drew upon the spoken and, in turn, had a considerable impact in structuring the form of the common vernacular stock.

Thus in Lowland Scotland, for example, the complex interaction between printed, manuscript and oral forms of transmission, is evident from the first introduction of the press to Edinburgh. In the second decade of the sixteenth century, Sir David Lindsay was a 'familiar' at the court of the young James V of Scotland (1513–42). In the 'epistle' prefacing his *Dreme* he referred to the way in which he would lull the boy king to sleep with a variety of 'stories amiabyll'. Some were part of the great tradition of classical mythology, including the legends of Hector and Alexander, of Hercules and Sampson. But his repertoire also incorporated narratives closer to home, such as the deeds of King Arthur, and 'the prophiseis of Rymour, Beid, and Marlyng', which were finding their way into print by this time. In addition, among the 'mony vther plesand storye' which he would tell his charge was that of 'the reid etin and the gyir carlyng'. In this case, no written text of the old Scottish fairytale 'The red giant and the old witch' survives from the period and it may actually have been the product of essentially oral dissemination, although certainly drawing upon motifs long known to literary tradition. Scribal copies were clearly made at some date but the tale was not printed until the 1820s when the Edinburgh publisher Robert Chambers transcribed it from a 'curious manuscript collection'. He found this refrain put in the mouth of the red etin, a three-headed ogre:

> Snouk but and snouk ben,
> I find the smell of an earthly man;
> Be he living, or be he dead,
> His heart this night shall kitchen my bread.

Clearly this rhyme, like its equivalent south of the border, had a long career before it ever made it to the press: 'Fy, fa, fum, I smell the bloud of an English-man' was first referred to in the 1590s but was not given full literary context until *The History of Jack and the Giants* was published as a chapbook in the early eighteenth century.[90]

Another frequenter of James V's court was the priest Sir James Inglis. It is he who probably wrote the treatise *The Complaynt of Scotlande* which was first printed in Edinburgh in 1548. In it he depicted a group of shepherds who decide that each one of them shall 'tel ane gude tayl or fabil, to pas the tyme quhil euyn'. Of these 'sum vas in prose, and sum vas in verse: sum var storeies and sum var flet taylis'. They too knew 'the taiyl of the reyde eyttyn viтht the thre heydis', together with the rest of the stories which Sir David Lyndsay had told his young master. Moreover, they were said to be conversant with other apparently indigenous Scottish fairytales, seemingly the preserve of oral transmission. Among them was 'the tail of the pure tynt', the native version of 'Cinderella', and 'the tayl of the velle of the varldis end', another classic type about a wicked queen and her horrid daughter who send the good daughter of the king to fetch a bottle of water. Both of these similarly evade literary form until Chambers transcribed them from word of mouth in nineteenth-century Fife as 'Rashie-Coat' and 'The wal at the warld's end'.[91]

At the same time, the remarkable repertoire of the shepherds included some tales which seem only to have been known from manuscript circulation, the references to them here predating their first known appearance in print. Still other items which they knew were clearly drawn from the stock of vernacular romances, histories and verses to be put in print in the late fifteenth and early sixteenth centuries. They told tales of 'the Bruce' which were first given literary expression in the late fourteenth-century verses of John Barbour, archdeacon of Aberdeen, but not known in a printed copy before about 1570. They related the acts and deeds of William Wallace, recorded in a single surviving manuscript of 1488 and first printed at the press of Walter Chepman and Andrew Myllar 'in the south gait of Edinbrugh' in 1508. Among the Arthurian tradition which was also finding its way from script to print, the shepherds knew 'The tail of Syr Euan, Arthours knycht', 'Arthour knycht he raid on nycht', and 'Arthour of litil bertangye'. Some of the great stories of Anglo-Norman romance literature, such as 'The tayl of the four sonnis of Aymon', 'Claryades and Maliades' and 'Beuis of Southamptoun' were equally said to be at their fingertips, perhaps derived from their earliest printed forms.[92]

Among the songs which the shepherds sang were those which were probably already known to the printed word. 'O lusty maye, vitht flora quene' was one such to have emerged from the press of Chepman and Myllar in 1508. 'Robene Hude' was in print at least as early as 1510 as *A Gest of Robyn Hode*. In 'The hunttis of cheuet', or *Chevy Chase*, they intoned a famous ballad which was probably another of those familiar in printed form by this time. Also in their repertoire was 'The battel of the hayrlau', commemorating an epic conflict of 1411 between feuding lairds, the earl of Mar and Donald of the Isles, while 'Ihonne Ermistrangis dance' probably celebrated the exploits of the notorious border reiver Johnie Armstrong of Gilknockie, hanged by

James V about 1529. Both of these ballads may also have been part of the printed stock. So, too, 'Stil vndir the leyuis grene', 'Cou thou me the raschis grene', and 'Brume brume on hil', which were among eight of the shepherds' songs or tunes said to have been works owned by the mason of Coventry, Captain Cox, as described by Robert Laneham in the 1570s.[93]

In a number of cases the shepherds sang refrains which had been included in the collection of *The Gude and Godlie Ballets* first compiled by John Wedderburn of Dundee around 1542. This anthology comprised translations of German psalmes and paraphrases but it also drew on traditional Scottish tunes and adapted the form of familiar native ballads. Thus the shepherds knew, as did Wedderburn, 'Allone i veip in grit distres', 'Rycht soirly musing in my mynde', 'O myne hart, hay, this is my sang', 'Greuit is my sorrou' and 'Allace, that samyn sueit face'. After the Reformation of 1560, the Scottish Kirk adopted a strategy of attempting to inculcate true doctrine among its semi-literate peoples by employing and appropriating the genres of popular culture such as music and drama, iconography and cheap print. As noted above, it was an endeavour common to many religious reformers across Europe, and Alexandra Walsham explores another manifestation of it in the English context in her contribution to this volume (Chapter 6). Thus the *Gude and Godlie Ballets* were actively disseminated in an effort, as the expanded edition of 1621 made plain, to replace the indigenous stock of 'prophane sanges' with a new repertoire of 'godlie sangis for avoyding of sin and harlatry'. Ironically, however, the evidence suggests that in recycling these well-known themes and melodies their effect was rather to reinforce the strength of the very 'bawdie songs and rymes' which they sought to expunge.[94]

Such examples indicate very clearly that the circulation of the printed word was not something that necessarily served to undermine the vitality of oral traditions or the independence of the spoken word, but could, instead, help to augment and invigorate it. It is less instructive to think in terms of inversely correspondent relationships between oral, scribal and print cultures, in which an advance in one must entail a consequent retreat in another, than to regard these three media as complementary and mutually sustaining. On investigation, the provenance and gestation of so many elements within the vernacular cultures of England, Scotland and Wales in the early modern period prove to owe much to the augmenting influence of writing. Equally, a great deal of that which found its way into the textual realm at this time drew upon the contents of common discourse.

The extent and nature of the English vocabulary, for example, provides a signal example of the infusion and enrichment of the spoken word through the circulation of print. During the Renaissance, with the international exchange of ideas across Europe and the ever-growing output of printed books, the size and capacity of the English language was enormously increased. Some 30,000 new terms were naturalized to English from ancient and modern European languages during the sixteenth and seventeenth centuries. The new genre of English dictionaries, which began with Robert Cawdrey's *Table Alphabetical* in 1604 and culminated in the early modern period with Samuel Johnson's famous *Dictionary of the English Language* (1755) reflected the need to record, explain and authorize this expanding lexicon.[95]

By the same token, many of the familiar sayings and proverbs of English and Welsh can be traced back to dicta derived from ancient Latin and Greek authors as disseminated by the ten editions of *Adages* which Erasmus published between 1500 and 1536. These alone were responsible for the propagation of over 4,000 proverbs and formulaic phrases in early modern Europe and for the ubiquitous status enjoyed by many of the household sayings of today's Britain. Erasmus spawned many imitators and followers, such as John Heywood, whose *Dialogue of Proverbs* (1546), was to prove the starting point for the genre of vernacular proverb literature which developed in England over the next two centuries.[96] In Wales, meanwhile, the 'Welsh Erasmus', William Salesbury, published *Oll Synnwyr pen Kembero ygyd* in 1547 to similar effect.[97] In Scotland proverbs found their way into print rather later but much of this purportedly indigenous stock was no less the product of an ancient and pan-European literary tradition.[98]

The same process may be observed with respect to many other aspects of the spoken word. Thus, in the case of popular tales and stories about the past, local folklore was often less the pure water of undiluted oral tradition and more the distilled product of narratives irrigated by script and print. Thus the broadside ballad accounts of King Arthur and his exploits, such as *A pleasaunte history of an adventurus knyghte of kynges Arthurs Couurte*, printed by Richard Jones in 1566, or *The noble Actes nowe newly found of Arthure of the round table* penned by Thomas Deloney in 1603, gave an added inspiration to parochial traditions of the ubiquitous hero. Passing Arthur's seat above Edinburgh in 1598, Fynes Moryson could describe the many such monuments associated with him as 'famous among all ballad-makers', and he might have added with no less justice that they were, in turn, made famous by them.[99]

Similarly, the tales of Robin Hood were not born so much of popular oral tradition as of the literary romances written for performance among the social elite during the later Middle Ages. Thereafter, it was the widespread dissemination of his story in the famous *Gest*, which was reprinted several times during the sixteenth century, together with broadsides such as *A ballett of Robyn Hod* (1562), which ensured the place of the famous outlaw in local lore. Thus, Robin Hood's Bay is not known to have been so named before 1544 and his many 'strides', hills and mills, or the examples of his butts which are to be found in at least six counties of England, are apparently attributed no earlier. Robin Hood's grave at Kirklees in the West Riding was not so described before 1565 while the resting places of Maid Marian at Little Dunmow, Essex, and Little John at Hathersage in Derbyshire were not designated as such before the seventeenth century.[100]

In parallel with this invention and stimulation of oral traditions by the written word went the reciprocal influence of the spoken word on what was recorded and printed. The early modern centuries witnessed fragmentary elements of the dialect, proverbs, traditional tales and many other aspects of vernacular culture from communities across England, Scotland and Wales being enshrined in print for the first time. The expansion in topographical, antiquarian and travel writing which is such a distinctive feature of the intellectual and publishing history of the period was one phenomenon responsible for capturing and freezing in texts elements of popular oral tradition as they were encountered and set down by the scholars and tourists. Histories of these three nations, or of their constituent counties, towns and parishes, together with the published accounts of itineraries through parts of Britain, occasionally referred in passing to snatches of vernacular tradition and local lore, thus affording glimpses of its lineaments in ossified form. At the same time the unpublished notes and correspondence of a number of antiquaries continued to record materials that they were somewhat more reluctant to put into print.[101]

Perhaps most notably, John Aubrey transcribed a number of such vernacular forms in the course of his investigations among the people of Wiltshire during the second half of the seventeenth century. He 'rakt up' scores of legendary tales and popular stories; he committed to paper nursery rhymes and bawdy jingles, sometimes centuries before anyone else thought them worthy of recording. He noted down, amid his often chaotic scribblings, various proverbs, 'the ancient and natural philosophy of the vulgar', samples of the speech of 'the common people (whose dialect and pronunciation antiquaries are not to slight)', and numerous examples of 'superstitions' and 'old wives' tales', for 'there may some truth and usefulnese be elicited out of them'.[102]

At the same time, Edward Lhwyd began work with a team of researchers on a monumental project to record and interpret the 'ancientest languages of Britain and Ireland' and to establish the relationships between them. His method was not only to travel through Wales and the Highlands of Scotland collecting ancient manuscripts and interviewing native speakers in order to compile catalogues of these tongues, but also to gather information by questionnaires sent out to informants in the localities. 'What words, phrases, or variation of dialect in the Welsh, seems peculiar to any part of the country?' he asked. 'What names of men and women uncommon? And wherein doth the English of the Vulgar in Pembrokeshire and Gowerland differ from the Western counties, etc., of England?' In the Highlands Lhwyd jotted down the first group of Scottish Gaelic riddles ever to be transcribed and he made a small collection of Gaelic proverbs, instigating a project which was taken up by Donald Mackintosh in the late eighteenth century and completed by Alexander Nicholson in the late nineteenth.[103] So it was, therefore, that print could feed into the oral repertoire helping to invent and refashion elements within it, and, in turn, an antiquarian interest in the folk traditions of the people became increasingly concerned to enshrine aspects of these vernacular cultures in writing.

As to the wider consequences of the spread of reading and writing skills and literary culture over the various parts of Britain during these centuries, these can be viewed in many different ways and remain the subject of debate among historians. It is possible, on the one hand, to stress the essentially incorporative nature of the changes in this period and to highlight the ways in which they conspired to draw people from around the regions and down through society into a more or less common world of letters, of standardizing English and of a homogenizing cultural repertoire. On the other hand, the more divisive implications of these developments might equally be emphasized. The penetration and the impact of literacy and of the printed word were not felt with equal force among all social groups; nor were their influences necessarily the same on men as on women, or experienced to the same degree in urban and rural areas, or evenly across the country.

Thus, in the seventeenth century Aubrey had identified certain superstitious beliefs and narrative practices which he associated particularly with women. Evidence from subsequent generations of the variable effects of printed literature on men and women suggests that it may have served to add another dimension to the gender differences in this respect. What appears significant, for example, about the visit which Richard Steele paid on the children of a friend in 1709 is not just that the 8-year-old boy, Robert, was reading chapbook histories of the great chivalric heroes, *Bevis of Southampton, Guy of Warwick* and *Saint George, Tom Hickathrift* and the *Seven Champions* among them, but that the little girl, Betty, as her mother told him, 'deals chiefly in fairies and sprights'. Already, it seems, the male imagination was being fired by a world of swashbuckling adventure as delivered from cheap print whereas the female mind was being nurtured on a magical lore as delivered from the mouths of maids and nurses.[104]

Several generations later the vivid testimony of John Clare, whose early experiences are dealt with in more detail by Bob Bushaway's essay (Chapter 9), suggests something of this same difference between men and women in their relationship to the printed word. Clare recalled his childhood in the remote Northamptonshire village of Helpston during the 1790s where his father, on the one hand, could read a little in the printed word and loved 'the supersti[ti]ous tales that are hawked about a sheet for a penny, such as *Old Nixons Prophesies, Mother Bunches Fairey Tales,* and *Mother Shiptons Legacy*', as also the ballads of which 'he was likewise fond'. His mother, on the other hand, 'knew not a single letter' and was steeped in 'superstition', just like the other 'gossips and granneys' of the neighbourhood. Clare was later able to evoke images of this female oral tradition and its formative influence. Thus the 'cottage evening in January' where the 'huswife', who 'knits and sues' before the fire, 'tells tales of magic wonders' and 'fairy feats'; or the field-work in spring and summer which became 'a delightfull employment, as the old womens memorys never faild of tales to smoothen our labour, for as every day came new Jiants, Hobgobblins, and faireys was ready to pass it away'.[105]

Although Clare's father and the other local men seemed to have been more literate and more directly influenced by popular literature than his mother and her 'gossips', however, there was apparently little difference in the essential content of their stories and songs, the one no less 'superstitious' than the other. Even the narratives learned from old women who could not themselves read were drawing upon centuries-old themes from popular print. The point was explicitly made when Clare 'met with a poetical story ... *The Foundlings Lamentation*' told to him by a female neighbour. 'Some of the things struck me so much as to copy them. She traced its origin to a 'penny book' from which she had gotten it by heart years afore ...'. Such evidence may caution, therefore, against too rigid an ascription of gendered relationships to the printed word, at least in the context of the cheap print circulating at this social level by this date.[106] In general, the impression given by Clare's reflections on childhood, corroborated by similar sources contemporary with them, is of just how widespread the cheaply printed page was by the late eighteenth and early nineteenth century, even among labouring folk in relatively isolated provincial villages, and of the great extent to which it structured their vernacular culture at almost every point.[107] But this had not always and everywhere been so. It could be argued that another feature of the ever-greater spread of an English-dominated literary production in Britain over the course of the early modern period was to marginalise the culture of 'peripheral' regions, or the 'provinces', as defined from a metropolitan or civic perspective. Large parts of Wales and the Highlands and Islands of Scotland, what Londoners often referred to dismissively as the 'dark corners of the land', were by virtue of their separate languages, geographical isolation and many other features of economic and cultural difference, thrown into even greater relief by their exclusion from an encroaching anglicization.

This exclusion also had a social dimension. For all that the mass medium of print served in some degree to reform the language, both spoken and written, and to infuse the common stock of phrase and fable for all social groups, regional dialects and Celtic tongues, together with much of the cultural product for which they were vehicles, came to be regarded among certain social groups and those responsible for the definition and arbitration of manners as being inferior and uncouth. Even in 1570 the English writer

George Puttenham had been able to draw a distinction between the kind of English 'spoken in the kings court, or in the good townes and cities', and that to be heard 'in the marches and frontiers, or in port townes'. And the latter was different again from that of 'any vplandish village or corner of a realme, where is no resort but of poore rusticall or vnciuill people'.[108] So the speech of uplandish rustics, the 'poorer sort', or denizens of the 'Celtic fringe' came to be deprecated in some quarters, no less than their proverbs, songs and parochial traditions which were to be regarded in due course as the expressions of 'vulgar error'. To the extent, therefore, that some of the many different uses of the spoken word became more socially variegated and determined over time, they may be said to offer a valuable perspective on the development of social prejudices and social relations in early modern Britain and beyond.

EXPLORATIONS OF THE SPOKEN WORD

The essays that follow attempt to highlight some of these possible differences in interpretation, even if they cannot hope to resolve them, by dealing with a variety of the themes raised here in more depth across different segments of the larger period, and with reference to different regions. Several of them examine aspects of the complex relationship between speech and literacy/ writing, and between the spoken and written or printed word. This is not a comprehensive treatment: we have been selective in our approach, preferring depth to breadth. Consequently by no means every aspect of oral culture that could be addressed is explored here (news, for example, a subject of much recent scholarship,[109] is here omitted) while others, such as oral traditions, figure in several essays. Nor are we able to cover every linguistic group. Cornish has been excluded, while systematic comparison with Ireland deserves separate treatment in another place.

Consistent with the volume's aim to be British in scope, we begin with an arena, education, in which two national tongues overlapped. Richard Suggett and Eryn White's contribution in Chapter 2 focuses on the relationship between speech and writing both within a single language, Welsh, and between two languages, Welsh and English. Welsh was in no danger of becoming extinct as a spoken language during the early modern period, but the increasing influence of English as the language of official and property transactions meant that Welsh, by default, was increasingly the tongue of the less privileged members of society. But the imperatives of religion – the need to make the Welsh into good Protestants first, and only secondarily into good English speakers – intervened to reinvigorate the study of Welsh. Throughout the eighteenth century, proponents of reform and education increasingly relied on written texts composed in the language of the majority,

Welsh, in order to increase popular literacy – and with it religiosity. The result, as Suggett and White conclude, is that far from being the twin enemies of speech, literacy and print culture may have actually reinforced the spoken tongue, by mandating the continued use of Welsh as an oral language of instruction linked to printed pedagogical texts written in that tongue.

Suggett and White allude in their chapter to several topics dealt with in more detail in ensuing essays. Donald Meek, in Chapter 3, provides a study that pursues the influence of religion on another minority language, Gaelic at the respective frontiers between Highland and Lowland, and between orality and literacy. Meek demonstrates that the eighteenth-century Scottish clergy, not unlike their earlier and contemporary Welsh counterparts, used the popular medium of Gaelic in oral and written form to advance the Gospel. A work such as the Rev. Ewen McDiarmid's collection of sermons, published posthumously in 1804, spread through the Highlands and across the Atlantic, providing material for domestic and emigré Scots preachers; it thereby allowed the printed text to influence the subsequent direction of the oral art of preaching.

It is an editorial tenet of this book that orality extends up and down the social ladder, though its manifestations and uses will vary according to stratum. One of the ways in which the written and spoken word continued to interact among the most highly literate members of society was in the phenomenon of reading aloud; another was the even more commonplace occurrence of conversations based upon texts. In Chapter 4, Daniel Woolf explores discussions of history in the later seventeenth and eighteenth centuries. Historians, as observed once or twice already in this Introduction, are highly partial to the written word, conventionally favouring the manuscript over the printed and particularly the oral source, while at the same time we assign a high value to print as the proper medium for presenting historical scholarship derived from those sources. These biases have a very long pedigree and there can be no doubt that reliance on written sources to the exclusion of the oral, and the use of print to present historical research both intensified between 1550 and 1700. Yet it is possible to overlook many contexts in which discussion about history continued to occur orally. Even in the eighteenth century, by which time the history book had become a commonplace fixture of private libraries, print remained for most educated people a supplement to speech rather than something read exclusively in silence and for private pleasure only. Published histories furnished topics of conversation and argument, and sources of learned anecdote, sometimes channeled from print to mouth by the intermediate step of collection in a manuscript miscellany, diary, or commonplace book: how they were used depended on the situation and also, to a considerable degree, on the ranks and genders of the interlocutors. The uses of spoken history could be both frivolous and serious. In lighter contexts, they provided a subject for discussion between courting couples, or for coffee-house amusement. More gravely, they figured in religious discussions, not least as fodder for preachers who increasingly referred to secular as well as biblical history in constructing their sermons, a point made within a Scottish setting by Meek's essay in Chapter 3.

Several essays move from oral communication and oral culture to the more specific problem of oral tradition, in both of the senses – the medium and its content – outlined above. These essays, too, range into Scotland and Wales as well as England, and collectively cover a similarly lengthy period from the sixteenth to the eighteenth century. In Chapter 5, Richard Suggett's second contribution to the volume examines the social role of minstrels in sixteenth-century Wales, demonstrating that the 'decline' of popular minstrelsy was considerably more complex than has previously been acknowledged. Although often associated with vagabonds, minstrels were not always prosecuted because they were vagabonds. Nor were all popular purveyors of tradition dealt with in the same way. Indeed, the *eisteddfodau* of 1523 and 1567 show a gap opening up between an approved minstrelsy, supported by the local elites, and a more vulgar, unlicensed class of performers, to be deemed rogues and beggars; this is roughly the same division noted above in connection with Highland bards over a century later. By the end of the sixteenth century the tastes of the elite had changed (with dance, for instance, supplanting extended poetic performance) and the locus of popular entertainment had shifted from household to alehouse. It was then that this strategy of 'social closure' failed, and with it for a time the holding of *eisteddfodau*. 'Festive culture, dominated by dancing, favoured new types of entertainers', Suggett concludes, 'but in the process the music and action of the dance silenced the spoken word of the professional poet.'

The social biases against oral stories, and in particular their association with vulgar error and superstition are the subject of Alexandra Walsham's essay in Chapter 6. Walsham begins by noting the well-known tendency of the advocates of Reformation to declaim against popish superstition and to contrast the truth of God's written word with the falsity of human traditions (here in the sense of 'unwritten verities' passed down through the Catholic Church). Yet the principle of relying on the written word was violated, of necessity, by its own architects in the interest of evangelism, as Protestantism was rapidly obliged to develop a set of traditions of its own. This 'reformed folklore' consisted of Lactantian tales of the grim deaths of popish persecutors and apostates, and the unpleasant torments providentially inflicted on the wicked. It played a crucial role in the spread of godliness in Britain, and in the reformation of morals and behaviour. Finally, Walsham cautions us appropriately that while it is an error to assume that the Reformation–literacy brought an end to Catholicism–orality, so it is also mistaken to explain the seventeenth century's scepticism toward oral traditions as exclusively a function of a growing rift between elite and popular culture. Ideological reasons –

particularly religion – drove many Tudor and Stuart critiques of vulgar error. As with several of the preceding essays, Walsham demonstrates that speech and both writing and print were interdependent, as oral tales found their way into written and printed texts, and were lifted thence back into conversation and newer traditions. 'Cultural traffic', she notes, 'did not travel in a single direction.'

Tradition is often contrasted with history, the one oral and fluid, the other written and fixed. This, however, is another example of a false dichotomy providing an easy, but misleading, picture of what in fact was a much more complicated relationship. The antiquaries of the seventeenth century, who often criticized the unreliability of tradition, are paradoxically our most important sources for it, since they were not willing to rule it out of court altogether, especially where it shed light on matters for which no documentary source survived. In this vein, Martin MacGregor, in Chapter 7, shows how tradition and history came together in the 'genealogical histories' of Gaelic Scotland after the Restoration. This distinctive genre appeared at the very time that an earlier and indigenous, aristocratic set of learned or 'classical' traditions, which had developed around clan and family origins, was drawing to a close. Written principally in the later seventeenth and early eighteenth centuries, predominantly in English, Scots or Latin, the newer genealogical histories nevertheless show familiarity with the Gaelic tongue. Typically, genealogical histories were an amalgam of four different types of historical material: original documents; earlier, indigenous Gaelic histories; material from the earlier 'classical' learned tradition of Gaelic culture; and oral tradition. The last component may well include elements going back centuries; it is exemplified in Alasdair or Alexander Campbell, author of *The Craignish History*, who wrote his work down for the first time between 1717 and 1722, in middle age, having 'listened with a greedy ear to all the traditions, and poems of my countrymen' while a lad in the 1680s. MacGregor suggests a typology of these genealogical histories, explains their relationship to earlier forms of both oral and written history, and provides a preliminary listing of the works that so qualify. His essay further undermines the elite–literate and vulgar–oral equivalences. Moreover, the presentation of previously Gaelic materials in English provides an excellent illustration of the cross-cutting between different media and different languages, as the act of writing for audiences geographically and temporally distant necessitated presentation in languages more widely understood further afield.

MacGregor's essay reminds us that these issues transcend not only the borders within Britain, but also the English Channel, and that we must be mindful of contemporary developments on the Continent. The construction of oral information as usable historical source, featured in the activities of many of the Scottish genealogical historians, is treated at a more general level by Nicholas Hudson in Chapter 8, in an essay on the eighteenth-century origins of the concept of 'oral tradition'. Medieval writers often made little distinction between oral and written sources, while Renaissance and especially seventeenth-century writers – as we have seen – frequently criticized the oral as an inferior and ephemeral form of the written. In contrast, eighteenth-century authors, swept up in the intellectual currents of the Enlightenment, began to recognize speech as not only not inferior to the written or printed, but as qualitatively different and non-comparable. Samuel Johnson, the great lexicographer, criticized as misguided earlier attempts to find a universal or natural language. Others pointed to the impossibility of replicating the force and range of the spoken word in graphical form. Linked to this was the emerging social critique of contemporary European society and its contrast with the simplicity of pre-literate cultures. Once seen as uneducated, heathen and savage, native societies were paradoxically, now praised for their very illiteracy which, like the satirical Houyhnhnms in *Gulliver's Travels*, allowed for a purer recollection of a more noble and rational past. Similar ideas soon spread to the interpretation of ancient texts, and it was this era that notably produced the earliest theories of the Homeric epics and parts of the Hebrew Bible as originating in primitive, pre-literate orality. It also generated the most egregious literary forgery of the eighteenth century, James Macpherson's *Fingal* (1761), followed fifteen months later by a companion epic, *Temora*. These poems their author proclaimed as genuine translations of ancient Gaelic historical song, passed down by tradition and literary fragment from the third-century bard Ossian or Oisin.[110] Leading into the later eighteenth and early nineteenth century, a valuing of the oral precisely because it was oral surfaces most acutely in romanticism. Sir Walter Scott's *The Antiquary* is a novel that well captures the meeting of Scots, English and Gaelic between tradition and writing, its protagonist at one point enraptured by his apparent discovery of a native, Gaelic tradition.[111]

Hudson's essay links the later years of the period covered by this book neatly with some of the very issues of orality and literacy raised at the beginning of this Introduction in connection with the work of Havelock, Parry and Lord. With Bob Bushaway's closing chapter, we shift to another aspect of oral culture: rural customs and recreations. At the same time, we move further forward chronologically, peering ahead from the end of the early modern period into the nineteenth century, the age of industrialization, to the eve of the First World War. While many of the contributions to the volume have suggested that oral culture was deeply affected by writing and that some aspects of it may have been altered beyond recognition, Bushaway argues strongly for the survival and endurance, rather than revival, of oral culture in rural England. His essay suggests that in popular customs, rituals and calendrical practices a form of life, and sense of local identity, were preserved in the face of modernization up to and perhaps past the First World War. Many of the features of orality that he describes for the nineteenth century are familiar to students of early modern popular culture. These include the importance of unwritten custom and the perseverance of memory. Bushaway's rural villagers sent off to Gallipoli may seem a far remove from the Welsh minstrels described by Richard Suggett, and the differences in their material and social worlds should not be underestimated. Yet in other ways, such as their reliance on the voice as the primary instrument of communication and collective memory, they are not so very far apart.

The editors have proposed in this introductory chapter that the relationship between spoken language and its graphical counterparts should not be viewed as fixed but dynamic. We have also suggested that the changes in these relations did not occur in a linear or unbroken fashion. In the *longue durée* of civilization, the few centuries covered in the essays that follow constitute a relatively brief, if significant, period in the history of the spoken word. Just as speech continues to evolve today in relation to a dizzyingly rapid pace of technological and social change, so current knowledge of how speech and other forms of communication interacted in previous times will need further elaboration and debate. The authors of this book hope to have made a contribution to that continuing conversation.

NOTES

1 Erving Goffman, *Forms of Talk* (Philadelphia: University of Pennsylvania Press, 1981), 77ff; Ronald Wardhaugh, *How Conversation Works* (Oxford: Blackwell, 1985), 1–23, 101–15.

2 Peter Burke, *The Art of Conversation* (Ithaca, NY: Cornell University Press, 1993); idem, 'A Civil Tongue: Language and Politeness in Early Modern England', in P. Burke, B. Harrison and P. Slack (eds), *Civil Histories: Essays Presented to Sir Keith Thomas* (Oxford: Oxford University Press, 2000), 31–48; Anna Bryson, *From Courtesy to Civility: Changing Codes of Conduct in Early Modern England* (Oxford: Clarendon Press, 1998), 153–9, 173–87; G. J. Barker-Benfield, *The Culture of Sensibility: Sex and Society in Eighteenth-century Britain* (Chicago, IL: University of Chicago Press, 1992).

3 Two helpful historical overviews of the philosophy of language are Alexander Miller, *Philosophy of Language* (Montreal and Kingston: McGill–Queen's University Press, 1998); and (for historical discussions) Hans Aarsleff, *From Locke to Saussure: Essays on the Study of Language and Intellectual History* (Minneapolis: University of Minnesota Press, 1982). Cf. an older overview in Albert Borgmann, *The Philosophy of Language: Historical Foundations and Contemporary Issues* (The Hague: Martinus Nijhoff, 1974), part 2.

4 Edward Sapir, *Language: an Introduction to the Study of Speech* (New York: Harcourt Brace & World, 1921); idem, 'Language', in *Culture, Language and Personality*, ed. D. G. Mandelbaum (Berkeley, CA: University of California Press, 1949), 1–44; Benjamin Lee Whorf, *Language, Thought, and Reality*, ed. J. B. Carroll (Cambridge, MA: MIT Press, 1956). For the opposing view, see Steven Pinker, *The Language Instinct: How the Mind Creates Language* (New York: HarperCollins, 1995), 57.

5 The literature on the key figures in modern linguistics is too vast to cite here. Some useful recent works are: *Chomsky: Selected Readings*, ed. J. P. B. Allen and Paul van Buren (London: Oxford University Press, 1971); Steven Pinker, *Words and Rules: the Ingredients of Language* (New York: Basic Books, 1999); Rosalind Horowitz and S. Jay Samuels (eds), *Comprehending Oral and Written Language* (San Diego: Academic Press, 1987), for developmental aspects of language.

6 See the helpful introductory essays on topics such as dress, gesture, humour, dance and other types of non-verbal communication in Richard Bauman (ed.), *Folklore, Cultural Performances, and Popular Entertainments* (New York and Oxford: Oxford University Press, 1992), xiii–xxi.

7 For a review of the history of the field, which emphasizes philosophical and sociological approaches and neglects historical ones, see Everett M. Rogers, *A History of Communication Study* (New York: Free Press, 1994).

8 Harold A. Innis, *The Bias of Communication* (Toronto: University of Toronto Press, 1951, repr. 1964), esp. ch. 1.

9 Ibid., 35, 55.

10 Michael E. Hobart and Zachary S. Schiffman, *Information Ages: Literacy, Numeracy, and the Computer Revolution* (Baltimore, MD: Johns Hopkins University Press, 1998), a book more concerned with information than communication but nonetheless offering insightful comments on the latter.

11 Plato, *Phaedrus*, 275a; Desiderius Erasmus, *De ratione studii*, trans. B. McGregor, *Collected Works of Erasmus* (Toronto: University of Toronto Press, 1974–), vol. 24: *Literary and Educational Writings*, 91.

12 Eric Havelock, *The Muse Learns to Write: Reflections on Orality and Literacy from Antiquity to the Present* (New Haven, CT: Yale University Press, 1986), 34–6, 50, 68; Jacques Derrida, *Of Grammatology*, trans. Gayatry C. Spivak (Baltimore, MD: Johns Hopkins University Press, 1976), 7–10 and passim; idem, *Writing and Difference*, trans. A. Bas (Chicago, IL: University of Chicago Press, 1978), 12. The primacy of orality is assumed by recent cognitive scientists, for instance in Pinker, *The Language Instinct*, 16: 'writing is clearly an optional accessory; the real engine of verbal communication is the spoken language we acquired as children'.

13 Brian Stock, *The Implications of Literacy: Written Language and Models of Interpretation in the Eleventh and Twelfth Centuries* (Princeton, NJ: Princeton University Press, 1983); M. T. Clanchy, *From Memory to Written Record: England 1066–1307*, 2nd edn (Oxford and Cambridge, MA: Blackwell, 1993). See also Mary J. Carruthers, *The Book of Memory: a Study of Memory in Medieval Culture* (Cambridge: Cambridge University Press, 1990).

14 Marshall McLuhan, *The Gutenberg Galaxy: the Making of Typographic Man* (Toronto: University of Toronto Press, 1962); idem, *Understanding Media: the Extensions of Man* (New York: McGraw-Hill, 1964). An early critique can be found in Sidney Finkelstein, *Sense and Nonsense of McLuhan* (New York: International Publishers, 1968). For more recent evaluations and critiques of McLuhan, see Graeme Patterson, *History and Communications: Harold Innis, Marshall McLuhan, the Interpretation of History* (Toronto: University of Toronto Press, 1994); Philip Marchand, *Marshall McLuhan: the Medium and the Messenger* (Toronto: Vintage Books, 1989), esp. 120–37; Glenn Willmott, *McLuhan, or Modernism in Reverse* (Toronto: University of Toronto Press, 1996), 153 (whence comes the quotation).

15 Walter J. Ong, SJ, *Ramus, Method and the Decay of Dialogue* (Cambridge, MA: Harvard University Press, 1958); idem, *The Presence of the Word: Some Prolegomena for Cultural and Religious History* (New Haven: Yale University Press, 1967); idem, *Orality and Literacy: the Technologizing of the Word* (London and New York: Methuen, 1982). On Ong's work, see Bruce E. Gronbeck, Thomas J. Farrell and Paul A. Soukup (eds), *Media, Consciousness, and Culture: Explorations of Walter Ong's Thought* (Newbury Park, CA: Sage Publications, 1991), esp. 25–43.

16 Dennis P. Seniff, 'Ong, Ramism, and Spain: the Case of Pedro de Navarra's Dialogues on the Differences between Speaking and Writing', in Gronbeck, *et al.* (eds), *Media, Consciousness, and Culture*, 121–32; D. R. Woolf, 'Speech, Text, and Time: the Sense of Hearing and the Sense of the Past in Renaissance England', *Albion*, 18 (1986), 159–93, in which Ong's writing is evaluated in somewhat greater detail than present space permits.

17 Marchand, *Marshall McLuhan*, 67. Ong's influence has been nearly as potent as McLuhan's (it indeed may even have inspired *The Gutenberg Galaxy*), and his works continue to be cited in a variety of disciplines.

18 H. J. Chaytor, *From Script to Print: an Introduction to Medieval Vernacular Literature* (Cambridge: Heffer, 1945) is a good example.

19 Harold A. Innis, *Empire and Communications* (first published Oxford: Oxford University Press, 1950), ed. D. Godfrey (Victoria and Toronto: Press Porcepic, 1986); S. H. Steinberg, *Five Hundred Years of Printing* (Harmondsworth: Penguin, 1955), and many subsequent editions; Lucien Febvre and Henri-Jean Martin, *L'Apparition du livre* (Paris, Editions A. Michel, 1958), trans. D. Gerard as *The Coming of the Book* (New York: Verso, 1997). The notion of print as one of the modern marvels of the age was of course abroad as early as the Renaissance; at that time it was frequently cited (along with gunpowder and the compass) as a technological achievement unknown to the otherwise superior ancients.

20 Elizabeth L. Eisenstein, *The Printing Press as an Agent of Change*, 2 vols (Cambridge: Cambridge University Press, 1979).

21 See especially Adrian Johns, *The Nature of the Book: Print and Knowledge in the Making* (Chicago, IL: University of Chicago Press, 1998).

22 Eisenstein cites Innis's *Empire and Communications* and consulted but does not specifically cite *The Bias of Communication*: see Eisenstein, *Printing Press*, bibliographical index.

23 Miriam U. Chrisman, *Lay Culture, Learned Culture: Books and Social Change in Strasbourg, 1480–1599* (New Haven, CT: Yale University Press, 1982); R. W. Scribner, *For the Sake of Simple Folk: Popular Propaganda for the German Reformation*, 2nd edn (New York and Oxford: Clarendon Press, 1994); Robert Darnton, *The Kiss of Lamourette* (New York: Norton, 1990); Natalie Zemon Davis, *Society and Culture in Early Modern France* (Stanford, CA: Stanford University Press, 1975); Sandra Hindman (ed.) *Printing the Written Word: the Social History of Books* ca. *1450–1520* (Ithaca, NY: Cornell University Press, 1991).

24 For instance, Carlo Ginzburg, *The Cheese and the Worms: the Cosmos of a Sixteenth-century Miller*, trans. J. and A. Tedeschi (Baltimore, MD: Johns Hopkins University Press, 1980); Paul Seaver, *Wallington's World: a Puritan Artisan in Seventeenth-century London* (Stanford, CA: Stanford University Press, 1985).

25 In addition to Febvre and Martin, *The Coming of the Book* (cited above), see H.-J. Martin, *Le Livre français sous l'Ancien Régime* (Paris, Promodis–Editions

du Cercle de la librairie, 1987) and *Print, Power, and People in Seventeenth-century France*, trans. David Gerard (Metuchen, NJ: Scarecrow Press, 1993); Roger Chartier, *The Cultural Uses of Print in Early Modern France*, trans. Lydia G. Cochrane (Princeton, NJ: Princeton University Press, 1987) and *The Order of Books: Readers, Authors and Libraries in Europe between the Fourteenth and Eighteenth Centuries*, trans. Lydia G. Cochrane (Oxford: Blackwell; Cambridge: Polity Press, 1994); Robert Mandrou, *De la culture populaire aux XVIIe et XVIIe siècles: la bibliothèque bleue de Troyes* (Paris, Stock, 1964).

26 See especially Harold Love, *Scribal Publication in Seventeenth-century England* (Oxford: Clarendon Press, 1993); Arthur F. Marotti, *Manuscript, Print, and the English Renaissance Lyric* (Ithaca, NY, and London: Cornell University Press, 1995); H. R. Woudhuysen, *Sir Philip Sidney and the Circulation of Manuscripts, 1558–1640* (Oxford: Clarendon Press, 1996).

27 Margaret J. M. Ezell, *Social Authorship and the Advent of Print* (Baltimore, MD, and London: Johns Hopkins University Press, 1999), 12.

28 Marotti, *Manuscript, Print, and the English Renaissance Lyric*, 135–208 usefully terms this interactive process 'social textuality'. On interactive reading and annotation there is a spreading literature including Anthony Grafton and Lisa Jardine '"Studied for Action": How Gabriel Harvey Read His Livy', *Past and Present*, 129 (1990), 30–78; William H. Sherman, *John Dee: the Politics of Reading and Writing in the English Renaissance* (Amherst, MA: University of Massachussetts Press, 1995); Kevin Sharpe, *Reading Revolutions: the Politics of Reading in Early Modern England* (New Haven, CT: Yale University Press, 2000).

29 R. S. Schofield, 'The Measurement of Literacy in Pre-industrial England', in Jack Goody (ed.), *Literacy in Traditional Societies* (Cambridge: Cambridge University Press, 1968), 311–25; David Cressy, *Literacy and the Social Order: Reading and Writing in Tudor and Stuart England* (Cambridge: Cambridge University Press, 1980); but cf. Keith Thomas, 'The Meaning of Literacy', in G. Baumann (ed.) *The Written Word: Literacy in Transition* (Oxford: Clarendon Press, 1986); and Harvey J. Graff, 'On Literacy in the Renaissance: Review and Reflections', in his *The Labyrinths of Literacy: Reflections on Literacy Past and Present* (London, New York, and Philadelphia: Falmer Press, 1987), 133–52. An excellent if now somewhat dated overview of the literature and theory concerning literacy may be found in Brian V. Street, *Literacy in Theory and Practice* (Cambridge: Cambridge University Press, 1984).

30 Margaret Aston, *England's Iconoclasts* (Oxford: Clarendon Press, 1988, vol. 1); Margaret Spufford, *Small Books and Pleasant Histories: Popular Fiction and its Readership in Seventeenth-century England* (London: Methuen, 1981); Tessa Watt, *Cheap Print and Popular Piety, 1550–1640* (Cambridge: Cambridge University Press, 1991); Ian Green, *Print and Protestantism in Early Modern England* (Oxford: Oxford University Press, 2000). In an interesting cautionary remark at the outset of his lengthy book, Green notes (p. v) that print, for all its profound impact on piety, was 'by no stretch of the imagination the only or the most crucial means by which the Protestant message was conveyed to those who were illiterate or had only limited reading skills'.

31 This is a suggestion first made by Thomas, 'Meaning of Literacy'.

32 Ruth Finnegan, 'Communication and Technology', in her *Literacy and Orality: Studies in the Technology of Communication* (Oxford: Blackwell, 1988), 15–44, and elsewhere in that volume.

33 Walter J. Ong, 'Oral Residue in Tudor Prose Style', in Ong, *Rhetoric, Romance and Technology* (Ithaca, NY, and London: Cornell University Press, 1971), 23–47.
34 Finnegan, *Literacy and Orality*, 174. Ian Dyck has made a similar comment concerning early nineteenth-century England, with respect to speech and print: 'Print and orality, the rational and the non-rational, were not mutually exclusive genres or world-views within rural popular culture.' Ian Dyck, *William Cobbett and Rural Popular Culture* (Cambridge: Cambridge University Press, 1992), 85. From a literary perspective, Leah S. Marcus has warned against the tendency not only to constitute writing and speech as a binary, but to 'invest speech as opposed to writing with an almost mystical wholeness, integrity and "presence" supposedly lost to human communication in our own culture.' See Marcus, 'From Oral Delivery to Print in the Speeches of Elizabeth I', in Arthur F. Marotti and Michael Bristol (eds), *Print, Manuscript, Performance: the Changing Relations of the Media in Early Modern England* (Columbus, OH: Ohio State University Press, 2000), 33–48.
35 Harvey J. Graff, 'Reflections on the History of Literacy', in Graff, *Labyrinths of Literacy*, 15–43, at p. 25.
36 Viv Edwards and Thomas J. Sienkewicz, *Oral Cultures Past and Present: Rappin' and Homer* (Oxford: Blackwell, 1990), 6.
37 Claude Lévi-Strauss, *Structural Anthropology*, trans. Claire Jacobson and Brooke Grundfest Schoepf (New York: Basic Books, 1963), 208–10; idem, *Anthropology and Myth: Lectures 1951–1982*, trans. Roy Willis (Oxford: Blackwell, 1987), 118–23; Edmund Leach, *Lévi-Strauss* (London: Fontana, 1970).
38 Albert B. Lord, *The Singer of Tales* (New York, 1965); idem, *Epic Singers and Oral Tradition* (Ithaca, NY, and London: Cornell University Press, 1991). Lord and Parry's theories on the composition of oral poetry have also been applied, not without criticism, to Old English epic: John Miles Foley, 'The Oral Theory in Context', in John Miles Foley (ed.), *Oral Traditional Literature: a Festschrift for Albert Bates Lord* (Columbus, OH: Slavica, 1980), 27–123, esp. 51–60. For a more recent cross-cultural exploration of epic orality, focusing on Beowulf rather than Homer, see John D. Niles, *Homo Narrans: the Poetics and Anthropology of Oral Literature* (Philadelphia: University of Pennsylvania Press, 1999).
39 Eric Havelock, *Preface to Plato* (Cambridge, MA: Harvard University Press, 1963); Havelock refined his views in *The Muse Learns to Write*, which among other features contains a useful history of the study of orality since the 1950s. Cf. criticisms of Havelock in Hobart and Schiffman, *Information Ages*, ch. 1. Rosalind Thomas has pointed out that ancient Athens was an oral society in many respects but also relied on record-keeping: Thomas, *Oral Tradition and Written Record in Classical Athens* (Cambridge: Cambridge University Press, 1989), 2–3.
40 Edwards and Sienkewicz, *Oral Cultures Past and Present*, 7–8.
41 The tradition of rigorous documentary criticism of course goes back via German *Quellenkritik* and classical philology through Jean Mabillon and the late seventeenth century, back to the Renaissance humanists. More recently, working historians (and not merely postmodern exponents of the extreme view that the past is unknowable and no reality exists beyond texts) have begun to question the general reliability and completeness of documentary evidence more generally. See for instance Natalie Zemon Davis's exposure of the constructed stories in sixteenth-century pardon tales in *Fiction in the Archives: Pardon Tales and their Tellers in Sixteenth-century France* (Stanford, CA: Stanford University Press, 1987),

or Patrick J. Geary's discussion of selective archival preservation (an early precursor of current 'document management') by medieval monastic scholars, in *Phantoms of Remembrance: Memory and Oblivion at the End of the First Millennium* (Princeton, NJ: Princeton University Press, 1994).

42 Jan Vansina, *Oral Tradition as History* (Madison, WI: University of Wisconsin Press, 1985); David Henige, *The Chronology of Oral Tradition: Quest for a Chimera* (Oxford: Clarendon Press, 1974); idem, *Oral Historiography* (London and New York: Longman, 1982). For an anthropological treatment, see Ruth Finnegan, *Oral Traditions and Verbal Arts: a Guide to Research Practices* (London and New York: Routledge, 1992).

43 Alex Haley, *Roots* (Garden City, NY: Doubleday, 1976).

44 Ruth Finnegan, *Oral Literature in Africa* (Oxford: Oxford University Press, 1970); Thomas A. Hale, *Griots and Griottes: Masters of Words and Music* (Bloomington and Indianapolis: Indiana University Press, 1998), esp. 59–113; Stephen Beecher, *Epic Traditions of Africa* (Bloomington: Indiana University Press, 1999), 7–8, 110.

45 Finnegan, *Oral Literature in Africa*, 14–15; idem, 'Transmission in Oral and Written Traditions: Some General Comments', in Finnegan, *Literacy and Orality*, 139–74, esp. 154–8.

46 Edwards and Sienkewicz, *Oral Cultures Past and Present*, 1.

47 Jack Goody, 'Oral Culture', in Bauman (ed.), *Folklore, Cultural Performances, and Popular Entertainments*, 12–20. Cf. the classic early formulation of Goody's position in his essay, with the late Ian Watt, 'The Consequences of Literacy', *Comparative Studies in Society and History*, 5 (1963), 304–45. Goody's views are discussed and evaluated in Street, *Literacy in Theory and Practice*, 44–65.

48 James Obelkevich, 'Proverbs and Social History', in *The Social History of Language*, ed. Peter Burke and Roy Porter (Cambridge: Cambridge University Press, 1987), 43–72; Donald F. Bond, 'English Legal Proverbs', *Proceedings of the Modern Language Association*, 51 (1936), 921–35; Adam Fox, *Oral and Literate Culture in England 1500–1700* (Oxford: Clarendon Press, 2000), ch. 2.

49 Finnegan, *Oral Traditions and Verbal Arts*, 7 and sources cited therein.

50 Glanville Price (ed.), *Languages in Britain and Ireland* (Oxford: Blackwell, 2000) is a useful collection of essays covering the range of languages spoken, past and present, including newer minority 'community languages'.

51 C. W. J. Withers, *Gaelic in Scotland, 1698–1981: the Geographical History of a Language* (Edinburgh: John Donald, 1984), 25; *Johnson's Journey to the Western Islands of Scotland and Boswell's Journal of a Tour to the Hebrides*, ed. R. W. Chapman (London: Oxford University Press, 1924), 22; *Early Travellers in Scotland*, ed. P. Hume Brown (Edinburgh: 1891; repr. New York: Burt Franklin, 1970), 174, 262; Thomas Pennant, *A Tour in Scotland; MDCCLXIX*, 3rd edn (Warrington: 1774), 183. Cf. *Beyond the Highland Line: Three Journals of Travel in Eighteenth-century Scotland*, ed. A. J. Youngson (London: Collins, 1974), 41.

52 *A Collection of Highland Rites and Customes Copied by Edward Lhuyd from the Manuscript of the Rev James Kirkwood (1650–1709) and Annotated by him with the Aid of the Rev John Beaton*, ed. J. L. Campbell (Cambridge: D. S. Brewer for the Folklore Society, 1975), 21. Cf. *Johnson's Journey to the Western Islands of Scotland and Boswell's Journal of a Tour to the Hebrides*, ed. Chapman, 106.

53 Geraint H. Jenkins (ed.), *The Welsh Language before the Industrial Revolution* (Cardiff: University of Wales Press, 1997); Glanmor Williams, *Renewal and*

Reformation: Wales, c. *1415–1642* (Oxford: Oxford University Press, 1993), 93–5, 149, 269, 277–8; George Owen, *The Description of Pembrokeshire*, ed. Dillwyn Miles (Llandysul: Gomer Press, 1994), 13–14, 36, 41–3; Geraint H. Jenkins, *The Foundations of Modern Wales: Wales, 1642–1780* (Oxford: Oxford University Press, 1987), 214, 219–22. For early modern English reactions to Welsh speech, see Bruce R. Smith, *The Acoustic World of Early Modern England* (Chicago, IL: University of Chicago Press, 1999), 301–2.

54 John Aubrey, *Brief Lives*, ed. Andrew Clark, 2 vols (Oxford: Clarendon Press, 1898), II. 329; 'Parochialia: Being a Summary to Answers to Parochial Queries in Order to a Geographical Dictionary, etc., of Wales issued by Edward Lhwyd', ed. Rupert H. Morris, *Archaeologia Cambrensis* (Supplements, 3 parts in 1, London, 1909–11), I: x; Richard Gough, *The History of Myddle*, ed. David Hey (Harmondsworth: Penguin, 1981), 110, 150, 247; Richard Carew, *The Survey of Cornwall* (London, 1602), fol. 56r. Cf. A. L. Rowse, *Tudor Cornwall: Portrait of a Society* (London: J. Cape, 1941), 21–4; Philip Payton, 'Cornish', in Price, *Languages in Britain and Ireland*, 109–19.

55 Hart quoted in Joseph M. Williams, '"O! When Degree is Shak'd": Sixteenth-century Anticipations of Some Modern Attitudes Toward Usage', in T. W. Machan and C. T. Scott (eds), *English in its Social Contexts: Essays in Historical Sociolinguistics* (New York and Oxford: Oxford University Press, 1992), 73; Alexander J. Ellis, *On Early English Pronunciation*, 5 vols (London: Chaucer Society Publications, 2nd ser., vols 1, 4, 5, 11, 25, 1869–89), vol. 5; Martin F. Wakelin, *English Dialects: a Survey*, 2nd edn (London: Athlone Press, 1977), 51. The latest research is presented in Harold Orton *et al.* (eds), *Survey of English Dialects*, 4 vols (Leeds: E. J. Arnold for the University of Leeds, 1962–71) and Harold Orton, Stewart Sanderson and John Widdowson, *The Linguistic Atlas of England* (London: Croom Helm, 1978).

56 Daniel Defoe, *The Great Law of Subordination Consider'd* (London, 1724), 48; William Marshall, *The Rural Economy of Norfolk*, 2nd edn, 2 vols (London, 1795), II. 373. For further comment to this effect see Fox, *Oral and Literate Culture in England*, 79–83.

57 *Fergusson's Scottish Proverbs from the Original Print of 1641 Together with a Larger Manuscript Collection*, ed. Erskine Beveridge (Edinburgh and London: Scottish Text Society, new ser., 15, 1924), 2.

58 Alan Everitt, 'River and Wold: Reflections on the Historical Origin of Regions and Pays', *Journal of Historical Geography*, 3 (1977), 1–19; idem, 'Country, County and Town: Patterns of Regional Evolution in England', *Trans. Royal Historical Society*, 5th ser., 29 (1979), 78–108; Charles Phythian-Adams, *Re-thinking English Local History* Occasional Papers in English Local History (Leicester: Leicester University Press, 1987); idem (ed.), *Societies, Cultures and Kinship, 1580–1850: Cultural Provinces and English Local History* (London and New York: Leicester University Press, 1993), 9–18 and figs 1.1–1.4. The cultural distinctions between *pays* in France is vividly evoked in Eugen Weber, *Peasants into Frenchmen: the Modernization of Rural France, 1870–1914* (Stanford, CA: Stanford University Press, 1976), 45–9.

59 British Library (hereafter BL), MS Add. 24539, fo. 31r. On the region in the early modern period, see D. Hey, *The Fiery Blades of Hallamshire: Sheffield and its Neighbourhood, 1660–1740* (Leicester: Leicester University Press, 1993).

60 On each of these regions in turn, see S. J. Watts, *From Border to Middle Shire:*

Northumberland 1586–1625 (Leicester: Leicester University Press, 1975), chs 1–2; Peter Clark, *English Provincial Society from the Reformation to the Revolution: Religion, Politics and Society in Kent, 1500–1640* (Hassocks: Harvester Press, 1977), 120–1; Nicholas Tyacke, 'Popular Puritan Mentality in Late Elizabethan England', in Peter Clark, A. G. R. Smith and Nicholas Tyacke (eds), *The English Commonwealth, 1547–1640* (Leicester: Leicester University Press, 1979), 77–92; John Walter, *Understanding Popular Violence in the English Revolution: the Colchester Plunderers* (Cambridge: Cambridge University Press, 1999), 34–5, 243–5.

61 John Smyth, *The Berkeley Manuscripts*, ed. J. Maclean, 3 vols (Gloucester: Gloucester Archaeological Soc., 1883–85), III. 30. For discussion see David Rollison, *The Local Origins of Modern Society: Gloucestershire 1500–1800* (London and New York: Routledge, 1992), ch. 3.

62 David Buchan, *The Ballad and the Folk* (London: Routledge & Kegan Paul, 1972), 1–47.

63 Ibid., 62–73. See also Hamish Henderson, 'The Ballad, the Folk, and the Oral Tradition', in Edward J. Cowan (ed.), *The People's Past: Scottish Folk, Scottish History* (Edinburgh: EUSPB, 1980), 65–101.

64 Bodleian Library, Oxford (hereafter Bodl.), MS Aubrey 3, f. 30; John Aubrey, 'Remaines of Gentilisme and Judaisme', in *John Aubrey: Three Prose Works*, ed. John Buchanan-Brown (Fontwell, Centaur Press, 1972), 445, 289. For further detail, see Fox, *Oral and Literate Culture in England*, ch. 3; D. R. Woolf, 'A Feminine Past? Gender, Genre, and Historical Knowledge in England, 1500–1800', *American Historical Review*, 102 (June 1997), 645–79.

65 Aubrey, 'Remaines of Gentilisme and Judaisme', in *Three Prose Works*, ed. Buchanan-Brown, 284; *A Collection of Highland Rites and Customes*, ed. Campbell, 49; W. Chappell, *Popular Music of the Olden Time* (London: Cramer, Beale, & Chappell, 1859), 579–84; [John Case?] *The Praise of Musicke* (Oxford, 1586), 44.

66 Keith Thomas, *The Perception of the Past in Early Modern England*, Creighton Trust Lecture (London: University of London, 1983), 4–5; Jennifer Westwood, *Albion: a Guide to Legendary Britain* (London: Granada, 1985); D. R. Woolf, 'The "Common Voice": History, Folklore and Oral Tradition in Early Modern England', *Past and Present*, 120 (1988), 25–52; idem, 'Of Danes and Giants: Popular Beliefs about the Past in Early Modern England', *Dalhousie Review*, 71 (Summer 1991), 166–209; Fox, *Oral and Literate Culture in England*, ch. 4; Jacqueline Simpson, 'The Local Legend: a Product of Popular Culture', *Rural History*, 2 (1991), 25–35; James Fentress and Chris Wickham, *Social Memory* (Oxford: Blackwell, 1992), 87, 93, 113, 121, 166.

67 A. H. Dodd, *Studies in Stuart Wales* (Cardiff: University of Wales Press, 1952), 13; Jane Dawson, 'Calvinism and the *Gàidhealtachd* in Scotland', in Andrew Pettegree, Alastair Duke and Gillian Lewis (eds), *Calvinism in Europe, 1540–1620* (Cambridge: Cambridge University Press, 1994), 236; *A Memoir of Thomas Bewick Written by Himself*, ed. Iain Bain (Oxford: Oxford University Press, 1979), 8.

68 Derick S. Thomson, 'Scottish Gaelic Folk-poetry ante 1650', *Scottish Gaelic Studies*, 8 (1955–58), 3; John Bannerman, 'Literacy in the Highlands', in Ian B. Cowan and Duncan Shaw (eds), *The Renaissance and Reformation in Scotland* (Edinburgh: Scottish Academic Press, 1983), 217–18, 222, 224–8, 229–31; Williams, *Renewal and Reformation: Wales* c. *1415–1642*, 442–50.

69 'Professor James Garden's Letters to John Aubrey, 1692–1695', ed. Cosmo

A. Gordon, *Miscellany of the Third Spalding Club* (Aberdeen: Third Spalding Club, 1960), III. 18–20. Cf. John Aubrey, *Monumenta Britannica*, ed. John Fowles and Rodney Legg (Sherbourne: Dorset Publishing Co., 1980–82), 171–2. The affiliation of bards with powerful families is also addressed in Martin MacGregor's study of Scottish genealogical histories below.

70 On these common minstrels, see Aubrey, 'Remaines of Gentilisme and Judaisme', in *Three Prose Works*, ed. Buchanan-Brown, 284; Edward J. Cowan, 'Calvinism and the Survival of Folk', in Cowan (ed.), *The People's Past*, 35.

71 Derick S. Thomson, *An Introduction to Gaelic Poetry* (London: Gollancz, 1974), ch. 1; *A Collection of Highland Rites and Customes*, ed. Campbell, 46; Martin Martin, *A Description of the Western Islands of Scotland* circa *1695* (Glasgow: T. D. Morison; London: Hamilton, Adams, 1884), 152–3, 217, 219, 220.

72 Rachel Bromwich, A. O. H. Jarman and Brynley F. Roberts (eds), *The Arthur of the Welsh: the Arthurian Legend in Medieval Welsh Literature* (Cardiff: University of Wales Press, 1991); J. S. P. Tatlock, *The Legendary History of Britain: Geoffrey of Monmouth's* Historia Regum Britanniae *and its Early Vernacular Versions* (Berkeley and Los Angeles: University of California Press, 1950).

73 T. D. Kendrick, *British Antiquity* (London: Methuen, 1950), 87–98; F. J. Levy, *Tudor Historical Thought* (San Marino, CA: Huntington Library, 1967), 130–3; Sydney Anglo, 'The *British History* in Early Tudor Propaganda', *Bulletin of the John Rylands Library*, 44 (1961–62), 17–48; R. F. Brinkley, *Arthurian Legend in the Seventeenth Century* (Baltimore, MD: Johns Hopkins University Press, 1932). On the Scottish appropriation of the Arthurian legend, see David Allan, '*Arthur Redivivus*: Politics and Patriotism in Reformation Scotland', in James P. Carley and Felicity Riddy (eds), *Arthurian Literature XV* (Cambridge: D. S. Brewer, 1997), 185–204.

74 William Camden, *Britannia*, ed. Edmund Gibson (London, 1695), 620, 628–9; James Brome, *Travels Over England, Scotland and Wales* (London, 1700), 22; Westwood, *Albion: a Guide to Legendary Britain*, 274–8; Aubrey, *Monumenta Britannica*, ed. Fowles and Legg, 809. Cf. *Parochialia ... by Edward Lhwyd*, ed. Morris, I. xi, II. 97–8, III. 72, 73, 83, 121; Thomas Pennant, *A Tour in Wales. MDCCLXX*, 2 vols (London, 1778–81), I. 375, 390, 412, II. 77, 254, 263-4. For sites similarly associated with Arthurian legend in Scotland, see *A Collection of Highland Rites and Customes*, ed. Campbell, 46; Stuart Piggott, *Ruins in a Landscape: Essays in Antiquarianism* (Edinburgh: Edinburgh University Press, 1976), 142–4; on England see, for example, Westwood, *Albion: A Guide to Legendary Britain*, 5–8.

75 For England see Schofield, 'The Measurement of Literacy in Pre-Industrial England', and Cressy, *Literacy and the Social Order*, both cited above; for Scotland, see R. A. Houston, *Scottish Literacy and the Scottish Identity: Illiteracy and Society in Scotland and Northern England 1600–1800* (Cambridge: Cambridge University Press, 1985).

76 On the evidence of signatures as a significant underestimate of reading ability, see Margaret Spufford, 'First Steps in Literacy: the Reading and Writing Experiences of the Humblest Seventeenth-century Spiritual Autobiographers', *Social History*, 4 (1979), 414; T. C. Smout, 'Born Again in Cambuslang: New Evidence on Popular Religion and Literacy in Eighteenth-century Scotland', *Past and Present*, 97 (1982), 121–3; Thomas, 'The Meaning of Literacy', 102–3.

77 Cressy, *Literacy and the Social Order*, 72–4, 136, 150–1, 176–7.

78 H. S. Bennett, *English Books and Readers 1475 to 1640*, 3 vols (Cambridge: Cambridge University Press, 1965–70); J. A. Sharpe, *Early Modern England: a Social History, 1550–1760*, 2nd edn (London: Arnold, 1997), 263; Watt, *Cheap Print and Popular Piety*, 11; Laurence Hanson, 'English Newsbooks, 1620–1641', *Library*, 4th ser., 18 (1938), 355–84; Spufford, *Small Books and Pleasant Histories*, 118; Bernard Capp, *Astrology and the Popular Press: English Almanacs 1500–1800* (London: Faber, 1979), 44; idem, 'Popular Literature', in Barry Reay (ed.), *Popular Culture in Seventeenth-century England* (London: Croom Helm, 1985), 198–243.

79 G. A. Cranfield, *The Press and Society from Caxton to Northcliffe* (London and New York: Longman, 1978), chs 1–2; Joad Raymond, *The Invention of the Newspaper: English Newsbooks 1641–1649* (Oxford: Clarendon Press, 1996); James Sutherland, *The Restoration Newspaper and its Development* (Cambridge and New York: Cambridge University Press, 1986); G. A. Cranfield, *The Development of the Provincial Newspaper 1700–1760* (Oxford: Clarendon Press, 1962).

80 See, for example, Isabel Rivers (ed.), *Books and the Readers in Eighteenth-century England* (Leicester: Leceister University Press, 1982); John Feather, *The Provincial Book Trade in Eighteenth-century England* (Cambridge: Cambridge University Press, 1986); James Raven, *Judging New Wealth: Popular Publishing and Responses to Commerce in England 1750–1800* (Oxford: Clarendon Press, 1992).

81 R. M. Wiles, *Serial Publication in England before 1750* (Cambridge: Cambridge University Press, 1957); Paul Kaufman, *Libraries and Their Users* (London: Library Association, 1969); D. R. Woolf, *Reading History in Early Modern England* (Cambridge: Cambridge University Press, 2000), 177–202, 273–81.

82 See, for example, John Ashton, *Chapbooks of the Eighteenth Century* (London: Chatto & Windus, 1882); Leslie Shepard, *The History of Street Literature* (Newton Abbot: David & Charles, 1973); Victor E. Neuburg, *Popular Literature: a History and a Guide* (London: Woburn Press, 1977); Sheila O'Connell, *The Popular Print in England 1550–1850* (London: British Museum Press, 1999). On Wales see Jenkins, *Literature, Religion and Society in Wales*, 161–4; Prys Morgan, *The Eighteenth-century Renaissance* (Llandybïe: Christopher Davis, 1981), 44–6; on Scotland, see *A Catalogue of the Lauriston Castle Chapbooks* (Boston, MA: G. K. Hall, 1964).

83 Tessa Watt, 'Piety in the Pedlar's Pack: Continuity and Change, 1578–1630', in Margaret Spufford (ed.), *The World of Rural Dissenters, 1520–1725* (Cambridge: Cambridge University Press, 1995), 235–72; Margaret Spufford, 'The Pedlar and the Historian: Seventeenth-century Communications', in her *Figures in the Landscape: Rural Society in England, 1500–1700* (Aldershot: Ashgate, 2000), 197–217; A. R. B. Haldane, *Three Centuries of Scottish Posts: an Historical Survey to 1836* (Edinburgh: Edinburgh University Press, 1971), chs 1–3, offers a suggestive Scottish parallel; G. Dyfnallt Owen, *Elizabethan Wales: the Social Scene* (Cardiff: University of Wales Press, 1964), 67–8; Richard Suggett, 'Pedlars and Mercers as Distributors of Print in Early-modern Wales', in Peter Isaac and Barry McKay (eds), *The Mighty Engine: the Printing Press and its Impact* (New Castle, DE: Oak Knoll Press, 2000), 23–32; *The Autobiography of Richard Baxter*, ed. N. H. Keeble, Everyman edn (London: J. M. Dent, 1985), 7.

84 Eryn M. White, 'Popular Schooling and the Welsh Language 1650–1800', in Jenkins (ed.), *The Welsh Language before the Industrial Revolution*, 317–41; and see ch. 2 by Suggett and White below.

85 *The Bible in Welsh and in the Vernacular* (Aberystwyth: Y Llyfrgell, Coleg Prifysgol

Cymru, 1988); Glanmor Williams, 'Unity of Religion or Unity of Language? Protestants and Catholics and the Welsh Language 1536–1660', and Jenkins, 'The Cultural Uses of the Welsh Language 1660–1800', in Jenkins (ed.), *The Welsh Language before the Industrial Revolution*, 212–18, 371; Jenkins, *Literature, Religion and Society in Wales, 1660–1730*, 34–5; Morgan, *The Eighteenth-century Renaissance*, 40–4.

86 Houston, *Scottish Literacy and Scottish Identity*, 89–91, 46–7. On the development of the Scottish book trade in this period, see Alastair J. Mann, *The Scottish Book Trade, 1500–1720* (East Linton: Tuckwell Press, 2000), 214–24.

87 Withers, *Gaelic in Scotland, 1698–1981*, 43–5; Dawson, 'Calvinism and the *Gàidhealtachd* in Scotland', in Pettegree, Duke and Lewis (eds), *Calvinism in Europe, 1540–1620*, 231–53; Donald Meek, 'The Gaelic Bible', in David F. Wright (ed.), *The Bible in Scottish Life and Literature* (Edinburgh: St Andrew Press, 1988), 9–23; Houston, *Scottish Literacy and the Scottish Identity*, 72, 78, 80.

88 *Johnson's Journey to the Western Islands of Scotland and Boswell's Journal of a Tour to the Hebrides*, ed. Chapman, 104–5.

89 Bannerman, 'Literacy in the Highlands', in Cowan and Shaw (eds), *The Renaissance and Reformation in Scotland*, 214–35; Houston, *Scottish Literacy and the Scottish Identity*, 70–83.

90 *Heir Follovis the Dreme of Schir David Lyndesay* (London: Early English Text Society, orig. ser., 11, n.d.), 264; Robert Chambers, *Popular Rhymes of Scotland, 3rd edn*, (London and Edinburgh: W. & R. Chambers, 1870 [1826]), 89–95; Westwood, *Albion: a Guide to Legendary Britain*, 363–7; Iona and Peter Opie, *The Classic Fairy Tales* (London and New York: Oxford University Press, 1974), 47–65.

91 *The Complaynt of Scotlande*, ed. J. A. H. Murray (London: Early English Text Society, extra ser., 17, 1872), lxxiii–xci, 62–5; Chambers, *Popular Rhymes of Scotland*, 66–70, 105–7.

92 On Wallace, see Walter Scheps, 'From The Acts and Deeds of Sir William Wallace', in *Medieval Outlaws: Ten Tales in Modern English*, Thomas H. Ohlgren ed. (Stroud: Alan Sutton, 1998), 253–87; on Bruce, 'Introduction' to John Barbour, *The Bruce*, ed. A. A. M. Duncan (Edinburgh: Canongate, 1997), 1–38; on Robin Hood, R. B. Dobson and J. Taylor, *Rymes of Robin Hood: an Introduction to the English Outlaw* (Gloucester: Sutton, 1989); on Arthur, Flora Alexander, 'Late Medieval Scottish Attitudes to the Figure of King Arthur: a Reassessment', *Anglia*, 93 (1975), 17–34; on Bevis, Laura A. Hibbard, *Mediaeval Romance in England* (New York: Oxford University Press, 1924), 115–26; and on the similar case of Guy of Warwick, see V. B. Richmond, *The Legend of Guy of Warwick* (New York: Garland, 1996). For a recent discussion of the romance tradition, see W. R. J. Barron, *English Medieval Romance* (London: Longman, 1997).

93 *The Complaynt of Scotlande*, ed. Murray, lxxxii–xci, 64–6; Robert Laneham, *A Letter* (London, 1575), 34–6.

94 *A Compendious Book of Godly and Spiritual Songs, Commonly Known as 'The Gude and Godlie Ballatis', Reprinted from the Edition of 1567*, ed. A. F. Mitchell (Edinburgh and London: Scottish Text Society, 39, printed for the Society by W. Blackwood & Sons, 1897), 147–8, 61–2, 139–40, 151–7, 63–4; Chambers, *Popular Rhymes of Scotland*, 13; Cowan, 'Calvinism and the Survival of Folk', in Cowan (ed.), *The People's Past*, 36–51.

95 Charles Barber, *Early Modern English* (London: Deutsch, 1976), ch. 6; Manfred Görlach, *Introduction to Early Modern English* (Cambridge: Cambridge University Press, 1991), 136–9, 166–9; De Witt T. Starnes and Gertrude E. Noyes, *The English Dictionary from Cawdrey to Johnson 1604–1755* (Chapel Hill, NC: University of North Carolina Press, 1946).

96 Margaret Mann Phillips, *The 'Adages' of Erasmus: A Study with Translations* (Cambridge: Cambridge University Press, 1964); *John Heywood's 'A Dialogue of Proverbs'*, ed. Rudolph E. Habenicht (Berkeley and Los Angeles: University of California Press, 1963). Among the major collections of English proverbs which followed were William Camden, *Remaines, Concerning Britaine*, 2nd edn (London, 1614), 301–15; James Howell, *Proverbs or Old Sayed Saws and Adages* (London, 1659); Thomas Fuller, *The History of the Worthies of England* (London, 1662); John Ray, *A Collection of English Proverbs* (Cambridge: 1670; 2nd edn, 1678); Francis Grose, *A Provincial Glossary with a Collection of Local Proverbs and Popular Superstitions* (London, 1787), sigs K5–S6.

97 William Salesbury, *Oll Synnwyr pen Kembero ygyd*, ed. J. Gwenogvryn Evans (Bangor and London: Jarvis, 1902); John Davies, *Antiquae Linguae Britannicae* (London, 1632), sigs Hhh2v–Iiii4v; Howell, *Proverbs or Old Sayed Saws and Adages*, 1–40 (second pagination); Jenkins, *Literature, Religion and Society in Wales*, 165–8. For later compilations see Henry Halford Vaughan, *Welsh Proverbs* (London: K. Paul Trench, 1889); T. R. Roberts, *The Proverbs of Wales* (Penmaenmawr: T. R. Roberts, 1885).

98 *The Bannatyne Manuscript Written in Tyme of Pest 1568*, ed. W. Tod Richie, 4 vols (Edinburgh and London: Scottish Text Society, new ser., 22, 23, 26, third ser., 5, 1928–34), III. 8–10; *Fergusson's Scottish Proverbs*, ed. Beveridge; *The James Carmichaell Collection of Proverbs in Scots*, ed. M. L. Anderson (Edinburgh: Edinburgh University Press, 1957); Pappity Stampoy, *A Collection of Scotch Proverbs* (London, 1663); R. B., *Adagia Scotica, or a Collection of Scotch Proverbs and Proverbial Phrases* (London, 1668); Ray, *A Collection of English Proverbs*, 2nd edn (1678), 356–95; James Kelly, *A Complete Collection of Scottish Proverbs, Explained and Made Intelligible to the English Reader* (London, 1721); Allan Ramsay, *A Collection of Scots Proverbs* (Edinburgh, 1737).

99 Hyder E. Rollins, 'An Analytical Index to the Ballad-entries (1557–1709) in the Registers of the Company of Stationers of London', *Studies in Philology*, 21 (1924), 169, 183; Fynes Moryson, *An Itinerary Containing his Ten Yeeres Travell*, 4 vols (Glasgow: J. MacLehose, 1907–8), II. 118; Aubrey, *Monumenta Britannica*, ed. Fowles and Legg, 543.

100 P. R. Coss, 'Aspects of Cultural Diffusion in Medieval England: the Early Romances, Local Society and Robin Hood', *Past and Present*, 108 (1985), 38–40; Westwood, *Albion: a Guide to Legendary Britain*, 206–8, 118–19; J. C. Holt, *Robin Hood*, 2nd edn (London: Thames & Hudson, 1989), 176–9, 41; *Elias Ashmole (1617–1692). His Autobiographical and Historical Notes, his Correspondence, and Other Contemporary Sources Relating to his Life and Work*, ed. C. H. Josten (Oxford: Clarendon Press, 1966), 625.

101 See, for example, Kendrick, *British Antiquity*, chs 7–8; F. Smith Fussner, *The Historical Revolution: English Historical Writing and Thought 1580–1640* (London: Routledge & Kegan Paul, 1962); May McKisack, *Medieval History in the Tudor Age* (Oxford: Clarendon Press, 1972); David C. Douglas, *English Scholars 1660–1730*, 2nd edn (London: Eyre & Spottiswoode, 1951); D. R. Woolf, *The Idea of*

History in Early Stuart England (Toronto: University of Toronto Press, 1990); idem, '"The Common Voice"', passim.

102 Michael Hunter, *John Aubrey and the Realm of Learning* (London: Duckworth, 1975), ch. 3; Fox, *Oral and Literate Culture in England*, 65–6, 68, 135–6, 154–5, 173, 179–81, 203–5.

103 'Parochialia ... by Edward Lhwyd', ed. Morris, part I. xi–xii; J. L. Campbell and Derick Thomson, *Edward Lhuyd in the Scottish Highlands 1699–1700* (Oxford: Clarendon Press, 1963), 220–2; Donald Mackintosh, *A Collection of Gaelic Proverbs, Apothegms, and Old Sayings* (Edinburgh, 1785; new edn 1819); Alexander Nicolson, *A Collection of Gaelic Proverbs and Familiar Phrases* (Edinburgh: MacLachlan & Stewart, 1881), xvi.

104 *The Tatler*, ed. Donald F. Bond, 3 vols (Oxford: Clarendon Press, 1987), II. 93.

105 *John Clare's Autobiographical Writings*, ed. Eric Robinson (Oxford: Oxford University Press, 1983), 2, 3, 8; John Clare, *The Shepherd's Calendar*, ed. Eric Robinson and Geoffrey Summerfield (Oxford: Oxford University Press, 1966), 10–21. A good impression of the separate spheres and traditions occupied by men and women in this context is conveyed in Flora Thompson, *Lark Rise to Candleford* (Harmondsworth: Penguin, 1973), 56–7, 64–75.

106 George Deacon, *John Clare and the Folk Tradition* (London: Sinclair Browne, 1983), 24.

107 See, for example, Samuel Bamford, *Early Days* (London: Simpkin, Marshall & Co., 1849), 90; James Hogg, *Memoir of the Author's Life; and Familiar Anecdotes of Sir Walter Scott*, ed. Douglas S. Mack (Edinburgh: Scottish Academic Press, 1972), 9; David Vincent, *Bread, Knowledge and Freedom: a Study of Nineteenth-century Working Class Autobiography* (London and New York: Methuen, 1981), ch. 6; idem, *Literacy and Popular Culture: England 1750–1914* (Cambridge: Cambridge University Press, 1989), esp. ch. 6; Jan Fergus, 'Provincial Servants' Reading in the Late Eighteenth Century', in James Raven, Helen Small and Naomi Tadmor (eds), *The Practice and Representation of Reading in England* (Cambridge: Cambridge University Press, 1996), 202–25; Dyck, *William Cobbett and Rural Popular Culture*, ch. 4.

108 George Puttenham, *The Arte of English Poesie* (London, 1589), 120.

109 For instance C. John Sommerville, *The News Revolution in England: Cultural Dynamics of Daily Information* (New York: Oxford University Press, 1996); Brendan Dooley and Sabrina Baron (eds), *The Politics of Information in Early Modern Europe* (London: Routledge, 2001); Richard Cust, 'News and Politics in Early Seventeenth-century England', *Past and Present*, 112 (August 1986), 60–90; Kevin Sharpe, 'Crown, Parliament and Locality: Government and Communication in Early Stuart England', *English Historical Review*, 101 (1986), 321–50; F. J. Levy, 'How Information Spread Among the Gentry, 1550–1640', *Journal of British Studies*, 21 (1982), 11–34; idem, 'Staging the News', in Marotti and Bristol (eds), *Print, Manuscript, Performance*, 252–78; Andrew Mousley, 'Self, State, and Seventeenth Century News', *The Seventeenth-century*, 6 (1991), 189–204; Steve Pincus, '"Coffee Politicians Does Create": Coffee Houses and Restoration Political Culture', *Journal of Modern History*, 67 (1995), 807–34, at p. 822; Fox, *Oral and Literate Culture in England*, ch. 7. One might also consider libels and other informal pieces of news circulated to and from London; these are well-covered in A. J. Bellany, 'The Poisoning of Legitimacy? Court Scandal, News Culture and Politics in England' (PhD dissertation, Princeton University, 1995).

110 Nicholas Hudson, *Writing and European Thought 1600–1830* (Cambridge: Cambridge University Press, 1994), 101–2.
111 Walter Scott, *The Antiquary* (Edinburgh, 1886), 44, 157, 208–9, 367.

Chapter 2

Language, literacy and aspects of identity in early modern Wales

Richard Suggett and Eryn White

INTRODUCTION

The history of the spoken word in early modern Britain involved the changing fortunes of seven or eight languages. The related English and Scots tongues expanded socially and geographically eroding Scottish Gaelic and reducing Cornish and Norse (spoken in Orkney and Shetland), and later Manx, to the point of extinction. Irish and Welsh proved the most resilient of the non-English languages of the British Isles and their speakers increased in number between the sixteenth and eighteenth centuries. However while Irish collapsed in the nineteenth century, Welsh entered a new phase of success with secure domains of language use. By the mid-nineteenth century rural and industrial parts of Wales were united by a Welsh-speaking and Welsh-reading Nonconformist culture that has subsequently deeply influenced definitions of Welshness. The elaboration of Welsh identity in the nineteenth century had much in common with the emergence in the same period of the 'buried' nationalities of central Europe and the rediscovery or invention of national traditions.[1]

The history of decline of the other Celtic languages suggests that the resilience of the spoken word in Welsh occurred against the odds. Why was Welsh different? The history of the spoken word is inseparable not only from the interaction between different languages but also the interrelation between spoken and written forms of the same language. Wales alone among the Celtic languages developed a vigorous print culture in the vernacular that built upon a written tradition reaching back into the Middle Ages. It is our contention that the survival and development of the written language, culminating in the print culture of the nineteenth century, became an essential condition for the reproduction of the modern spoken language.

This chapter examines some aspects of the interrelations between writing and speaking in Wales in the period covered by this book, broadly between about 1500 and 1800. It is hoped that a broad-brush treatment of oral and literate culture over this long period can bring out significant shifts in the relationship between literacy, language and aspects of identity in Wales. Speech and writing in Wales related dynamically throughout this period, as it did in England. However the relationship between the written and spoken word had an additional complexity in Wales because of the cross-cutting hierarchy of the English and Welsh languages. The changing relationship between the spoken and the written word and between English and Welsh has been considered in three broad periods. Much has been omitted, but it is hoped that the dynamic between language, literacy and identity will clearly emerge.

The first period extends broadly from the fifteenth-century recovery after the revolt of Owain Glyndŵr to the Acts of Union (1536 and 1543). Reaction to the revolt included an attack on the language and customs of the Welsh. Nevertheless, despite disabling statutes against the Welsh, there was probably a marked social and geographical expansion of the spoken language, and an extension in the domains of written Welsh in the fifteenth century. In particular, some oral genres, especially praise poetry and genealogy, found vigorous written expression and incidentally demonstrated the increasing accommodation of urban and rural elites of English origin within Welsh-speaking communities. The second period, extending from the Act of Union (1536) to the Restoration (1660), saw the institutional dominance of the new Court of Great Sessions. The court was an agency of anglicization, actively eroding custom and promoting the use of English. This period witnessed a general expansion of domains of literacy but contraction in the use of written Welsh. Despite the inheritance of Welsh as a written language, and the numerical predominance of Welsh speakers, literacy was increasing equated with reading and writing in English only. English became the dominant literate language for commercial and administrative purposes; Welsh as a literary language declined in significance and the status of professional bards and musicians, and other professionals literate in Welsh, was undermined by cultural shifts. However, crucially, the language of public worship was Welsh and the translation of the Bible into Welsh gave the language in its spoken and written forms new status in the religious domain.

Lastly, the period from the Restoration to about 1830 is considered. At the beginning of the period traditionalist (mainly clerical) intellectuals 'felt that the life blood was ebbing away from Wales, Welsh history was regarded as an irrelevance, the language was becoming a mere patois, and traditional culture ... was waning even among the more isolated common folk'.[2] The religious imperative, however, promoted schemes for literacy in Welsh. Although a relatively low rate of literacy existed in the seventeenth century, by the mid-eighteenth century Wales had been transformed into one of the most literate countries in Europe. Constructing literacy in Welsh through teaching in the medium of Welsh provided the basis for a new consciousness of *being* Welsh. The written word was a common standard uniting groups of dialect speakers. Welshness was increasingly defined in terms derived from literate Nonconformity, and the organization of religious societies and chapels provided a new awareness of the terrain of Wales. The majority of Welsh men and women regarded themselves as a people of the Book and with renewed linguistic confidence sometimes (with tongue only slightly in cheek) referred to their language as 'the language of heaven'.

SPEAKING AND WRITING IN LATE MEDIEVAL WALES

The diversity of language in late medieval Wales needs to be emphasized. There were many different voices in late medieval Wales but not all of them found written expression. English-language communities were to be found in the towns where they formed legally privileged islands in a sea of Welshness and also in rural communities, especially in the south, which had originated in the period of Anglo-Norman settlement. Pembrokeshire was particularly diverse with clearly defined Englishries and Welshries as well as the remnants of Flemish communities, and a continually replenished Irish population who tended to adopt English rather than Welsh as their language. But, unquestionably, Welsh was the dominant language within Wales and the only language spoken by the majority of its inhabitants whose speakers were increasing numerically throughout the late medieval and early modern periods and spilled over into some areas historically regarded as English.[3]

Diversity of speech was paralleled by diversity in writing. Four languages of record may have been used within Wales. When William Herbert was created Earl of Pembroke and a knight of the garter in 1460, a commission from the Crown was apparently directed to 'learned men' of south Wales, who included three bards, to certify the lineage of the earl because English heralds could not agree upon his descent. They assembled at Pembroke Castle and consulted ancient documents that included court records, histories, monastic registers and pedigree books and rolls. The agreed genealogy was sent to the king written in four languages: Latin, Welsh (*Bryttish*), French and English. This document may in fact have been a sixteenth-century fabrication but, if so, it was a clever forgery. It accurately revealed the existence of a whole range of records generated in literary, religious and administrative contexts, stressed the importance of specialists – especially bards of high status – needed to interpret them, and identified four languages used in Wales: two trans-national languages of record and two vernaculars.[4]

The use of written Welsh by no means reflected the dominance of the spoken language. In fifteenth-century Wales, however, there was growing use of the vernacular as a written language which paralleled the growth of English as a written language in new contexts and the slippage of Latin and Anglo-French as languages of record in some domains. Llinos Smith's indispensable survey of the evidence concludes that there was 'a marked intensification' of the process of creating a literate mentality in later medieval Wales. In fifteenth-century Wales literacy was widespread but what types of record were generated in which languages, and by and for whom? For the later medieval period, especially, we need to appreciate that characteristic expressions of literacy were not only the book or the roll but also painted and inscribed funerary monuments, inscriptions on artefacts, and wall-paintings in churches and domestic buildings. The prestige of the document means that historians can be neglectful of the written word in other media. Paper and parchment were expensive but other materials were available that may have been used for writing intended to have only a temporary significance.[5]

In this respect the archaeological discovery of an accumulation of shattered slate writing tablets, probably of late fifteenth-century date, in the debris of the ruined Cistercian abbey of Strata Florida helps us to understand the uses of cheaper writing materials. Some of the inscribed slates had lettering trials, others were used for verse composition, and some served as temporary administrative records. In particular, a ruled tablet re-used as a roofing slate recorded a bailiff's account for a monastic grange and is carefully inscribed in Welsh. One may suppose that in addition to libraries in the conventional sense, the abbey may have had collections of stone tablets used in routine administration which were regarded as temporary rather than permanent records. Three languages occur on these tablets – Welsh, Latin, and English – although the dominant language is Welsh and two of the scribes appear to have been, characteristically, a monk (David Gwyn, *monachus*) and a minstrel (David Grythor, a crowder).[6]

Relatively few Welsh language manuscripts survive from the first half of the fifteenth century. It appears that there was a long hiatus in manuscript production in the aftermath of Owain Glynd r's rebellion. However, from the mid-fifteenth century a new literate phenomenon is apparent: the production of autograph poems and the compilation of household books of poetry for patrons. These books were often rather 'home-made' productions, not the work of the scriptorium, or professional scribes, and written on paper rather than parchment. Characteristically, as Daniel Huws has argued, the poetry they contained was taken directly from oral tradition. Huws has drawn attention to the paradox that although a new poetic style (the *cywydd*) had developed in the mid-fourteenth century that was subsequently to dominate poetic composition, this new poetry did not find a written form until a century later. Huws arrives at the hypothesis that 'there were no manuscript collections of the poetry of the *cywyddwyr* earlier than about 1450 for the reason that oral tradition was so predominant'. But he suggests that by 1450 a barrier – 'a taboo almost' – had been broken and the written transmission of poetry became increasingly important between the mid-fifteenth century and the collapse of bardic culture in the late sixteenth century.[7]

There seem to have been tensions between the written and the spoken word that were probably closely related to conventions of bardic training and performance, especially the 'secret' nature of some aspects of bardic knowledge and the public recitation of verse by poets and professional reciters. Composition and performance were in some respects separate skills. Poets composed but did not necessarily recite their own poetry, but there were professional reciters (*datgeiniaid*) who recited poetry composed by others. Some poets and all reciters depended for their livelihoods on committing poetry to memory, and were accordingly threatened by written texts that made this poetry more widely accessible. Collections of poetry might be jealously preserved. 'Truly I say to you Sir John', runs a cautionary note from scribe to owner of a substantial manuscript of poetry, 'guard your book well from *datgeiniaid* because there are many good things in it.' Presumably the book had a scarcity value that would have been devalued by *datgeiniaid* committing its contents to memory and reciting them. However autograph manuscripts by poets of high status have survived and it seems probable that poets who could not read and write, or were hostile to poetry in manuscript form, were disadvantaged in their relations with literate patrons. The high status of the expert bards needs to be appreciated, as does the companionable quality of the relationship between poets and patrons, some of whom were amateur versifiers and musicians. Although praise poetry was essentially an oral genre, the distinction between bards of high status and those of low status may have been defined increasingly in terms of literacy as well as proficiency in strict-metre poetry.[8]

The public recitation of poems before patrons remained of central importance but the transmission of poetry shifted partly from an oral to a written mode in the Tudor period. It seems to have become the practice of some poets to present patrons with written copies of their poems after performance. Indeed, for some poets the written text may have displaced the importance of the memorized version of a poem. A revealing anecdote related how Meurig Dafydd (*floruit c.* 1550) came to a great house to 'singe songes and receave rewardes', and presented his patron with a new poem containing 'partelie the praises of the gentleman, and partelie the pettygrees and matches of his auncesters'. The patron perused the poem and asked Meurig if there were other copies. 'No by my fayth (sayd the rhymer) but I hope to take a copie of that which I delivered you.' The patron then gave the poet his reward but at the same time rebuked the bard for an unsatisfactory composition and consigned the text to the hall fire, saying, 'By my honestie I swere yf there bee no copie of this extante, none shall there ever bee.'[9]

The sheer quantity of these late medieval poems, principally praise poems that enhanced the status of patrons by emphasizing their gentility, leadership and generosity, should be noted. Some thousands exist in manuscript and many are of 'local' rather than 'national' interest, expressing the regional context of patronage by numerous 'freemen' descended from noble families (*uchelwyr*) who were influential in their own districts. This surviving corpus of vernacular literature is difficult to parallel elsewhere in Europe. It is also important to appreciate that this poetic culture flourished alongside a renewed and vigorous post-Glyndŵr material culture. The new timber houses of a great late medieval rebuilding that took place between 1430 and 1550 provided the physical – including acoustic – context for oral poetry. Material and poetic culture were two sides of the same coin of conspicuous consumption.[10]

Praise poems and elegies contained much genealogical material and the late medieval poets were increasingly authorities on genealogy and heraldry. Siddons has traced the development of heraldry in Wales from a more-or-less decorative system to a disciplined system with a distinctive vocabulary and heralds licensed by the College of Arms. Pedigree rolls commissioned from the herald bards and other experts by the sixteenth-century Welsh gentry combined heraldry and genealogy in a strikingly visual way.[11] The bards made numerous compilations of genealogies and may have gathered fresh genealogical information in a systematic way. An account of *c.* 1600 claims that the bards were present at the christenings, marriages and burials of the gentry families and registered these events in their books. The genealogy of a patron was integrated into a final elegy (*marwnad*) that was recited by the poet before kin and neighbours. A written version of the elegy was then lodged with the kin of the deceased and 'thousands' of these 'ancient epitaphs' were safely preserved. This may be a somewhat idealized account, composed when the bardic system was in decline, but numerous *marwnadau* survive and genealogical manuscripts reveal the systematic recording of descents relating to several thousand individuals in the fifteenth and sixteenth centuries.[12]

In the domain of genealogy we may note the interplay between the spoken and written word. The poets were to have ready on the day of burial the elegy as well as the genealogy of the deceased which, it is reasonable to suppose, may have been prepared for some time. These were solemn occasions relating to the dissolution of an individual whose social position was defined genealogically in terms of his ancestry and posterity. The elegy describing the merits of the deceased was recited publicly ('openly') with 'a loud and clear voice' before those attending the funeral, principally 'the chief gentlemen of the country who would hear it and judge it'. The genealogy of the deceased was evidently also recited as well as the names of the deceased's spouse and their children. The genealogy extended to eight generations, a pattern of relationships called in Welsh *yr wyth rhan rhieni.* The bard was expected to declare this mournfully 'in manner of bemoaning', presumably using a distinctive rhythm and voice colouring.[13]

In many ways genealogy defined the person because of its relation to status and inheritance. A gentleman's extended patronymic was not simply a string of names but also a record of the descent of his estate from a noble ancestor. Accordingly, as an antiquary explained, a gentleman 'of the meaner sort' in Wales would have in his house not only the written pedigree of his family but was also expected to be able to name his four great-grandfathers and their wives. This feat would probably have been impossible for most English gentlemen of the period, but a Welsh gentleman unable to demonstrate his ancestry in this way was accounted 'an obscure and carelesse man' who was 'out of love with himselfe'. It was acknowledged that this interest in genealogy, socially widespread in Wales, would be 'a strange and rare thinge' if found 'in the meaner sort of people in England'. But in Wales knowledge of one's kindred had practical significance for inheritance and other aspects of Welsh customary law.[14]

The recitation from memory of complex genealogies was an oral genre, although it is not apparent how they were recited and what mnemonics were employed. Sir John Wynn's celebrated history of the Gwydir family seems in some ways a late literary recension in English with occasional documentary 'proofs' of a Welsh oral genre of event-structured genealogy that paid special attention to feuding and inheritance. Numerous anecdotes revealed the genealogical awareness of Wynn's neighbours. 'Conferring often with the freeholders of the parish of Llanrwst', Wynn found that 'most of them are descended lineally from Ednyfed Fychan'. The professional genealogist (*achwr*) who knew genealogies on a regional basis also appears in Wynn's family history. In an enlightening anecdote, Wynn described how his great-grandfather asked Robin Achwr ('the greatest antiquary of our country') to present a nosegay to the best-descended gentlemen at a country assembly. To Wynn's ancestor's chagrin the nosegay was delivered to another, the obscure Llywelyn ap Dafydd, before the assembled gentlefolk. Other sources confirm that there were public demonstrations of genealogical learning, including assemblies where the bards would recite ('rip up') pedigrees and related traditions of the saints.[15]

Genealogical and poetic manuscripts, closely related to oral genres, reveal a new scribal consciousness in late medieval Wales that co-existed with routine administrative record keeping in Latin. The relationship between Latin as a language of record and the vernacular languages was probably shifting. Llinos Smith shows that the steadily increasing use of English as a medium of literacy in England was also mirrored in Wales where English rather than Welsh was sometimes used for documents that would previously have been written in Latin, especially deeds, arbitration awards, marriage settlements, wills and petitions. Nevertheless Welsh might be used for more personal estate memoranda or temporary administrative records, and occasionally Welsh was used in formal parchment administrative records. Remarkably, a mid-Tudor (1549) survey and rental of Crown lands in a part of Anglesey made, according to the Latin preamble, by the oath of named freeholders, is actually a listing in Welsh of tenements according to 'beds' (*gwelyau*) or agnatic holdings which had descended to tenants from common ancestors, and presumably reflected oral tradition and its expression in current place names. We do not know the language of its predecessor survey, but its early seventeenth-century successor two generations later was in Latin.[16]

The variety of language in record keeping reflected in part the amalgam of custom and practices in the courts of the Marcher lordships. Variability of custom was in the nature of the Marcher lordships and each lordship had its own mix of English and Welsh customary law. Welsh judges were present in some Marcher courts and Welsh law was appealed to in extra-curial arbitrations up to and beyond the Act of Union. The oral procedure in many Marcher courts was in the Welsh language although the final written record of a court was in Latin. Some of the Welsh procedural terms have been preserved, including verdicts in cases of life and death, and the substitution of oral procedures in English after the Act of Union was a profound change.[17]

In many lordships the custom of partible inheritance was recognized and land was inherited by and divided equally between male co-heirs. Inherited land could not be sold but a distinctive form of mortgage (*prid*) developed in medieval Wales that circumvented the obligation to retain lands within a kin group. Welsh mortgages were theoretically perpetually renewable. Land was transferred for a fixed term, usually four years, and at the end of the period the land was either redeemed or re-mortgaged for a further term.[18] This system of permanently redeemable mortgages provided a practical reason for preserving genealogies since land was never (in theory) permanently alienated from a kin group. As an Elizabethan authority noted, 'this law among the Welshmen did move some very earnestly to study theire own descents' hoping to redeem land mortgaged by a member of their kindred.[19]

There was an expanding land market in late medieval Wales. Deeds, while surviving unevenly, are almost without exception in Latin – the universal language of public record – although more private memoranda of land transactions, especially Welsh mortgages, might be recorded in books and rolls in Welsh. Lordships varied in the way land was transferred but in great tracts of west and mid-Wales tenements were surrendered by the rod. This was regarded as a Welsh custom although it was not unknown in England. Those who had inherited land or were mortgagees were handed a rod by a bailiff or steward in open court in token that they were admitted tenants in a lordship. These transactions were not necessarily supported by deeds and charters, and Llinos Smith has noted the corresponding absence of deeds in some Welsh regions.[20] Land disputes in these areas were probably frequently settled extra-curially by arbitrators expert in Welsh land law who depended as much on the memory of witnesses as on the written word. A complex and revealing mid-Tudor arbitrators' award, written entirely in Welsh in 1540 between first and second Acts of Union, survives for the Caeo area in west Wales. The award clearly suggests that evidence was taken orally from the disputants according to certain procedural steps before final judgment was made by two arbitrators familiar with Welsh law. Again, the linguistic complexity of the situation must be appreciated. The bond binding the parties to litigation was written in English on parchment; evidence was given orally in Welsh; the judgment of the arbitrators was given in writing in Welsh on paper.[21]

A literate culture centred on the monastic houses co-existed with the bureaucratic administration of lordships and Principality. The books of the monastic libraries largely – but not entirely – disappeared with the dissolution of the religious houses. Reminders of the ubiquitous former existence of liturgical books can be provided archaeologically, as at Carmarthen Greyfriars where book clasps were found scattered throughout the monastic church, especially in the choir.[22] Religious houses were not only centres of religious learning but also of secular learning. In particular some heads of religious houses were patrons of the bards and experts in heraldic and genealogical learning. Important literary and historical manuscripts were lodged in monastic libraries. The sources of William Herbert's pedigree, mentioned above, were said to have included 'bookys of remembrans founde in the auncyent abbeye of Strata Florida' as well as 'the rowls of Morgan Abbot'. These manuscripts have disappeared, but a significant survivor of the lost Welsh monastic libraries is the oldest-known European ordinary of arms which was kept at Greyfriars, Carmarthen, in the fifteenth century. This interest in heraldry and genealogy was no doubt partly informed by a pragmatic interest in patrons' and founders' kin who were often buried in religious houses.[23]

The late medieval Welsh religious houses and greater parish churches were full of memorials and other monuments with genealogical and heraldic information. In this context the written word was part of a broadly based visual culture whose non-verbal elements had also to be read. The badge (an eagle's claw and fish) repeatedly carved on the rood screen at Conwy parish church, for example, announced that Sir Richard Pole, constable of the castle, had commissioned the screen. It was usual for memorials to contain several visual elements. A window of *c.* 1500 which survives in Llangadwaladr parish church, Anglesey, contains the heraldry of the donor, several inscriptions and a depiction of the donor kneeling before an open book.[24]

Inscriptions provide one of the best indications of the growing status of the written vernacular in the fifteenth century, although extant examples are few in number and often difficult to fully interpret. Surviving inscriptions are generally in stone but a unique Welsh inscription in timber at Llanfair Waterdine (now in Shropshire) suggests that some of the elaborate Welsh rood screens, mostly destroyed at the Reformation, carried vernacular inscriptions. A medieval school of stone carving in north Wales had used Latin for the memorial inscriptions of the fourteenth-century Welsh aristocracy, but in the fifteenth and sixteenth centuries Welsh memorials were found alongside Latin inscriptions. Most notably, the entrance to Llanfihangel Esgeifiog church, Anglesey, has a Welsh inscription in bold relief asking all those who passed through the doorway to say a paternoster for the donor's soul and other Christians; above the doorway two niches contain figures holding books. The solemn request reveals the new status of Welsh in an ecclesiastical context and presupposes both a laity who could read the inscription and, of course, a relationship between written (inscription) and oral (prayer) genres.[25]

The most interesting surviving late-medieval memorial inscription commemorates Adam of Usk (*ob.* 1430), the clerical lawyer whose Latin chronicle is an important source of information for events between 1377 and 1421. His memorial brass, surviving but no longer in its original location in Usk priory church, has a black-letter inscription in Welsh of four couplets. The inscription is an early expression of the fifteenth-century enthusiasm for giving new Welsh verse a written form. Moreover, the use of a Welsh inscription in a town that was 'English' and had been attacked by Owain Glyndŵr is revealing. Owain Glyndŵr's rebellion and the Crown's reaction had reinforced the identity of Welshness with the Welsh language. Adam himself records his shock that Welsh had become a proscribed language during the war and he may have suffered personally because of his Welsh sympathies. There can be little doubt that the vernacular inscription was an expression of Adam's identity as a Welshman.[26]

Tombs and memorials provided the most concentrated expressions of the late medieval and Tudor links between verbal and visual culture and history and genealogy. Poetic descriptions of funerary monuments show that the tombs of the ruling families were admired and contemplated by contemporaries, illuminating details that are not now readily apparent. The most elaborate altar tombs had naturalistic carvings of the deceased set above inscriptions, painted coats of arms and emblematic figures holding books and scrolls. A herald's visitation of south Wales made in 1531 shows that a large number of memorials existed in Welsh churches and religious houses on the eve of the Reformation. They included tombs and coats of arms attributed to significant historical figures and founders of families. In Carmarthen Greyfriars, for example, over thirty armorial monuments were recorded as well as important altar tombs in the choir, where reposed, among others, Edmund, Earl of Richmond, father of Henry VII. In the Marches at Wigmore Abbey, the herald was shown the tomb of Gwladus Ddu, daughter of Llywelyn the Great, 'which Gladius the Welshmen take for a goddesse'.[27] Tombs and shrines provided physical pegs on which to hang the historical and genealogical traditions which were an important part of oral culture. The destruction of so many monuments at the Reformation inevitably involved an assault on Welsh historical mythology.[28]

The relationship between identity and language was complex in late medieval and Tudor Wales. In addition to a hierarchy of languages there was a hierarchy of media for recording these languages. The available evidence, which includes inscriptions as well as paper and parchment, suggests that there was an expansion in the use of written Welsh, which in the case of poetry and genealogy directly related to oral genres associated with the bards. Bardic learning, which was probably substantially oral, related deeply to definitions of Welshness. A late tract on the 'office and function' of the bards neatly brings out the elements which defined Welshness: language, history and custom; these were 'the three memorials' (*y tri chof*) which the bards were expected to maintain. The bards were to preserve the purity of the ancient tongue, accounting for every word and syllable they used, by avoiding any foreign words. The bards were also to know the notable acts of the Welsh kings and princes, and required to keep the genealogies of the Welsh nobility who descended from them, including their division of lands and their coats of arms.[29] Welsh identity was not only a matter of maintaining the spoken word but entailed maintaining those customs and the historical mythology which also constructed a sense of separate identity.[30] The attack on custom after the Acts of Union was as much a deliberate erosion of Welshness as was the explicit exclusion of the Welsh language from certain domains of use.

LANGUAGE AND LITERACY AFTER THE ACTS OF UNION

In Wales the mid-Tudor reformation of religion and the reformation of custom had profound consequences for the status of the Welsh language, domains of literacy, and the definitions of identities – both personal and national. The preamble to the Act of Union (1536) was uncompromising: in Wales there were divers rights, usages, laws and customs 'far discrepant from the Laws and Customs of this Realm'. Furthermore, the speech of the Welsh people was 'nothing like nor consonant to the natural Mother Tongue used within this Realm'. All courts were to be held in English, and all office-holders were to be English speakers. The aim was 'utterly to extirp' all the 'sinister Usages and Customs' in Wales now that it was fully incorporated within the realm of England. The primary instruments for establishing uniformity were new assize courts, the Courts of Great Sessions, which were to become immensely busy.[31]

The drive for legal and linguistic uniformity in the Tudor state-building process meant not only an attack on custom but also an erosion of oral and written genres in Welsh that related to custom. Significant areas of Welsh-language learning, particularly genealogy, became devalued, partly because their relevance to status and inheritance within an extended kindred had been lost with the abolition of partible inheritance and the new freedom to alienate land inherited from ancestors. Welsh land law and inheritance, an important marker of the difference between the English and the Welsh, had been killed almost stone-dead by the Act of Union. Inheritance claims by kin relating to gavelkind land held by those dying before the second Act of Union, specifically by the Feast of the Nativity of St John the Baptist 1541 in the thirty-third year of Henry VIII's reign, were entertained by the Court of Great Sessions. However it was a measure of the assimilation of custom that the number of these claims rapidly declined in the second half of the sixteenth century.[32]

A decline in learning in Welsh – especially bardic learning which combined both written and spoken genres – occurred in the second half of the sixteenth century, but it was a prolonged and nuanced process. As is explained in Chapter 5 of this volume, the decline in the status of the bards was a complex combination of changes in taste, the emergence of an increasingly anglicized gentry class, and the redefinition of itinerant entertainers as vagabonds and their rewards as begging. By the beginning of the seventeenth century the capacity of professional bards to earn a living had been seriously curtailed and poetic, historical and genealogical learning became the preserve of a small number of antiquarian-minded gentlemen and clerics. There was a sense of finality about the ending of the older order and the loss of learning in the Welsh language. As one antiquary put it at the beginning of the seventeenth century, 'at this time all the greate knowledge of the bards, there credit and worth is altogether decayed and worne out, soe that at this time they are extinguish[ed] amongst us'.[33]

There can be little doubt that there was a consequential decline of literacy in Welsh. The erosion of domains of literacy was accompanied by the loss and destruction of manuscripts generated by the old centres of literacy. The literary, administrative and religious books of the religious houses mostly disappeared at the Reformation, with a few important exceptions. The routine administrative documents of the Marcher lordships suffered similarly after the Act of Union. It was no longer necessary to register transfers of land in the books of the Marcher courts; this could now be done without the lord's knowledge simply by levying a fine in the Court of Great Sessions. As manuscripts lost their relevance they were jettisoned. Genealogies compiled before the Act of Union were already 'rare and decayed' by about 1600. Surviving Welsh-language manuscripts reveal the selective nature of preservation. Very little devotional, administrative and later legal material has survived. Literary manuscripts have survived unevenly and the older part of the Welsh literary 'canon', especially the pre-1400 poetry and *Mabinogion* tales, rests on a slender thread of unique texts in four or five 'ancient books'.[34]

The peripatetic Courts of Great Sessions emerged as a central domain of language use from which by and large Welsh was excluded. Welsh was not recognized by the court as a formal language of procedure or record. As there was a hierarchy of languages, so there was a hierarchy of media. Welsh-language business in the courts was confined to oral statements that were translated into English. The English language was admitted into the record of the court, especially in the form of examinations, as paper records. Finally, the record of the court was made in Latin on parchment. It may be noted, however, that certain points in the criminal procedure linked the spoken and written word theatrically. As in England, convicted felons could claim 'benefit of clergy' by demonstrating in open court their ability to read in Latin like a clerk. Those who successfully claimed benefit of clergy were discharged after branding on the brawn of the thumb; those who failed to read were executed. These public demonstrations of literacy and non-literacy were dramatic, and sometimes produced unexpected results attributed to God's intervention. In 1602 Thomas Bull was convicted of poisoning, and claimed benefit of clergy at the Radnorshire Great Sessions. He was brought a book 'to assaye and to rede upon', but although literate ('lettered') found 'he could not reede any Whitt, but said that there was a Miste before his eyes so that he could not decerne the letters'. But there were numerous successful claims to benefit of clergy in Tudor and Stuart Wales. It was a procedure that could be manipulated by both court and those convicted.[35]

However, outside the formal English and Latin procedures of the court there existed a largely hidden Welsh-language system of compromise and arbitration dominated by the spoken word. Civil actions rarely proceeded to trial and judgment although very large numbers of writs were issued between sessions. Numerous accusations of felony were made but acquittals were high and a large proportion of bills of indictment were thrown out by the grand jury before trial for lack of evidence. Writs and bills of indictment induced defendants to compromise with plaintiffs and suspects to 'compound' with accusers. Numerous early modern arbitrators' awards have survived and they show that large numbers of disputes were settled extra-curially through a complex interplay between written and oral procedures in English and Welsh. Dispute settlement took place orally in Welsh using arbitrators and sworn testimony, occasionally using large numbers of 'oath-helpers', but the final outcome took the form of written awards in English that sometimes became the subject of litigation because of non-performance.[36]

The records of the Great Sessions reveal that commercial transactions in Wales were increasingly regulated by written agreements in English. A flood of actions for debt were grounded upon written transactions ranging from entries in mercers' shop-books to formal agreements for leasing land, selling stock and produce, building and repairing houses and numerous other circumstances. The written agreement was probably the rule rather than the exception and provided work for the scriveners who can sometimes be identified in taxation documents and other records as a moderately prosperous occupational group. Most agreements were supported by conditional bonds that entailed a financial penalty if the terms of the agreement were not kept. This was an interesting situation linguistically. Welsh society, rural and urban alike, was increasingly enmeshed in a nexus of debt recorded in a language most would not be able to understand, let alone read. It emerges from pleadings that the written and spoken word were linked by unnamed translators. It was the practice for the terms and conditions of these English bonds to be recited in Welsh (perhaps by scriveners or attorneys) before sealing.[37]

The experience of literacy in early modern Wales was often an expression of legal and religious authority reinforced by the spoken word. This included the hearing of proclamations and other black-letter texts publicly read. Literacy was rarely the direct experience of education or entertainment. Basic work on measuring literacy remains to be done but the evidence, such as it is, suggests that rates of illiteracy were higher in Wales than in England. It has been bravely estimated that by the 1640s less than a fifth (about 18 per cent) of the population in Wales could read. Readers were unevenly distributed both socially and geographically. There was a pronounced rural–urban literacy divide that ran parallel with the linguistic divide between town and country. This is clearly conveyed by the pattern of jurors' marks and signatures on coroners' inquisitions in the seventeenth century. In urban locales, jurors – mostly tradesmen – were overwhelmingly literate in the sense that most signed their names; conversely in rural locales, jurors were overwhelmingly illiterate in the sense that most made a cross or some other mark. The growing numbers of jurors who signed with their initials and presumably were therefore able to recognize letters probably indicates a steadily increasing proportion of rural jurors who could read but not write. This information relates of course to male jurors; the extent of female literacy is unknowable.[38]

The expansion of the use of English for all legal and quasi-legal documents was probably accompanied by a contraction in the literate use of Welsh. Given the nature of schooling it was to be expected that even the most personal of documents composed by Welsh speakers would be in English. Letter writing in Wales was almost exclusively an English-language genre even though the author and recipient of a letter might be Welsh speakers. Wills were not required to be in Latin or English, but they were very rarely written in Welsh until the eighteenth century. In a revealing late sixteenth-century encounter, a mortally sick Montgomeryshire yeoman asked Hugh Pennant to write his will because the curate of the parish was absent. Hugh Pennant, a bard and graduate of the 1568 *eisteddfod*, obliged but 'did write the same in the welche tongue for that as he saied hee could not write the same in Englishe'.[39] The incident is particularly interesting because it confirms that the older literacy in Welsh could be independent of literacy in English. The Preface to the first printed Welsh book (1546/47) had referred to the 'many Welshmen who could read Welsh but not a word in English or Latin'.[40]

However, literacy in Welsh was probably a declining skill in the century after the Act of Union because it was considered less practically useful in a worldly sense than literacy in English. By the mid-seventeenth century it was alleged that few people were able to read Welsh apart from the clergy, and even they found it difficult.[41] Reading and writing in Welsh were rarely formally taught. Indeed in certain circumstances literacy in Welsh might be regarded as a suspect skill and there were sometimes searches for seditious books that were both Welsh *and* Catholic. The Denbighshire grand jury was asked to locate books that contained doctrine contrary to the established religion, and searches for seditious books were authorized at the Flintshire assizes. Catholics in Wales made an effort to circulate literature in the vernacular, including satirical songs, and had a short-lived clandestine press.[42]

The adverse consequences of the Act of Union for a sense of separate Welsh identity based on language and custom were profound. Welsh custom and language were both deemed 'uncivil' or even 'sinister'. A new word – 'civility' – entered the discourse of power to describe the superiority of English language and custom on which the unity of the peoples of the British Isles under the Crown was to be based. Towards the end of the sixteenth century the reforming activities of the Court of Great Sessions was deemed to have brought Wales 'to knowe civilitie'. Petitions to the court from 'mere' Welshmen, who were described as simple and illiterate, unable to speak or write English, reveal a sense of inferiority among some Welsh speakers and the growing reality of the dominance of the English language in many domains of language use.[43]

However although the English language dominated legal and commercial domains, religion remained a contested domain in terms of language use. The state's language policy of uniformity was tempered by acknowledgement of the necessity for people to gain knowledge of religion in their own tongue. The 1563 Act authorizing the translation of the Bible and *Book of Common Prayer* into Welsh, and permitting the use of Welsh in divine service, also ordered that English versions should be placed in churches where Welsh Bibles were needed so that people 'by conferring both Tongues, [may] the sooner attain to the Knowledge of the English tongue'. The status of Welsh in this domain was expressed publicly by painted black-letter texts derived from the *Book of Common Prayer*. An Elizabethan (1583) episcopal visitation of the diocese of St Davids enquired whether altars, rood lofts and other 'signs and monuments of superstition and idolatory' had been removed and 'sentences of Holy Scripture written in their places'. The written word had replaced the image in the post-Reformation churches of Wales and, crucially, in this domain the words were in Welsh. The erosion of custom meant that language was to become increasingly important as a signifier of difference, especially within the religious domain where it acquired special status.[44]

LANGUAGE, LITERACY AND RELIGION IN EARLY MODERN WALES

Religion has frequently been identified as one of the major driving forces behind the growth of literacy during the early modern period.[45] In Wales religion was a fundamental motivation for the spread of literacy and – alone among the Celtic languages of Britain – the development of a vigorous print culture in the vernacular. From the mid-sixteenth century, the authorities recognized that unity of religion had to take priority, for the time being at least, over unity of language.[46] It was more important to make the Welsh into good Protestants than to make them into good English speakers. The aim in the long term may well have been to convert them into good English-speaking Protestants. In the meantime, however, it was realized that Welsh was the most effective means of communication to ensure their conversion. The translation of the Bible and *Book of Common Prayer* into Welsh ensured the development and maintenance of a standard literary language that was read aloud in the parish churches of Wales and heard week in and week out by the majority of Welsh men, women and children.[47]

The inter-relationship between language, religion and education would have profound implications for the survival of the Welsh language. Welsh was seldom the language of formal instruction during the early modern period. The urban grammar schools, established from the sixteenth century onwards, used English as the medium of instruction and were intended primarily for the sons of the gentry, burgesses and well-to-do yeomen farmers. The Dissenting academies, initially established during the period of persecution to provide an alternative form of higher education for Dissenters who were banned from attending the universities, also used English as the medium of instruction.[48] In the wake of the Acts of Union, English increasingly came to be considered the language of prestige and advancement, whereas Welsh was the language of the marketplace and the farmyard. Ultimately the saving grace for the language in terms of education was that the educational initiatives of the early modern period were all prompted by a single concern: the need to instil saving knowledge of the Gospel. With the spread of print culture, religious reformers of the period became acutely aware of a fundamental truth, perhaps best expressed by David Maurice in 1700: *I mae'r llais, a glower, yn darfod yn ddisymmwth, ond yr scrifen a beru byth* (The voice, which is heard, ends suddenly, but writing lasts forever).[49] The statement expresses a perception of the transience of the spoken word, and the growing authority of the more permanent printed word.

From the mid-seventeenth century onwards attempts were made to encourage literacy among substantial sections of the population in Wales. The first of these endeavours was the work of the state, in the form of the Act for the Better Propagation of the Gospel in Wales (1650–53), passed by a Puritan regime which regarded Wales as 'one of the dark corners of the land', where superstition, popery and ignorance ruled.[50] This first attempt to establish free elementary education for the children of Wales began with the best of intentions, but ultimately failed to fulfil its ambitions and the last of the schools established under the Act were abolished with the Restoration of the monarchy in 1660. Subsequent efforts to promote education and literacy came as the result of various voluntary movements, including the Welsh Trust (1674–81), the Society for the Promotion of Christian Knowledge (SPCK) (1699–1737) and Griffith Jones's circulating schools (1731–79). The Welsh Trust was the brainchild of Thomas Gouge, a London minister who, despite his own strong Puritan tendencies, was able to appeal to moderates among both the Anglicans and the Nonconformists. By summer 1675 over eighty schools had been established in some of the major market towns of the country, with over 2,000 children attending them. However, despite the initial success, decline soon set in and by 1678 only thirty-three schools remained open. Hostility grew as people became suspicious that the Trust aimed to revive Puritanism. The influence of the schools was also limited by the decision to use English as the medium of instruction. Most of the schools tended to be located in major towns and in the border areas, where knowledge of English was more widespread. Even so, Stephen Hughes, the Trust's leading figure in Wales, was vehemently opposed to the language policy of the schools. The Trust was eventually wound up after the death of Thomas Gouge in 1681.

It would appear that any remaining funds were ultimately transferred to the coffers of the SPCK. This organization was fuelled by the same Pietist influences as other societies from this period, such as the Society for the Reformation of Manners. Its aim was to establish elementary schools to improve educational facilities in Wales and to publish improving literature. The drive to establish schools met with some initial success. It is significant that thirty of the first schools set up by the SPCK were located in places where Trust schools had previously been established. Like the Trust, the SPCK concentrated on setting up schools in the major market towns, particularly in the south of the country. Ninety-six schools were set up by the SPCK, sixty-eight of which were established by 1715. Support dwindled subsequently, partly as a result of the Schism Act of 1714 and partly because the SPCK was suspected of harbouring a secret Jacobite agenda. Once again, their influence had been limited by the continued insistence on the use of English, although many of the schools in north Wales appear to have been conducted in Welsh. Ultimately, the SPCK's greatest success may well have been its contribution in terms of publications. Despite its reluctance to use Welsh as a medium of instruction, it was willing to publish religious literature in Welsh. In particular the Society played an important role in producing substantial copies of the Welsh Bible, which would be of paramount importance to subsequent educational initiatives. The 1718 edition of the Bible ran to 10,000 copies, 1,000 of which were distributed free to the poor.

The real breakthrough in terms of popular literacy came with the work of Griffith Jones and the circulating schools. Born in Carmarthenshire in 1684, Jones's name is inextricably linked with the parish of Llanddowror, which he served as rector from 1716 until his death in 1761. It may well have been an outbreak of typhus in south-west Wales between 1727 and 1731 that spurred Griffith Jones into action. He was acutely aware that many of those who died during this epidemic were woefully ignorant of the basic principles of their faith. Like David Maurice, he realized all too well that preaching alone could never be sufficient to combat this ignorance. His initial response was to establish a school in his own parish of Llanddowror in 1731. It is not clear precisely when he embarked on the circulating system, but by 1738 the first annual report on the progress of the schools, *Welch Piety*, was published. The circulating schools basically consisted of a schoolteacher sent to an area for some three months at a time to conduct classes in any available building. The schools were invariably established between September and May, so as not to clash with the busiest months of the agricultural calendar.

These attempts to increase literacy were by no means completely detached from orality. Indeed, the spoken word remained at the heart of Griffith Jones's educational initiative, which relied to a large degree on mnemonic devices and reading aloud. The greater emphasis on reading over and above writing ensured that this was the case. The curriculum was severely curtailed to concentrate primarily on reading. The pressing aim was to teach as many people as possible to read the Bible in as short a time as possible. Writing, arithmetic and other subjects favoured by the SPCK were jettisoned as superfluous to the primary intention of the schools. Thus, with a streamlined syllabus, it was possible to achieve more in a short space of time. It was Griffith Jones's proud boast that in his schools a child could be taught to read in Welsh within the space of three months. Lessons began with learning the alphabet, but much of the subsequent instruction was based on the repetition of sentences read aloud by the teacher, as Jones himself explained:

> I am credibly informed, that it has, in England, been found a good Method, to bring Children to read soon, without Hesitation, to have some Sentences first read

> by the Teacher, and then for the Scholar to read them; and this to be repeated over and over again, till the Scholar reads them readily, and without Hesitation. It is for want of this most rational Practice that many Children are long in learning to read readily, without Hesitation, and are therefore thought dull, when, in reality, it is not their Fault.[51]

This method explains how some blind scholars were taught, since they could recite and memorize sections of the Scriptures, even though they could not read the letters. In Gelli-gaer in Glamorgan, for example, an old blind woman of eighty attended the school to receive instruction in 'the Principles of Religion'. She was motivated to attend after a visit to the school during which she heard the children going through the responses to the catechism.[52] Reciting the catechism was given a high priority in these classes and it is significant that Griffith Jones referred to his schools in *Welch Piety* as the Circulating and Catechising Schools. Jones himself provided Welsh-medium catechisms to be used by his scholars, such as *Esponiad Byr ar Gatecism yr Eglwys* (1752; A Brief Explanation of the Church Catechism).

At the end of the quarter, the teacher would move on to begin the process again in another area. However, in many parishes, teachers would return for a second or third visit to consolidate their work, instruct new recruits and impart further instruction to the most advanced pupils. The schools were open free of charge to pupils of all ages and every social status. Additional classes were conducted during the evening for those whose work did not allow them to attend during the day. It is estimated that two-thirds of the total number of scholars were adults, many of them advanced in years. Reports in *Welch Piety* contain numerous accounts of elderly men and women moved to tears of joy at gaining access to the printed word for the first time and tears of regret that they had not had this opportunity earlier in life.

In many ways, Jones's ideas were not particularly new. The idea of ambulatory schools had previously been advocated by the SPCK in the Highlands of Scotland. In 1719, Sir Humphrey Mackworth, a patron of the SPCK in Wales, suggested that the use of itinerant teachers might have some value. What was new was the combination of inspiration, dedication and practicality that prompted Griffith Jones to decide upon the use of the Welsh language as the medium of instruction. Previous efforts by the Welsh Trust and the SPCK had foundered at least partly because of their insistence upon using English in their schools. English was used in the circulating schools located in more anglicized areas, such as south Pembrokeshire, Gower and Monmouthshire, but Welsh was the language of the vast majority of the schools. This caused some concern amongst English philanthropists and also among critics within Wales itself. Griffith Jones was forced to defend his policy and did so partly on the grounds of pragmatism and economy. Welsh was the language of the majority of the population, as Jones stated: 'Welsh is still the Vulgar Tongue and not English'.[53] Whilst that remained true, it was the logical choice to educate the mass of the population in Wales. Since the main aim was the salvation of souls, it was imperative to employ the quickest and most effective methods to introduce the scholar to the Bible. Otherwise, countless souls might be condemned to ignorance, as Griffith Jones pointed out:

> For how much better is it that the Welsh People should forever be ignorant of the English Language ... than that they should live and die ignorant of what is necessary to their salvation, and which they cannot be instructed in ... but in Welch only?[54]

Pupils could be taught to read in Welsh in three months; indeed, it was claimed that one seven-year-old child in Cynwyl Elfed in Carmarthenshire was taught to read Welsh in less than three weeks.[55] But it might take three to four years to teach them to read through the medium of English.[56] This was time they could ill afford. In addition, the shorter the process of instruction, the cheaper it was. Griffith Jones took pride in the fact that for every twenty-shilling donation he received, six poor children were taught to read in Welsh. He was therefore able to put forward a sound and practical defence for the use of Welsh. The main reason behind the decision to make Welsh the medium of instruction was the simple fact that it was the language of the spoken word for the majority of the population. If the decision was governed by the strength of the Welsh language, then the fact that Welsh, and not English, became the medium of education in these schools in turn reinforced that strength. It helped ensure that the English language would not be regarded exclusively as the language of schooling and literacy in Wales.

After Griffith Jones's death in 1761, the schools continued under the management of Madam Bridget Bevan. She proved to be a most efficient and business-like manager. The number of schools actually increased under her supervision, particularly in English-speaking areas. Madam Bevan intended the schools to continue after her death in 1779, with the help of a £10,000 bequest in her will. Unfortunately, however, some members of her family contested the will and, with the money tied up in legal wrangling, the schools went into a sharp and inexorable decline.

During their heyday, the schools had provided many tenant farmers, cottagers and labourers, along with their wives and children, with their first real opportunity to acquire basic literacy. Local clergy were asked by Griffith Jones to testify to the benefits they had witnessed in their parishes as a result of the schools. They were invariably able to do so because of the emphasis on reading aloud and catechizing in the schools, which enabled visitors to judge the progress of the scholars. As a result, David Morris, vicar of St Lawrence in Pembrokeshire, was able to give this account of the changes wrought amongst his parishioners by 1747:

> To our Shame be it spoken, I can very well remember that the grey Hairs of Persons arrived to the full Age of Man, Sixty Years old and upwards, were so ignorant and illiterate, as not to be able to read the Lord's Prayer in the Mother Tongue; but now, by the Grace of God, a beardless Boy distinctly reads the Welch Bible; a Blessing entirely owing to the Welch Schools.[57]

He and other witnesses expressed their joy at the remarkable experience of hearing the pupils reading and responding to the catechism. The best indication of the extent of the influence of the circulating schools may be gained from the figures. By the time of Griffith Jones's death in 1761, over 200,000 pupils had received instruction in some 3,325 schools, at a time when the population of Wales was an estimated 489,000. Wales could be counted amongst the most literate countries in Europe in this period. News of this success reached as far as Russia where Catherine the Great instructed her ministers to make further enquiries about the schools. There is a consensus amongst historians of Wales that the circulating schools did much to revive the fortunes of the Welsh language. According to Glanmor Williams, Griffith Jones's contribution 'did more than anything else to preserve and fortify the Welsh language and literature, of which the Bible was the corner-stone'.[58] Geraint H. Jenkins agrees that the circulating schools 'were the chief means by which the native tongue was strengthened and preserved during the eighteenth century'.[59] The momentum of the circulating schools was to some extent maintained by numerous petty schools, some of which were presided over by schoolteachers trained in Griffith Jones's service. One such was William Thomas, of Michaelston-super-Ely in Glamorgan, whose diary includes several references to keeping school in a number of locations in the area of the Vale of Glamorgan.[60] By the end of the century, Thomas Charles of Bala had begun his pioneering work with the Sunday schools, which would do much to continue the tradition of the circulating schools.

There seems little doubt that rates of literacy had increased by the end of the eighteenth century, despite a possible contraction following the decline of the circulating schools. There is some evidence to confirm this from the visitation returns for the Diocese of St David's in 1804, in which the parish clergy were required to indicate what proportion of the poor in their parishes were able to read.[61] One indication of the growth of literacy was the notable increase in the number of books published in Welsh during the eighteenth century. Up until 1695, the business of printing books had been restricted to London, Oxford and Cambridge. The production of books in Welsh was a laborious process fraught with difficulties. Errors were all too common when printers were unfamiliar with the Welsh alphabet and language. However, with the lapsing of the Licensing Act after 1695, presses were soon to be established in Shrewsbury, which was much more convenient for both authors and purchasers within Wales. The first printing press in Wales itself was set up by Isaac Carter at Trefhedyn near Newcastle Emlyn in 1718. Other presses were soon established in market towns, including Swansea, Carmarthen and Brecon. During the eighteenth century over 2,500 books, excluding ephemera, were published in Welsh, and in the nineteenth century the Welsh press continued to expand; by 1820 there were over 50 printers in Wales.[62]

It must be remembered, however, that solitary book reading was by no means the only aspect of print culture.[63] The custom of reading aloud, as described by Erasmus Saunders in 1721, was certainly popular at this time:

> [T]here are many, even of the common People, who gladly make the best use of what little Knowledge they have gain'd, and take the Pains privately, by Reading or Discoursing to instruct one another in their Houses. And it is not uncommon to see Servants and Shepherds, as they have an Opportunity, strive to do these good Offices to each other.[64]

From the mid-seventeenth century onwards, it became increasingly common practice to include in published works a guide to the illiterate to help them learn to read. This was particularly true of those works edited by Stephen Hughes during the mid–late seventeenth century. In his Introduction to his edition of *Tryssor i'r Cymru*, Hughes urged those familiar with written works to guide the less familiar over the difficult words.[65] In 1683, Thomas Jones went a step further in his *Llyfr Plygain* and produced a guide for those learning to write, including instructions on how to fashion a pen and advice about ink and about the ideal seated posture for the exercise. The work also included examples of italic, round and mixed hand for the uninitiated.[66]

There was apparently a tradition of reading aloud and discussing texts in craftsmen's workshops. Craftsmen had an advantage over farmers and agricultural labourers in that their work was not always as physically demanding and therefore in some instances allowed such discussion groups to take place. It is not clear, however, how prevalent the custom of silent reading had become. There are occasional clues, as in William Williams's elegy to Mrs Grace Price of Watford, which describes her sitting in her chair by the fire reading, making a note of which of Williams's hymns appealed to her most, or pointing out sections of printed sermons that had served to inspire her.[67] She could, however, be classed as a member of the minor gentry and may not have been wholly representative of the population at large. The growth of literacy and printing in some ways might even have helped to revive some elements of the oral tradition. The publication of medieval *cywyddau* during the late seventeenth and early eighteenth centuries encouraged a revival of interest in strict-metre poetry. Free verse, however, was apparently less likely to be preserved in print during this period. Examples do appear, however, in manuscript form and many ballads, carols and other forms of popular verse are noted in commonplace books from this period.

It seems that the least likely to survive was the work of women poets.[68] It has been suggested that women's preference for free-verse poetry partially accounted for this, since it was not afforded the same respect as strict-metre poetry. Even the work of Ann Griffiths, now regarded as one of the most important hymn writers of the eighteenth century, was not recorded in print during her lifetime and only one verse survived in Ann's own hand. Instead, it was memory that preserved her verse. Her maidservant, Ruth, had memorized all her mistress's hymns and was able to dictate them so that they might be published for posterity.[69]

The growing value placed on the written word did not immediately eradicate the importance of oral transmission. Many people read in order to commit to memory. Editions of Rees Prichard's religious verses remained popular throughout the eighteenth century. Motivated by his concern for the welfare of his parishioners, Vicar Prichard of Llandovery composed numerous catchy verses with an obvious moral or religious message, which were intended to be easily memorized. The first printed version of his work appeared in 1658 and numerous subsequent editions proved to be remarkably popular.[70] His rough and ready verses are peppered with colloquialisms and seem to have been originally written in the dialect of the area of Carmarthenshire, bordering with Glamorgan, where he lived and worked. There is no doubting their immense appeal. It is a mark of the Vicar's success that beggarwomen knew his verses on the duty of charity by heart and were apt to recite them to encourage those reluctant to part with their money.[71] Nesta Lloyd suggests that Rees Prichard's verse lost its popularity by the twentieth century simply because it was so firmly rooted in the oral tradition. These were verses designed to be heard, whose rhyme scheme may appear strange on the printed page but works when they are read aloud in the appropriate dialect, as initially intended.[72] In addition, folk-tales, traditions, ballads and carols continued to be passed on by word of mouth. Howel Harris, the Methodist revivalist, may have been greatly influenced by reading the Welsh versions of Puritan classics, but he was also captivated by the many folk-tales and traditions recounted to him on his travels. For instance, he was told of a woman of sixty who visited a holy well at Llanwennog and was subsequently able to breastfeed her infant granddaughter.[73] Harris also heard several accounts of the appearance of corpse candles which he judged to be 'truth real'.[74] In 1770 in Pembrokeshire Harris encouraged his listeners, 'ye old Brittons', not 'to swallow ye English Pride & Language & despise their own'.[75]

The growing romanticizing of Wales by patriots and travellers prompted increasing interest in language and folk tradition. Scholars and romantics scrambled to record – and sometimes elaborate – remaining folk-tales and traditions, songs and dances for future generations.[76] There was anxiety that traditions might be lost forever if not preserved in print. These concerns prompted William Owen Pughe to found the *Cambrian Register*, a periodical that appeared in three volumes between 1795 and 1818. According to the editorial Preface, its aim was to preserve the oral tradition before it vanished forever:

> Since the revival of learning in Europe, most nations have been emulous of bringing forward their respective stores of ancient memorials, in order to enrich the common stock; but a vast treasure is contained in the Welsh language, in manuscripts, and the oral traditions of the people, of which barely a notice has hitherto been given to the world.[77]

This treasury of Welsh antiquarian and literary traditions was produced in English, published in London, and ultimately folded through lack of support. However, at the same time there were numerous ventures in publishing Welsh-language periodicals, often with denominational links and a high religious content. *Seren Gomer* (The Star of Gomer) was established as a weekly journal in 1814 and distributed throughout Wales, and has some claim to be the first national newspaper in one of the 'non-official' languages of Europe.[78]

The overwhelming majority of the material produced in print was of a religious nature. There seems to be little doubt that the emphasis on learning to read the Bible and the number of religious works published in this period had a profound impact on the Welsh language. The growth of Methodism and Nonconformity emphasized the need for a common standard that would overcome the divisions of regional dialects. Substantial numbers travelled to Llangeitho in the south-west to hear Daniel Rowland preach and later in the century to Bala in the north to hear Thomas Charles. Rarely, if ever, had such mass meetings, drawing people from north and south, east and west, been held in Wales. Initially, the Methodist preachers from the south had received a poor welcome in the north, partly at least because their accents and dialects had marked them out as strangers. It was imperative, therefore, that the revivalists should be understood by all their hearers. They were acutely aware of the need to communicate in a dialect that would be intelligible to all. Hence the development of a 'pulpit language' which would unite the entire audience and a 'Welsh style' of preaching by peripatetic preachers which was expressed most dramatically in periodic religious revivals.[79]

Preachers were by no means the only group of people to wrestle with the problem of uniting an audience without a common dialect. The north–south linguistic divide proved to be especially troublesome to authors. Many of the early books printed in Welsh referred to this problem and some seventeenth-century authors included glossaries explaining the meaning of regional words which might be unfamiliar to their readers.[80] As Stephen Hughes remarked in 1688, this was necessary so that the inhabitants of the north and south should not be as 'barbarians' to each other.[81] It was perhaps inevitable that the Methodists, who used the Bible as their guide and inspiration in so many matters, would turn to the Scriptures in this respect also. The evolution of Methodist and Nonconformist imagery and language owed much to the Bible. The Methodists in particular developed their own idiom of religious experience when attempting to discuss their spiritual condition in their societies. In the early years of the movement during the 1740s the local superintendent, who oversaw the spiritual welfare of a number of individual societies, was expected to write regular accounts of the condition of each member. These reports were then sent to the Association, the movement's governing body. There was a marked tendency to categorize members according to their spiritual experience and development. The terms used to do so were largely derived from the Bible. Some were described as being 'under the Law', others as 'searching for the pearl', and these scriptural references would be immediately intelligible to the Methodist community. The Scripture then supplied them with a form of shorthand which could be used to describe members. In one instance, Anne David of Dyffryn-saith society in south Cardiganshire was categorized with a simple reference to the Gospel of St Luke, chapter fifteen, which contains the reference to the 'joy in the presence of angels of God over one sinner that repenteth'.[82] Such efforts to analyse and express religious experiences undoubtedly served to enrich the language. It is notable that many composite Welsh words beginning with the prefix *hunan-* (self-) appeared in print for the first time during the eighteenth century in works by religious writers and in translations of English Puritan works of the seventeenth century.[83]

As aspects of Welsh culture bound up with the oral tradition seemed to be dying out, Methodism and Nonconformity replaced them with an alternative culture in which orality in other forms was a vital element. Field preaching was an important feature of the Methodist revival and one of the main methods by which converts were attracted to the movement. Although Griffith Jones had on occasion preached out of doors when his congregation proved too large to be contained within a church, it was the Methodists who truly developed itinerant field preaching. The fervour and enthusiasm of Methodist sermons, frequently lasting two to three hours, was new to the majority of their audiences. Word of mouth, therefore, proved to be the most effective means of communicating the Methodist gospel. Despite being so thoroughly grounded in the Book, the Methodist movement relied heavily on the spoken word. Methodist societies were termed 'experience meetings' because their essential activity was to relate and analyse experiences. It was this that led Saunders Lewis to describe them as 'clinics of the soul', where those who had gone through the overwhelming experience of conversion could discuss their feelings with their fellow members.[84] Extempore prayers and hymn singing were also popular elements in the activities of the societies. Hymns were not sung from books, but repeated line by line after the individual member entrusted to pitch the tune. These activities set the foundations for the numerous prayer meetings, sermons, society meetings, Sunday schools, the Band of Hope, choirs and the *Cymanfa Ganu* (hymn-singing festival) which would become part and parcel of a new 'chapel civility' during the nineteenth century.[85]

From the sixteenth century onward, the Bible had been the cornerstone of standardized literary Welsh and its influence continued into the nineteenth century.[86] By the early nineteenth century, the growth of Nonconformity had particularly fostered the importance of religion as a focus for Welsh identity and the development of a chapel-based social culture in the Welsh language. The religious census of 1851 revealed that nearly 60 per cent of the Welsh population attended a place of worship and that the overwhelming majority of worshippers – almost 90 per cent – belonged to Nonconformist denominations. Nonconformity was in the ascendancy in most of the forty-eight Poor Law districts used as the basis for enumeration. The Established Church was strongest along the borders with England and in the more anglicized areas of the south and was weakest where the Welsh language was strongest.[87] This intensified the belief in the association between Nonconformity and Welsh language and identity that would be emphasized increasingly by Nonconformist leaders as the century progressed. Nonconformity came to be seen as an essential part of Welsh identity, and literacy in Welsh as a fundamental part of Nonconformist identity. The growth of the institutions of Liberal Nonconformity in the second half of the nineteenth century coincided with the spectacular growth in the number of Welsh speakers. In 1911 nearly 1 million Welsh speakers were enumerated, although numbers of Welsh speakers have declined substantially subsequently. In the twentieth century alternative and competing definitions of Welshness emerged that did not depend on religious allegiance and the Welsh language.[88]

NOTES

1 See generally the volumes in the series 'The Social History of the Welsh Language', general ed. Geraint H. Jenkins (Cardiff: University of Wales Press, 1997–2000). Important contextual essays include: Brynley F. Roberts, 'The Celtic Languages of Britain', in Jenkins (ed.), *The Welsh Language before the Industrial Revolution* (Cardiff: University of Wales Press, 1997), 407–40; R. J. W. Evans, 'Language and Society in the Nineteenth Century: Some Central-European Comparisons', in Jenkins (ed.), *Language and Community in the Nineteenth Century* (Cardiff: University of Wales Press, 1998), 397–424.

2 Prys Morgan, 'Keeping the Legends Alive', in Tony Curtis (ed.), *Wales: the Imagined Nation. Studies in Cultural and National Identity* (Bridgend: Poetry Wales Press, 1986), 26.

3 See generally, Llinos Beverley Smith, 'The Welsh Language Before 1536' and Geraint H. Jenkins, Richard Suggett and Eryn M. White, 'The Welsh Language

in Early Modern Wales', in Jenkins (ed.), *The Welsh Language before the Industrial Revolution*, chs 1 and 2.

4 Text in Richard Fenton, *A Historical Tour Through Pembrokeshire* (Brecon: Davies & Co., 1903), 340–1. Objections to its authenticity are noted in P. C. Bartrum, 'Notes on the Welsh Genealogical Manuscripts', *Trans. Hon. Soc. Cymmrodorion*, Session 1968 (1969), 70. As M. T. Clanchy observes, forgery is at the centre rather than the margin of a literate culture: *From Memory to Written Record. England 1066–1307* (London: Edward Arnold, 1979), 248–57. Cf. also the commission of Henry VII to examine the pedigree of Owen Tudor, discussed by Sidney Anglo, 'The *British History* in Early Tudor Propaganda', *Bulletin of the John Rylands Library*, 44 (1961), 24–5, 46–7.

5 David Wallace (ed.), *The Cambridge History of Medieval English Literature* (Cambridge: Cambridge University Press, 1999), passim; Helen Suggett, 'The Use of French in England in the Later Middle Ages', *Trans. Royal Hist. Soc.*, 4th ser., 28 (1946), 61–83; Llinos Beverley Smith, 'Inkhorns and Spectacles: the Impact of Literacy in Late Medieval Wales', in Huw Pryce (ed.), *Literacy in Medieval Celtic Societies* (Cambridge: Cambridge University Press, 1998), 202–22.

6 E. D. Jones, 'Inscribed Slates from Strata Florida', *Ceredigion*, 1 (1950–51), 103–5. Cf. Alan J. Bliss, 'The Inscribed Slates at Smarmore', *Proceedings of the Royal Irish Academy*, 64, sec. C (1965), 28–37.

7 Daniel Huws, *Medieval Welsh Manuscripts* (Cardiff: University of Wales Press and National Library of Wales, 2000), passim, esp. 16–17, 83, 91. On the earlier manuscript tradition, see generally Brynley F. Roberts, 'Writing in Wales', in Wallace (ed.), *Cambridge History of Medieval English Literature*, 182–207.

8 Daniel Huws, *Medieval Welsh Manuscripts*, ch. 6, esp. 89–90 and n. 15 citing 'yn wir dewedaf i chwi Sir John kadw du lyfr yn dda rag dadgainiait kanys y may indo ef lawer o bethau da'. On *datgeiniaid*, see below, ch. 5 in this volume.

9 John Stradling, 'The Storie of the Lower Borowes of Merthyrmawr', *South Wales and Monmouth Record Society Publications*, 1 (1932), 70–1.

10 R. F. Suggett, 'The Chronology of Late-medieval Timber Houses in Wales', *Vernacular Architecture*, 27 (1996), 28–37.

11 M. P. Siddons, *The Development of Welsh Heraldry* (Aberystwyth: National Library of Wales, 1989–93), I–III; P. C. Bartrum, 'Notes on the Welsh Genealogical Manuscripts', parts I–III, *Trans. Hon. Soc. of Cymmrodorion*, Session 1968 (1969), 63–98, Session 1976 (1976), 102–18, Session 1988 (n.d.), 37–46; M. P. Siddons, *Welsh Pedigree Rolls* (Aberystwyth: National Library of Wales, 1996).

12 National Library of Wales (hereafter NLW), MS 9853E, 100–1 (a transcript of George Owen Harry's, 'The Wellspringe of True Nobility'); E. D. Jones, 'Presidential Address', *Archaeologia Cambrensis*, 112 (1963), 3–4.

13 NLW, MS 9853E, 100–1.

14 Ibid.

15 Sir John Wynn, *The History of the Gwydir Family and Memoirs*, ed. J. Gwynfor Jones (Llandysul: Gomer Press, 1990), passim, esp. 34–5; see p.15, this volume, for assemblies where pedigrees were recited.

16 T. Jones Pierce, *Medieval Welsh Society*, ed. J. Beverley Smith (Cardiff: University of Wales Press, 1972), ch. 4.

17 R. R. Davies, *Lordship and Society in the March of Wales* (Oxford: Clarendon Press, 1978), passim; R.F. Suggett, 'The Welsh Language and the Court of Great Sessions', in Jenkins (ed.), *The Welsh Language before the Industrial Revolution*, 154–5.

18 On this complex subject, see Llinos Beverley Smith, 'The Gage and the Land Market in Late Medieval Wales', *Economic History Review*, 2nd ser., 29 (1976), 537–50; A. D. Carr, '"This my Act and Deed": the Writing of Private Deeds in Late Medieval North Wales', in Pryce (ed.), *Literacy in Medieval Celtic Societies*, 223–37.

19 NLW MS 9853E, 104.

20 Smith, 'Inkhorns and Spectacles', 215–16. Smith notes the relationship between power and closely controlled access to the curial record of land transfers; NLW MS 1388D, f. 10.

21 T. Jones Pierce, 'The Law of Wales – the Last Phase', *Trans. Hon. Soc. Cymmrodorion* (1963), 7–32. The bond specifically required the parties to obey the judgment of 'ii men learned in the Welsh law': NLW, Edwinsford Deeds & Documents 1913.

22 Dee Brennan, 'The Small Finds and Other Artefacts', Topic Report of *Excavations at Carmarthen Greyfriars 1983–1990*, ed. Terrence James (Carmarthen: Dyfed Archaeological Trust, 2001): for book-clasps and fittings, nos. 32–42; for page-holder, no. 41.

23 Cf. David H. Williams, *The Welsh Cistercians*, 2 vols (Caldey: Cistercian Publications, 1984), I. 159–63; 'William Fellow's Visitation of South Wales and Herefordshire, 1531', in M.P. Siddons (ed.), *Visitations by the Heralds in Wales*, (Publications of the Harleian Soc., new ser. 14, 1996), 23–103. Most of the monuments recorded by Fellow have disappeared.

24 F. H. Crossley, 'Screens, Lofts and Stalls Situated in Wales and Monmouthshire, [part] II', *Archaeologia Cambrensis*, 97 (1945), 80; Richard B. White, 'The Llangadwaladr East Window – an Examination of the Inscription and its Personae', *Transactions of the Anglesey Antiquarian Society* (1969–70), 80–110.

25 John Rhys, 'The Welsh Inscriptions of Llanfair Waterdine, *Y Cymmrodor*, xxvi (1916), 88–114; Royal Commission on Ancient and Historical Monuments in Wales and Monmouthshire, *An Inventory of the Ancient Monuments in Anglesey* (London: HMSO, 1937), appendix vii, for Welsh inscriptions described by Ifor Williams, esp. at p. cxliii (Llanfihangel Esgeifiog).

26 J. M. Lewis, *Welsh Monumental Brasses* (Cardiff: National Museum of Wales, 1974), 38–9; *The Chronicle of Adam Usk, 1377–1421*, ed. and trans. C. Given-Wilson (Oxford: Clarendon Press, 1997).

27 D. J. Bowen, 'Gwladus Gam a'r Beirdd', *Ysgrifau Beirniadol XXV* (Denbigh, Gwasg Gee, 1998), 84–8 (descriptions of the tomb of Sir William ap Thomas at Abergavenny); 'William Fellow's Visitation', ed. Siddons, 65–71, 85.

28 Occasionally there were attempts to create alternative historical mythologies. In particular, the marble armorial tomb of Edmund, Earl of Richmond, father of Henry VII, was removed from Carmarthen Greyfriars after the dissolution and re-erected in front of the high altar at St David's Cathedral. This was an extraordinary secular translation of relics that attempted to displace the cult of St David (whose shrine had been despoiled) with the cult of the Tudors. See Heather James, 'The Cult of St. David in the Middle Ages', in Martin Carver (ed.), *In Search of Cult: Archaeological Investigations in Honour of Philip Rahtz* (Woodbridge: Boydell Press, 1993), 105–12, at p. 111.

29 Ceri W. Lewis, 'Einion Offeiriad and the Bardic Grammar', in A. O. H. Jarman and Gwilym Rees Hughes (eds), *A Guide to Welsh Literature 1282–c. 1550* (Cardiff: University of Wales Press, 1997), 45; D. J. Bowen, 'The Bardic Functions', in

D. M. and E. M. Lloyd (eds), *A Book of Wales* (London and Glasgow: Collins, 1953), 104–8 (a transcript of part of NLW, Llanstephan MS 144).

30 Cf. R. R. Davies, 'The Peoples of Britain and Ireland, 1100–1400: [part]IV Language and Historical Mythology', *Trans. Royal Historical Society*, 6th ser., 7 (1997), 1–24, esp. 22–3.

31 Act 27 Henry VIII, c. 26, *Statutes of the Realm* III (1817; repr. 1963), 563–9; R. F. Suggett, 'The Welsh Language and the Court of Great Sessions', in Jenkins (ed.), *The Welsh Language before the Industrial Revolution*, ch. 4.

32 Act 34 & 35 Henry VIII, c. 26, *Statutes of the Realm*, III, 926–37, paras xxxvi, lxiv.

33 On the decline of poets, see this volume, ch. 5; extract from NLW, Llanstephan MS 144, 16–17, in D. J. Bowen, 'Y Cywyddwyr a'r Dirywiad', *Bulletin of the Board of Celtic Studies*, 29 (1981), 492 (no. 96).

34 NLW MS 9853E, 98; Graham C. G. Thomas, 'From Manuscript to Print – I. Manuscript', in R. Geraint Gruffydd (ed.), *A Guide to Welsh Literature, c. 1530–1700*, (Cardiff: University of Wales Press, 1997), 241–62; Huws, *Medieval Welsh Manuscripts*, esp. chs 1 and 5.

35 Suggett, 'The Welsh Language and the Court of Great Sessions', 161–4; G. Dyfnallt Owen, *Elizabethan Wales* (Cardiff: University of Wales Press, 1964), 224. It is not impossible that a proportion of professional thieves formed a subculture of readers. It was certainly in their interests to have a reading ability when their lives could depend on it. A few cases actually reveal that some thieves were habitual book carriers, but this may have related less to a literate mentality and more to the nature of the oath regarded as binding when sworn on the Gospels. It seems that some Welsh men who had committed a robbery or an assault forced their terrified victims to swear on a book not to divulge the circumstances of the crime. See R. Suggett, 'Pedlars and Mercers as Distributors of Print in Early Modern Wales', in Peter Isaac and Barry McKay (eds), *The Mighty Engine. The Printing Press and its Impact* (Winchester and Delaware: Oak Knoll Press, 2000), 23–32.

36 Suggett, 'The Welsh Language and the Court of Great Sessions', 164–7; see also Llinos Beverley Smith, 'Disputes and Settlements in Medieval Wales: the Role of Arbitration', *English Historical Review*, 106 (1991), 835–60. The arbitrators' award written in Welsh, discussed earlier, is an exceptional survival.

37 Litigation enrolled on the plea rolls of the Court of Great Sessions.

38 William P. Griffith, 'Schooling and Society', in J. Gwynfor Jones (ed.), *Class, Community and Culture in Tudor Wales* (Cardiff: University of Wales Press, 1989), 108–9; information derived from coroners' inquisitions filed on the gaol files of the Court of Great Sessions.

39 George Owen, *The Description of Penbrokshire*, ed. Henry Owen Cymmrodorion Record Series no. I (London: Cymmrodorion, 1892), 36; John Fisher, 'Three Welsh Wills', *Archaeologia Cambrensis*, 6th ser., 19 (1919), 189–92.

40 Glanmor Williams, 'The Renaissance and Reformation', in P. H. Jones and E. Rees (eds), *A Nation and its Books* (Aberystwyth: National Library of Wales, 1998), 41–54, at p. 47.

41 The view of the Puritan Oliver Thomas cited in P. H. Jones, 'Wales 1546–1695', *The Cambridge History of the Book in Britain* (Cambridge: Cambridge University Press, forthcoming), IV.

42 Suggett, 'The Welsh Language and the Court of Great Sessions', 174–5; Geraint

Bowen, 'Roman Catholic Prose and its Background', in Gruffydd (ed.), *A Guide to Welsh Literature c. 1530–1700*, ch. 9.

43 Suggett, 'The Welsh Language and the Court of Great Sessions', 153, 156–7 (references to petitions). For civility and the Welsh, see Prys Morgan, 'Wild Wales: Civilizing the Welsh from the Sixteenth to the Nineteenth Centuries', in Peter Burke, Brian Harrison and Paul Slack (eds), *Civil Histories: Essays Presented to Sir Keith Thomas* (Oxford: Oxford University Press, 2000), ch. 15.

44 Act 5 Eliz. c. 28, *Statutes of the Realm*, IV. 1 (1819; repr. 1963), 457; W. P. M. Kennedy, *Elizabethan Episcopal Administration*, Volume III: Visitation Articles and Injunctions, 1583–1603 Alcuin Club Collection, 27 (London: Alcuin Club, 1924), 140.

45 F. Furet and J. Ozouf, *Reading and Writing: Literacy in France from Calvin to Jules Ferry* (Cambridge: Cambridge University Press, 1982); Keith Thomas, 'The Meaning of Literacy in Early Modern England', in G. Baumann (ed.), *The Written Word* (Oxford: Clarendon Press, 1986), 97–131, at p. 111.

46 See Glanmor Williams, 'Unity of Religion or Unity of Language? Protestants and Catholics and the Welsh Language 1536–1660', in Jenkins (ed.), *The Welsh Language before the Industrial Revolution*, 207–33.

47 Jones, 'Wales 1546–1695'; Glanmor Williams, *Wales and the Reformation* (Cardiff: University of Wales Press, 1997), 338–60.

48 Dewi Eurig Davies, *Hoff Ddysgedig Nyth* (Swansea: Tŷ John Penry, 1976), 124–25; R. Tudur Jones, 'The Puritan Contribution', in Jac L. Williams and Gwilym Rees Hughes (eds), *The History of Education in Wales* (Swansea, Christopher Davies, 1978) I. 42–4.

49 David Maurice, *Cwnffwrdd ir Gwan Gristion, neu'r Gorsen Ysyg Mewn Pregeth* (London, 1700), vi.

50 Christopher Hill, 'Puritans and "the Dark Corners of the Land"', in *Change and Continuity in Seventeenth-century England* (London: Weidenfeld & Nicolson, 1974), 3–47; Geraint H. Jenkins, *Protestant Dissenters in Wales 1639–1689* (Cardiff: University of Wales Press, 1992), 9–10.

51 *The Welch Piety* (London, 1752), 21.

52 Ibid., 41–2.

53 Ibid., 44.

54 Ibid., 1.

55 Ibid., 47.

56 Ibid., 44.

57 Ibid., 59.

58 Glanmor Williams, 'Religion, Language and the Circulating Schools', in *Religion, Language and Nationality in Wales* (Cardiff: University of Wales Press, 1979), 215.

59 Geraint H. Jenkins, *The Foundations of Modern Wales* (Oxford: University of Wales Press, 1987), 380.

60 *The Diary of William Thomas of Michaelston-super-Ely, near St Fagans, Glamorgan, 1762–1795* ed. R.T.W. Denning (Cardiff: South Wales Record Society and South Glamorgan County Council Libraries and Arts Department, 1995).

61 NLW, Records of the Church in Wales, SD/QA/3; SD/QA/63; SD/QA/120; SD/QA/183.

62 Jenkins, Suggett and White, 'Welsh Language in Early Modern Wales', 92; Eiluned Rees, 'The Welsh Book Trade from 1718 [to] 1820', in Jones and Rees (eds), *A Nation and its Books*, 123–33.

63 Roger Chartier (ed.), *The Culture of Print: Power and the Uses of Print in Early Modern Europe*, trans. Lydia G. Cochrane (Princeton, NJ: Princeton University Press, 1989), 1–9.
64 Erasmus Saunders, *A View of the State of Religion in the Diocese of St David's About the beginning of the 18th Century* (1721; repr. Cardiff: University of Wales Press, 1949), 32.
65 Stephen Hughes (ed.), *Tryssor i'r Cymru* (London, 1677).
66 Thomas Jones, *Llyfr Plygain* (Shrewsbury, 1683); G. H. Jenkins, *Thomas Jones yr Almanaciwr 1648–1713* (Cardiff: University of Wales Press, 1980), 95–9.
67 N. Cynhafal Jones (ed.), *Gweithiau Williams Pantycelyn* (Holywell: P. M. Evans, 1887), I. 525.
68 For further discussion of these themes, see C. Lloyd-Morgan, 'Oral Composition and Written Transmission; Welsh Women's Poetry from the Middle Ages and Beyond', *Trivium*, 26 (1991); C. Lloyd-Morgan, 'Women and Their Poetry in medieval Wales', in Carol M. Meale (ed.), *Women and Literature in Britain 1150–1500*, 2nd edn (Cambridge: Cambridge University Press, 1996); Nia Watcyn Powell, 'Women and Strict-metre Poetry in Wales', in M. Roberts and S. Clarke (eds), *Women and Gender in Early Modern Wales* (Cardiff: University of Wales Press, 2000), 129–58.
69 Dyfnallt Morgan (ed.), *Y Ferch o Ddolwar Fach* (Caernarfon: Gwasg Gwynedd, 1977); A. M. Allchin, *Ann Griffiths* (Cardiff: University of Wales Press, 1976); A. M. Allchin, *Ann Griffiths: the Furnace and the Fountain* (Cardiff: University of Wales Press, 1987).
70 No copy of the 1658 edition, *Rhan o waith Rees Prichard*, has survived.
71 G. H. Jenkins, *Literature, Religion and Society in Wales, 1660–1730* (Cardiff: University of Wales Press on behalf of the History and Law Committee of the Board of Celtic Studies, 1978), 154.
72 Nesta Lloyd, *Cerddi'r Ficer: Detholiad o gerddi Rhys Prichard* (Llandybïe: Cyhoeddiadau Barddas, 1994), xxii–xxiii; idem, 'Sylwadau ar Iaith rhai o Gerddi Rhys Prichard', *National Library of Wales Journal*, 29 (1996), 257–80; Siwan Non Richards, *Y Ficer Prichard* (Caernarfon: Pantycelyn Press, 1994), 14–26.
73 NLW, Calvinist Methodist Archive, Diaries of Howel Harris, Diary 41, 28 February 1739.
74 Ibid., Diary 41, 1 March 1739; Diary 70, 26 February 1741.
75 Diary 262, 24 May 1770.
76 Prys Morgan, 'From a Death to a View: the Hunt for the Welsh Past in the Romantic Period', in E. J. Hobsbawm and T. Ranger (eds), *The Invention of Tradition* (Cambridge: Cambridge University Press, 1983), 46–7.
77 Quoted in Prys Morgan, *The Eighteenth Century Renaissance* (Llandybïe: Christopher Davies, 1981), 41.
78 See generally Gwyn Walters, *Y Wasg Gyfnodol Gymreig 1735–1900: the Welsh Periodical Press 1735–1900* (Aberystwyth: National Library of Wales, 1987).
79 See generally, W. P. Griffith, 'Preaching Second to No Other under the Sun': Edward Matthews, the Nonconformist Pulpit and Welsh Identity during the Mid-Nineteenth Century', in R. Pope (ed.), *Religion and National Identity: Wales and Scotland* c. *1700–2000* (Cardiff: University of Wales Press, 2001), 61–83. On preaching and public prayer as oral genres, see the remarks of Brynley F. Roberts, 'Oral Tradition and Welsh Literature: a Description and a Survey', *Oral Tradition*, 3 (1988), 79–80.

80 For instance, Charles Edwards, *Gwyddorion y Grefydd Gristianogol* (London, 1679); Robert Llwyd, *Llwybr Hyfforddd yn cyfarwyddo yr anghyfarwydd i'r Nefoedd* (London, 1682); John Davies, *Llyfr y Resolusion* (London, 1684).
81 John Bunyan, *Taith y Pererin*, ed. Stephen Hughes (London, 1688). This work is a Welsh translation of Bunyan's *Pilgrim's Progress*.
82 NLW, Calvinist Methodist Archive, Trefeca MS 3004, 4–5. The passage referred to is Luke 15:10.
83 *Geiriadur Prifysgol Cymru: a Dictionary of the Welsh Language* (Cardiff: University of Wales Press, 1950), *sv* 'hunan–'.
84 Saunders Lewis, *Williams Pantycelyn* (London, 1927), passim.
85 'Chapel civility' is Prys Morgan's helpful phrase, 'Wild Wales: Civilizing the Welsh from the Sixteenth to the Nineteenth Centuries', in Burke *et al.* (eds), *Civil Histories*, 279–80.
86 See, for instance, D. Ll. Morgan, *Y Beibl a Llenyddiaeth Gymraeg* (Llandysul: Gomer Press, 1998).
87 Ieuan Gwynedd Jones, *Explorations and Explanations: Essays in the Social History of Victorian Wales* (Llandysul: Gomer Press, 1981), 217–35; E. T. Davies, *Religion and Society in the Nineteenth Century* (Llandybïe: Christopher Davies, 1981), 27–34.
88 Kenneth O. Morgan, *Rebirth of a Nation: Wales 1880–1980* (Oxford: Clarendon Press, 1981); Gwyn A. Williams, *The Welsh in Their History* (London: Croom Helm, 1982), esp. ch. 8; R. Merfyn Jones, 'Beyond Identity? The Reconstruction of the Welsh', *Journal of British Studies*, 31 (1992), 330–57; Jenkins (ed.), *Language and Community in the Nineteenth Century*, passim; Graham Day and Richard Suggett, 'Conceptions of Wales and Welshness: Aspects of Nationalism in Nineteenth-century Wales', in Gareth Rees, Janet Bujra, Paul Littlewood, Howard Newby and Teresa L. Rees (eds), *Political Action and Social Identity* (London: Macmillian, 1985), 91–115.

Chapter 3

The pulpit and the pen: clergy, orality and print in the Scottish Gaelic world

Donald E. Meek

THE CLERGY have been of great importance to the creation, maintenance and growth of literacy within the Celtic cultures of Britain and Ireland. This observation applies across the centuries from the early Middle Ages to the period after 1870, when (in Britain) the Education Acts and the consequent nationalizing of educational systems laid the foundations of mass literacy. Even in the twentieth century clergymen have continued to enjoy considerable status in their communities, standing shoulder to shoulder alongside schoolmasters and doctors as the beneficiaries of formal education and its associated literary skills, acquired in their college and university training.

This chapter proposes to examine primarily the role of the Protestant clergy in the Scottish Highlands as practitioners of the written word, especially in relation to the Gaelic language. The extent to which the clergy stood at the boundaries of oral and literary traditions in the Scottish Highlands, as in other parts of Britain and Ireland, is worthy of detailed examination. However, the chapter is no more than a first step in that direction. It will explore the manner in which literate clergymen governed and shaped the Gaelic culture of their time by acting as the bridge-builders between oral and literary traditions, and as arbiters of literary taste and the providers of reading material for newly literate people. It will also reflect on the ways in which the oral and literary traditions, working in different directions, influenced the corresponding products of the clergy, whether in the pulpit or at the writing-desk.

ORALITY AND LITERACY IN THE CELTIC AND GAELIC CONTEXTS

It is a commonly held popular 'myth' that the Celtic areas of Britain and Ireland had little or no access to the written word before *c.* 1870. This interpretation appears to rest partly on an external view of the 'Celtic Fringe' propounded by apologists for anglocentric perspectives of history, although at different stages it has also suited the arguments of Celtic scholars, as well as non-specialists, to stress the outright predominance of oral rather than literary tradition. In fact, the Celtic areas of Britain and Ireland developed a literate dimension in the early Middle Ages, and did so as a result of the arrival of the Christian faith. This does not, however, imply that literacy was widespread; literacy functioned alongside orality, but, in the early Middle Ages, before *c.* 1100, it was restricted to an elite class of scribes and penmen, whose representatives consisted initially of monks and other ecclesiastical personages.[1]

From the twelfth century, literacy and the learning that accompanied it were gradually disseminated more widely, and were in effect secularized to a large extent. In Scotland, as in Ireland, literacy was usually to be found within the ecclesiastical sphere, but after 1200 it was evident within the domains of the 'learned orders' of poets, historians, medical men, craftsmen and sculptors, who were sustained by the medieval Gaelic world until *c.* 1600. Acting as the civil servants of their day, these men ensured that the literary needs of the Gaelic upper classes were met, in monument and muniment, on parchment, paper and stone.[2] We thus need to envisage Celtic cultures which incorporated both literary and oral dimensions across many centuries. These impinged on one another to varying degrees.

THE MEDIEVAL LITERARY TRADITION

The medieval literary activity of the Gaelic world is well attested in Scotland. In broad terms, it extends across a millennium from the foundation of the monastery at Iona in *c.* 563 until the eve of the Reformation. The monastery at Iona recorded annals, transcribed Latin texts, and produced illuminated books of various kinds, including (possibly) the Book of Kells. This literary activity was shared with other monasteries of similar type, some of them founded by Columba, in Ireland.[3] Although the record is by no means complete, the work of the monastic scribes associated with early Gaelic churches appears to have been sustained in Scotland until the twelfth century. It appears saliently in a pocket gospel-book, associated with the monastery of Old Deer in Buchan, Aberdeenshire, in the early years of that century.

The north-eastern provenance of the manuscript is worth noting. While it is by no means clear that the book itself was compiled at Deer, it contains in its margins six deeds which were written in Gaelic and are closely linked to the area. These relate to the granting of land to the monastery: they define the extent of the land granted to the monastery by noblemen, and confirm the privileges (from dues and exactions) enjoyed by it. The recording of the deeds of grant and privilege in the margins of a gospel-book of this kind demonstrates at once the importance of these deeds in the eyes of the monks at Old Deer, and also the significance of the gospel-book itself, which was deemed a fit repository for such important records. Although it is common to refer to the language of the deeds as Middle Irish, they are in fact in Middle Gaelic, the language shared by both Ireland and Scotland in this period. The Deer entries do, however, contain evidence of the emergence by that date of linguistic features that are distinctively Scottish, and for this valuable glimpse of the developing language we are deeply indebted to the scribes at Old Deer. The recording of these features demonstrates the overlapping of orality and literacy, since they are inherently phonological and thus part of the spoken language, but they are preserved for us in a manuscript.[4]

A much more expansive view of the Gaelic world of the later Middle Ages, embracing the Classical Gaelic poetry of Ireland and Scotland, is provided four centuries later by a manuscript compiled by clergy associated with Fortingall in Perthshire and Lismore in Argyllshire. James MacGregor, titular dean of Lismore, and his brother Duncan, natives of Fortingall, appear to have been the principal scribes involved in the compilation of the Book of the Dean of Lismore. This major collection of Gaelic verse extends, in effect, across the single Gaelic literary province formed by the Gaelic regions of Scotland and Ireland, extending geographically from Perthshire in the east to County Clare in the west, and from Lewis in the north to the Shannon in the south. The northern mainland of Scotland is not represented, nor (curiously) is the north of Ireland to any great extent. Beyond the Hebrides and the southern Highland mainland, the western side of Ireland, from Connacht southwards, is the source of the largest proportion of surviving poems. The book appears to owe much of its sparkle and energy to the impetus provided by Campbell patronage of the MacGregors after the downfall of the Lordship of the Isles (*c.* 1200–1493). It is, however, difficult to know whether the MacGregors had a particular purpose in compiling their manuscript. The mixture of genres within the manuscript – from stray sayings and chronicles to shopping lists – gives the impression that it may have been a fairly casual compilation, and it would be unwise to read too much into the work in its surviving format; but it is legitimate to wonder whether it may have been at least a first draft of an ambitious project to capture some of the finest verse products of the medieval Gaelic world, from western Scotland to western Ireland. Some of the oldest poems in the book can be dated to the thirteenth and early fourteenth centuries, while the latest were composed close to the time of compilation of the book itself. The range of verse – formal bardic verse to patrons of the poets, ballads about the heroes of the Fianna, religious poetry of very high quality, and occasional poems on various themes, including courtly love – is impressive, as is the overall standard of the poetry.[5]

The Book of the Dean of Lismore has some well-known peculiarities. The most notorious is the spelling system which the scribes, based in their Fortingall scriptorium, close to the frontier with the Lowlands, consistently applied to their texts. This spelling system is based on the conventions of Middle and Early Modern Scots, and not on the standard conventions of Gaelic tradition. Elsewhere, it has been argued that Gaelic scribes in Scotland had two spelling systems to choose from, the one represented in the Book of the Dean of Lismore and the other in the many Gaelic manuscripts compiled by scribes operating in the Gaelic heartlands of Ireland and Scotland, where Scots and English spelling conventions were less pervasive.[6]

The second peculiarity of the Book of the Dean of Lismore – on this occasion one which is more warmly welcomed by Gaelic scholars – is the extent to which its scribes have represented dialectal features of Early Modern Scottish Gaelic in their transcriptions. From time to time – though not by any means consistently – they depart from the strict grammatical conventions of the Classical Gaelic tradition which would have been used by the trained poets and prose writers of both Ireland and Scotland. They allow aspects of the language as spoken to determine the shape of their words, and this provides another major vantage point for viewing the development of distinctively Scottish forms of Gaelic. It is not clear whether the scribes themselves are solely responsible for this practice; it seems likely that they obtained at least some texts in which linguistic weathering of this kind was already evident, and it is, of course, likely that they added their own Perthshire peculiarities to the material as they transcribed it. The material in the Book of the Dean of Lismore is thus linguistically complex and multi-layered, representing the fusion of different orthographic, morphological and grammatical conventions.[7]

One of the many questions raised by this perplexing Gaelic manuscript is the extent to which it is based on oral or literary sources. When it was first examined in some detail by scholars in the late nineteenth and early twentieth centuries, it was generally claimed that the scribes had obtained their material from oral sources. More recent scholars have been much more cautious, and, while arguing for the influence of oral conventions at various levels, have been inclined to consider the possibility that the MacGregor scribes at Fortingall were, in the main, likely to have had access to manuscript versions of their poems. This makes it easier to understand how the scribes could have set about the detailed emendation which appears in certain poems in the manuscript. Their principles of emendation and concern for altering their texts, so as to provide what was a 'correct' text in their eyes, may also be indicative of humanist influence in the southern and eastern areas of the Highlands on the eve of the Reformation.[8]

The Book of the Dean of Lismore is important not only as a window on Gaelic literary tradition in the period from 1200 to 1500; it is also a sobering reminder of what might have happened to the spelling conventions of Scottish Gaelic if the MacGregor scribes of Fortingall had been the first to harness print for the purposes of publishing Gaelic texts. The power of the clergy, particularly through major religious texts, to determine the spelling used by minority languages is demonstrated in the case of Manx, a form of eastern Gaelic closely related to Scottish Gaelic. The application of a spelling system based on that of Early Modern English is evident in Bishop Phillips' Manx translation of the *Book of Common Prayer*, undertaken between 1605 and 1610, but not actually printed though preserved in manuscript. The first Manx printed book, a bilingual version of Bishop Thomas Wilson (of Man)'s *Principles and Duties of Christianity*, published in the early eighteenth century, was similarly in an English-based non-Gaelic spelling, and ensured that non-Gaelic orthographic conventions would be the norm for the Manx language thereafter.[9] The Manx clergy, employing variations of this kind of spelling system, translated the Bible into Manx, and also a range of significant religious texts (e.g. Paul Crebbin's translation of John Rawlet's *Christian Monitor* of 1686, known in Manx as *Yn Fer-raauee Creestee*, and published in 1763[10]). This set Manx apart from other forms of Gaelic – Scottish Gaelic and Irish – and made it (in T. F. O'Rahilly's phrase) 'that Cinderella of Gaelic tongues'.[11] A similar fate might have befallen Scottish Gaelic, if the first printed book had turned its back on Classical Gaelic spelling conventions. In the event, the first printed book in Gaelic – including Irish and Scottish Gaelic – appeared in 1567. It was the work of John Carswell, a Reformation clergyman who was deeply imbued with the classical conventions of the Gaelic world, and who transferred the practices of the Gaelic scribes to the new world of print.

GAELIC AND THE REFORMATION

John Carswell's book was a translation of *The Book of Common Order*, the directory of the Reformed Church in Scotland. The BCO had been authorized in Scotland in 1563, and the appearance of Carswell's translation, no more than four years later, was a remarkable achievement. Protestant doctrine was thereby given validation in the language of the Gaelic west. It is important to note the kind of Gaelic used by Carswell: it was not the Gaelic language as spoken by the 'ordinary' Gaels of Scotland, but the Classical Gaelic literary language, employed by the literate classes of both Ireland and Scotland. For

John Carswell, this was not only a natural choice, it also ensured that the book would have the best possible opportunity to circulate among influential members of the learned class in Ireland and Scotland. Pre-Reformation clergymen who, like Carswell himself, had accepted benefices in the reformed Church would have inherited much of the Classical Gaelic literary tradition, including literacy in the classical *lingua franca*. Carswell himself was apparently trained at a Gaelic bardic school, where diction and writing according to the old classical standards would have been inculcated, but he had also received a university education at St Andrews. In this way, his education reflects a fusion of Lowland and Gaelic culture, a fusion which is likewise at the heart of his book, in that it contains doctrines that first entered the Lowlands, and would have been unknown to most Gaels, although they were couched in a language which they would have recognized readily.[12]

Of course, most Gaels in Ireland and Scotland would have been unable to read Carswell's book. To cross this barrier, it would have been expected that the ministers would read and declaim the relevant sections of the book to their congregations. Carswell's style is, in fact, made for oral recitation and ready memorization in an oral context. He uses earlier stylistic devices, such as alliteration, in some profusion and to good effect. He also provides a catechism which is largely his own composition, and which lends itself to dramatic rendition. The aim of the catechism is to demonstrate the unacceptability of earlier Catholic practices. This is achieved by means of two speakers, the one an interrogator and the other a novice in the Protestant faith. The novice, however, is seen to be much more knowledgeable than the teacher. Carswell's catechism, while employing formal Classical Gaelic at the literary level, contains distinct cadences of spoken Scottish Gaelic.[13]

Carswell adds further material to the original *Book of Common Order*, notably his Dedicatory Epistle to his patron, the fifth earl of Argyll, his Epistle to the Reader, and his final Lawful Apology. These are key chapters which seek to accommodate the book to Gaelic conventions, but they also make a brave attempt to pull traditional Gaelic scribes into the new world of the printed book, by pointing out the speed with which the latter can be produced. In his Epistle to the Reader, Carswell challenges the old scribes to re-order their priorities by moving from manuscript to print, thus saving themselves time and effort. He also makes it clear that he would prefer them to move away from the 'mendacity' encapsulated in traditional tales to the 'truth' which the Reformation and the Bible have brought to the Gaelic world.[14]

The post-Reformation literary activity of Gaelic Scotland, then, did not come out of the blue. It had its roots in much earlier medieval scribal activity and in a stable set of Gaelic literary conventions. These were applied to a new cause, and provided a bridge between the old world and the new. The Reformation, as perceived in its Gaelic guise by John Carswell, was not intended to cause division in either cultural or religious terms. Although it did not unite Ireland and Gaelic Scotland, it did have the effect of creating a particular linguistic style for Scottish Gaelic Protestantism. On the other hand, Carswell's book also challenged traditional perspectives by going to the heart of the domain of the scribes who wrote secular poems and tales laboriously in manuscript. The advance of information technology, then as now, was a challenge to established patterns. Since they lacked the motivation of Protestant apologists who were alive to the power of the press, secular Gaelic scribes did not make an early and effective transition to print as Carswell recommended, and the Gaelic world was much the poorer.[15]

Despite the conservatism of the secular scribes, Carswell's cultural brokering had far-reaching implications for the future of Gaelic. It is fair to state that, since the Reformation, the Protestant Church has acknowledged the importance of Gaelic as a medium for its ministry, and that it has used the language fairly consistently as a medium for the Christian message proclaimed from its pulpits. There have been times when the commitment of the Church to Gaelic has faltered. This has happened largely because the language is often perceived as no more than a route to gain access to the minds and souls of Highlanders. Despite such a utilitarian view of Gaelic, the Church of Scotland has acknowledged the importance of the language, and throughout the centuries it has tried to preserve a Gaelic ministry in its Highland charges. All other Protestant churches and denominations active in the Highlands have employed Gaelic preachers – the Episcopal Church of Scotland, the Free Church of Scotland, the Free Presbyterian Church, and also the smaller nonconformist bodies, such as Baptists and Independents (also known as Congregationalists).[16]

Since 1560 the Protestant churches have been the main users of Gaelic as a preaching medium, but the Roman Catholic Church has likewise employed Gaelic in its services in the Highlands and Islands, and continues to do so. Since the Second Vatican Council, it has made much more extensive use of Gaelic in preaching and worship. The diocese of Argyll and the Isles has a small but well-sustained body of Gaelic-speaking priests who serve charges in the islands of Barra, South Uist and Eriskay, and on the western edge of the Highland mainland. The Gaelic priests of the Highlands and Islands are usually natives of the islands that they serve, and are very close to the everyday lives of their people and their communities. Their preaching is immediately recognizable to the Protestant Gaelic ear, not only by its different doctrinal emphases, but also by its register and diction. Put simply, Roman Catholic preaching style is generally closer to ordinary spoken Gaelic than is Protestant preaching.[17]

Protestant preachers use a more elevated style of Gaelic, based on the Classical Gaelic dialect which the Protestant Church inherited from the Middle Ages. This may seem slightly paradoxical, but it is, in fact, the case that Protestants have been much more wedded to upper register than Catholics.

When the old order of scribes declined after 1600, along with the conventions of Classical Gaelic, the Protestant Church became, by default, the principal custodian of the type of Gaelic closest to that of the medieval world. Classical style and diction were transferred to Protestant religious books, thus setting them apart from secular books, but, as Gaelic literacy spread, a gradual adjustment towards vernacular practice had to take place. The classical features of 'Protestant Gaelic' were thus modified by allowing more of the vernacular language into religious texts. The decline of the classical tradition meant that the style of 'Protestant Gaelic' was liable to be influenced not only by the vernacular, but also by external models, particularly since translation from English to Gaelic was at the heart of the Protestant educational programme. Ministers were among the most influential translators of key religious books, including catechisms and Puritan works, though they were aided increasingly after 1800 by Gaelic schoolmasters.[18]

CATECHISMS AND PURITAN TEXTS

Carswell's translation of the *Book of Common Order* preceded the provision of a specifically Scottish Gaelic Bible. The primary concern of the reformed church in the Highlands before 1650 was to lay a firm doctrinal foundation. This is evident in the priority given to the translation of Gaelic catechisms. Dating from 1631, the catechisms were a most important bridge between the laity and the Protestant Church. Consequently, language level required to be pitched as close as possible to spoken, oral Gaelic, while retaining essential technical terms. The catechisms, beginning in a strongly classical mode, do show a gradual 'lowering' of linguistic level as the years pass. Adjustments had to be made to language and style to ensure that basic Christian doctrine could be assimilated easily within the wider community. Assimilation certainly occurred. The *Westminster Shorter Catechism*, translated by the Synod of Argyll and first published *c.* 1653, had reached a second edition by 1659. It was reprinted almost thirty times in the course of the eighteenth century, and, in a suitably vernacular style, it became part of the oral culture of the Highlands and Islands.[19] Recited and quoted as required, it may have compensated to some extent for the lack of liturgy and litany in the reformed context.

From the middle of the eighteenth century, the catechisms were supplemented by a steady stream of translations of Puritan works into Gaelic, beginning with Richard Baxter's *Call to the Unconverted* in 1750, which was translated by the Rev. Alexander MacFarlane of Arrochar (who was later asked to undertake the translation of the New Testament into Gaelic, but was unable to do so). As translation developed, Gaelic religious texts lost some of their Classical Gaelic flavour, but moved closer to the style of their

English Puritan exemplars, thus creating a hybrid 'Puritan–Westminster Gaelic', with tight articulation and long sentences which were not always easy to read or absorb. The opening sentence of MacFarlane's translation, in which the author (Richard Baxter) explains the purpose his work, will give the flavour of the whole:

> Anns an eolas ghoirid a bha agam air seirbhiseach urramach agus foghlumta Chriosd, Easpuig Usher, bu tric leis, o àm gu h-àm bhi 'g am bhrosnachadh, chum riaghailt sdùiridh a sgriobhadh, do gach inbh fa leth, do luchd-aidmheil a chreidimh Chriosduidh, a shonraicheadh amach do gach neach a chuibhrionn fein; a' toiseachadh leis na daoinibh neo-iompaicht' agus a' gabhail air m' aghaidh cum nan leanaba ann an Criosd, agus 'na dhiaigh sin, chum nan daoine neart-mhor, a' coi-measgadh cuideachaidh shonraicht an aghaidh gach peacaidh fa leth, air am bheil iad teomadh.[20]
>
> (In the brief acquaintance that I had with that honourable and learned servant of Christ, Bishop Ussher, it was his frequent practice on different occasions to exhort me to write a guide, for each level individually, for the professors of the Christian faith, which would set out for each person his own portion; beginning with the unconverted people and keeping on my way to the babes in Christ, and after that, to the strong people, intermingling specific help against each individual sin, to which they are prone.)

Gaelic translation of this kind reached a high point in the nineteenth century. Perhaps the most ambitious of all Puritan translations into Gaelic was John Owen's treatise *On Communion with God, the Father, Son and Holy Ghost*, published in 1876.[21] This was undertaken by a schoolmaster, Alexander MacDougall of Glen Urquhart. Of the man and his work, Professor Donald MacLean has written as follows:

> Among the translators of English prose, none has laboured with more painstaking industry than Alexander Macdougall of Glenurquhart. In the upper reaches of that Strath this teacher spent his evenings, summer and winter alike, in translating the works of Dr John Owen. The translations are as severely accurate and unbending as the theology of the famous Puritan.[22]

As MacLean suggests, such translations tended to sacrifice lively, vernacular Gaelic to doctrinal precision and stylistic imitation. Some concession to the idiom of vernacular Gaelic would certainly have brightened their appeal, at least to modern minds. In fairness, however, it requires to be noted that theological works were technical treatises, the laboured efforts of the study rather than the spontaneous outputs of the pulpit, and it is only to be expected that, like present-day translators of important scientific textbooks, the Gaelicizers of Puritan works would have afforded a high priority to semantic precision. A sample of MacDougall's translation of Owen – a single sentence in all – will be sufficient to indicate the tenor of the work as a whole:

> Air an stéidh so, ma seadh, ged a thigeadh an saoghal gu léir air aghaidh – ma dh'fheudas sinn labhairt mar sin – a dh'òl suas tròcair, saoir ghràis agus maitheanas pheacanna, a' tarruing uisge gun tàmh à tobraichibh na slàinte, – seadh, ged a luidheadh iad uile a stigh ri aon ghealladh agus aingeal o nèamh a' brosnachadh suas an ìotaidh, ag ràdh, 'Olaibh, a chàirdean, seadh, òlaibh, gu pailt, tàirnibh gu saoibhi[r] gràs agus maitheanas peacaidh na dh' fhòghnas airson an tobair aingidheachd a th' ann an uchd gach aoin dibh;' – cha bhitheadh e comasach dhoibh doimhne ro phailt a ghràis a th' anns a' ghealladh sin a lughdachadh anns an tomhas as lugha.[23]

> (On this foundation, therefore, if the whole world should come forward – if we may speak like that – to drink up mercy, free grace and forgiveness of sins, drawing water ceaselessy from the wells of salvation, – yea, though they should all adhere to the one promise and though an angel from heaven should exacerbate their thirst, saying, 'Drink, my friends, yea, drink plentifully, draw richly as much grace and forgiveness of sin as will suffice for the well of wickedness that there is in the breast of each one of you'; – it would not be possible for you to diminish in the smallest measure the exceeding plenty of the grace that there is in that promise.)

Printed translations of Puritan treatises, heavy with imported doctrine, were thus influencing Gaelic style in the eighteenth and nineteenth centuries. Yet 'Puritan Gaelic' was by no means uniform. Even when the subject matter was sober, it was possible to reproduce it in a lively style, especially if the original work had a strong element of narrative. This is evident in the case of John Bunyan's celebrated *Pilgrim's Progress*, which was translated into Gaelic in 1812. The fluency of the translation was such that it entered into oral narrative as the shared spiritual biography of the Gaelic people, and Bunyan himself was often regarded as if he were a native Gael.[24] The translator of *Pilgrim's Progress*, Patrick MacFarlane (1758–1832), was a schoolmaster in Appin, who also produced fluent Gaelic texts of works by Philip Doddridge and William Guthrie.[25] Much therefore depended on the skills of the translator and the nature of the original text. Some further stylistic variety was achieved when the whole Bible became available in Gaelic in 1801. Naturalization of Gaelic religious writing was facilitated thereafter not only through the pulpit, but also through the creation of Gaelic Schools Societies which operated in the Highlands and Hebrides from 1811, and taught the people to read the standard Scottish Gaelic Bible.[26]

TRANSLATING THE BIBLE

The translation of the Bible into Scottish Gaelic was long delayed. As early as 1567, John Carswell recognized the need for a printed Gaelic Bible, but Gaels in Scotland were to wait for more than two centuries before a complete Scottish Gaelic Bible was produced. The first Gaelic Bibles were translated in Ireland, and were the product of the Classical tradition of both Ireland and Gaelic Scotland – the same tradition as that which had shaped Carswell's translation of the *Book of Common Order*. The Classical Gaelic version of the New Testament, completed by William Ó Domhnaill, was published in 1602–3. The corresponding version of the Old Testament, translated by William Bedell, Bishop of Kilmore, with the assistance of Gaelic scribes of the traditional kind, was completed *c.* 1640, but not published until 1685.[27] In the mid-seventeenth century the Synod of Argyll tried unsuccessfully to undertake a translation of the Old Testament into Gaelic; the project appears to have perished because of the political and ecclesiastical instabilities of the time.[28] Copies of the two Classical Gaelic Testaments were sent to Scotland, and distributed to a number of churches in the Gaelic-speaking areas. These early volumes employed the scribal conventions of the Classical period, and also a type-face based on Gaelic script. Consequently, Scottish clergy, who had generally lost their familiarity with the Classical tradition by the later seventeenth century, had difficulty in reading the texts. In an attempt to achieve a working compromise, Robert Kirk, the Episcopalian minister of Aberfoyle, converted the Classical texts into Roman type and expanded the scribal conventions. By so doing, he produced a pocket Bible which was published in London in 1690. It was widely used in the Highlands, but, despite Kirk's adaptation, it was not a distinctively Scottish text.[29]

The translation of the Bible into Scottish Gaelic was achieved in two stages – the New Testament was completed in 1767 and the Old in 1801. The translations were sponsored by the Society in Scotland for Propagating Christian Knowledge (SSPCK), a body which began to establish schools in the Highlands in 1709. The SSPCK initially aimed to eradicate Gaelic by teaching English in its schools, but by the mid-eighteenth century it had changed its tactics, and by 1755 it was making plans to translate the Bible into Scottish Gaelic. It arranged for the translation and ultimate publication of the Gaelic New Testament in 1767. Though the SSPCK tried initially to enlist the services of Alexander MacFarlane, minister of Arrochar, the translation of the New Testament was eventually entrusted to the minister of Killin, James Stuart. His son John, minister of Luss, was closely involved in the production of the Old Testament. The Old Testament was translated in portions.[30]

The styles of the two Scottish Testaments were surprisingly different. Both were unquestionably indebted to the Classical language and style of the earlier versions, but they were nevertheless Scottish Gaelic in terms of their syntax and morphology. However, the New Testament was noticeably stricter in its verbal relationship to the underlying Greek text, conceding little to natural Gaelic idiom, particularly in the Epistles, while the Old Testament, after some fairly radical adjustment of certain sections, achieved a more natural stylistic flow. The narrative style of much of the Old Testament eased the translators' work. The Gaelic Bible as a whole employed a lean and sinuous style which, while reflecting the natural variations in different types of Greek and Hebrew prose, was very different from the convoluted structures of earlier Puritan translations.[31] Indeed, it could be said that, among its many beneficial effects, the Gaelic Bible, and especially the Gaelic Old Testament, helped to steer Gaelic writing away from the repressive corsetry of catechisms and doctrinal treatises. 'Westminster Gaelic', however politically and doctrinally correct, was challenged and displaced as the preeminent register of Gaelic prose. The Goliath of stylistic philistinism – and Puritanism – was neatly slain by the David of the vernacular Gaelic world, as the description of Goliath indicates (1 Samuel 17:4–7):

> 4. Agus thàinig curaidh a mach a camp nam Philisteach d'am b' ainm Goliath o Ghat, anns an robh sè làmhan-coille agus rèis air àirde.
>
> 5. Agus bha clogaid umha air a cheann, agus bha e air éideadh le lùirich mhàilich: agus b'e cothrom na lùiriche cùig mìle secel umha.
>
> 6. Agus bha coisbheirt umha air a chosaibh, agus targaid umha eadar a ghuaillibh.
>
> 7. Agus bha crann a shleagha mar gharmain figheadair, agus bha ann an ceann a shleagha sè ceud secel iaruinn; agus bha fear a' giùlan sgéithe ag imeachd roimhe.[32]
>
> (4. And a warrior came out of the camp of the Philistines, who was called Goliath from Gath, who measured six cubits and a span in height.
>
> 5. And there was a helmet of bronze on his head, and he was attired with a mail breastplate; and the weight of the breastplate was five thousand shekels of bronze.
>
> 6. And there were bronze shoes on his feet, and a shield of bronze between his shoulders.
>
> 7. And the shaft of his spear was like a weaver's beam, and there were six hundred shekels of iron in the head of his spear; and a man carrying a shield walked before him.)

Such concise depiction stands in sharp contrast not only to the long sentences of Puritan works, but also to Gaelic literary conventions for the description of warriors. Yet this stylistic victory was not immediate or total. The new text was not readily accepted by everyone. It ran into dialectal difficulties, and for a while there were rumours of competing versions, ready for publication. It also had to displace a range of 'substitutes' which had appeared in the course of the sixteenth and seventeenth centuries, and continued well into the nineteenth. What were in effect oral Bibles had been made available, in whole or in part, across the centuries, and were deeply etched in people's memories. Some of these were adaptations made by ministers, employing either the English Authorized Version of 1611 or the Classical Gaelic Testaments as their basic texts. Ministers and parishioners often preferred the improvized translations to which they had grown accustomed.[33]

FROM PULPIT TO PRINT

Despite initial antipathy, the gradual availability of a Scottish Gaelic Bible gave a boost to Gaelic preaching. The provision of the full Scottish Gaelic Bible helped to create a more literate ministry, and also a broader readership. The influence of Bible-based literacy, reflecting the gradual use and absorption of the new translations, probably stimulated the appearance of printed Gaelic sermons. The transferring of the preached word to the printed text had a significantly liberating effect on Gaelic prose.

Social change, and particularly migration and emigration, were among the initial factors in transferring the oral word to the printed page. Gaelic preaching was heard not only in Highland pulpits; it also found a place in Lowland pulpits, notably the pulpits of the Gaelic chapels which were built in Scotland's cities from the late eighteenth century in order to provide spiritual nourishment for the many Highlanders who found their way to the cities for employment. In Aberdeen, for instance, a Gaelic congregation was established in 1785, largely for the benefit of Highlanders who came to work in the granite quarries in Rubislaw. The chapel which the congregation later erected, and which was located for a number of years in Gaelic Lane (where the old building can still be seen), was a focal point of Gaelic activity. Pre-eminently it provided a platform for Gaelic preachers, among them some distinguished graduates of King's College and Marischal College.[34]

Highlanders, of course, went farther afield than the Lowlands and the eastern fringes of Scotland; they emigrated in substantial numbers from the early years of the eighteenth century, and sometimes took their preachers with them. Much more frequently, however, they had to search for new preachers.[35] Preaching had a very important place in the migrant and emigrant context, and it was there that the earliest attempts were made to print Gaelic sermons. The emigrant experience hastened the transition from orality to print, since Gaelic ministers in the new colonies were in very short supply, and the availability of printed sermons helped to distribute the Christian message more widely among emigrants, who lacked easy access to the means of grace. Literate laymen could read the printed sermons to groups assembled in homes, and the press could act to some extent as a substitute for the missing preacher.

It is therefore not entirely surprising that the first Gaelic sermons to have survived in print were published far from the Highlands, by Sibley, Howard and Roulstone in Fayetteville (formerly Cross Creek), North Carolina, in 1791.[36] Both were preached in the Raft Swamp district of North Carolina, inland from Cape Fear, in 'the first month of autumn 1790' by the Rev. Dougal Crawford (1752–1821), a native of Arran, who had arrived in the area about 1784.[37] His congregations would have consisted of a large number of his Highland compatriots, who had been creating, since the mid-1730s, a substantial Gaelic colony in that part of what is now the USA.[38] No fewer than three prayers were also included in the book, one preceding the first sermon, and two preceding the second. This in itself makes a significant point. The book was evidently intended to provide a set of useful materials for both private devotion and (when necessary) public worship. In addition, it was apparently expected that the book would be read in both Arran and North Carolina. The prefaces to the sermons are dedicated respectively to Crawford's home congregation in the parish of Kilmorie in Arran,[39] and to 'the congregation in Raft Swamp and the congregations in Robeson County and in Mr MacKay's place'[40] – possibly a reference to the congregation of an Argyllshire man, Archibald MacKay, who became an elder in the Longstreet church, Cumberland County.[41]

The themes of the Raft Swamp sermons appear to have been chosen with particular relevance to the context of the emigrant communities. In the absence of a plentiful supply of ministers, parents had a particularly onerous responsibility for the correct instruction of the young. The first sermon is therefore on Proverbs 22:6, 'Tog suas an leanabh ann san tslighe ann san coir dha gluasachd, 'nuair a bhios e og; & 'nuair a thig e gu haois, cha treig e i' (Bring up the child in the way he should go, when he is young; and when he comes of age, he will not forsake it).[42] The second sermon drew its theme from Micah 2: 10: 'Eiribh agus imichibh, oir cha 'ne so bhur tamh' (Arise, and go, for this is not your rest) – a text which must have had considerable poignancy in the emigrant context, particularly for second-generation emigrants who had become settled in their ways.[43] Crawford, in fact, warns his hearers of the dangers of settled living, and particularly those which come in the wake of prosperity. People must remember that they have to face death. Crawford majored on the need to forsake the things of this world. This was to become one of the keynotes of Highland evangelical preaching during the next century. In the following extract, the preacher's point is made by a cumulative listing of those things which perish, and the rhetoric, which represents that of the typical Gaelic preacher in its pulse and rhythms, culminates by laying emphasis on the enduring qualities of Godly virtue:

> Criochnachui' onoir agus urram, basaichi maise agus gach dealbh is fionalta a chuaidh riamh a sgeudacha le feòil, falbhaidh beartas as an tsealladh le sgiatha grad, imichidh foghlum agus gliocas air falbh, agus dichuinichear gach ni a chuireas a bheatha so fa chomhair 'ar suilean; ach mairidh subhailce gu siorruidh, se onoir amhain beatha agus sonas gach ni tha iomlan, mor, agus maith.[44]

> (Honour and privilege will perish, beauty and every finest image which was ever bedecked by the flesh will die, wealth will vanish from sight with swift wings, knowledge and wisdom will depart, and everything that this life puts before our eyes will be forgotten; but virtue will last forever – honour consists solely in the life and joy of every thing that is perfect, great and good.)

The preaching verses for both sermons are slightly different from their forms in portions of the Gaelic Old Testament which were published in 1786–87. Crawford's version of Proverbs 22:6 employs *gluasachd* for *imeachd*, and adds the clause *'nuair a bhios e og*, while Micah 2:10 employs *tàmh* for *còmhnuidh* (dwelling). This may point to some degree of fluidity in the Gaelic Bible versions (between printed and oral forms, with concessions to dialect) which were available to Gaels before the 'official' version of the Old Testament was finalized and accepted after 1807.[45] Nevertheless, Crawford was evidently skilled in writing Gaelic, and his printers were apparently no less familiar with the language. Although the punctuation is unusual at times, the grammar, syntax and orthography of each sermon show a high degree of consistency, and relatively few misprints.[46] The important place given to preaching as part of late eighteenth-century worship is underlined by both Raft Swamp sermons, each of which comprises some sixteen pages of tightly packed print, and (if we can discount the possibility that Crawford may have expanded his work for publication) each must have taken at least an hour-and-a-half to deliver.[47] The prayers, which reproduce in print the normal phrasing and rhythms of public prayer in Gaelic, range from one to two pages in length.[48] By declaiming this remarkable set of Presbyterian sermons and prayers from the *Gàidhealtachd* of North Carolina, it is still possible to 'hear' the voice of the preacher as he addresses his various congregations far from his native Gaelic community.

By 1795 Crawford had returned to Arran, and was assistant at Kilmorie. In that year he published another homiletic text, this time addressed to women, and published by James Gillies of Glasgow.[49] The target readership/audience for Crawford's second publication suggests that the motivation to print Gaelic homiletic material in Scotland was a concern for those seen to be 'at risk' and in need of spiritual strengthening, because of their age, role, profession or location. Children came within this category, and were offered a Gaelic translation of Isaac Watts's *Sermon to Young People* (1795).[50] Highland soldiers in the British regiments were likewise targeted in a sermon by the Rev. Thomas Broughton, which was translated and published in 1797 as a small booklet with an extensive preface. The sermon was specifically composed for soldiers, and entitled in Gaelic *An Saighidear Criosduidh no na dleasdnais iomchuidh chaum beatha dhiadhaidh chaithe, air an sparradh air an armailt: o eisempleir Chornelius* (The Christian Soldier, or the duties appropriate to living a Christian life, urged upon the army: from the example of Cornelius).[51] This theme, which combined Christian values with a military profession, reflected the revamping of the old warrior ideal, once central to Gaelic society, in response to both Christian morality and British expansionism. The preface to the translated work was composed in Gaelic by the unidentified translator, and makes no bones about what is expected of the soldiers who read or hear the sermon:

> B' ard cliu nan gaidheal, na 'n linne fa leath, air sinnsearan, airson mor-mhisneach, chum onoir na 'n Righ, agus na 'n duthaich dhionadh tearainte. Tha duil agam nach toir an sliochd mi-chliu orra le caochladh cleachdain.[52]
>
> (The Gaels had a high reputation, in another generation, our ancestors, for great courage, to honour the king, and to defend their country securely. I hope that their descendants will not bring disrepute upon them with a different practice.)

Religious literature in Gaelic, both poetry and prose, stood not only on the frontier between orality and print, but also on the frontier between external British supremacy and the civilizing of an allegedly barbarous people by redirecting their lives into other, more constructive, avenues. The goal of 'improving' the Gaels – spiritually, politically, morally and socially – was never far from the minds of writers of Gaelic prose in the eighteenth and (especially) the nineteenth centuries.

As key people in bringing spiritual improvement to the Highlands, divinity students and budding Gaelic preachers were a group whose needs were recognized, and this encouraged the printing of sermons. A collection of the sermons of the Rev. Ewen MacDiarmid was published in 1804, with new preachers directly in view.[53] MacDiarmid was, for a period, the minister of Glasgow Gaelic Chapel. He was also an important collector of Gaelic songs and lore.[54] Although MacDiarmid has been regarded as a moderate because of his contribution to the collecting of Gaelic folklore, his theological sympathies appear to have lain with evangelicals. The sermons published posthumously under his name are certainly warmly evangelical, though Professor Donald MacLean claims that 'MacDiarmid's sermons are understood to be translations from a Scottish divine'.[55] His book was well used, nevertheless; copies crossed the Atlantic with emigrant Highlanders, and those in Scotland sometimes show evidence that they were indeed employed as models by preachers, who pored over their texts and annotated their vocabulary in the margins.[56] In this way, the printed text aided the maintenance of an oral art, and doubtless influenced its direction.

Whatever their source, MacDiarmid's sermons are stylistically very different from the stiff formality of Broughton and of Puritan translations. Sentences are shorter, and the more natural phrasing and cadences of the vernacular Gaelic pulpit are very evident. This is illustrated by the opening of MacDiarmid's sermon on Hebrews 4: 16, a verse which is rendered in the 1767 Gaelic New Testament and in MacDiarmid's heading as 'Thigeamaid uime sin le danachd gu righ-chaithir nan gras, chum gu faigh sinn trocair, agus gu 'n amais sinn air gras chum cobhair ann an am feuma' ('Let us therefore come with boldness to the throne of grace, that we may obtain mercy, and attain grace to help in time of need'):

> 'S iomadh cuireadh càirdeil, agus earrail dhian, a tha Dia 'na fhreasdal, agus gu h-àraidh 'na fhocal a' toirt dhuinn teachd gun dàil 'na ionnsuidh fein. Cuireadh is cairdeile, agus comhairle is fhearr, cha d' fhuair sinn riamh, agus cha 'n fhuigh gu brath air talamh no am briathraibh steidh mo theagaisg. Am bheil cuireadh chum biadh a ghabhail, a' toirt sòlas do 'n duine ocrach; am bheil chum deoch fhaotainn do'n neach a tha paiteach; am bheil chum fois a mhealtuinn, do 'n dream a tha sgìth; am bheil chum slainte a shealbhachadh dhoibh-sin a tha tinn; 's mugha gu mòr an sòlas is còir dha a thoirt dhuinne, gu bheil sinn a' faotain cuirreadh teachd an ionnsuidh Dhe, chum 's gu 'm fuigh sinn tròcair agus gràs uaithe. Tròcair fhaotainn, 'se so ar saorsa o dhiteadh; gràs fhaotainn, 'se so ar naomhachadh air talamh, agus ar n' ullachadh fa chomhair neamh.[57]
>
> (There is many a friendly invitation, and ardent entreaty, that God in his providence, and especially in his word[,] gives us that we may come without delay to himself. A more friendly invitation, and better advice, we never received, and we will never get on earth[,] than in the words on which my exposition is founded. Does an invitation to take food give joy to a hungry man; to receive drink to the one who is thirsty; to enjoy rest to the one who is weary; to gain healing to those who are ill[?]; so much greater is the joy that it ought to give us, that we are receiving an invitation to come to God, in order that we may receive mercy and grace from him. To receive mercy, this is our freedom from condemnation; to receive grace, this is our sanctification on earth, and our preparation with a view to heaven.)

Despite MacDiarmid's volume, publication of sermons originally composed in Gaelic was not evident to any significant extent before 1830, and even after 1900 printed output was sluggish. The flow was stimulated initially by the Gaelic journals of the Rev. Dr Norman MacLeod (see below), and there was a clear connection between the growth of literacy, particularly through the Gaelic Schools Societies, and the provision of texts in an idiomatic form closer to that used by the people themselves.

The twentieth century witnessed the publication of a somewhat greater number of collections and anthologies of Gaelic sermons, among them Malcolm MacLeod's *An Iuchair Oir* (1950),[58] and *Dòrlach Sìl* (1931), edited by that exacting Free Church commentator, Professor Donald MacLean. In his Introduction, MacLean offers his views on why there had been such a dearth of printed Gaelic sermons hitherto:

> Ann an Litreachas Gàidhlig a tha ann an clò chan fhaighear ach glè bheag de shearmoinean. Chan e nach robh na Gaidheil ag cur meas agus miadh air searmoinean, oir bha, mar a tha iad a' deanamh sin fhathast, ach cha robh a h-uile ministeir ainmeil a bha aca cho ealamh ann an sgriobhadh na Gàidhlig ri an gibht-labhairt innte. Air chùl sin, cha robh an sluagh, am bitheantas, comasach air feum a dheanamh dhiubh ann an clò, agus bha am prìs trom is an t-airgead gann.
>
> An lorg sin tha a' Ghaidhealtachd is na h-Eileanan an-diugh dh'easbhuidh searmoinean nan diadhairean fiùghail sin a chruth-atharraich gu h-iomlan snuadh spioradail an luchd-aiteachaidh. Tha, gun amharus, dioghlum beag againn, thall sa bhos, de an teagasgan. Thàinig mìrean blasda agus puingean cothromach thugainn air beul-aithris an t-sluaigh bho bhòrd fialaidh an t-soisgeil sin a fhritheil iad gu dùrachdach agus gu h-eudmhor.[59]
>
> (In printed Gaelic Literature only comparatively few sermons can be traced. It is not that Gaels did not esteem or value sermons, for they did, as they still do, but not all of their famous ministers were as agile in the writing of Gaelic as they were in their gift of proclamation in the language. Furthermore, the people generally were not able to derive benefit from them in print, and the price was heavy and money scarce.
>
> As a consequence of that, the Highlands and Islands now lack the sermons of those worthy divines who transformed totally the spiritual appearance of their inhabitants. Undoubtedly, a small amount of their teachings has been gleaned, here and there. Tasty fragments and apposite points have come to us in the people's oral tradition from the generous table of that gospel that they served enthusiastically and zealously.)

ORALITY AND INSPIRATION

MacLean provides a number of interesting reasons for the absence of a rich homiletic literature in print in Scottish Gaelic, but he does place some emphasis on the paucity of a Gaelic reading public, and the lack of clerical confidence in the writing of Gaelic. It is, however, possible that the main reason for the scarcity of indigenous Gaelic sermons in printed form was the understanding among both clergy and laity that *real* Gaelic preaching was essentially an oral art, performed and transmitted by the spoken word. Sermons, delivered spontaneously (or seemingly so) from the pulpit, were esteemed very highly in the Highlands. The sermon was the centre-piece of worship. In many parts of the Highlands and Islands, the whole experience of Gaelic worship was focused in the phrase *aig an t-searmon* (at the sermon). *An robh thu aig an t-searmon an-diugh?* (Were you at the sermon today?) was the great Sabbath-day question.

The hallmark of the greatest Gaelic preachers was indeed their capacity to deliver sermons orally without reference to paper or notes. This, of course, reflected the fundamentally important place of oral skills in the Highland context; the telling of traditional Gaelic tales was likewise an oral art – an art to which the Gaelic sermon was indebted to some extent. However, the pre-eminence of orality was, to a significant degree, increased still further when evangelical Christianity began to penetrate the Highlands and Islands. The preacher was expected to deliver a message from God, a message which was spontaneous and given to preacher and people in the power of the Holy Spirit. The use of paper, and the reading of a learned and laborious discourse, became the hallmark of the moderate (that is, non-evangelical) preacher. One of the most dismissive Gaelic terms for a poor, note-bound preacher was that he was a *ministear pàipeir* – 'a minister of paper'. To use paper was to compromise a high spiritual calling with a low earthly standard.[60]

Of course, Highland ministers were not entirely free from paper. The very existence of the Raft Swamp sermons indicates that Dougal Crawford was a highly literate man who was able to write out his material longhand in a manuscript, and he may well have done so before he delivered the sermons. As a consequence, his sermons contain features of his native Gaelic dialect, that of the island of Arran. Since they may preserve features of the preacher's dialect which have not been levelled by complete conformity to 'Protestant Gaelic', printed sermons can be a very useful source of information for the Gaelic dialectologist, though this may not be appreciated by the theologian. Professor Donald MacLean pronounced a severe verdict on the published sermons of the Rev. John Macalister of Arran (1789–1845: publ. 1896): there, he claimed, 'we have the irritating peculiarities of the dialects and idioms of Arran in unrelieved faithfulness'.[61] MacLean thereby indicates that he had his own standard for the presentation of Gaelic sermons; disliking Puritan rigidity of style on the one hand, he was disinclined to admit too much of the preacher's natural dialect on the other, particularly if that dialect belonged to the southern Hebrides (rather than MacLean's native Lochcarron). In fact, Macalister's sermons contain comparatively little of the Arran dialect – no more than do those of Crawford – and it would seem that MacLean was reacting against style rather than language.

Traces of the two preachers' dialects in the printed sources are a healthy indicator of the slow but steady growth of a vernacular Gaelic literature. Other ministers also were recording their sermons in written form; some made outlines of their sermons before they delivered them; others used slates, on which they wrote in chalk, and then wiped off their notes; while still others wrote outlines on paper, or even drafted full texts, which they kept long after the sermon had exhausted its pulpit life.[62] Several manuscript collections of Gaelic sermons have survived from the eighteenth century, and the practice of writing sermons longhand was evidently fairly well established at an early period.[63] The most important consideration was that the preacher should not appear in the pulpit with a large and bulky manuscript, and proceed to read it to the expectant congregation. The same condition applied to English sermons too. It was not a question of language, but of inspiration.

Inspiration showed itself in ways other than spontaneity. The animation of the preacher, his body language, and the modulation of his voice were all part of the experience. We can appreciate some of the cadences of a sermon in its spoken form if we read the printed version aloud and study its phrasing, but printed sermons will never be anything more than a poor shadow of their original, orally delivered forms. The greatest defect in printed homilies is, of course, that they do not preserve any traces of the preacher's voice, his accent, or his mannerisms. It was normal for Highland preachers to project their voices by means of a heightening of pitch as the sermon progressed, as happened in Wales. This was known in Argyllshire as the minister's *duan*, 'song, tune', and in Lewis as his *sèisd* (likewise 'tune').[64]

Even if they do not catch the cadences, printed sermons at least give us an outline of what the preacher said, and here we can see a considerable variety of themes and approaches. There are many sermons, particularly those preached in the northern Highlands and Islands, which are in effect theological treatises, departing little from straight exposition of the Bible text, and closely resembling the Raft Swamp sermons of 1790. Less weighty evangelical preaching, putting more emphasis on personal response and decision making, and often leaning towards the vernacular language, was more common in the Inner Hebrides than the Outer Hebrides, and more likely to be found in revivalist contexts than in the regular proclamations of Calvinist ministers. As a result of variations in themes and contexts, there is no single type of sermon which can be called characteristically 'Highland'; there are many such types. Sermons were produced to meet a wide range of contexts across the years; in addition to what we regard as the normal church setting, they were regularly preached in the open air, especially at communion services, when thousands would gather together; and others were preached by enthusiastic itinerant preachers to small congregations in cottages, in the harvest field or by the shore. Itinerant preachers were particularly gifted in making sermons relevant to the contexts of their audiences. Themes like road building, harvesting, fishing and the burning of dead scrub, lent themselves readily to biblical illustration.[65]

Sermons were preached on special occasions also, such as times of communal sorrow or rejoicing, and occasionally the printed text allows us to catch a glimpse of a frequently forgotten aspect of orality, namely audience response and participation. A particularly poignant time for preaching was in the hours prior to the departure of emigrant ships, heading for America or Australia. In a celebrated essay, '*Long Mhór nan Eilthireach*' ('The Emigrant Ship'), perhaps dating to the late 1820s, Dr Norman MacLeod (see below) provides a picture of preaching on board an emigrant ship about to set sail from Tobermory. The venerable minister – a towering authority figure in the midst of an uncertain people – goes aboard the ship, and addresses his audience. MacLeod's printed narrative catches a situation-specific style of proclamation. The emigrants, who are frightened of the voyage, answer the preacher's rhetorical question derived from Scripture: *O! sibhse air bheag creidimh, c'ar son a tha sibh fo eagal?* (O! ye of little faith, wherefore are ye afraid?):

> 'Tha sinn a' fàgail ar dùthcha,' fhreagair iad. 'Tha gun teagamh', ars' esan; 'tha sibh a' fàgail an eilean 's an d' fhuair sibh 'ur togail 's ur n-àrach; gu cinnteach tha sibh a' dol air imrich fhada; cha ruigear leas a chleith gu-m bheil iomadh cruadal a' feitheamh oirbh; ach cha d' thàinig so oirbh gun fhios duibh. A' fàgail 'ur dùthcha! an dubhairt sibh; am bheil ceangal seasmhach aig mac an duine ri aon dùthaich seach dùthaich eile? Chan eil dùthaich bhunailteach againn air thalamh; cha 'n eil sinn air fad ach 'n ar n-eilthirich; agus cha-n ann 's an t-saoghal chaochlaideach so a tha e air a cheadachadh dhuinn le Dia an dachaidh sin iarraidh as nach bi imrich.'[66]

> ('We are leaving our country,' they answered. 'You are indeed,' he said; 'you are leaving the island in which you were reared and brought up; assuredly you are going on a long voyage; there is no need to conceal the many dangers that await you; but this has not come upon you unawares. Leaving your country, did you say? Does man have a lasting link with one country rather than another? We have no fixed country on earth; all of us are mere pilgrims, and it is not in this changeable world that it is permitted for us by God to seek that home from which there will be no more journeying.')

Despite variations in context, there were certain expectations which Highland and specifically Gaelic preachers tried to satisfy, as they still do. For one thing, within the predominantly Protestant tradition, it was considered important to hold to the Scriptures and to expound them. As we have noted, the second Raft Swamp sermon of 1790 (which hints at the theme of mutability and transience among emigrants, which was also developed more ornately by Norman MacLeod) is very much in the 'heavier' evangelical mould, and draws richly on Scripture. However, the weight of exposition was sometimes lightened by exemplum and illustration, and some ministers, like the celebrated eighteenth-century ministers Lachlan MacKenzie of Lochcarron and John Balfour of Nigg, were particularly well known for their parables and anecdotes.[67] MacKenzie's surviving Gaelic sermons show a lightness of touch and a free-flowing style which is used to convey word pictures in memorable form, as the following extract from his *Ròs o Shàron* (A Rose from Sharon) demonstrates:

> Tha an lili air son a' ghàraidh, ach 's e crioch an droighnich a losgadh. Tha sluagh Dhé anns an t-saoghal mar an lili ann am fasaich dhris agus dhroighnich, ach bithidh iad air an atharrachadh gu 'bhi air a' suidheachadh ann am Pàros shuas. 'Mheud 'sa tha na lilidhean 'san t-saoghal so bithidh iad air a' suidheachadh ann a' gàradh Dhè, far am bi iad fuidh ghathan grian na fìreantachd, agus làn chothrom aca air am blàthan a sgaoileadh a mach. Cha chuir an droigheann ni 's fhaide bacadh air am fàs, oir loisgear le teine e. Ann am freasdal glic Dhè, a reir a rùin iongantaich 's diomhair, tha e air cheadachadh dhoibh fàs còmhlath air thalamh.[68]

> (The lily is for the garden, but the end of the thorn is to be burnt. The people of God in the world are like the lily in the wilderness of briars and thorn, but they will be changed in order to be given a place in Paradise above. As many lilies as there are in this world will be situated in God's garden, where they will be under the rays of the sun of righteousness, with a full opportunity to spread out their blossoms. The thorn will no longer inhibit their growth, for it will be burnt by fire. In the wise providence of God, according to his wonderful and mysterious will, it is permitted for them to grow together on earth.)

Some later Highland ministers, like Robert Finlayson of Lochs, in Lewis, were more 'homely' in their styles, and were experts at locating biblical events and characters in their own communities. Noah himself could become a local worthy with a boat, like all other good crofters.[69] Ministers' pithy word-pictures and illustrations tended to survive longer in popular memory than the rest of their sermons, and were frequently recounted whenever and wherever sermon-loving Highlanders assembled. Highland sermons owed much to both the Bible and traditional forms of storytelling. Tales about ministers, their sermons, and especially their illustrations, became a narrative cycle in themselves, complementing a similar body of stories about catechists.[70]

Because the sermon was a central art form in the Highlands, it influenced a great deal of creativity, both oral and literary. It honed the mind and sharpened the expression of preacher and hearer alike. Preaching contributed much too to the shape of printed Gaelic prose; the earliest Gaelic periodicals were produced by ministers who were naturally inclined to homiletic styles of exposition even when dealing with everyday matters. Yet, these same ministers were also reading English magazines and literary journals, and listening (at a respectable distance) to the traditional tales which were narrated in the cèilidh-houses of the Highlands and Islands. Their output reflects the interaction of all of these different styles.

COMPILING THE JOURNALS

Nineteenth-century clergymen compiled and edited the earliest Gaelic periodicals, and none was more important in this respect than the Rev. Dr Norman MacLeod, whose first journal, *An Teachdaire Gaelach*, spanned the two years, 1829–30. It was followed in 1840–43 by *Cuairtear nan Gleann*.[71] Both periodicals attempted to provide a wide range of reading for those who had become literate through the various Gaelic Schools Societies. Diversification of Gaelic reading material was their overall aim. The journals published sermons, short stories, and moralistic and educational narratives, some of which had their roots in traditional forms of story-telling, as well as songs and more ambitious poems, sacred and secular.[72] The range and variety of styles are impressive. Norman MacLeod himself was a skilful writer who could command several different modes. It is sometimes claimed that his writing is heavily indebted to the Gaelic Bible, but this is scarcely true; MacLeod was as much influenced by contemporary early Victorian prose in English as he was by the Gaelic Bible.

In particular, he had a remarkably keen ear for the richly idiomatic Gaelic of the nineteenth century, and sought to convey its cadences, particularly in dialogues. Dialogues were a common feature of early journals, and frequently tried to represent the spoken word of the characters. It could be claimed that, in MacLeod's dialogues, between rustic characters and omniscient catechists or schoolmasters, we are in the world of social and stylistic control.[73] The link with oral culture may be regarded as contrived and artificial, serving the needs of the establishment rather than reflecting the world of ordinary people. Unquestionably, there is a strong element of ponderous pomposity in such dialogues. The tone reflects the voice of the minister, rather than that of the people, but it is equally clear that the people's voice is represented, however imperfectly. So too, apparently, is the people's opinion of Gaelic sermons. In the first dialogue in *An Teachdaire Gaelach*, *Lachainn nan Ceist* (Lachlan of the Questions [i.e. Lachlan the catechist]) presents the editorial manifesto, while the second, more rustic, character, *Eòghann Brocair* (Ewen the Badger-catcher), is the bemused recipient of the 'verbal flyer' for the new journal. He reacts unenthusiastically when he hears that sermons are to be published in it:

EOGH. – Cha-n 'eil fhios agam fhéin – na-n tuiteadh dhoibh searmoinean a chur a mach a b' urrainn daoine bochd' a thuigsinn, gun teagamh bhiodh iad feumail. Ach air mo shon fhéin, cha do thachair searmoin Ghàelic orm, ach ainneamh, ann an leabhraichean, as an tugainn mòran maith: tha 'Ghàelic tuilleadh a's domhain air mo shon, agus na smaointean air an leigeadh ris air uairibh air dhòigh nach eil mi 'g an tuigsinn.

LACH. – Thoir thusa fainear nach 'eil searmoin againn ach na dh'eadar-theangaicheadh as a' Bheurla, agus gu-m bu dùth dhoibh beagan de bhlas na Beurl' a bhi orra; ach na searmoinean ùra so, tha iad air an cur r'a chéile air tùs anns a' Ghàelic, agus uaithe sin tha dòchas agam gu-m bi iad freagarrach do staid na dùthcha.[74]

(EWEN – I do not know – if they should happen to issue sermons that poor people could understand, they would undoubtedly be useful. But for myself, I never came across a Gaelic sermon, but seldom, in books, from which I could derive much good: the Gaelic is too deep for me, and the thoughts expressed at times in such a way that I cannot understand them.

LACHLAN – You take note that we have no sermons other than those which have been translated from English, and that it would be natural for them to carry a little of the flavour of English; but these new sermons, they are composed in Gaelic originally, and because of that I am hopeful that they will match the condition of the country.)

When Ewen objects that it would be be more sensible for people to make better use of the sermons preached orally each Sunday, and to save their money for purposes other than buying journals, Lachlann stresses the superiority of the printed sermon over the oral model, since the former, rather than the latter, can be recited intact to the family, and can accompany the rustic reader to *fasgadh an tuim* (the shelter of the hillock).[75] Quite apart from the rather bizarre picture of Gaels resting behind hillocks while reading the latest homily in the *Teachdaire Gaelach*, this appears to underestimate the memory power of Gaelic listeners, while overestimating levels of Gaelic literacy generally in the Highlands. In a manner which recalls John Carswell's strictures on Gaelic scribes in 1567, MacLeod thus promotes the perception that the non-literate Gael is missing out on a 'full' experience of the world.

It is nevertheless beyond doubt that MacLeod tried, however patronizingly, to reach the level of 'the ordinary Gael in the glen'. He strove to make 'homiletic Gaelic' more reader-friendly, and he tried to extend the range of Gaelic registers which had hitherto found their way into print. It is clear too that vernacular Gaelic is well represented in his journals, especially in his dialogues. The colourful, idiomatic, somewhat overwrought Gaelic of excited natural speech is captured well in the following excerpt from a conversation in which the participants catch sight of a well-known nineteenth-century paddle-steamer, *Maid of Morven*, as they go out to meet her in the Sound of Mull, and set off for seasonal work in the Lowlands:

> A mach ghabh sinn 'an coinneamh soitheach na smùide, a' Mhaighdean-Mhorairneach, mar a their iad rithe. Bha i 'teannadh oirnn o Mhuile, a cur nan smùid d'i. Tha i so a' tighinn, arsa Pàra Mòr, an aigeannach mhaol ghrànda, le 'gleadhraich, 's le h-ùpraid; cha b' ìoghnadh leam ach a' Mhaighdean a ràdh rithe; b' i sin a' Mhaighdean gun mhodh, gun eisimeil. Tharruing i oirnn, le caoiribh bàna fo 'sròin – a' slachdraich, agus a' sloisreadh na fairge foipe, 'bha 'g èiridh 'n a h-iomairean bàna còbhragaich a nunn gu h-Aros. Thàinig i 'nuas oirnn a' bagradh ar smàladh fo 'cuibhleachan. Fa dheireadh stad a' bhèist – 'us cha luaith' a stad na cuibhleachan o 'dhol mu 'n cuairt, na 'thug feadan fada caol, a bha suas ri taobh an t-simileir mhòir, aon ràn as a shaoil mi 'sgàineadh mo cheann. 'S ann an sin a bha 'n ùinich 's an othail 'an dol ri cliathaich na Luinge, a h-uile beul 's a' bhàta fosgailte 's an aon àm – gun urram fear d'a chéile. Ma 's i Marsali mhòr thug i mach a' Bheurla sin nach do chleachd i o 'n a bha i 'n uraidh air a' Ghalldachd; cò ach ise – bha 'Bheurla 's a' Ghaelic 'am measg a chéile. Dean fodha, ars' an dara h-aon, nach imir thu a mhic do mhàthar, ars' an t-aon eile: a stigh an ràmh bràghad shuas, buille 'g a deireadh shìos: *Cani, cani* 'illean, arsa Marsali mhòr – gu rèidh ars' a h-uile h-aon.[76]

> (Out we went to meet the steamship, the *Maid of Morven*, as they call her. She was drawing closer to us from Mull, going full speed. 'Here she comes', said Big Patrick, 'the horrid, bluff-bowed, spirited one, with her clamour and commotion; I'm not surprised that they had to call her the Maid; some Maid she, with no manners or decency.' She bore down upon us, with white waves under her nose – walloping and splashing the sea beneath her, which was rising in foaming, white swathes across to Aros. She came down upon us, threatening to destroy us under her paddles. At last the brute stopped – and no sooner did the paddles cease turning than a long thin whistle that was up beside the great funnel emitted a roar that I thought would split my head. What huffing and puffing there was, going alongside the ship, and every mouth in the boat open at the one time, regardless of each other. As for big Marjory, she came out with English that she hadn't used since she was in the Lowlands last year; who but she – Gaelic and English mixed together. 'Down with the oar,' said one; 'won't you row, mother's son', said another; 'ship the bow oar up there, give a stroke to her stern down there'. 'Canny, canny, lads', said big Marjory; 'take it slowly', said everyone [else].)

In this passage we can hear the vigorous, vernacular Gaelic of Morvern, MacLeod's native area, combined with the story-telling style used of monsters and sea-beasts. Traditional register is being extended to embrace the idiosyncracies of a paddle-steamer. At the same time, MacLeod gives us a glimpse of how Gaelic speech is being infiltrated by English words and phrases, as part of the cultural exchange consequent upon Highlanders' growing dependence on seasonal labour in the Lowlands, at the harvests or in the 'big houses'. It is a picture of a changing world, captured superbly in a verbal photograph which demonstrates the critical role of the clergy not only as creators of a new social and religious order in the Highlands, but also as the chroniclers of the emerging transformation.

COLLECTING THE LORE

The clergy of the Highlands and Islands stood at the intersection of oral and literary tradition beyond the ecclesiastical sphere, and, as the preceding extract shows, they were appreciative of the rich variety of traditional creative genres attested within the communities which they served. They were, for instance, aware that prose was not the only medium for a sermon: song could be harnessed to preach evangelical messages or to inculcate higher virtues. Alexander MacFarlane, minister of Arrochar, took to the poetic air-waves in order to condemn the cattle-reiving activities of his kinsmen, and to remind them that the gibbet was one of the sure-fire ways to Hell.[77] Donald Sage's *Memorabilia Domestica* alone bears vivid witness to the daily interaction of clergymen with sacred and secular lore, and suggests strongly that, in the eighteenth and nineteenth centuries, the Highland clergy inhabited a world which was much better balanced, and less affected by rejectionist dualism, than that of their post-1900 successors.[78] Although Highland churchmen after 1690 strove to eradicate secular practices which were at variance with evangelical Christianity, their worries about doctrinal purity appeared to increase from *c.* 1870. In the debate over allegiance to the Westminster Confession which engulfed the churches in the late nineteenth century, influential Highland minorities within the wider groupings reasserted the Puritan creeds of the seventeenth century, while the broader bodies liberalized their doctrinal positions. The more conservative groups split, at different stages, from the mainstream. As the mainstream gradually lost its identity, the smaller churches claimed the doctrinal high ground, and called for a much stronger degree of differentiation between 'the world' and 'the church'.[79]

Because of this very late form of Protestant reclusiveness, it is sometimes thought that, across the centuries, evangelical clergy and schoolmasters had little interest in collecting Gaelic secular material of any kind, but this is an inaccurate picture. In fact, it seems that a schoolmaster who was closely allied to the evangelical thrust of the eighteenth-century Highland church was the first to call for the compilation of a wide-ranging Gaelic dictionary in the wake of the 'Ossianic translations' of James Macpherson.[80] This was no less a person than Dugald Buchanan (1716–68), the celebrated itinerant preacher, hymn composer and catechist stationed at Kinloch Rannoch, Perthshire.[81] Buchanan urged his employers, the Society in Scotland for Propagating Christian Knowledge, to compile a dictionary of 'the Terms used in Divinity'.

In so doing, argued Buchanan, they were to pay attention to the lexical riches of Gaelic poetry in the oral domain, and in 1767, while he was supervising the printing of the Gaelic New Testament in Edinburgh, he wrote to Sir John Clerk of Penicuik, an eminent figure of the Scottish Enlightenment, in an attempt to enlist his support for such a project:

> Some time in harvest last the Society for propagating Christian Knowledge proposed to me that while I was correcting the Galic New Testament just now in the press that I should arrange all the words in an alphabetical order as they intended to publish a small Dictionary for the use of their schools, I told them that all the words in the old as well as in the New Testament could be comprised in very little room when properly arranged and that such a Dictionary would be very defective even with respect to the Terms used in Divinity so that in my opinion they ought to add all the words in the Common prayer Book the Confession of ffaith & Catechisms with all the Galic words in Llhyd's Archaelogia Britannica and that even with all these materials before a tollerably perfect Dictionary could be made out it would be necessary that the Compiler should travel thro the Isles and western Coasts of Scotland and collect the work of the antient & modern Bards, in which alone he could find the Language in its purity. Whether the necessary expence of travelling which behoved to be very considerable deterred them from coming to any conclusion I know not but I have not heard any more of it since and imagine that this motion like many others that has been made to compose a Dictionary of this Language is crushed in the bud.[82]

Buchanan's vision, which combines the sacred and secular, as well as the oral and literary, dimensions of Gaelic culture, is deeply concerned with the survival and reinforcement of the Gaelic language 'in its purity'. It anticipates the need to provide a range of printed tools, including dictionaries and compendia of verse. His proposal was probably too ambitious and too secular to enjoy the patronage of the SSPCK, and it doubtless scared them into silence.

Though great in scale, however, Buchanan's proposal was not entirely novel in its perceptions. Alexander MacDonald, the Jacobite poet, had published his *Vocabulary* in 1741 while still an SSPCK schoolmaster in Ardnamurchan.[83] The collecting of traditional songs, as well as other aspects of Gaelic lore, was also established by 1767, and churchmen had played an important part in this process. From the late seventeenth century onwards, some Highland clergymen had acted as collectors of Gaelic folklore, thus replicating to a significant extent the function of medieval monks and priests (like the dean of Lismore) as compilers of manuscripts. Robert Kirk of Aberfoyle, who produced 'Kirk's Bible' of 1690, had a scholarly interest in fairy lore.[84] Yet the spirit of 'Ossian' and the Enlightenment, which had inspired Dugald Buchanan to envisage greater things than the works of MacDonald or Kirk, appears to have had an equally beneficial effect on his clerical contemporaries.

Their response led to the compilation of manuscripts of great value, some of which, in whole or in part, reached print in later years. Major ministerial collectors of Gaelic verse in the eighteenth century included Alexander Pope of Reay, James Maclagan of Amulree and Blair Atholl, Donald MacNicol of Lismore, and Ewen MacDiarmid of Glasgow and Comrie. All four made important collections of Gaelic verse, the largest of which is that of Maclagan.[85] Ministers also wrote down the verse of key eighteenth-century Gaelic poets, who composed their songs orally and carried them in their heads. MacNicol of Lismore wrote down the verse of Duncan MacIntyre of Glenorchy from the poet's capacious memory, and the preservation of the verse of Rob Donn MacKay, of Reay, in Sutherland, was deeply indebted to clerical intermediaries.[86] Gaelic tales were written down and edited by several clergymen, among them John Gregorson Campbell, minister of Tiree from 1861.[87]

Gaelic Scotland thus owes the survival of a considerable proportion of its vernacular ballads, songs and tales to the Protestant Church. Although several of these collectors were moderate clergymen, some prominent evangelical ministers are represented, among them MacDiarmid and MacNicol, and also, in the early nineteenth century, the redoubtable John MacDonald of Ferintosh, who gathered a number of Gaelic heroic ballads.[88] MacDonald was also a champion of evangelical orality, gifted with a particular power in preaching at open-air gatherings. He came to be admired as the finest Gaelic preacher of the first half of the nineteenth century, if not of the entire century.[89] Despite the popular stereotype of the world-rejecting Calvinist minister whose image tends to haunt the minds of present- day literary critics, commitment to evangelical theology did not necessarily preclude an enthusiasm for secular Gaelic literature, and particularly for the gathering of material from the oral domain. Indeed, it is worth noting that the Protestant clergy of the Scottish Highlands made a much more significant contribution to recording secular oral material than they did to writing original scholarly works of theology.

CONCLUSION: THE CONTRIBUTION OF THE CLERGY

I have considered aspects of the process whereby Gaelic-speaking clergymen, and literate schoolmasters too, contributed to the development of Gaelic culture at oral and literary levels, and especially at those points where orality and literacy intersected. It is no exaggeration to say that their contribution has been both central and major, and that it has covered virtually all the domains of Gaelic literary activity as we see it across the centuries. The literary input and output of the clergy have been among the mainstays of Gaelic cultural survival. We owe the literary tradition largely to the clergy. Clerical composers have contributed handsomely to enriching the variety of both prose and verse. Clerical collectors have likewise ensured that highly important dimensions of the oral tradition of Gaelic Scotland, both sacred and secular, have been preserved in manuscript and in print. If we remove the clerical contribution from extant Gaelic literature, some two-thirds of it will vanish before our eyes.

Not only have the Highland clergy enhanced the *variety* of Gaelic literature; they have also influenced the *style* of printed Gaelic prose. As practitioners of both the pulpit and the pen, they stood at the frontier of orality and literacy. On the one side of the frontier, they operated in the domain of literacy, while, on the other, they were dependent on oral means for the communication of their message to the people. In the course of their pastoral duties, they would have used the day-to-day Gaelic of their people. Yet it could be argued that, when they first took up the pen, they allowed extraneous styles and models considerable place in their literary aspirations, and this tended to inhibit the development of natural Gaelic expression. The vernacular language, together with vernacular style, was sacrificed to some extent in order to achieve conformity with wider religious, political and literary designs. From 1567 to *c.* 1800, the clergy undoubtedly had a key role as translators of foundational Gaelic religious texts which were based on Genevan and (later) Westminister Calvinism, and also as the translators of the Gaelic Bible (completed in 1801). Theological study, productive of original scholarly works in Gaelic, is scarcely attested in the clerical domain; reproduction of Protestant theology and its key works was the clergy's main literary concern until the closing years of the eighteenth century.

After 1800, however, the task of translating Puritan texts (other than catechisms) became largely the responsibility of schoolmasters, who were seldom the masters of pulpit oratory. With some honourable exceptions (such as Patrick MacFarlane), they tended to perpetuate rigidity of style, producing texts which moved from one printed form to another, and hardly ventured into creative writing. As the schoolmasters devoted themselves to translation, Gaelic-speaking clergymen apparently liberalized and widened their range of interests. Those with an eye for creativity, who also happened to be placed in a context conducive to literary enterprise (usually in the Lowland cities or in the colonies), became the principal bridge-builders between orality and literacy, and also between orality and print. Pulpit oratory was traditionally and pre-eminently the domain of the clergy, and it may well have been enhanced and ennobled as an oral art by the impact of the Ossianic debate. It is certainly clear that, when ministers' original Gaelic sermons and views on style and language did reach the printing press, they brought much-needed stylistic sparkle and liveliness to a prose tradition which was all too often in danger of succumbing to the tight corsetry of external imitation. Ministers like Dougal Crawford, whose printed sermons of 1791 mark the beginning of a new homiletic era for Gaels, could not afford to lose their readers' and hearers' attention by importing foreign styles: the emigrant communities in North Carolina would have expected 'normal' sermons. Later literary minded clergymen, consciously reacting against English models, were well aware of the need to redress the balance in favour of the spoken word. The desire to incorporate vigorous contemporary Gaelic, as spoken by the people themselves, is the rationale behind the journals of Dr Norman MacLeod in the first half of the nineteenth century. By diversifying Gaelic prose beyond doctrine and homily, MacLeod took the first significant steps to give status and independence to the voice of the Gaelic people on the printed page.

The Gaelic-speaking and Gaelic-writing clergy thus played different roles as Gaelic literacy developed. Overall, it can be said fairly that they laid the foundations on which later generations of creative writers could build. As they moved away from strict adherence to the conventions of medieval Classical Gaelic, and later of 'Westminster Gaelic', they affirmed the importance of the vernacular language, and helped to develop its power as a printed medium. Gaelic tradition as a whole, both oral and literary, thus owes the pulpiteers and clerical penmen at least a judiciously qualified debt of gratitude.

NOTES

In writing this article, I have been given much help and encouragement by my students and colleagues. I am very grateful to Mr David Allan for providing me with a loan of his collection of early Gaelic religious texts; in so doing, he was quite unaware of their timely appearance! Dr Adam Fox and Professor Daniel Woolf have been models of editorial patience and support, and I thank them for their comments on earlier drafts. As always, I am greatly indebted to my wife, Dr Rachel Meek, for her help in various areas, and not least for her willingness to discuss my literary thoughts and 'discoveries' at all hours of the day and night.

1 Huw Pryce (ed.), *Literacy in Medieval Celtic Societies* (Cambridge: Cambridge University Press, 1998).
2 K. A. Steer and J. W. M. Bannerman, *Late Medieval Monumental Sculpture in the West Highlands* (Edinburgh: HMSO, 1977); Martin MacGregor, 'Church and Culture in the Late Medieval Highlands', in James Kirk (ed.), *The Church in the Highlands* (Edinburgh: Scottish Church History Society, 1999), 1–36.
3 Thomas Owen Clancy and Gilbert Márkus, *Iona: the Earliest Poetry of a Celtic Monastery* (Edinburgh: Edinburgh University Press, 1995).
4 Kenneth Jackson, *The Gaelic Notes in the Book of Deer* (Cambridge: Cambridge University Press, 1972).
5 Donald E. Meek, 'The Scots–Gaelic Scribes of Late Medieval Perthshire: an Overview of the Orthography and Contents of the Book of the Dean of Lismore', in J. D. McClure and M. R. G. Spiller (eds), *Brycht Lanternis: Essays on the Language and Literature of Medieval and Renaissance Scotland* (Aberdeen: Aberdeen University Press, 1989), 387–404.
6 Dòmhnall E. Meek, 'Gàidhlig is Gaylick anns na Meadhon Aoisean', in W. Gillies

(ed.), *Gaelic and Scotland: Alba agus a' Ghàidhlig* (Edinburgh: Edinburgh University Press, 1989), 131–45, 233–5.
7 Ibid.
8 Meek, 'Scots–Gaelic Scribes'.
9 R. L. Thomson, 'The Study of Manx Gaelic', Sir John Rhys Memorial Lecture 1969, British Academy, *Proceedings of the British Academy*, 55 (1969), 177–210, esp. pp. 178–84.
10 R. L. Thomson (ed.), *Yn Fer-ravee Creestee (1763)* (Douglas: Yn Chesaght Ghailckagh, 1998).
11 T. F. O'Rahilly, *Irish Dialects Past and Present* (Dublin: Broune & Nolan, 1932), ix.
12 R. L. Thomson (ed.), *Foirm na n-Urrnuidheadh* (Edinburgh: Scottish Gaelic Texts Society, 1970).
13 Ibid., lxvi–lxxvii.
14 Ibid., 3–13, 173–81 (translation).
15 Donald E. Meek, 'The Reformation and Gaelic Culture: Perspectives on Patronage, Language and Literature in John Carswell's Translation of the *Book of Common Order*', in James Kirk (ed), *The Church in the Highlands* (Edinburgh: Scottish Church History Society, 1998), 37–62.
16 Donald E. Meek, *The Scottish Highlands: the Churches and Gaelic Culture* (Geneva: World Council of Churches, 1996).
17 Donald E. Meek, 'God and Gaelic: the Highland Churches and Gaelic Cultural Identity', in Gordon McCoy and Maolcholaim Scott (eds), *Aithne na nGael* (Belfast: Institute of Irish Studies and the ULTACH Trust, 2000), 28–47, at pp. 42–3.
18 The pattern of translating Puritan and other doctrinal texts from English into Gaelic was not unique; it is attested in the case of Manx (as in *Yn Fer-ravee Creestee*: see note 10), but more evidently in Welsh; see Geraint H. Jenkins, *Literature, Religion and Society in Wales, 1660–1730*, Studies in Welsh History, (Cardiff: University of Wales Press, 1978), II.
19 R. L. Thomson (ed.), *Adtimchiol an Chreidimh: the Gaelic Version of John Calvin's Catechismus Ecclesiae Genevensis* (Edinburgh: Scottish Gaelic Texts Society, 1962). This also contains (pp. 231–50) an edition of the Gaelic version of the *Westminster Shorter Catechism*. For subsequent editions of the *Shorter Catechism*, see Donald MacLean, *Typographia Scoto-Gadelica* (Edinburgh: John Grant, 1915), 68–82.
20 *Gairm an De Mhoir don t Sluagh Neimh-iompoichte iompochadh agus bith beo.* Le Richard Baxter (Glasgow: R. and A. Foulis, 1750), iii.
21 John Owen, *On Communion with God, the Father, Son and Holy Ghost* ... translated into Gaelic by Alexander M'Dougall, Teacher, Glen Urquhart, with a Preface by John Kennedy, D.D., Dingwall (Edinburgh: The Religious Tract and Book Society of Scotland, 1876). Interestingly, Kennedy's Preface is in English.
22 Donald MacLean, *The Literature of the Scottish Gael* (Edinburgh: William Hodge & Co., 1912), 61.
23 Owen (trans. M'Dougall), 77.
24 *Cuairt an Oilthirich; no Turas A Chriosduidh; o'n t-Saoghal so chum an Ath-shaoghail fo shamhladh Brudair* ... (Edinburgh: C. Stewart, 1812). This was re-edited in later years and published in popular editions. For these editions and translations of other works by Bunyan, see MacLean, *Typographia*, 40–6.

25 Nigel M. de S. Cameron (ed.), *The Dictionary of Scottish Church History and Theology* (Edinburgh: T. &. T. Clark, 1993), 513.
26 Victor Edward Durkacz, *The Decline of the Celtic Languages* (Edinburgh: John Donald, 1983), 96–153.
27 Breandán O. Madagáin, 'An Bíobla i nGaeilge (1600–1981)', in M. Mac Conmara (ed.), *An Léann Eaglasta in Eirinn 1200–1900* (Baile Atha Cliath: An Clòchomhar Teo., 1971), 176–86; Deasún Breathnach, *Bedell and the Irish Version of the Old Testament* (Baile Atha Cliath: Clódhanna Teo., 1971); D. MacKinnon, *The Gaelic Bible and Psalter* (Dingwall: Ross-shire Printing and Publishing Co. Ltd, 1930), 45–9; Donald E. Meek, 'The Gaelic Bible', in David F. Wright (ed.), *The Bible in Scottish Life and Literature* (Edinburgh: St Andrew Press, 1988), 9–23.
28 MacKinnon, *Gaelic Bible*, 42–4.
29 Ibid., 49–53.
30 Ibid., 54–62; Durkacz, *Decline*, 66–7.
31 Donald E. Meek, 'Language and Style in the Scottish Gaelic Bible (1767–1807)', *Scottish Language*, 9 (Winter 1990), 2–16.
32 *Leabhraichean an t-Seann Tiomnaidh (Edinburgh: William Smellie, 1787)*, II. Caib. 17:4–7.
33 MacKinnon, *Gaelic Bible*, 66–71.
34 Ian R. MacDonald, *Aberdeen and the Highland Church (1785–1900)* (Edinburgh: St Andrews Press, 2000); for Glasgow, see Ian R. MacDonald, *Glasgow's Gaelic Churches* (Edinburgh: Knox Press, 1995).
35 This important aspect of the emigrant experience requires to be studied in detail, but numerous works touch on it. Of particular relevance to the present chapter is Douglas F. Kelly and Caroline Switzer Kelly, *Carolina Scots: an Historical and Geographical Study of Over 100 Years of Emigration* (Dillon, SC: 1739 Publications, 1998), 99–105, at pp. 99–100.
36 *Searmoin a chuaidh a liobhairt aig an Raft-Swamp, air an fhichioda' latha don cheud mhios don fhoghmhar* 1790, le D. Crauford, Minister (Fayetteville, 1791). I am deeply grateful to Mr David Williams, San Francisco, for supplying me with photocopies of this very important volume.
37 Ibid., 28: Crawford claimed in the dedication of the second sermon that he had been getting to know the people in Carolina for seven years. Crawford was the son of David Crawford, farmer, Sisgan, Kilmorie, Arran. He was educated at Glasgow University, and licensed by the Presbytery of Dunoon on 27 March 1781. He was ordained on 3 October 1781 by the Presbytery of Edinburgh as deputy chaplain of a regiment in Dutch Service in America. He was assistant at Kimorie in 1795, and was successively minister at Saddell, Kintyre (1779–1815) and at Kilmorie (1815–21). He was accidentally drowned on 22 March 1821 while going out to a small boat, about a mile from Pladda Island. See Huw Scott *et al.* (eds), *Fasti Ecclesiae Scoticanae* (Edinburgh: Oliver & Boyd, 1866–), IV. 63, 65. Rev. Dr T. M. Murchison notes (in the Gaelic Supplement of *Life and Work*, March 1966, 5) that Crawford became the minister of Barbecue (or Barbeque) Presbyterian church, Olivia, NC, about 1784.
38 Duane Meyer, *The Highland Scots of North Carolina 1732–1776* (Chapel Hill, NC: University of North Carolina Press, 1957); Kelly and Kelly, *Carolina Scots*.
39 *Searmoin … aig an Raft-Swamp*, 5. The separate dedications suggest strongly that the sermons were originally intended to be published as two separate booklets, but the existing text shows the consecutive page numbering of a single

volume. *Searmoin* on the existing title page is probably a singular (feminine) noun, and not a plural. It is possible that the printer/publisher decided at a late stage that it was economically more prudent to issue the sermons as one book.

40 Ibid., 38.

41 Kelly and Kelly, *Carolina Scots*, 100, 168.

42 *Searmoin ... aig an Raft-Swamp*, 9.

43 Ibid., 34.

44 Ibid.

45 *Leabhraichean an t-Seann Tiomnaidh* (Edinburgh: William Smellie, 1786), IV.

46 It is not clear how or where Crawford learned to write Gaelic.

47 I am not aware that earlier handwritten drafts of these sermons have survived. A close textual analysis (which I intend to undertake as part of a forthcoming full edition of the sermons) may reveal post-delivery 'insertions'.

48 The printing of prayers was a bold step in the Gaelic evangelical context. The length of the prayers appears to correspond to normal conventions in the Highlands.

49 *Searmoin do Mhnai' chuaidh a sgriobhadh ann sa Bhliadhna 1795*, le D. Crauford (Glasgow: James Gillies, 1795).

50 MacLean, *Literature*, 28.

51 This was printed by John Moir, Edinburgh.

52 *An Saighidear Criosduidh*, 10.

53 *Searmona le Mr Eobhann MacDiarmad, Minister ann an Glascho, agus na dheigh sin, an Comrie* (Edinburgh: C. Stewart, 1804). MacDiarmid was the minister of the Ingram Street Gaelic chapel; see MacDonald, *Glasgow's Gaelic Churches*, 9.

54 Derick S. Thomson (ed.), *The MacDiarmid MS Anthology* (Edinburgh: Scottish Gaelic Texts Society, 1992).

55 MacLean, *Literature*, 35.

56 I have examined copies of MacDiarmid's book which were the treasured possessions of owners in both Canada and Scotland. The copy used for this chapter was extensively annotated by a theologically alert and 'involved' reader.

57 MacDiarmid, *Searmona*, 120–1.

58 Calum MacLeòid, *An Iuchair Oir: Searmoinean* (Stirling: Stirling Tract Enterprise, 1950).

59 Domhnull MacGilleathain (ed.), *Dòrlach Sìl: Searmoinean Le Caochla Mhinistearan* (Edinburgh: Free Church Publications, 1931), 5.

60 This is a well-acknowledged perspective in the Gaelic areas, and can be confirmed readily by consulting any minister who uses Gaelic as a regular preaching medium.

61 MacLean, *Literature*, 61. J. Kennedy Cameron (ed.), *Gaelic and English Sermons of the Late Rev. John Macalister* (Inverness: Northern Counties Printing and Publishing Co. Ltd, 1896).

62 This material affords useful material for future explorations of ministerial literacy in Gaelic.

63 See, for example, John Macdonald, 'The Rev. John MacKay's Gaelic Sermons', *Scottish Gaelic Studies*, Part 2 (March 1962), 176–202; Kenneth MacDonald, 'Prose, religious (eighteenth century)', in D. S. Thomson (ed.), *The Companion to Gaelic Scotland* (Oxford: Blackwell, 1983), 241–2.

64 Personal knowledge.

65 Donald E. Meek, 'Evangelical Missionaries in the Early Nineteenth-century Highlands', *Scottish Studies*, 28 (1987), 1–34, at p. 12.
66 A. Clerk (ed.), *Caraid nan Gaidheal: A Choice Selection of Gaelic Writings by Norman MacLeod* (Edinburgh: John Grant, 1910), 263–73, at pp. 269–70.
67 John MacInnes, *The Evangelical Movement in the Highlands of Scotland, 1688–1800* (Aberdeen: Aberdeen University Press, 1951), 69–78.
68 *'Ros o Sharon': Searmoin leis an Urr. Lachlann Mac Coinnich a bha ann an Lochcarron* (Glasgow: Archibald Sinclair, n.d.), 10.
69 Roderick MacLeod, 'The John Bunyan of the Highlands: the Life and Work of the Rev. Robert Finlayson (1793–1861)', *Transactions of the Gaelic Society of Inverness*, 54 (1984–86), 240–68.
70 Tale-swapping of this kind continues to the present.
71 Clerk, *Caraid nan Gaidheal*, xxxi–xxxiii.
72 Ibid.
73 Sheila Kidd, 'Social Control and Social Criticism: the nineteenth-century *còmhradh*', *Scottish Gaelic Studies*, 20 (2000), 67–87.
74 Clerk, *Caraid nan Gaidheal*, 11.
75 Ibid.
76 Ibid., 385–6. The paddle-steamer, *Maid of Morven*, was acquired by Robert Napier in 1827; see C. L. D. Duckworth and G. E. Langmuir, *West Highland Steamers* (Glasgow: Brown, Son & Ferguson, 1987), 4.
77 *Sean Dain, agus Orain Ghaidhealach* (Perth: John Gillies, 1786), 132–3; Michael Newton, *Bho Chluaidh gu Calasraid* (Stornoway: Acair, 1999), 260–3.
78 Donald Sage, *Memorabilia Domestica* (Wick: W. Rae, 1889), 1–49.
79 Meek, *Scottish Highlands*; Meek, 'God and Gaelic'.
80 Fiona Stafford, *The Sublime Savage* (Edinburgh: Edinburgh University Press, 1988).
81 *The Spiritual Songs of Dugald Buchanan*, Donald MacLean, ed. (Edinburgh: John Grant, 1913), vii–xiii, provides the 'traditional' outline of Buchanan's life. This requires substantial modification; I am currently at work on a new Gaelic edition of Buchanan's verse and a reassessment (to be published in English) of his life and work in their eighteenth-century context.
82 SRO GD 18/4529. I am very grateful to Dr Donald William Stewart, Department of Celtic, University of Edinburgh, who is assisting me in the Buchanan project (see note 81), for bringing this document to my attention; and also to Sir John Clerk of Penicuik, Bt, for giving me permission to reproduce the letter in print. Edward Lhuyd (1660–1709), who is mentioned in the letter, made a grand tour of the Celtic countries in 1697–1701. He assembled material of archaeological, historical and linguistic significance; see Derick Thomson and John Lorne Campbell, *Edward Lhuyd in the Scottish Highlands* (Oxford: Oxford University Press, 1963).
83 Ronald Black, *Mac Mhaighstir Alasdair: the Ardnamurchan Years* (Coll: Society for West Highland and Island Historical Research, 1986), 24–30.
84 Robert Kirk, *The Secret Commonwealth of Elves, Fauns and Fairies* (Edinburgh, 1815). The work was completed in 1691.
85 For MacDiarmid, see note 52 above. For the other collectors, see Thomson, *Companion*, 177, 188, 240, under individual names.
86 Ibid., 188, 250.
87 Cameron, *Dictionary*, 129.

88 John Kennedy, *The Apostle of the North* (Glasgow: Free Presbyterian Publications, 1978), 22–4.
89 Ibid., passim.

Chapter 4

Speaking of history: conversations about the past in Restoration and eighteenth-century England

Daniel Woolf

FOR the past two or three centuries we have become rather used to thinking of history as something found in books. Just as we ourselves are trained to read and criticize documents, and to take these as the basis of all historical knowledge, so we tell our students which books to go off and read, what 'authorities' to rely on, which journals to consult, and so on. The advent of the Internet has changed the way in which written texts circulate, but has not altered our perception of history as something that is textualized rather than heard about. There were certainly history 'books' (or at least graphical equivalents to books) as far back as Herodotus, but it is only since the eighteenth century that the book has become the vessel *par excellence* for conveying stories about the past. It was then that history really became a commercially successful genre, with every bookseller and publisher having to lay in a good stock of the most famous modern and ancient historians from Gibbon and Voltaire via Clarendon and Guicciardini back to Livy and Thucydides.

This bookishness is likely to make us forgetful of the oral and oratorical origins of history, and of the fact that Clio was, originally, a muse – a performative goddess rather than a scholar. There's not much left of the era when Herodotus stood in the middle of Athens to read his *Histories*, or of that time, 2,000 years later, when the Italian *condottiere* Federigo da Montefeltro assembled his courtiers to listen to readings from ancient historians. Public readings today are usually of poems or novels, and few people would turn up at Blackwell's or Waterstone's to hear a chapter of the latest thing in historical erudition trip resonantly off an Oxford don's tongue. And yet there are still some contexts in which we do prefer to speak, rather than read, about history. Our students hear us lecture, and discuss what they have read in classrooms and tutorials (and, we like to think, among themselves); we listen to papers and lectures ourselves, attending international colloquia and inviting guest speakers. Many books and articles first enter the public domain as conference papers, and among the highest honours that can be bestowed on a British historian is to be Ford's lecturer at Oxford for a term. Less formally, chat about history in our offices, in the halls, and with our friends; we go to conferences not merely to listen to our colleagues' papers but to *discuss* them at the hotel bar afterwards, at least when we are not comparing our teaching loads and griping about salary problems, the insensitivity of academic administrators, or the decline of standards.

The early modern era, the age of the great transition to print culture, was perhaps the only point in human history when there has been a near equilibrium between the speaking of history and its silent reading.[1] Although the number of history books available to be read increased steadily through the sixteenth and early seventeenth centuries, exploding from 1660 on, there were still nearly as many contexts in which history could be listened to, heard about and discussed. And despite the authority that writing, and especially print, were beginning to confer on statements about the past, the two modes of presenting the past, oral and graphical were still seen as complementary rather than as competitive or mutually exclusive. The social origins of a tale or anecdote about the past, or of what we now call a 'fact' – a notion whose modern history also begins in the seventeenth century – counted for much more in terms of its claim to veracity than did the method of its delivery.[2] The purpose of this chapter (which itself has been read aloud to colleagues once or twice before being trapped on the typeset page) is to offer some illustrations of the ways in which history continued to be spoken aloud, in various social contexts, in early modern England. With occasional backward glances toward the Renaissance, the focus is on the period from the Restoration to the late eighteenth century, the era when the printed history book (and its narrative rival, the novel) made their greatest inroads into the book-selling market. I do not attempt to deal with every type of oral discussion of the past. The matter of 'oral residue' in Renaissance prose has been explored adequately by Father Walter J. Ong, and in another essay I have examined the implications of this for the perception of the past during the Renaissance.[3] Early modern oral tradition, the subject of several chapters in the present volume, has also been studied elsewhere, and scholars such as Adam Fox and Laura Gowing have written extensively about the oral presentation of the past in 'everyday' settings such as the ecclesiastical courts.[4] Finally, there is no space here for the role of the history play, perhaps the most obvious context for the oral presentation of the past, but scarcely one suffering from scholarly neglect.

HISTORY READ ALOUD

While it was not as common a practice as it had been in antiquity and in the early Renaissance, public readings of history books continued to occur in early modern Europe, though there are relatively few documented occurrences of this in England.[5] By the seventeenth century, with plenty of books available and private homes furnished with libraries and closets, there was little necessity for this among the literate, and the English have in any case never possessed much in the way of a *piazza* sociability. The most obvious exception is the university classroom where the first Camden Professor of history, the inestimable Degory Whear, bored his pupils for a quarter-century with Latin recitations of and commentaries upon ancient historians such as Lucius Florus.[6] Less formal public recitations – rather than readings proper – of history occurred on ceremonial occasions. When the Lord Chancellor, Lord Somers, visited St Catherine's Hospital in London on 1698, he insisted on giving his captive audience what one observer called 'a large historical account of all the steps and parts in the visitation, which lasted about an hour', before the proceedings even began.[7] In the 1740s, the bluestocking Elizabeth Carter heard Thucydides read aloud, in the Hobbes translation, but while we learn that 'he did not answer my expectations', it is not clear the degree to which this was a public reading.[8]

In truth, the English never had a strong tradition of public history readings, in comparison with the courts and marketplaces of the Continent, though the kind of intense studying and re-studying of ancients like Livy that Gabriel Harvey is known to have undertaken with successive companions may be seen as quasi-public, at least in the sense that they were intended to provide political advice to public figures.[9] Private and domestic reading, however, was another matter. In the mid-eighteenth century, for instance, Elizabeth Carter reports reading a translation of Livy 'in a family way', while a year later her 'family book' was Dio Cassius's *Roman History*.[10] There are numerous references to this sort of thing in the diaries and letter-books of the later seventeenth and eighteenth centuries. Samuel Pepys, whose appetite for history books at times exceeded his sexual longings, had his own collections on the history of the navy read aloud to him at supper, and he and his wife Elizabeth read other books together in bed.[11] A few decades further on, the history enthusiast Henry Prescott of Chester had his son Jack and his wife Suzy read to him. 'Jack reads Speeds Account of the Popish Plott and part of the History of Cataline', recorded Prescott on 5 November 1704, the ninety-ninth anniversary of Gunpowder Plot Day. On 30 January 1706, the fifty-seventh anniversary of the death of the Blessed Martyr of Glorious Memory, Charles I, Jack read aloud 'Nelson's Introduction to the King's Tryall'.[12]

Servants were also pressed into service to read history to their employers. An especially interesting example of this is Prescott's older contemporary Lady Sarah Cowper, an embittered matriarch who lived in a state of constant warfare with her husband, looking for solace in books. Failing eyesight threatened to remove this pleasure. A terrible quarrel with her husband in 1702 was precipitated by Sarah's request that she be accompanied to London by a servant who 'cou'd read well which would comfort me much now my sight is near gone'. Indeed, the prospective reader would have to be an educated woman who could not, therefore, dine with the other servants: 'Now such as are so well bred will think themselves too good (and indeed so do I) to dine in the kitchin therfore I desired she might sitt at our table ffor moreover I can scarce see to carve my meat decently.' By the beginning of 1705 Sarah had her way. Having acquired 'to wait on mee a woman that reads well', her new companion immediately began to read to her from the earl of Clarendon's newly-published *History of the Rebellion*. We can follow Sarah's reactions to hearing this read through successive entries in her diary, which is dominated by reflections on Clarendon for the better part of two months.[13]

Wives often had the task of reading history to their husbands, whether or not the works were of any personal interest. Mary Rich, Countess of Warwick, tells us in her diary that she regularly ministered to her ailing spouse by reading him extracts from history. On 11 February 1669 Rich notes 'After dinner my Lord that day againe falling ill of the gout, of which he kepte his bed, I was constantly with him and red to him history.' Her function there was entirely as entertainer and palliative care-giver; there is no suggestion that this unnamed work was being read by her choice rather than the earl's. Similarly, a week later 'After dinner I was constantly with my Lord and red in a history to him', an act repeated the following day.[14] Sometimes, it is even clear that this was a demanding chore, a marital duty akin to unwelcome sex and from which she fled at the earliest opportunity (usually when his lordship dozed off) in order to return to her private devotions. 'In the after noone [I] red to my Lord in a history, and after super I comited my soule to God.' And, even more cheerily: 'After diner red in History to my Lord; at evening reatired and red in a good booke, and aftwardes meditated upon death.'[15]

Mary Rich's readings aloud of secular history are devoid of any comment on the quality of what she read, nor does she even tell us the name of the historian; there is no sign of intellectual response to the matters discussed, as if a story were being recited with no attention to its content.[16] In contrast, the deeply religious countess was considerably more enthusiastic about Foxe's Book of Martyrs, which she sometimes retreated to read by herself, but on occasion heard read by a member of her household or her husband. During the afternoon of 19 December 1666, for instance, she 'hearde red bichop Latimers and Ridleys martyrdome, with which my heart was very much affected to read the courage and resolution with which thay dide'. On hearing the passage she retreated to pray to God 'that if he called me too I might as willingly suffer for his trueth'.[17]

Not all women found secular history a bore, and it had made considerable headway with them, as an alternative to romances and novels, a century later, when we find Lady East of Hall Place, Hurley, and her husband, both invalids, engaged in reading to each other from Gibbon. 'I was very ill all day & did not go out. Began to read the 4th Vol. of Gibbon Roman History.' She continued with Gibbon the next few days, interspersed with walks when she and her husband were able: 'We read Gibbon – walk'd a little ... A wet morning & worse weather all day than we have had some time; read all the morning in Gibbon.' Sometimes guests were included in this domestic decline and fall. On 20 February, which fell on a Sunday, Rome had to take a back pew to religion, if not to barbarism: 'I read aloud in the morning to Mr Clyfford & Sir William – from the moral part of Elegant Extracts, & Mr Holroyd's Translation of Reflections for every day in the year. In the evening we read the Roman His[tory by] Gibbon.'[18]

By the beginning of the nineteenth century, such scenes of men and especially women reading history books together, in mixed- or single-sex pairs and larger groups, is a familiar one, found in novels like Elizabeth Hamilton's *Memoirs of Modern Philosophers* (1800), in which the heroine Harriet is described 'quietly seated at her work with her aunt and sister, listening to Hume's *History of England* as it was read to them by a little orphan girl she had herself instructed'.[19] More famously, in Jane Austen's *Mansfield Park* the child Fanny Price is given daily rations of history to read aloud and later, as a young woman, embarks on readings of history and biography with her sister Susan. The dullness of the bare text of history is considerably enlivened in Fanny's oral summations. 'Fanny was her oracle', Jane Austen writes of Susan. 'What Fanny told her of former times, dwelt more on her mind than the pages of Goldsmith.'[20]

WHAT'S GOOD TO READ?

The advertising of history books, generally in the form of lists published at the end of other books, was in its infancy, and those curious to know which histories they should read relied much more on word of mouth in selecting titles, or even in learning of their publication. When Pepys took the historian and divine Thomas Fuller to The Dog, an alehouse, in 1661, he was told by the cleric about his forthcoming *Worthies of England*, a 'history of all the families of England', while its author boasted he could tell Pepys more about his own family than he knew himself. Pepys was to be severely disappointed when he first encountered the book in print, for Fuller made no mention of his family at all.[21]

The advent of circulating libraries in the mid-eighteenth century made this *viva voce* shopping more rather than less necessary, especially for recent works which might be blandly advertised in *The Gentleman's Magazine* and were not likely to be mentioned at all in courtesy literature, the historical prescriptions which tended to favour the classics. Lady Mary Coke, a keen reader, often spent her evenings in female company immersed in history, and freely dispensed her tastes to her friends. On 27 March 1769, with a friend in residence, she recorded with some frustration that 'I don't find Frances has read so much History as I thought She had. I have recommended some books to her.'[22] Coke herself learned of books by conversation, as on the occasion when Horace Walpole dropped by the house in 1773 and left her with a copy of his newly published *Memoires du comte de Gramont*, while on a previous day she had discussed with Lord Lyttelton 'the History of Henry the second, which he has just publish'd', and the author's fears that it would not be well received.[23] Elizabeth Carter, whose family had made Lyttelton their 'after supper book' in July 1767, told her confidante Catherine Talbot to advise Archbishop Secker, with whom Talbot lived, 'that I hear a bookseller at Maidstone is going to publish a new edition of [John] Philpot's history of Kent, with some additions that have been found amongst his papers'.[24]

Opinions on specific authors, historians as much as novelists, are increasingly a feature of genteel Georgian conversation: the sociable study of books for the purposes of sharing their contents was often contrasted with a more selfish, 'bookish' form of private study.[25] Mary Coke records a discussion concerning the virtues of Clarendon's *History of the Rebellion* and Horace Walpole's attack on it. Coke suggested to Lady Mary Forbes, the great-great granddaughter of Clarendon, that she thought Walpole merely to be saying 'what every one allowed, that his History was a very fine one, but that it was not a singular opinion to say that it was a partial history'. Forbes's defensive response that 'misrepresentation was very different to partiality' inclined Coke to drop the conversation rather than argue further and risk a scene.[26] Fanny Burney was asked by Dr Johnson, 'Miss Burney, what sort of Reading do you delight in? – History? – Travels? – Poetry? – or Romances?' She declined to answer for fear that any choice would be the wrong one.[27] On another occasion, however, Burney was more forthcoming. When discussing with William Seward a play they were jointly plotting, the latter suggested to Fanny that they begin a scene with the hero, Mr Dry, in his study, picking up a book. Burney records the exchange as follows:

> 'For Example, *this*,' cried I, giving him Clarendon's History.
>
> He took it up *in Character*, & flinging it away, cried, 'No, – this will never do, – a History by a Party writer is odious.'
>
> I then gave him Robertson's America [*History of America*, 2 vols, 1777].

'This', cried he, 'is of all reading the most melancholy; an account of Possessions we have lost by our own folly.'

I then gave him Baretti's Spanish Travels.

When Seward declined this, also, as shot through with falsehoods, she changed genres altogether, giving him *Clarissa* (which he disliked, thinking the only readable novel Burney's own *Evelina*). Burney then continued to present her companion with other books on which he continued to make 'severe, splenetic, yet comical comments'.[28]

Certain historians – Robertson, Gibbon, Hume, for example – because socially prominent as well as commercially successful, were especially common subjects of and occasional participants in conversation; as living historians, they could literally speak to readers outside of their own texts. Perhaps no one was more discussed and with greater animation than Catharine Sawbridge Macaulay. The 'republican virago's' life and political views attracted attention, with her own sex holding especially strong views on her character and historiographical talents.[29] Elizabeth Carter 'defended' Macaulay ambivalently on the grounds that she came across much better in person than in her books, and in spite of her 'extraordinary conduct' in marrying a much younger husband late in life.[30] 'Poor Mrs Macaulay!' Carter wrote to Elizabeth Montagu, who was less impressed with the historian's work. 'So you will not read her book, I cannot help it; I will, as I have a much higher opinion of her talents than you have. I am but very little acquainted with her, but in a tête-à-tête conversation of between two and three hours that we once had; she appeared to me to have [a] very considerable share both of sense and knowledge.'[31]

Quite aside from her unorthodox political views, Macaulay was already the object of suspicion among female as well as male readers simply for being that highly unusual creature, a woman historian. Mary Coke, for one, had a low view of Macaulay's talents, while conceding her knowledge. 'In the evening I read Sherlock upon Providence, & then the fourth volume of Mrs Macaulay's History. She shews herself Mistress of great learning, but with it has such strong prejudices as makes her unfit for the office of an historian.' A few days later, Coke and the Princess Amelia engaged in conversation about Macaulay, and a week after that Coke busied herself preparing for a visit from Macaulay's great rival, David Hume, by studying the latter's more conservative history. 'This evening I've been comparing Mr Hume's History with Mrs Macaulay's, not to the advantage of the latter, tho' I really think a Lady of her great learning an honor to the Sex, & lament her being so prejudiced.' When Hume showed up in person five days later, he and Coke 'talk'd then about Mrs Macaulay's history, & on that subject we agreed'.[32] Yet despite her grudging sympathy for Macaulay's victimization, a rumour that Coke and Macaulay were cohabiting proved too much to bear.'The Princess Amelia said she had hear'd I lived with Mrs Macaulay. I cou'd not help smiling at so strange an invention, & assured Her Royal Highness I was not positive whether I knew her by sight, but cou'd affirm I never spoke to her, & tho I thought her writings proved her to have genius, yet her ideas of government were so unreasonable & so absurd that I had no patience with her.'[33]

ANECDOTES AND NAME DROPPING

It was not necessary, however, for a history book to be read collectively, or for a historian to come to tea, for history to become an item in conversation. In fact, one did not need a book at all, since education still encouraged the memorizing of the most important facts about the past. These were often digested in textbooks and cheap chronologies in a manner calculated to encourage the most rudimentary rote learning. The number of historians appreciated for their great style, and who were read as master narrators of the past, was tiny in comparison to the enormous number of authors whose books simply contained historical trivia which the socially adept were expected to have at their command. A long line of works stretches from Renaissance titles such as *A Thousand Notable Things* and *The Varietie of Memorable and Worthy Matters* to Richmal Mangnall's enormously popular *Historical and Miscellaneous Questions* in the early nineteenth century. These were standard issue first for sixteenth-century students, then for a broadening urban and rural elite and middling sort. Those lower down the social ladder could find in broadsheets and almanacs all manner of reproducible historical information, from the names of the Nine Worthies to the regnal years of English kings and Roman emperors, to the year in which boots were invented.[34]

There is a long-standing 'history' to this, reaching back to the medieval and Renaissance emphasis on the study of particular characters and episodes of the past for the purpose of comparison, and for their deployment in rhetoric. As early as the 1590s Shakespeare provided a humorous take on Plutarchian parallels in a battlefield discussion between Fluellen and Gower on the character of 'Alexander the Pig', or Great as compared with Henry V (*Henry V*, IV, 7, 1–56). The commonplace books of the early modern period are littered with incidents wrenched from their temporal contexts to provide illustrations of moral or political points. Once collected, they furnished the speaker with a *copia* of examples with which to argue, either by precedent or analogy, the rightness of a particular action. The parliamentary debates of the seventeenth century show that Members of Parliament had regular recourse to the chronicles of the Middle Ages and sixteenth century to provide ammunition for political argument. These occasionally included blistering denunciations of particular historians, such as Edward Littleton's denunciation of the Tudor historian Polydore Vergil as a liar on the floor of the Commons in 1628.[35] The past similarly figured in sermons, which most obviously drew material regularly from biblical 'histories', a point taken up in Donald Meek's chapter on the Scottish clergy. By the end of the seventeenth century, preachers were also paying much more attention to secular history, especially on occasions such as anniversaries. Bishop White Kennett, a historian in his own right, gave an oral account of the Gunpowder Plot in one such sermon in 1713; several years earlier he had preached on the causes of the Civil Wars.[36] On 29 May 1705 Henry Prescott heard a similar sermon preached by a Mr Kippax of Ormskirk. 'The sermon is historicall out of Lord Clarendon, plain, honest but rustick.' On another occasion Prescott records 'Mr Lancaster has in the parish church a sermon on Ps. 115 v. 1 mixt with English History'.[37]

Congregants, like Members of Parliament, may be expected to have either nodded piously or nodded off as uplifting and enlightening episodes from history wafted through the air around them. Yet despite the arguments of contemporaries that history was a serious genre, much of what was lifted from the pages of histories and then floated in conversation was amusing rather than grave. In a recent study of a sixteenth-century history, Holinshed's *Chronicles,* Annabel Patterson has usefully commented on the 'portable' quality of many of the tales to be found in Tudor chronicles. Some of these involved very minor or domestic events rather than the great deeds that were normally expected from historians, at least according to the canons of humanist historiography, which continued to be accepted throughout the eighteenth century.[38] A memorable tale, once learned, was liberated from its paper and vellum prison, to be recounted again and again, the way jokes and urban folk-tales circulate today. Anecdotes became social tools, used to make points not only in private correspondence, but also in civil conversation.

It was not unusual to find the facts of history, or the virtues and vices of a particular figure, the subject of animated discussion. In old age Mary Wortley Montagu complained of the ill manners of the Italian Catholics with whom she had to debate religious issues. Their attacks on at least one English national figure were a particular irritant. 'As I do not mistake exclamation, invective, or ridicule for argument, I never recriminate on the lives of their popes and cardinals, when they urge the character of Henry the Eighth; I only answer, good actions are often done by ill men through interested motives, and 'tis the common method of Providence to bring good out of evil: history, both sacred and profane, furnishes many examples of it.'[39] Just as often, history was produced for a lighter purpose, to entertain friends and visitors. Ambrose Barnes, alderman of Newcastle in the late seventeenth century, was, his biographer records, 'furnisht for all manner of conversation in history. He entertained men to admiration by reciting the times, places, occasions and precise actions, as if he had seen them.'[40] Facts of history could be produced at the supper table, like salt, to enliven otherwise dull and stiff encounters. The day after her sixty-seventh birthday Sarah Cowper, who *was* easily bored, hosted a Kentish parson who amused her with the tale of an Elizabethan nobleman having a minister buried alive for refusing to perform a funeral service without advance payment, 'for which the earl was try'd and condemnd to dy. But the Queen pardon'd him.'[41] She herself collected many such 'histories' she had heard in her commonplace books.

Discussion of history often went hand in hand with conviviality. The already-mentioned Henry Prescott, who served as deputy registrar of the diocese of Chester in the early eighteenth century, conversed on history in settings outside church and hearth. Indeed, he was as fond of the alehouse as the study, and found many opportunities to combine his two favourite pastimes, discussing history with friends and associates in surroundings more redolent of Bacchus (coincidentally the name of one of his haunts) than of Clio. 'I take 3 hours and 2 pints at the Fountain. Roman Antiquity our discourse', we hear on one occasion; on another Prescott prevailed upon the chancellor of the diocese to stay late in the evening at the same tavern to discuss 'Books, learning, [and] Lives'. On 14 July 1706, again at The Fountain, he encountered two travellers, 'Sir Richard of Lincolnshire and Mr Worsley of ... a Member of Parliament' who asked him about several local antiquities they'd seen including the church altar. 'I give them account of that and the antiquity of Chester'. They soon fell to arguing about the merits of hereditary succession and primogeniture and Prescott suspected them 'of the deprav'd humor of the age as to religion and the Church of England'. During a particularly heavy evening of drinking and jollity, in November 1706, 'the wine, Church of England history, discourse, healths go on till 11 when the Archdeacon and I (the last men) return in a cold and rugged temper of the night'. During a severe winter storm in 1707 Prescott and his antiquarian friend Mr Davies repaired for warmth to the coffee house and then The Bacchus where they had three pints and discussed the life of the Elizabethan scholar Dr John Rainolds. With equal attention to detail in matters of history and libation, Prescott notes on another evening: 'Wee go to the Bacchus where wee (over 2 pints of white and ½ pint of sack) have an History of the House of Derby and the Island, with the Healths concurrent, past 10.'[42] A meeting in the same venue involved a discussion of a two-century old squabble as to which of the two universities, Oxford or Cambridge, had been founded first. At The Fountain, his favourite watering hole, he was entertained with some friends by a Mr Poole of Liverpool who tells 'long and great stories'. At The Ship, another pub, Prescott and several companions chatted about 'Mr Cloptons Genealogy' while drinking in the evening.[43] Sometimes private homes were the scenes of such discussions, as when Prescott and a friend were received by the antiquary Davies in his study; there they were entertained 'with indifferent claret but with gratefull variety of books and learning, especially ecclesiastical antiquity'. Personal reminiscence often figured in such encounters. On one occasion Prescott met 'with Mr Daniel Chadwick of Preston who was present at the barberous execucion of the earl of Derby, hee [*sic*] remembers the History of the Time and the Officers in and aginst Lathom House'.[44]

This last example is a reminder that there was a category of 'facts about the past' which might best be termed 'privileged' – details about persons, principally from recent history, known to only a few, and not to be found in books. Memories and tales of interest passed informally in conversation and sometimes by tradition across generations, long before they were consigned to the written record. The seventeenth century produced a whole series of 'Thomas More jokes' and witticisms involving other famous lawyers, many of which appear to have had oral rather than written origins.[45] At the end of the eighteenth century Hester Thrale Piozzi repeated for a friend a story involving Queen Caroline of Anspach. Attempting to acquaint herself with English history, the queen had told Sir Woolston Dixie, Bart, that she knew of his connection with Bosworth Field, the site of Richard III's defeat and death, near which Dixie lived. The baronet immediately became embarrassed and fled the room, because, being a brute with an 'utter ignorance of historic literature' he had assumed the queen was referring to a recent incident in which Dixie had been thrashed within an inch of his life by a tinker he had provoked while crossing Bosworth.[46]

The ability to recount such details conferred on the speaker a higher, 'in-the-know', status among his or her peers; it gave the listeners, afoot or at table, the pleasure of microhistories, revealed only to them, which in turn could be passed on selectively to chosen companions. A good example of this process is the attention paid by a late seventeenth-century northern antiquary, Abraham de la Pryme, to the tales told by his parishioners and others, including an elderly civil war veteran, Cornelius Lee (1629–1702). From Lee the young Pryme heard such 'facts' of history as that the French king Henri IV had been assassinated by Jesuits in 1610 for warning James I of the Gunpowder Plot. 'This relation', noted Pryme, 'he says, he had from the mouth of a great popish lord, in King Charles the First's time, who had it discover'd to him by his confessour.'[47]

There are many such instances of people recording, late in life, stories that they heard when much younger. In 1701, the very old Cuthbert Bound, who had been minister of Warmwell in Dorset at the Restoration, reported an incident he had witnessed in 1661. This involved a delirious prophet, visited by spirits who allowed him to predict both who would visit him later that day and political events such as the 1665 Plague, the Great Fire and the invasion of William of Orange in 1688. Bound, having been convinced in the fullness of time that these prophecies were legitimate, reported them to the Cambridge scholar John Covel in 1701. Thence they passed to Covel's brother-in-law Philip Traheron, who determined to interview Bound, 'who is decayed of late' before he died and extract further information.[48] Famous literary names often figure in such exchanges. Mary Coke, when riding in Hyde Park with the octogenarian Lord Bathurst in 1767, began to converse about her companion's relations with Pope, Swift, Bolingbroke and Atterbury half a century previously; Bathurst told her 'many things of them I had not heard; his memory never cou'd have been more perfect'.[49] The greater suspicion with which oral sources were often greeted after the middle of the seventeenth century did not always extend to personal recollections, especially when passed by members of the elite among themselves. On the other hand, there was no reason to accept a story, even from a family member, if he or she had a reputation as a liar or blowhard. When Sir Denny Ashburnham came calling on his cousin John he 'told a great many incredible stories' at dinner, but he got a cool reception from his host. John, the grandson of a royalist, disliked his kinsman on principle as a member of the parliamentarian side of the family, and he also thought Sir Denny 'a great prevaricator, and not to be trusted by me or myne'.[50]

The converse of this sort of private information, valued principally because it could not be found in books, was the type of detail about the historical past that was well-documented in books, yet was also so well known that it did not require a written authority. We would call this 'common knowledge'. The learned would make claims about the past while at table, many of which were matters of opinion rather than fact. Sir Edward Walker, the quarrelsome Garter King of Arms, asserted to Samuel Pepys 'that there was none of the families of princes in Christendom that do derive themselfs so high as Julius Caesar, nor so far by a thousand years, that can directly prove their rise'.[51] Disputed facts were sometimes the occasion of arguments, and by the early eighteenth century Richard Steele found it possible to satirize club-and-coffee-house wagers over history in a bet between two gentlemen, one a recognized authority on ancient sex scandals, 'upon a point of history, to wit, that Caesar never lay with Cato's sister'.[52]

Real-life arguments could turn on points nearly as pedantic. Hester Thrale Piozzi sought the aid of the antiquary Daniel Lysons in order to resolve her argument with a male associate as to whether Cardinal Wolsey had once, as suggested in Hume, stopped at Esher, the site of her own grandson's estate.[53] A few years later Piozzi turned to Lysons's brother Samuel to resolve the question of some 'disputants' as to what 'authority' could be adduced for the occurrence of a great frost on the Thames during the third century AD. 'Do me the very great kindness to let me know, and where you read the fact, whether in Holinshed, Stowe, Speed, or Strype's Annals and from what record the incident is taken, it having been averred that no records would then have been kept. I mean in 260 or 270 A.D.'[54] Lady Mary Coke notes in her journal an argument with David Hume about Oliver Cromwell's religion: 'I said he was as great a hypocrite in that as he was in every thing else, but he wou'd not allow it & insisted he was religious.'[55] On another occasion, in 1771, Coke found herself involved in a wager with Anne Pitt, whom she disliked. 'Mrs [Anne] Pit[t] & I had another violent dispute: I said that the Emperor Rodolphus the first was in possession of Austria, Stiria, &c.: she affirm'd the Family were not in possession of those Country's till long after, in the reign of Albert the second.' In order to resolve this important matter, the two women 'agreed to lay a crown, & when She came to me on monday I presented her with a history of the Empire'. Mary Coke won the point. Poor Mrs Pitt, to add insult to injury, then embarrassed herself publicly. 'With her eagerness to find herself in the right, She forgot She wanted to blow her nose, & as it wou'd not wait for her, it dropt, or rather let fall a drop, not at all to the advantage of my book, just upon the place where She found herself in the wrong: upon which She cry'd out, my nose has dropt, & will remain a mark of my infamy, yet notwithstanding this confession She wou'd only pay me half a crown. She is a droll Creature that is certain.'[56]

As this last example suggests, women were as apt as men to make history the subject of conversations with either sex, though the highly gendered character of history made women's relationship to the formal record of the past – which few of them actually wrote about – an ambiguous one.[57] Hume himself had strongly recommended historical knowledge for women, principally as a conversational tool rather than to encourage either deep scholarship or public life (the reasons men usually read it). Without a basic familiarity with the facts of national, and classical, history, he wrote, 'it is impossible her conversation can afford any entertainment to men of sense and reflection'. Hester Chapone's *Letters on the Improvement of the Mind, Addressed to a Young Lady* (1773), perhaps the most widely reprinted advice book to women of the eighteenth century, similarly associated historical knowledge principally with conversation rather than scholarship.

> The principal study I would recommend, is *history*. I know of nothing equally proper to entertain and improve at the same time, or that is so likely to form and strengthen your judgment, and, by giving you a liberal and comprehensive view of human nature, in some measure to supply the defect of that experience, which is usually attained too late to be of much service to us. Let me add, that more materials for conversation are supplied by this kind of knowledge, than by almost any other.[58]

For women, however, trimming a course between a Lady Knowall pedantic display of knowledge on the one hand and trivial discussions of frivolity on the other was not an easy task. Elizabeth Carter, for instance, uses the term 'historiettes' to pillory the gossip of 'the good gentlewomen of Ealing'.[59] Carter, who loved polite conversation but despised idle banter in the empty-headed, found history a subject she could hold forth on at great length in writing or in person. As she remarked to Elizabeth Montagu:

> O dear, O dear, why will you set me to talking over history, when there is so much danger that I may not stop till you are tired to death of the subject. I must, however, at even that risk, add a few words more on this subject, just to ask you, whether the brutality of the Sicilian character in this dreadful transaction, in which fathers murdered their own daughters, because they had married Frenchmen, does not bear a strong resemblance to their ancient stamp, and remind you of their behaviour with regard to the daughter of Hiero, so many centuries before. I have not read Constanza's History, though I have been looking out for it a long while. I know where to borrow it; but, by all accounts, it is a book worth having in one's possession.[60]

Men, for their part, were expected to have a commanding knowledge of history, to respond with authority when questions arose about the past in discussion; we recall the above-cited reference to the Lysons brothers of questions by Hester Thrale Piozzi. History was even considered to be among the decorous topics suitable for courting couples. In Jane Austen's *Northanger Abbey*, the oft-cited dispute between the heroine, Catherine Morland, and her friend Eleanor Tilney as to the utility and appeal of history is resolved by Eleanor's brother Henry, to whose arguments (and eventually marital overtures) Catherine assents.[61] While the modern undergraduate male is unlikely to have his way with women by displaying his familiarity with Tacitus or Toynbee, we have an excellent example of the conversational uses of history, principally for sexual purposes, in the young law student Dudley Ryder. A future chief justice of King's Bench, Ryder was the son of a dissenting draper. He kept a diary in 1715 and 1716, one of the explicit purposes of which was to record what he read every day and his moods on that day, so that he could review it later and 'know what best suits my own temper'. Most of all it would help him remember what he read. The diary gives us a very good sense of what a law student thought he should read and how best to do so. An added bonus derives from the fact that, like Samuel Pepys half-a-century earlier, he kept the diary in shorthand, revealing that he shared with Pepys both a strong libido and a proclivity for hanging about with whores – though in Ryder's case a bit more nervously, his emotions confused by fear of infection and by his concurrent infatuation with a tailor's daughter, Sally Marshall.[62] Also like Pepys, young Dudley read history books in a variety of contexts, at his lodgings, at booksellers' stands, and while travelling from place to place, taking Sallust's *Conspiracy of Catiline* – a topical book in the year of the Fifteen – to dinner on one day, dipping back into it after practising his viol on another. Feeling ill after a bad night's sleep he consoled himself by reading both Virgil and a modern, Perizonius's *Universal History*.[63]

Ryder's interest in reading in general and history in particular derived, however, largely from social rather than intellectual concerns. Above all, the compulsively shy Dudley saw history as a great way to meet women. Sometimes his tactics may not have worked: he read Burnet's *History of the Reformation* to the women at his lodging-house, though privately admitting that he found the bishop's style 'too stiff and formal'. A pleasant walk with some ladies along the marsh at Hackney turned Ryder's conversation to love, his thoughts to 'gallantry and knight-errantry and enchanted castles and cruel giants who barbarously treated the Fair', and his eyes away from Sallust or Sir Edward Coke and in the direction of *The Adventures of Lindamira, a Lady of Quality*.[64] Above all, what he craved was *stories*, true or false, to be able to haul out of his mental bag of tricks at a moment's notice; his colourless and sketchy memories of a trip to Paris proving unequal to a witty conversation about France, for instance, he decided to refresh them by reading someone else's printed travel accounts.[65]

CONCLUSION

This essay has only pointed out a few of the contexts within which men and women read history together and aloud, or discussed it conversationally. While much more could be said on each of these, and others, a few tentative generalizations may be in order. For a start, it is clear that oral and written modes of discourse about the past cannot be viewed in opposition. Although scholarly tradition, by 1700, had already vested greater authority in the written text for two centuries, no book ever remains exclusively the subject of silent reading and individual contemplation; certainly not the sorts of books that were being read by the educated populace outside the college chambers. A very long tradition of rhetoric, which had once used the matter of the past as the 'invention' for formal oratory, now provided the framework within which detailed knowledge of historical events, and familiarity with the greatest historical writers, ancient and modern, could be used in social intercourse. Secondly, it is equally evident that however overwhelming the number of history books from which ladies and gentlemen could choose, the knowledge to be gleaned from them was intended not to be used principally for the advancement of historiography, as modern historians are too apt to think, nor even for the furtherance of public and private virtue, as the courtesy literature and advice books of the era proclaimed. Rather, history was intended to be a *lingua franca* among and between the sexes, a serious but also an entertaining tool, much like religion, philosophy, politics and fiction, to be employed in the art of conversation.

NOTES

This chapter was delivered as a lecture in the Department of English at Dalhousie University in January 1999, and I am grateful for comments received therein; some of the examples have been used, though in a different form, in my book *Reading History in Early Modern England* (Cambridge: Cambridge University Press, 2000).

1 Andrew Taylor, 'Into His Secret Chamber: Reading and Privacy in Late Medieval England', in James Raven, Helen Small and Naomi Tadmor (eds), *The Practice and Representation of Reading in England* (Cambridge: Cambridge University Press, 1996), 41–61; cf. N. Tadmor, '"In the Even my Wife Read to Me": Women, Reading and Household Life in the Eighteenth Century', in ibid., 162–74.
2 Lorraine Daston, 'Baconian Facts, Academic Civility, and the Prehistory of Objectivity', *Annals of Scholarship*, 8 (1991), 337–63; M. Poovey, *A History of the Modern Fact: Problems of Knowledge in the Sciences of Wealth and Society* (Chicago and London: University of Chicago Press, 1998); Barbara J. Shapiro, *A Culture of Fact: England, 1550–1720* (Ithaca, NY, and London: Cornell University Press, 2000).
3 Walter J. Ong, 'Oral Residue in Tudor Prose Style', *Rhetoric, Romance and Technology: Studies in the Interaction of Expression and Culture* (Ithaca, NY, and London: Cornell University Press, 1971); D. R. Woolf, 'Speech, Text, and Time: the Sense of Hearing and the Sense of the Past in Renaissance England', *Albion*, 18 (1986), 159–93; see also the very interesting treatment of the sound of language in Bruce R. Smith, *The Acoustic World of Early Modern England* (Chicago, IL: University of Chicago Press, 1999), esp. 127–9 on the relation between reading and oral cues.
4 D. R. Woolf, 'The Common Voice: History, Folklore and Oral Tradition in Early Modern England', *Past and Present*, 120 (1988); this will be handled at greater length in my forthcoming book *The Social Circulation of the Past*; Adam Fox, 'Custom, Memory and the Authority of Writing', in P. Griffiths, A. Fox and S. Hindle (eds), *The Experience of Authority in Early Modern England* (Basingstoke: Macmillan, 1996), 89–116; idem, *Oral and Literate Culture in England 1500–1700* (Oxford: Clarendon Press, 2000); Laura Gowing, *Domestic Dangers: Women, Words and Sex in Early Modern London* (Oxford: Clarendon Press, 1996)
5 On reading aloud in general, see Roger Chartier, 'Leisure and Sociability: Reading Aloud in Early Modern Europe', in Susan Zimmerman and Ronald F. E. Weissman (eds), *Urban Life in the Renaissance* (Newark, DE: University of Delaware Press, 1989), 103–20; Alberto Manguel, *A History of Reading* (New York: Viking, 1996), 109–23.
6 J. H. M. Salmon, 'Precept, Example, and Truth: Degory Wheare and the *ars historica*', in Donald R. Kelley and David Harris Sacks (eds), *The Historical Imagination in Early Modern Britain* (Cambridge: Cambridge University Press and Woodrow Wilson Centre Press, 1997), 11–36.
7 Arthur Charlett to Thomas Tanner, 1 October 1698, Bodl. MS Tanner 22, fo. 86r.
8 *A Series of Letters between Mrs Elizabeth Carter and Miss Catherine Talbot from the Year 1741 to 1770*, 2 vols (London: F. C. and J. Rivington, 1808), I. 56–7 (6 January 1745).
9 Lisa Jardine and Anthony Grafton, 'Studied for Action: How Gabriel Harvey

Read his Livy', *Past and Present*, 129 (1990), 30–78; for a similar approach see William H. Sherman, *John Dee: the Politics of Reading and Writing in the English Renaissance* (Amherst, MA: University of Massachussetts Press, 1995); Kevin Sharpe, *Reading Revolutions* (New Haven, CT: Yale University Press, 2000).

10 *Letters between Mrs Elizabeth Carter and Miss Catherine Talbot*. I, 30 (27 December 1743); I. 67 (6 January 1745).

11 *The Diary of Samuel Pepys*, ed. R. Latham and W. Matthews, 11 vols (Berkeley and Los Angeles: University of California Press, 1970–82), IX. 506 (2 April 1669).

12 *The Diary of Henry Prescott, LL.B., Deputy Registrar of Chester Diocese*, ed. John Addy, 3 vols (Record Society of Lancashire and Cheshire, 1987–97), 30. 'Nelson' is actually John Nalson, *A true copy of the Journal of the High Court of Justice, for the tryal of K. Charles I, as it was read in the House of Commons, and attested under the hand of Phelps, clerk to that infamous court. Taken by J. Nalson, LL D. Jan. 4, 1683. With a large introduction* (1684). Cataline is certainly Sallust's account of the conspiracy of Cataline, and Speed probably the account of the Gunpowder Plot in an edition of John Speed's *Historie of Great Britaine*, first published in 1611 and republished several times during the seventeenth century.

13 Sarah Cowper, Diaries, 7 vols, Herts. Record Office, Panshanger MSS, D/EP F. 29–35 Diary I. 265; III. 10 ff.

14 British Library (hereafter BL) Add. MS 27351, fos 292v (11 February 1669), 295r (18–19 February 1669).

15 BL Add. MS 27351, fo. 297r (25 February 1669); Add. 27352, Diary, II. fo. 5v (26 November 1669), emphasis mine. For an explicit complaint of the time taken attending her husband and the brief moments seized for personal reading and meditation, see ibid. fos 87r and 229v.

16 Other examples: BL Add. MS 27352 fos 27r (28 December 1669), 54r (8 February 1670), 54v (10 February 1670), 55r (11 February 1670), 145v (4 February 1671), 147r (8 February 1671); a 'French history' is as precise as Rich gets in naming the works read: Add. 27358, fo. 33r (8 January 1669).

17 BL Add. MS 27351,fo. 47r, 19 December 1666. Two months earlier, on 17 October, she rose from dinner and 'heard some storys out of ye Book of martyrs read, w[i]th w[hi]ch my heart was much affected': MS 27358, fo. 4v.

18 Berkshire Record Office, Reading, D/EX 1306/1, Diary of Lady East, 1791–92, unfoliated, entries from 7 to 20 February 1791.

19 Elizabeth Hamilton, *Memoirs of Modern Philosophers*, 3 vols (Bath and London, 1800), 1. 107–8.

20 Austen, *Mansfield Park* (Harmondsworth: Penguin, 1989), 363.

21 *Diary of Samuel Pepys*, II. 21 (22 January 1661); III. 26 (10 February 1662).

22 *The Letters and Journals of Lady Mary Coke*, 4 vols (Edinburgh: D. Douglas, 1889–96), II. 28 (Lyttelton); III. 51.

23 Ibid., IV. 163 (7 January 1773).

24 *Letters between Mrs Elizabeth Carter and Miss Catherine Talbot*, I. 459 (19 April 1760); II. 46 (9 July 1767).

25 Adrian Johns, *The Nature of the Book* (Chicago, IL: University of Chicago Press, 1998), 470. For a useful introduction to social discourse in early modern Europe, see Peter Burke, *The Art of Conversation* (Ithaca, NY: Cornell University Press, 1993) and, more recently, Peter Burke, 'A Civil Tongue: Language and Politeness in Early Modern England', in P. Burke, B. Harrison and P. Slack (eds), *Civil*

Histories: Essays Presented to Sir Keith Thomas (Oxford: Oxford University Press, 200), 31–48; cf. Smith, *The Acoustic World of Early Modern England*, 252–61. For contemporary notions of 'civil' conversation (in both its modern, narrower sense and the older, broader meaning of 'public conduct'), see Anna Bryson, *From Courtesy to Civility: Changing Codes of Conduct in Early Modern England* (Oxford, 1998), 153–9, 173–87; and Peter N. Miller, *Peiresc's Europe: Learning and Virtue in the Seventeenth Century* (New Haven, CT: Yale University Press, 2000), 51–63. I have also found helpful the theoretical discussions in Ronald Wardhaugh, *How Conversation Works* (Oxford: Blackwell, 1985).

26 *Letters and Journals of Lady Mary Coke*, II. 191.

27 *The Early Journals and Letters of Fanny Burney*, ed. Lars E. Troide and Stewart J. Cooke (Oxford: Clarendon Press, 1994), vol. III: *The Streatham Years, part I, 1778–1779*, 106 (August 1778).

28 Ibid., 322 (*c.* 15–26 June 1779).

29 Bridget Hill, *The Republican Virago: the Life and Times of Catharine Macaulay, Historian* (Oxford: Clarendon Press, 1992).

30 *Letters from Mrs Elizabeth Carter, to Mrs Montagu, between the years 1755 and 1800*, ed. Montagu Pennington, 3 vols (1817), III, 98 (no. 218, 7 December 1778).

31 Ibid., II. 309 (no. 181, 3 June 1775).

32 *Letters and Journals of Lady Mary Coke*, III: 4, 8, 11, 18 (8–19 January 1769).

33 Ibid., III, 18, 22.

34 Thomas Lupton, *A Thousand Notable Things of Sundrie Sortes* (1627); Walter Owsold, *The Varietie of Memorable and Worthy Matters* (1605); Richmal Mangnall, *Historical and Miscellaneous Questions: for the use of young people with a selection of British and general biography*, 11th edn (London: Longman, Hurst, Rees, Orme & Brown, 1814).

35 *Commons Debates, 1628*, ed. Mary Frear Keeler, Maija Jansson Cole and William B. Bidwell (New Haven, CT, and London: Yale University Press, 1977–83), IV. 42 (31 May 1628).

36 White Kennett, *A memorial to Protestants on the fifth of November, containing a more full discovery of some particulars relating to the happy deliverance of King James I. and three estates of England, from the massacre by gunpowder, anno 1605* (1713); idem, *Moderation maintain'd, in defence of a compassionate enquiry into the causes of the civil war, &c. In a sermon preached the thirty-first of January, at Aldgate-church* (1704).

37 *Diary of Henry Prescott*, I. 52, 67. For another example from 1709, see ibid. p. 222.

38 A. Patterson *Reading Holinshed's Chronicles* (Chicago, IL: University of Chicago Press, 1994); idem, 'Foul, his Wife, the Mayor, and Foul's Mare: the Power of Anecdote in Tudor Historiography', in Kelley and Sacks, *Historical Imagination in Early Modern Britain*, 159–78.

39 *The Letters and Works of Lady Mary Wortley Montagu*, ed. W. Moy Thomas, rev. edn, 2 vols (London: Bell & Sons, 1887), II. 296 (Wortley Montagu to Lady Bute, 20 October 1755).

40 M.R., *Memoirs of the Life of Mr Ambrose Barnes* (Surtees Soc., 50, Newcastle, 1866), 151.

41 Sarah Cowper, Diary, V. 279 (15 February 1711).

42 *Diary of Henry Prescott*, I. 38, 82, 84, 107, 125, 131, 155.

43 Ibid., I. 81, 147, 193. The work referred to is possibly Hugh Clopton (ed.), *Historical discourses, upon several occasions ... By Sir Edward Walker* (1705).
44 Ibid., I. 149, 229.
45 Robert Parker Sorlien, 'Thomas More Anecdotes in an Elizabethan Diary', *Moreana*, 34 (May 1972). Sorlien notes the first written appearance of one of these anecdotes in Cresacre More's *Life of Thomas More*, composed about 1615.
46 *Autobiography, Letters, and Literary Remains of Mrs Piozzi*, ed. A. Hayward, 2nd edn, 2 vols (London: Longman, Green, Longman, and Roberts, 1861), I. 340.
47 *The Diary of Abraham de la Pryme, the Yorkshire Antiquary*, ed. Charles Jackson (Surtees Soc., 54, Newcastle, 1869–70), 233, 258.
48 CUL MS Mm. 6.50 (Covel letters), fos 251, 253, Covel to Traheron 25 July 1701.
49 Coke, *Journals*, I. 236 (8 May 1767).
50 East Sussex Record Office (Lewes), MS Ash. 931, p. 33, Diary of John first Lord Ashburnham for 3 August 1686.
51 *Diary of Samuel Pepys*, V. 319 (11 November 1664).
52 *Spectator*, ed. Donald F. Bond, 5 vols (Oxford: Clarendon Press, 1965), II, 72 (no. 145, 16 August 1711).
53 *Autobiography, Letters, and Literary Remains of Mrs Piozzi*, II. 70 (Piozzi to D. Lysons, 9 July 1796).
54 Ibid.; II. 89 *(Piozzi to S.* Lysons, 17 February 1814).
55 *The Letters and Journals of Lady Mary Coke*, III. 19 (7 February 1769).
56 Ibid., III. 440–1.
57 D. Looser, *British Women Writers and the Writing of History, 1670–1820* (Baltimore, MD,: Johns Hopkins University Press, 2000); Mark S. Phillips, *Society and Sentiment: Genres of Historical Writing in Britain, 1740–1820* (Princeton, NJ: Princeton University Press, 2000); D. R. Woolf, 'A Feminine Past? Gender, Genre and Historical Knowledge in England, 1500–1800', *American Historical Review*, 102 (1997), 645–79.
58 See Woolf, 'A Feminine Past?', 666–7, for Hume and Chapone, and for the differences between their views, which are inconsequential in the present context.
59 *Letters from Mrs Elizabeth Carter, to Mrs Montagu*, I. 84. Compare Mary Coke's reference to the 'terrible Historys' she heard walking the streets of London, tales of recent murders and crimes: *Letters and Journals of Mary Coke*, II. 66.
60 *Letters from Mrs Elizabeth Carter, to Mrs Montagu*, II. 140, (no. 145, 20 June 1772); II. 239 (no. 167, 24 December 1773).
61 Jane Austen, *Northanger Abbey*, Introduction by M. Drabble (New York and London: Penguin–Signet, 1989), 111.
62 *The Diary of Dudley Ryder 1715–1716*, ed. W. Matthews (London: Methuen, 1939), 29 (n.d. 1715), 72 (8–9 August 1715), 171 (23 January 1716).
63 Ibid., 67 (3 August 1715), 70 (6 August 1715), 130 (3 November 1715, for his reading at the booksellers). Sallust was a favourite of his; the next month he continued with the *Jugurthine War*: ibid., 92 (8 September 1715).
64 Ibid., 337 (27 September 1716), for his reading of De la Rivière Manley's *The Secret History of Queen Zarah and the Zarazians* (1705); ibid., 209–10 (31 March to 2 April 1716); ibid., 357 (1 November 1716) for the *Art*.
65 Ibid., 282 (23 July 1716); 297 (15 August 1716).

Chapter 5

Vagabonds and minstrels in sixteenth-century Wales

Richard Suggett

THROUGHOUT much of late medieval and early modern Europe, from Poland and Russia in the east to Wales and Ireland in the west, itinerant minstrels entertained noble and plebeian audiences. Wandering entertainers may well have provided (as Burke has suggested) one of the unifying elements within European popular culture. A pan-European tradition of minstrelsy, crossing social and cultural boundaries, is an appealing idea, but the differences as well as the similarities between minstrels need to be appreciated. A diversity of vernacular terms for minstrels conveyed status differences as well as different performance skills among the entertainers. Some performance genres travelled better than others. Low-status physical performers – acrobats, jugglers and dancers – probably moved more easily between different language and cultural groupings than verbal performers, who might have high status within their own speech communities. Traditions of minstrelsy that gave high prestige to oral poetry and the music that accompanied recitation, and were tightly related to internal social structures, may have been important for defining local solidarities but might be regarded externally as ludicrously unmusical. However it is clear that, despite a diversity of performance genres, minstrels considered as a professional occupational grouping shared recognizably similar historical experiences of itinerancy, episodic persecution, and attempts at self-protection through membership of fraternities. Minstrels were culturally important as entertainers, social commentators and remembrancers but their mobility, communication in oral rather than written genres, and increasingly marginal position in the sixteenth century have made entertainers particularly elusive for the historian. Understandably, since sources are generally meagre and difficult to locate, there have been few regional studies of itinerant entertainers and their genres of performance.[1]

This chapter is a case study of entertainers in a particular locale – Wales – during a period of rapid social and cultural changes, and it attempts to answer some basic questions about performers and performance: who were the minstrels; what were their genres of performance; was there legal discrimination against entertainers and, if so, when; and did minstrels have strategies for professional survival? Wales is particularly significant for the history of late medieval and early modern European minstrelsy because there has been extensive preservation in manuscript of poetry, particularly praise poetry, that was, initially at least, declaimed by professional performers before an audience.[2] Moreover, abundant legal records, a bureaucratic consequence of the Acts of Union with England, have survived, providing uniquely in the British context a view of minstrels from the administrative as well as the literary perspective.

VAGABONDS AND MINSTRELS

Information about minstrels in the sixteenth century often derives from hostile sources, generally by the exponents of 'high' or courtly traditions seeking to distance themselves from a 'low' tradition of minstrelsy, and from legal and administrative records, especially statutes and proclamations that viewed entertainers – broadly defined – as troublesome and idle wanderers, regarding them as 'vagabonds' who were to be punished with increasing severity. Tudor anxiety about vagabonds was sharply expressed in several coercive statutes between 1530 and 1597.[3] The later Tudor vagrancy legislation has been suggested as a cause of the decline of minstrelsy in England and Wales. In particular, the 1572 Vagrancy Act specifically redefined minstrels and other unlicensed entertainers (fencers, bearwards, common players, and jugglers) as vagabonds; a proviso to safeguard Welsh minstrels was rejected by the Commons.[4] Rather perplexingly, given this discrimination against entertainers, few minstrels have been identified as victims of the legal process in England, although this may be an aspect of the uneven survival of the legal record.[5] However, clearer documentary evidence survives for campaigns against minstrels in Wales, and also in Ireland.

Locating vagabonds and minstrels and other wanderers on the margins of settled society depends on the survival of the appropriate historical record. In Wales the survival of a substantial proportion of the records of the assize courts or Great Sessions, established by the second Act of Union (1543), exceptionally allows the recovery of a series of sixteenth-century prosecutions of vagabonds and minstrels. There are inevitably chasms in the record but it is clear that a campaign of legal harassment against minstrels was begun a generation before the 1572 Act and involved the multiple prosecutions of entertainers as vagabonds.

Minstrels were indicted at the new Welsh assize courts in the decade immediately following the second Act of Union. Prosecutions were initially concentrated on the Chester circuit, that is in the three counties of north-east Wales (Flintshire and the newly-shired counties of Denbighshire and Montgomeryshire) and in the adjoining English county of Cheshire. The first prosecutions occurred in 1547, the year of Edward VI's accession, when a bill of indictment was laid against twelve minstrels in Flintshire. Three years later, in the spring sessions 1550, more than thirty minstrels were prosecuted throughout north-east Wales: four minstrels were indicted in Flintshire, eight or more in Denbighshire and at least nineteen in Montgomeryshire. The mid-Tudor prosecutions concluded in 1552–53 with the grand-jury presentment of eighteen or more minstrels in Cheshire and of sixteen 'vakabonds cawllyng them selyffs mynstrells' in Denbighshire. These indictments reveal a regional core of more than fifty professional entertainers working in mid-sixteenth-century north-east Wales.[6] The minstrels' sense of shock and betrayal was clearly expressed in a poetic complaint – a remarkable survival – specifically prompted by the indictment of the 'craftsmen in poetry and music'. The anonymous author regards Denbighshire as cursed and condemns those who had indicted the minstrels instead of supporting them. The poet emphasizes the traditional role of the bards and urges the men of Gwynedd to call the minstrels home where their craft is still respected.[7]

It must be emphasized that the evidence for the multiple prosecutions of vagabond–minstrels in mid-Tudor Wales appears to be unique among surviving legal records of the British Isles. This is not to say, of course, that parallel campaigns against minstrels did not occur outside Wales. However, discrimination against vagabonds is hard to chart, partly because of the uneven survival of the legal record and partly because the summary punishment of vagrants permitted by the legislation before 1572 could leave little or no trace in the formal legal record. There are occasional hints of organized local searches for minstrels in England. In 1556 a general order was made by the Marian Council against 'players and pipers' strolling through the kingdom spreading sedition and heresy, but if this instruction resulted in multiple prosecutions the evidence has disappeared with the destruction of the greater part of the mid-sixteenth-century assize records.[8]

There are grounds, however, for thinking that the administration in Wales was disposed to view minstrels with particular disfavour. There were numerous wanderers in sixteenth-century Wales, but it is very striking that by and large minstrels were the only type of vagabond prosecuted at the mid-Tudor assizes. Sixteenth-century Welsh minstrels fell foul of general reforming concerns about vagrancy but, additionally, they could be regarded as suspect persons because of their adherence to Welsh language and custom. Fifteenth-century minstrels had been suspected of sedition and their sixteenth-century successors still cultivated the poetry, genealogy and history that helped sustain a sense of a separate Welsh identity. In this sense minstrels maintained 'sinister usages and customs' which the Act of Union (1536) resolved to 'extirpate' because they tended to undermine the unity of the realm. It was probably not coincidental therefore that minstrels were prosecuted so soon after the Act of Union.[9]

Minstrels were prosecuted sporadically in Elizabethan Wales but it becomes increasingly difficult, especially after the 1572 Act, to distinguish entertainers from other wanderers who were regularly indicted as vagabonds. Multiple prosecutions of vagabonds, wanderers and suspect persons, including vagrant women, took place in Glamorgan in 1560, 1577 and 1586 but minstrels were not separately identified among them. In addition, new itinerant groups, which may have included entertainers, were discriminated against. A band of forty 'vagrant personnes terming themselfes Egiptiens' was rounded up in Radnorshire in 1579 for prosecution under the 1562 Act that had made travelling as a gypsy a capital crime. Their fate is unknown, but two wayfarers arrested in Glamorgan in 1599 were indicted as 'egypytians', convicted and sentenced to hang as felons.[10] The last clearly identifiable campaign against minstrels occurred in early seventeenth-century west Wales when a determined effort was made to rid Pembrokeshire of strolling musicians. In 1620 the grand jury made a presentment of the fiddlers, harpers, crowders, tabor-players and pipers who wandered up and down the country like rogues. One minstrel was ordered to keep to his parish, but six musicians were sent to the house of correction which must then have become something of a minstrels' academy before the musicians were taken into service.[11]

WHO WERE THE MINSTRELS?

Who were the minstrels? A first step towards answering this fundamental question is to recognize the diversity of entertainers in Wales beyond the poets of high status who inevitably dominate the literary sources. Nevertheless, it is not particularly easy to distinguish between different types of entertainer, especially as ambiguity was inseparable from the terms used to designate minstrels. Minstrels were commonly called *clêr* in Welsh and the term could be used inclusively, to refer to all poets and musicians, but in other contexts the term designated lesser entertainers, especially versifiers of low standing. Status differences among the minstrels were important, and numerous terms were used to disparage entertainers regarded as inferior, including the expressive *clêr y dom*, or 'dung-flies'.[12]

The overwhelming majority of minstrels in Tudor Wales were professional entertainers who were masterless and itinerant, without the retainer's livery or badge, and sought patronage and employment wherever they could. There were many minstrels but, generally speaking, little is known about their social origins, ways of life and genres of performance. Numerous minstrels are simply names; many more have been completely forgotten. The mid-Tudor indictments of minstrels at the Court of Great Sessions are therefore particularly important since, exceptionally, they identify by name some sixty entertainers and other wanderers, most of whom would be otherwise unknown. The parallel with Ireland in the same period is striking. About fifty or so versifiers and other entertainers have been found in 'fiants' or warrants for pardon after indictment or outlawry, but less than a dozen of these minstrels can be identified with any certainty from literary sources.[13]

The recovery of long-forgotten minstrels from archival oblivion is doubly rewarding: not only are the identities of individual minstrels restored but, more generally, their names disclose some details about the structure of minstrelsy. The entertainers who were prosecuted were, without an exception, men, and it appears that in sixteenth-century Wales women were excluded from minstrelsy and public performance.[14] Names are revealing about the specialisms, origins and 'personas' of the male minstrels. Minstrels shared with other wanderers, including outlaws, a fondness for by-names that touched on different aspects of wayfaring life and obscured, doubtless sometimes deliberately, a former identity. The romantic identification of the minstrel's independent, mobile and masterless life with the outlaw, who belonged to no particular place and lived from day to day, is suggested by the name sported by one poet – Robin Hwd. In 1550 the indictments against several minstrels carefully distinguished between official and unofficial names: Thomas Tyvie alias 'Brythyll Brych', Owen ap David alias 'Oweyn Trovednoth' and Robert ap John ap Rheinallt alias 'Hodyn Siglen'.[15]

The professional names that entertainers adopted reveal different aspects of the minstrels' life although the meanings of some aliases remain ambiguous or obscure. Some epithets referred to the elusive and striking creatures of the wild with which the wandering minstrels may have fancifully compared themselves: *Brythyll Brych* or 'speckled trout'; *Hodyn Siglen* or (probably) 'wagtail youth'. The sobriquets of *Rees Du Cwrw*, presumably a lover of beer (*cwrw*), and *Richard Penhayarn* or 'Ironhead' convey the comforts and knocks of vagabond life. The names of a few minstrels reveal former or dual occupations: Richard 'Grydd' or shoemaker and David 'Talyer' or tailor. This was to be expected as the tailor's occupation, and sometimes the cobbler's, was peripatetic. The physical appearance of some minstrels, especially their hair colour, was denoted by common descriptive terms (*du* 'black'; *melyn* 'yellow'); blindness (*dall*), a disability widely associated with minstrelsy, is sometimes referred to.[16] Several vagabonds were called *bedlem*, from the English 'bedlam', and *gwyllt*, literally 'wild'. These names presumably referred to the wandering insane or persons of unpredictable behaviour rather than minstrels, but there was a loose association between wandering, wildness, and minstrelsy.[17] Those who chose to spend the night on *Gwely Idris*, a bed of stone on the summit of Cadair Idris, one of the wildest mountains, would be transformed (according to a late sixteenth-century source) into either a poet (*prydydd*) or a lunatic.[18] The muse (*awen*) might appear to a man in a dream and drive him to lead a wandering life as a poet. The muse, according to one account, appeared like a hunter in the wild 'with a garland of green leafs' about his head, a quiver of arrows on his back, and a hawk upon his fist whose quarry was the sleeping future bard.[19]

Frequently a minstrel – like numerous other craftsmen – was known simply by his specialism: *Ffowc Ffidler* – Fulk the fiddler; *Dafydd Llwyd Delynor* – David Lloyd the harper; *Henry Grythor* – Henry the crowder; *Ieuan Brydydd* – Ieuan the poet; and so on. Sometimes a wandering minstrel's name revealed the area he originally hailed from. Thomas *Tyvie*, indicted three times in north-east Wales in the 1550s, presumably came from the Teifi Valley in the south-west; Huw *Arwystl* identified himself with the extensive lordship of Arwystli in Montgomeryshire; Thomas *Gwynedd* adopted the ancient territorial name for north-west Wales; several notable minstrels were called *Penllyn* after a particular district in north-west Wales. The locational names adopted by the bards tended to be tracts of country or rivers, rather than the more specific settlement names more characteristically adopted as nascent surnames in the same period.[20] This of course expressed the wandering nature of the minstrel's profession. The late medieval poets had had a somewhat ambivalent attitude towards those boroughs regarded as centres of English influence, but towns were increasingly important to the sixteenth-century Welsh minstrels as centres of patronage and bases for perambulations, and several poets and musicians can be identified as town dwellers.[21]

Welsh minstrels were indicted collectively, but this was not because they travelled in troupes. However, pairs of minstrels commonly travelled together for musical considerations as well as for companionship and safety. An account of payments made to minstrels in Anglesey at the end of the sixteenth century shows that the pairing of poet and musician in various combinations was rewarded: poet and harper, reciter and harper, poet and crowder. Apprentices were formally recognized among the bards and might travel with experienced master poets or musicians. Rowland David of Narberth was prosecuted in 1615 not only for wandering up and down the country with his 'fiddell or crowde' but also for keeping two 'preety' youths whom he was training 'in the same trade or scyence'.[22]

Using the names and styles recorded in some indictments, and relating them to literary sources, a picture can be built up of the different skills of the minstrels. Poets, harpers and crowders predominated. These were the minstrels (*gwŷr wrth gerdd*) with skills regarded as traditional, some of whom were recognized as 'graduates' in the 1523 and 1567 *eisteddfodau*. David Powel in 1584 succinctly described the three sorts of minstrels 'in vse in the countrie of Wales to this daie'. The *beirdd*, or bards, were 'makers of songs and odes of sundrie measures, wherein not onlie great skill and cunning is required; but also a certeine naturall inclination and gift'. The poet's calling in particular was regarded in some ways as involuntary – an unpredictable gift from God that was sometimes taken back. As Aubrey was told, 'In Wales are some bards still who have a strange gift in versyfying: but the fitt will sometimes leave them, and never returne again.' The accomplished poets were also *arwyddfeirdd* (herald–bards) who kept records of '[g]entlemens armes and petegrees' and were 'best esteemed and accounted of among them'. Equal in status to the poets were the 'plaiers vpon instruments, cheefelie the Harpe and the Crowth'. Minstrels of the third type were reciters or declaimers (*datgeiniaid*) 'which doo sing to the instrument plaied by another' or (according to another source) declaimed while beating time with the end of a staff (*datgeiniaid pen pastwn*).[23] The structure of minstrelsy in Ireland and Scotland, which also privileged the spoken or (more probably) chanted or sung word of the poet, was similar.[24]

The records of the Great Sessions also reveal the lively presence of other types of entertainers who are rarely mentioned in the literary record – dancers, acrobats, and jugglers or magicians. Two dancers were included in the first prosecution of minstrels in 1547: Richard *Dawnsiwr* of Ruthin and Huw *Dawnsiwr* of Beaumaris; and others were subsequently indicted. There are no clues to the type of dancing they performed, unless the nicknames of some minstrels – 'wagtail', 'trout', and 'barefoot' (*troednoeth*) – referred to barefooted leaping and jumping. The names of several jugglers have been preserved, and the interesting epithet *hudol* ('magician', 'conjuror') which has late medieval resonances occurs several times. John Hudol was arrested on three occasions. In 1547 he was styled vagabond of Ellesmere; in 1550 he was called a juggler from Welshpool; later, in 1553 in Denbighshire, he was described as a fiddler. This case is instructive: it illustrates the mobility of minstrels, reveals the importance of towns to them, and suggests that some minstrels would have had more than one performing skill.[25]

The indictment of eighteen minstrels at Chester in 1552 provides an illuminating inventory of the instruments favoured in mid-Tudor Cheshire that contrasted with the specialisms of exactly contemporary Welsh minstrels.[26] In Cheshire there were equal numbers of fiddlers and pipers (eight are named), three taborers as well as two harpers, one luter, and two 'seggers', a term that probably designated reciters or storytellers ('sayers'), about whom it would be interesting to know more. The dominance of the fiddle, pipes (most probably bagpipes) and tabor, essentially instruments for the dance, clearly emerges. The most popular Welsh instruments were either poorly represented in Cheshire, in the case of the harp, or completely absent, as with the crowd. Crowders and harpers are the most frequently named musicians in Welsh legal documents in the second half of the sixteenth century and their stringed instruments often accompanied the voice of the poet.[27]

Welsh entertainers formed a relatively closed group. Significantly, no Welshman was included among the seventeen minstrels indicted in Cheshire in 1552 and, conversely, very few English entertainers appear to have wandered the Welsh countryside.[28] Some Welsh minstrels travelled in England but they were probably not numerous. Although Welsh harpers might have a curiosity value, Welsh singer–poets were liable to find themselves treated as inferior minstrels in England or denied a reward.[29] Minstrels have been regarded as an exceptionally mobile occupational grouping, straddling different languages and cultures, but the Welsh and English minstrels occupied different aural as well as geographical spaces. Crucially, in Wales there was an emphasis on the spoken word among entertainers. Poems were declaimed to the specialist accompaniment of the harp or crowd. This was an aural delight in Wales, but to mid-Tudor English ears the Welshman's voice accompanied by the plucked horse-hair strings of the harp sounded 'much lyke the hussyng of a homble be.'[30]

The names of several poets have been preserved among the vagabond–minstrels. Ieuan Brydydd, indicted in Denbighshire in 1553 for 'going about with a harpe', and his namesake Ieuan Brydydd y Coweyneon, indicted in Montgomeryshire, were poets whose names are not otherwise recorded. But Richard Brydydd Brith (Richard the 'speckled' or 'freckled' poet) was indicted twice, possibly three times, as a vagabond before graduating as a licensed poet at the 1567 *eisteddfod*. The compositions of several other vagabond–poets can be identified in literary sources. The best-known of these versifiers was Robert or Robin Clidro, indicted in 1547, a complex figure with a considerable reputation whose wit and popularity were perhaps threatening to the poets of high status, one of whom composed a mock obituary on the vagabond–poet while he was still alive.[31]

Usually vagabond–minstrels appear socially undifferentiated in the legal record, but the 1550 prosecution of minstrels in Montgomeryshire conceded that there were status differences among them. Some minstrels were prejudicially referred to as vagabonds, others were neutrally called harper or crowder according to their specialisms; a few were termed yeoman, but two minstrels were styled gentlemen: the accomplished poet Huw Arwystl and the harper Dafydd Llwyd Delynor. Both are also named in a broadly contemporary list of expert musicians and their apprentices working in north-east Wales.[32] These bards were exceptions that proved a general rule: there was a minstrel élite, the technically accomplished poets and musicians, especially the graduates of the *eisteddfodau*, who by and large managed to escape prosecution as vagabonds.

The occasions for performance brought together the vagabond–minstrels and the bards and musicians of high status. The statute of Gruffudd ap

Cynan specifies the seasons and occasions when the poets and other minstrels were to visit patrons: the Christmas, Easter and Whitsun seasons, patronal festivals, weddings and funerals. Elegies, some probably commissioned and composed in advance, were 'brought home' following the death of a patron and publicly recited. The circuits (or *clera*) of gentlemen's houses, theoretically at least, were undertaken at intervals of three years. At the appropriate season, especially 'the loytring time betweene Christmas and Candlemas', the minstrels, expert and inexpert alike, converged on the hospitable halls to 'singe songes and receave rewardes'.[33] Contemporary references show that numerous minstrels could be rewarded at the same house at the same time. Five named *mynstrells* were paid sums varying from two to ten shillings each for providing Christmas entertainment at Lleweni (a major Denbighshire house) in 1555, and forty years later thirteen minstrels celebrated Christmas at the same place. In the mid-sixteenth century, Wiliam Penllyn, the chief harpist, recorded in his patron's poem-book the names of eight other minstrels who had visited Moelyrch, Denbighshire, during the Christmas holidays. Revealingly, they included three crowders who had been indicted as vagabonds in 1550. A generous and hospitable patron would be much visited. The memoranda of an Anglesey gentleman show that he rewarded nineteen minstrels on twelve separate occasions between Christmas Eve and Candlemas 1594–95.[34]

Although several minstrels might gather at a patron's house, performance was not collective but essentially an individual (or dual) affair. Minstrels were in competition with each other and this meant that there was antagonism and rivalry between them. Tension between poets found expression in 'debate poems', and sometimes ill-feeling between minstrels led to violent confrontations. The Montgomeryshire grand jury in 1561 made separate presentments of two Welshpool crowders, James Grythor and Robert Jones, for assaulting each other, considering one as bad as the other. In 1600 there was grave suspicion that a harper, Jenkin ap Syr David, had been involved in the death of the poet Hugh ap John alias Prydydd, whose corpse had been found under Llanidloes bridge the morning after a Mayday 'merry-night'. The harper, who seems habitually to have carried a 'crab-cudgel', had quarrelled with the poet at the merry-night but, by his own account, had remained with the company until dawn when he went out into the streets and roused some of the townsfolk, one after another, with the serenade *Hwntus Up*, that is 'The Hunt Is Up'.[35]

A number of minstrels were accused of capital felonies. One may instance Griffith ap Howell alias Dawnsiwr, a Cardiganshire entertainer, who was hanged for the murder of a Cardigan burgess in 1546, and Philip ap Rees ap Howel Pibydd, a Pembrokeshire piper, who was found guilty of grand larceny with judgment of death in 1550. Robert ap Huw, a young Anglesey harper, was suspected in 1600 of a catalogue of offences, mostly hanging felonies, that included abduction, burglary, and gaol-break, but he evaded recapture long enough to benefit from James I's general pardon and subsequently became a notable musician sporting the royal badge in silver on his harp.[36]

The uncertainties and opportunities of life on the road, as well as the financial cost of the sociability of the tavern, may have tempted minstrels to theft and other crimes. But, of course, not all minstrels were thieves, drunkards, or quarrelsome. The systematic prosecution of minstrels as suspect persons in mid-Tudor Wales shows that entertainers were rounded up as a matter of policy rather than for crimes committed by them as individuals. It is important to explore why this was so.

WHY WERE MINSTRELS PROSECUTED?

Why were minstrels prosecuted as vagabonds in Wales? The question requires a number of related answers rather than a single explanation. There was certainly a moral panic about vagabonds in the mid-sixteenth century and the ruling class sometimes expressed contempt for them in the most extreme language. The mid-Tudor multiple prosecutions in Wales may have been prompted by circular letters from the Privy Council to all justices requiring them to enforce the vagrancy laws.[37] But it needs to be emphasized that minstrels were prosecuted not because they were simply regarded as a type of vagabond. Itinerant and masterless men of different definition were numerous in mid-sixteenth-century Wales, but it is significant that the mid-Tudor wanderers prosecuted as vagabonds were almost exclusively minstrels. The mid-Tudor prosecutions of entertainers in Wales seem to have been an initiative from the Council in the Marches and the Welsh judges that reflected not only the circumstances of the time but also the historical experience of the English administration in Wales which had explicitly linked minstrels and vagabonds as suspect persons since the fifteenth century.

More immediately, the indictment of minstrels has to be understood in the broad context of Tudor social and moral reform.[38] Minstrels were unlucky in that they straddled in a negative way a whole series of overlapping administrative concerns about suspect strangers, rumour-mongers, unlawful assemblies, vagrants, alehouses and unlawful games. The mid-Tudor State regarded the proliferation of alehouses and their link with illegal games and 'light persons' as a fundamental social problem requiring reform. Sir William Herbert (one of the twelve privy councillors) appointed lord president of the Council in the Marches in April 1550, strictly instructed the sheriffs and justices of the peace of the new Welsh shires to put into execution the statutes against vagabonds, unlawful games, alehouses and 'blynd innes'.[39] The subsequent campaign against the alehouse and its way of life can be reconstructed from the record of crown business at the Great Sessions. Prosecutions of unlicensed alehouse-keepers, players of unlawful games and those who lodged rogues and vagabonds are regularly found in the gaol files. Minstrels were in part casualties of the campaign against unlicensed alehouses and unlawful games. Alehouses provided places of rest for the minstrels (especially if access was denied at the great houses) and places to entertain where a ready-made audience was collected. When minstrels were prosecuted at the assizes there were generally indictments in the same session against other representatives of the alehouse culture. Sometimes minstrels were themselves prosecuted for playing unlawful games or keeping unlicensed alehouses. Three separate indictments can be traced against William Goch, a crowder prosecuted in 1550 as a vagabond–minstrel, for keeping 'tables' and other unlawful games at his alehouse in Welshpool.[40]

Sir William Herbert seems to have secured the co-operation of the Welsh élite for the implementation of the Council's reforming policy. However, reform was not a uniform process. The concentration of prosecutions in north-east Wales is striking and reflects the geographical closeness of the counties of the Chester circuit to Ludlow, the seat of the Council in the Marches, and the position of the chief justice of Chester as the premier Welsh judge and *ex officio* a senior member of the Council (usually the president's associate or deputy).[41] The prosecution of seventeen Cheshire minstrels at the Great Sessions in 1552 seems to have been an extension of the concerns in Wales.[42]

Sir William Herbert drew a distinction between 'evel and seditious people', who were the enemies of good order and obedience and should be sharply punished, and 'good and obedient people' who observed the king's ordinances and commandments and must be 'comformably used'. There was a pervasive sense in which minstrels could be regarded as suspect and potentially dangerous persons who challenged the established social order. Simply as wanderers, the minstrels touched a raw nerve in a society whose rulers saw vagabonds as threatening social stability. Even by their clothes, minstrels may have challenged social hierarchy and the sumptuary laws forbidding excess in apparel. Above all, participation in the alehouse culture rendered suspect the adherence of the minstrels to good order. As a memorandum from the Council in the Marches put it, the resort of vagabonds, sturdy beggars and other idle persons to the alehouse left no kind of disorder unattempted.[43]

But minstrels were also suspect persons because of their capacity for social comment. The bards in their praise poems emphasized the traditional duties and behaviour appropriate to their gentlemen patrons.[44] The other side of the poetic coin was satire which eroded personal authority and social standing. The significance of satire in the later medieval and early modern periods cannot be doubted although a vast amount of poetic invective has certainly been lost.[45] Satire was inseparably associated with the wandering bards, particularly those of low status. The succinct description of the Highland 'jockies' as strolling minstrels who 'go up and down using Rythmes and Satyrs and are plentifully rewarded' approximates to a description of the life of a wandering poet in Wales.[46] In Wales those wanting entertainment (recalled a Catholic exile writing in the 1560s) would call for a harper and a declaimer who would either praise virtuous actions or satirize 'evil tricks', whichever was wished for. It was considered demeaning for a poet of high status to indulge in satire needlessly; silence or the lack of praise was enough. But, of course, theory and practice might not coincide, especially as poets were expected to be witty and scabrous as entertainers. Repartee between poets was much enjoyed as a performance genre. The 'butt of the bards' (*cyff clêr*) was a chief poet who was set to compose a poem on a frivolous subject at a feast, and who had to withstand the lampoons of his fellow but lesser bards. Two poets (*clerwyr*) would stand before the company at a feast, 'the one to give in rime at the other extempore to stirre mirth and laughter with their wittie quibbes'.[47]

The temptation to satirize was personal or financial. Firstly, poets would satirise those who had displeased them: ungenerous patrons, rival poets, and so on; this was characteristic and personal to the poet. But, secondly, satire was also composed to order, for a fee, to ridicule people against whom the poet might have no personal animosity. This amoral practice was particularly associated with versifiers of low status. Satire and slander, even when devoid of political content, was an expression of unruly and anti-social behaviour by minstrels that displeased the authorities, and sometimes prompted legal action both for the punishment of rhymers and for compensation by aggrieved parties. Complaints about libellous verse can be found in the surviving records of most courts of any consequence and the versifiers are sometimes named. In 1590, for example, Rosser ap Rosser, 'a vacabound and a loyttringe person', was accused of making songs and rhymes 'sclaundringe and dispisinge' divers men and women on the borders of Brecknock and Radnorshire.[48]

The subversive power of satirical verse, especially when it was political in nature, was well understood by the State. There was a connection between satire and sedition, and the composers of satirical rhymes might also try their hands at irreverent poems about the great public figures of the day, challenging the established social order. Richard Edwards, the author of libellous poems in Welsh about his Shropshire neighbours, was also accused in the Star Chamber of composing political libels in English against the late Queen Elizabeth, the Scottish lords associated with James I, as well as a biting epitaph on Sir Robert Cecil, the Secretary of State, who had taken a close interest in libellers.[49] Rhymes, libels, and 'pasquils' became an increasingly popular vehicle for generally anonymous social and religious comment in sixteenth-century London and the provinces, but by and large political verse seems to have been an English-language genre.[50] However rhymes and songs by schismatics and Catholics were an instance of dangerous verses that might be composed in Welsh, sometimes by quite humble songsters. One of the damaging accusations at the trial of Richard Gwyn, the future Catholic martyr, was that he had recited certain rhymes of his own making against married priests and other matters (subsequently circulated in manuscript) and had bestowed a nickname on the chief justice of Chester. Satirical rhymes and nicknames were of course part of the stock-in-trade of minstrels. Richard Gwyn was not a minstrel but his later life as a wanderer and suspect person was in some ways an exaggerated version of the fugitive existence of the vagabond–minstrel.[51]

Minstrels were wanderers and therefore people with news, and probably disseminators of rumour and sometimes of prophecy. But it would be forcing the evidence to argue that minstrels were seditious in a consistent political sense. The poets' generally pragmatic attitude to the religious changes of the sixteenth century after the Edwardian Reformation is particularly instructive. The transition to Protestantism involved a fundamental adjustment for the poets, and included the loss of monastic patronage, but it is particularly striking that the minstrels, with a few exceptions, followed their secular patrons in abandoning Catholicism.[52]

Nevertheless the poets did maintain a consciousness of the Welsh as a separate people with their own language and traditions, and in this deep if rather diffuse sense minstrels could be regarded as subversive. Indeed the historical experience of the crown administration in the Principality and March since the fifteenth century gave the idea of the minstrel as a suspect person a much sharper definition in Wales than in England. Henry IV's punitive legislation against the Welsh in the aftermath of Owain Glyndŵr's rebellion, enacted in 1402 and confirmed in 1446–47, included, significantly, a statute against minstrels who were classified as a type of vagabond. The Act referred to the 'many diseases and mischiefs which have happened before this time in the land of Wales by many Wasters, Rhymers, Minstrels and other Vagabonds', and ordained that no minstrel should make 'gatherings upon the Common people there'.[53] There were several important ideas here. Minstrels were clearly regarded as seditious. In particular, the bards wrote prophetic poems (*brudiau*) that were anglophobic in sentiment, foreseeing the defeat of the English by the Welsh and the restoration of freedom.[54] Additionally, the fees and gifts expected by minstrels as a reward for their services were viewed as a kind of extortion and their itinerant way of life as a type of vagabondage.

These late medieval administrative worries about minstrels were still recognizable in mid-Tudor Wales and Ireland. The prosecution of minstrels in Wales was paralleled in Ireland. Ordinances of 1534 decreed that 'no Iryshe mynstrels, rymours ... ne bardes' should demand rewards within the

Englishry upon pain of forfeiture of goods and imprisonment. Official policy was especially directed against poets who praised as 'valiauntes' the gentlemen who indulged in extortion, robbery and other abuses. The Irish statute of 1549 ordered that no poet should compose any praise poems to any person except the king. In the mid- and late Elizabethan drive against Irish malefactors and rebels, the bards, rhymers and harpers were specifically included among the vagabonds, 'horse-boys', and other masterless and idle men who were to be whipped, banished, and, in extreme cases, punished by death.[55]

Welsh minstrels in the sixteenth century were certainly capable of sustaining a kind of counter-culture at communal meetings reminiscent of medieval gatherings that had challenged English authority and were akin to contemporary Irish hill-top assemblies that attracted (according to Spenser) 'all the scum of the country'.[56] If a report to the Council in the Marches on the state of religion in north Wales *circa* 1600 can be taken at face-value, on Sundays and holidays men, women and children from every parish would meet at hill-side gatherings arranged by chief minstrels (*pencars*) where harpers and crowders would 'singe them songs of the doeings of theire auncestors', especially of the wars against the English, declaim their pedigrees at length to show their descent from the Welsh princely houses, and relate the lives of 'prophets and saincts of that cuntrie'. 'There could be no more convincing picture', comments Rees Davies on this passage, 'of the cultivation and transmission of a historical mythology, and its natural links with genealogy, amongst the population at large.' The detail of this account cannot be corroborated, but the mid-Tudor poetic complaint on the indictment of minstrels asserted the traditional role of the poets in Gwynedd as maintainers of prophecy and remembrancers of the genealogies of 'chieftains' and heroes (including Llywelyn, Bleddyn, the otherwise forgotten Rhys Hefaid, and Emrys) who had lived before 'foreigners' settled among them and were also praised.[57] Other sources of the period confirm that communal gatherings, particularly of youth groups, took place at 'playing-places' in north Wales.[58]

These gatherings might well have been considered unlawful assemblies in the mid-Tudor period. Sir William Herbert's instructions to the Welsh justices bade them 'geve good heede that no assembles or gathering togethers be suffered' without good cause. The new statute (1549–50) for the punishment of unlawful assemblies was to be put into execution and the statute read in every market town once every three weeks. These instructions have to be understood in the context of an insecure government shaken by revolt. The Welsh justices were given a policing role. They were to make diligent search for 'tellers of newes, berers of tales, secrete whisperers of the kynge or the counsaille' and purveyors of 'blynd and false p[ro]phises'. These 'naughtie and p[er]niciouse p[er]sones' were to be apprehended, secretly examined, and punished without delay in a public place.[59]

The State's concern with 'blind and false prophecies' was understandable because of their association with rebellion. The very serious revolts of 1549 in Yorkshire and East Anglia had been buoyant with prophecies. Less than a generation before in Wales, the revolt of Rhys ap Gruffydd which ended with his execution in 1531 had been encouraged by a prophecy that played upon the significance of the raven as Rhys's family badge. The prophecies of Merlin and Taliesin were enduring. At the hill-side gatherings in north Wales, already mentioned, the traditions of these 'intended prophets' were recited.[60] Prophetic sayings and millennial rumours were on the lips of many people in late sixteenth-century Wales – an opaque 'babble of the base sort' who included vagabonds. A Welsh vagabond wandered to Oxford in 1599 bringing the rumour that Edward VI, the boy–king, had not died but yet lived in Scandinavia.[61] So addicted were the Welsh to the prophecies of Merlin and the 'fond fables' of Taliesin, and other *Bardi Brytannorum*, that an aspiring Cardiganshire sheriff promised to bring Sir Robert Cecil 'such volumes of prophecies' as would make a memorable bonfire in London. This may have been an exaggeration, but a vast quantity of written prophecy was in circulation. In the major collections of Welsh manuscripts some twenty large compilations of prophetic verse and gnomic sayings still survive from the sixteenth century, as well as earlier and later volumes.[62] The compiler of one mid-Tudor collection made in central Powys noted the sources of several prophecies, some of which were oral. 'Thomas Gwynedd & Edward Powel sayd yt' is glossed against a characteristically opaque prophecy on the destruction of three lions by an arrow. Thomas Gwynedd may be identified as a vagabond–minstrel prosecuted in 1547 and again in 1550 under the intriguing alias 'John Newydd' or 'New John'.[63]

Minstrels were professional remembrancers who serviced the collective memory that related to events, the genealogies of the living, and the voice of prophecy. In some ways minstrels, more specifically poets, were regarded as inheritors of special – if fragmentary – ancient knowledge that had been dissipated by wars and the destruction of bardic books. According to William Salesbury, 'the commune answere of the Walshe Bardes', when anyone 'cast in their teath' the 'folysh vncertaintie and the phantasticall vanities of theyr prophecies' and other matters, was to allege in excuse that most of their 'bokes and monuments' had perished in the Tower of London or had been destroyed in Owain Glyndŵr's rebellion. Not one volume had escaped that was not 'vncurablye maymed, and irrecuparablye torne and mangled'. The bards themselves had been persecuted. Sir John Wynn of Gwydir, a leading power-broker, explained that Edward I 'caused our bards all to be hanged by martial law as stirrers of the people to sedition; whose example, being followed by the governors of Wales, until Henry the Fourth's time, was the utter destruction of that sort of man'.[64]

The story of the Edwardian massacre of the bards, first recorded in the sixteenth century, expressed both the idea of the continuity of minstrelsy in

Wales from an early period, but also the dangerous nature of the bardic calling whose practitioners could be suspected of sedition. A dual challenge faced the bards for much of the sixteenth century: how to preserve and protect their arcane knowledge and how best to present themselves as loyal subjects who should be adequately rewarded for practising their craft skills.

STRATEGIES: THE SESSIONS OF THE BARDS (THE 1523 *EISTEDDFOD*)

It is important to appreciate that while minstrels might be viewed from the outside, especially by administrators and legal officials, as an undifferentiated group, there were long-established status differences and tensions among the poets, musicians and other entertainers. There are disparaging late medieval bardic references to unnamed 'worthless' poets and musicians, the minstrels of the dung-heap (*clêr y dom*), who seem, nonetheless, to have been welcomed in the halls of the gentry.[65] The idea of two types of minstrelsy – a distinction between respectable and disreputable minstrels – was clearly expressed in the 'statute' prepared for the *eisteddfod* or sessions of minstrels. The first (1523) and second (1567) *eisteddfodau* were key events in the perception, organization and control of poets and musicians and other entertainers. Although 'degrees' were awarded, the primary aim of these sessions was not competitive but aimed to regulate the minstrels and their craft according to the provisions of a bardic 'statute'.

The ordinances for the *eisteddfodau* were included in the grandly called 'Statute of Gruffudd ap Cynan' (*Ystatud Gruffudd ap Cynan*), after the twelfth-century king of Gwynedd. Numerous manuscript versions of the bardic statute are extant, and they testify to the interest of patrons and performers in the rights and privileges of the poets and minstrels and their anxiety to maintain them.[66] The 'roll' of the *eisteddfod* begins with the proclamation of a session to be held at Caerwys, a Flintshire borough, by commission of Henry VIII 'to bring order and control to the craftsmen in poetry and music' according to the statute of Gruffudd ap Cynan and to certify and confirm those judged to be master craftsmen and apprentices of various degree. It then recites the statute, giving the requirements for degrees or 'grades' in poetry and music and the restrictions and privileges of the master craftsmen and their apprentices, including the fees payable to them. An important section considers the conduct appropriate to minstrels and the penalties for those who misbehaved.[67]

The statute, although it probably contains some archaic elements, was essentially a 'pseudo-antique' document, presumably specially prepared in advance of the 1523 *eisteddfod* where it was ratified.[68] The attribution of the ordinances to Gruffudd ap Cynan gave authority to a document which, while purporting to be ancient precedent, was actually an innovative instrument for regulating the bards. The statute of Gruffudd ap Cynan can be understood in part as an early sixteenth-century attempt to organize the bards which drew on some of the features of the late medieval craft guilds or associations. Minstrelsy – because it was a peripatetic occupation – was difficult to organize as a fraternity but in late medieval continental Europe there were urban-based organizations of minstrels with regulatory statutes. Guilds of minstrels with ordinances had been established or refounded in sixteenth-century England, notably the Company of Musicians of London (1500) and the Fraternity of Minstrels in Beverley (1555). Minstrels' courts ratified entertainers in Cheshire and Staffordshire (the Honour of Tutbury), and the Beverley Fraternity purported to control minstrels in the northern English counties between the rivers Trent and Tweed. The mid-sixteenth-century restatement of the privileges of the Beverley fraternity, entered in the 'great book' of the town, invoked the authority of King Athelstan in much the same way as the bardic statute was legitimized by Gruffudd ap Cynan's name.[69]

Craft associations organized their members hierarchically into masters and apprentices and privileged them by excluding non-members from practising their crafts. The protection of the interests of the bardic fraternity is clearly discernible in the detailed provisions for apprenticeship in the bardic statute. The bardic statute emphasized the mystery of the poetical and musical crafts, the craft of the tongue (*cerdd dafod*) and the craft of the string (*cerdd dant*), and the long apprenticeship with three grades needed to attain full understanding of a craft before qualification as a master craftsman. A bardic apprenticeship might last nine years, two years longer than the theoretical length of a craft apprenticeship. The bardic statute and the *eisteddfod* recognized the separate specialisms of poet and musician (harper and crowder) with apprentices, and also the occupation of declaimer (without an apprenticeship). Other entertainers were by implication excluded from the dignity of recognition as craftsmen in poetry and music. A late sixteenth-century hierarchy of minstrels contrasted the four types of graduate minstrel (poet, harper, crowder, reciter) with four *ofergerddorion* or inferior entertainers: the piper, the taborer, the fiddler (or player on the three-stringed *crwth*), as well as the juggler or magician.[70]

The named patrons of the *eisteddfod* were key officials in the administration of north Wales who controlled a vast swathe of territory from Anglesey to the Marches. The *eisteddfod* was held before the sheriff of Flintshire, with the consent of the chamberlain of Gwynedd and the steward of the lordship of Denbigh. They had the counsel of Tudur Aled, the pre-eminent master–poet, and Gruffydd ap Ieuan ap Llywelyn Fychan, a gentleman bard, as well as many unnamed 'gentlemen and wise men' who may have assisted (perhaps in the manner of juries) in verdicts and judgments.[71] A list of the graduates of the *eisteddfod*, which is probably incomplete, has been preserved. Sixteen apprentices of various grades were recognized and the award of silver prizes or trophies confirmed the status of the most eminent practitioners of each craft: the silver harp to the best harper; the silver *crwth* to the best crowder; the silver tongue to the best declaimer. Tudur Aled's status as chaired poet was acknowledged by the award of a silver chair. The silver prizes were probably worn at the neck as symbols of the authority of the master craftsmen.[72]

The 1523 *eisteddfod* was a remarkable demonstration of regional dominance by Welsh power-brokers on whose authority the crown's administration in Wales depended. Understandably, the *eisteddfod* has been discussed largely in a literary context. But the *eisteddfod* has also to be understood in a political sense as an expression of the status of its patrons as influential administrators, a demonstration of their power to command, which showed their concern for order and government within their sphere of influence.

The bardic statute prepared for the *eisteddfod* expressed the dual interests of both minstrels and their patrons in much the same way as craft guild ordinances reflected not only the interests of craftsmen but also the reality of municipal control.[73] The statute authoritatively recognized the separate crafts of poet, crowder and harper and the long apprenticeship needed to learn the mysteries of each craft. Musicians and poets who had not been apprenticed or entertainers of other types were by implication to be excluded from the rewards of the minstrels' craft. But, for their part, the accredited poets and musicians were to behave peaceably and to be of service to all faithful subjects of 'the prince' (that is, Henry VIII) and his officials. Detailed and revealing regulations for the conduct of the minstrels were set out: they were not to get drunk or to brawl; they were not to propagate insulting or scandalous songs, especially those disparaging women; they were not to frequent taverns or hidden places to play dice, cards and other games. An extraordinary passage suggests that if a minstrel offended, he was to be punished by losing the contents of his purse to those who apprehended him. It is difficult to know how this precept was interpreted in practice.[74]

The prohibition against playing dice and other games, it may be noted, is entirely consistent with an early sixteenth-century date, and other elements of Tudor reforming policies seem to be reflected in the statute. Early Tudor legislation on unlawful games and vagabonds (1495) was comprehensively restated in 1511–12, made perpetual in 1514–15, and reinforced by several proclamations between 1526 and 1528.[75] Crucially, minstrels were enjoined by the bardic statute not to follow the practices of vagabonds (*arveroedd vacabwndys*). This seems to have been the first use of the quasi-legal and pejorative English term 'vagabond' in a Welsh-language text.[76] The maintenance of a clear distinction between vagabonds and minstrels was to become increasingly vital for the craftsmen in poetry and music and it is significant that the mid-Tudor prosecutions of vagabond–minstrels took place between the first (1523) and second (1567) sessions of the bards.

LICENCES AND REWARDS

According to David Powel (1584), the bardic statute or decree (glossed as 'a verie good lawe against abuses in musicians') was 'oftentimes allowed by publike authoritie of the cheefe magistrats' in Wales, 'as appeareth by sundrie commissions directed to diuers Gentlemen in that behalfe'.[77] This was a reference both to the *eisteddfodau* and to the licensing system that arose from them.

Between the first and second *eisteddfodau* a licensing system developed. The surviving licence issued to Gruffudd Hiraethog, a herald–bard, is a document of great interest dated 1545/46 (year 37 of Henry VIII). The date may have been significant: it coincided with a proclamation ordering all vagabonds including common players to the galleys. The licence recited in Welsh that Gruffudd had served his apprenticeship, was competent, and able to go forth and receive gifts from noblemen and commoners. The document was signed and sealed by two squires and by Gruffudd's teacher, the master–poet (*pencerdd*) Lewys Morgannwg, who was recognized as the pre-eminent bard in Wales.[78] Gruffudd seems to have carried on his bardic itineraries not only the licence – a prudent precaution – but also an impressive copy of the statute of Gruffudd ap Cynan engrossed on a parchment roll some seven feet long when unfurled that became worn from constant perusal.[79]

In broad terms, despite its special context, the bardic licence was not greatly different from other licences or 'placards' issued in the same period authorizing the collection of benevolences from place to place. By statute (1534) it was expressly forbidden to gather any 'comortha' (Welsh *commorth:* 'aid') or benevolence within Wales and the March without the written licence of the king's commissioners. This was a restatement of earlier ordinances against 'comorthas'. In July 1526 the Instructions to the Council at Ludlow expressly required it 'to punish all persons who levied any comortha or other exaction' that were contrary to the king's former instructions. These former instructions cannot now be traced, but the ordinances against *commorthau* stemmed from orders made in 1494 and promulgated at the Sessions for North Wales which in their turn had drawn on Henry IV's anti-Welsh legislation.[80]

'Comortha' was an ill-defined but deeply entrenched term in the Anglo-Welsh legal vocabulary of the Principality and March and covered a wide range of customary gifts, loans, rents, exactions, and collections made at specially organized bid-ales and games. It is clear from contemporary sources that the minstrels' reward could be regarded as a form of 'comortha' and therefore, presumably, forbidden unless licensed. The 1402 statute had explicitly ordered 'that no waster, rhymer, minstrel nor vagabond be in any way sustained in the land of Wales to make comorthas or gathering upon the common people there'. Nearly 200 years later the rewards given to minstrels were still included among a list of payments bestowed 'by way of commortha'. One thousand pounds a year was said to be 'consumed' in this way.[81]

Crown administrators in the second half of the sixteenth century regularly expressed concern about the gathering of 'comorthas'. The practice was viewed as a 'grett hurte and extorcion done to the people' in mid-Tudor Wales. 'Comorthas' were regarded as pernicious partly because they were often a disguised form of extortion by local élites, revealing the weakness of the State, and partly because the constant levying of money, livestock and other goods impoverished the country. The payments for protection and other favours demanded by officials, especially sheriffs and their bailiffs, resulted in numerous prosecutions for 'comortha' throughout the sixteenth century. This was extortion of an obvious kind. However, the dominant meaning of 'comortha' gradually shifted from the exactions levied by the powerful to the collections made by the poor, that is from extortion to begging. By the early seventeenth century 'Comorthaes and beggeinge or vnlawfull gatheringe of Money' were explicitly linked as offences to be enquired into by the Council.[82] Elizabethan prosecutions for 'comorthas' increasingly concerned customary loans and payments reinterpreted as disguised forms of begging that encouraged the increase and mobility of the idle poor.

By the mid-Elizabethan period itinerant minstrels were in a very difficult position – not only could they be apprehended as vagabonds but they were also vulnerable to accusations of soliciting for unlicensed *commorthau*. The second *eisteddfod* (1567) has to be understood as a renewed attempt by the bards of high status to protect their position by excluding the less accomplished minstrels and legitimately claiming the rewards of the bardic itinerary through a licensing system. It seems from the commission for the *eisteddfod* that the lord president of the Council, Henry Sidney, had been petitioned while travelling in Wales and had 'perfect understanding' of the accustomed place and rewards of the of the *eisteddfod*. No doubt the herald–bards had made much of Sidney's ancestry: he could claim descent from Gruffudd ap Cynan who was credited with the statute for regulating the bards and minstrels.[83]

The commission, given in the queen's name at Chester, recited that 'vagraunt and idle persons naming theim selfes mynstrelles, rithmers and barthes' had grown into an intolerable multitude. The 'shameless disorders' of these vagabond minstrels had often 'disquieted' gentlemen in their houses and also hindered the expert minstrels 'in tonge and con[n]yng' from gaining their living by discouraging them from travelling. The commission gave a year's warning to all those who intended to earn their living by minstrelsy that they should attend an *eisteddfod* at Caerwys and 'showe furthe their learninges'. Open proclamation was to be made in the towns and markets of the five shires of north Wales that the assembly of minstrels was to be held at Caerwys on the Monday after the Feast of the Blessed Trinity 1567. Twenty-one commissioners drawn from the north Wales gentry were appointed who had 'experience and good knowledge' in the bardic 'scyence'. The silver harp was to be awarded and the expert poets and musicians granted degrees appropriate to their skill. Those deemed unskilful were to be given 'straight monycion and commandment' in the Queen's name to return to honest labour or risk being taken as sturdy and idle vagabonds and punished according to statute.[84]

It is impossible to know now how many minstrels attended the 1567 *eisteddfod*; only the names of the successful have been preserved. Eighteen minstrels were recognized as master-poets and musicians, together with thirty-five apprentices of various degrees. The proceedings of the assembly were to be certified to the Council; presumably this would have incorporated a list of those minstrels confirmed by the commissioners as graduates and licensed to go on the bardic itinerary. A copy of the certificate from the commissioners granting the degree of *pencerdd* or chief bard to Simwnt Fychan has survived. The certificate, signed by several commissioners, ordered that the poet was to be welcomed in all appropriate places and rewarded according to his grade.[85]

The purpose of the degrees and licences awarded at the *eisteddfod* was to restrict the rewards of the bardic itinerary to the accredited minstrels. This was a strategy of 'social closure' that emphasized the training, knowledge and respectability of the accredited bards and musicians and introduced scarcity into the profession by driving out the unlicensed entertainers who formed an 'intolerable multitude of minstrels'.[86] A rough-and-ready calculation based on the number of minstrels named in the legal record suggests that for every licensed bard there may have been three or four vagabond–minstrels. It is difficult to know to what extent unlicensed minstrels were subsequently taken up as rogues and vagabonds. Minstrels were not distinguished in the Elizabethan legal record from other wanderers who were regularly indicted at the Great Sessions, but there were certainly some casualties among the unlicensed entertainers. In the year after the *eisteddfod* ten vagabonds, mostly apparently minstrels, were apprehended in Flintshire and there were prosecutions in successive years. Dr Elis Prys, the principal commissioner of the *eisteddfod*, proved to be a harrier of vagabonds. A group of six vagabonds arrested at Ysbyty Ifan in June 1578 were questioned by Prys. Five confessed without further explanation that they led idle lives as rogues or beggars wandering 'from countrey to countrey'. The sixth, Owen ap Thomas of Denbigh, explained that he had 'wandered abroade' for three years as a 'rhymer' because 'he can make songs or rymes'. Prys was unimpressed and promptly committed the unlicensed poet to gaol to await indictment as a vagabond at the next sessions.[87]

BARDIC CRISIS

In 1594 the Council in the Marches was petitioned for a commission to hold a third *eisteddfod*. According to the petitioners, eleven of the north Wales gentry, the 'worthier sorte' of minstrels, had been 'earnest suters' for the *eisteddfod* that would distinguish skilful, honest and sober poets and musicians from 'loyterers and drones'. The petition emphasized the three categories of the worthier sort who were to be maintained and encouraged: the *byrdh* or 'Welshe poetes' who also knew the truth of pedigrees, arms and descents, the players on the harp and *crwth*, and the reciters who sang to instruments played by musicians. The various degrees of proficiency and experience were to be recognized and the silver prizes – the chair, harp, crowd and tongue – awarded to the most skilful as masters or doctors of their 'science'. The unskilful were to be taken up as rogues and driven to labour, or punished if they continued to wander. Only the skilful were to be permitted to travel among men of 'worshipp, gentillitie and power' who would maintain them.[88]

The commission for a new *eisteddfod* was not awarded. It is likely that an assembly of the bards was by then considered something of a legal and cultural anachronism. The 1572 vagrancy legislation already specifically provided a mechanism for licensing minstrels. More fundamentally, minstrels had become vulnerable to the consequences of changing values among their patrons. By 1594 it was probably too late to protect the status and rewards of the skilful bards. The petition recognized a change in attitude but blamed it on the importunate inferior minstrels: 'by the multitude of the unskillfull their [the bards'] callinges & sciences are not studied or regarded'. Crucially, the social system that had sustained the music and poetry of the bards of high status had been changing since the mid-sixteenth century. The poetic complaint on the indictment of minstrels had attributed their prosecution to 'misers' who presumably wanted to avoid the social obligation of giving feasts and rewarding minstrels.[89] The decline in hospitality offered to the bards had the appearance of individual acts of meanness; it was, however, an expression of deep-seated social changes. Honour and reputation for the gentry were no longer directly linked with feasting, giving entertainment and earning a reputation for generosity. As a consequence, hospitality and rewards were not offered as a matter of course to the itinerant bards who had formerly amplified the reputations of their hosts. The poets complained increasingly that they were without honour, that Welsh-language learning was no longer respected and that the doors of the mansions were closing against them.[90]

The process of change was surprisingly rapid as the decline in hospitality was compounded by the anglicization of the gentry.[91] Shortly before the petitioning for the third *eisteddfod* an Anglesey gentleman–poet, Robert ap Ifan of Brynsiencyn, had concluded his transcription of a bardic grammar bitterly conscious that poetic knowledge was a fading interest for his class. He contrasted the poor status of the minstrel of his own time with the golden age of the bards when Gruffudd ap Cynan's statute had established the rewards and courtesies due to poets and musicians. At the time of writing (in 1587) it was more profitable to be a pilferer or pickpocket than a good minstrel practising his craft. The poor minstrel wandered here and there seeking company but people avoided him lest they would have to reward him with more than a halfpenny's worth of ale.[92] Within a generation after 1594 the professional poet able to earn a living from visiting gentry houses had more-or-less vanished, and bardic lore and the appreciation of strict-metre poetry became the preserve of a small minority of antiquarian-minded gentlemen and clerics. As one antiquary explained, writing in the first half of the seventeenth century, 'at this time all the greate knowledge of the bards, there credyt and worth is altogether decayed and worne out, so that at this time they are extinguish[ed] amongest us'.[93]

MINSTRELS AND FESTIVE CULTURE

However some professional musicians were able to flourish outside the walls of the great houses, especially in the context of the alehouse, the fair and the revel. The details of six musicians prosecuted as rogues in Pembrokeshire in 1620 provide a profile of the professional wandering minstrel in early seventeenth-century Wales. These minstrels were variously described as a fiddler, a piper and fiddler, a crowder, two harpers, a taborer and harper, and a taborer. Two significant facts need to be emphasized. Firstly, there were no poets or rhymers among the minstrels. Secondly, these musicians were not indicted for seeking rewards from the gentry but had been wandering up and down the country, particularly at 'sheer[ing] time' or 'wool time', which were presumably communal or neighbourly seasonal tasks.[94]

Changing musical taste was reflected in the preference for new types of musical instrument. Professional crowders, once numerous and some of great repute, faded quickly from the scene in the first half of the seventeenth century as the crowd was replaced by the fiddle. There was only one crowder among the strolling musicians prosecuted in Pembrokeshire in 1620; in north-east Wales, once the stronghold of the *crwth*, John Lewis Mone (Siôn Lewys Môn), crowder, listed among several 'idell p[er]sons, loyterers and nightewalkers' in Denbighshire in 1612, appears to have been one of the last professional crowders.[95] Harpers were more resilient as popular entertainers within Wales, or as household musicians to romantic or conservative gentry families, although the nature of the instrument changed as the single-strung harp was eventually replaced by the larger triple-harp.[96]

There are more references in seventeenth-century sources to fiddlers, pipers, drummers and taborers, some of whom wandered the countryside, than to harpers and crowders. The combination of pipe and tabor was to become 'exceeding common' in the seventeenth-century border counties where 'many Beggars begd with it' and 'the Peasants danced to it'. Taborers and pipers were rarely found among the sixteenth-century Welsh minstrels but they seem to have become more numerous in the seventeenth century. Two of the six entertainers prosecuted in Pembrokeshire in 1620 were taborers, one of whom was also a harper. By the mid-seventeenth century the classic combination of pipes and tabor was found in Cardiganshire where Griffith ap Evan of Caron was prosecuted for 'wandringe up & downe' the county 'w[i]th a taber, & pipe, roguinge & begginge'.[97]

The tension between traditionalist poet–minstrels and non-traditional musicians was expressed in a number of poems. In a satire on the fair, Siôn Mawddwy (*fl.* 1560–1613), an itinerant bard, described the alien music and dancing at a shire-town where the Great Sessions were held. The town was crowded with people and entertainers but the poet remained empty-handed there. In revenge he satirized the Englishness of the town, the undignified minstrels, their excruciating music and absurd instruments: the rebec, lute, tabor, bandor and pipes. According to the poet, one piper (perhaps a former soldier) wore a filthy breast-plate or cuirass; another minstrel with a 'dung-pipe' (*bawbib*) clenched between his teeth had the fixed smile of a scarecrow.[98] Poets reserved particular venom for the bagpiper whose windbag and pipes invited many ludicrous comparisons. Poets and pipers were in competition and the music of the pipes was increasingly preferred to the poets' words. 'By the saints of heaven' – exploded Lewys Dwnn – 'every Englishman [or anglophile] calls for a pipe rather than a poet of high repute'.[99]

The instruments that the bards detested – fiddle, pipe and drum or tabor – were louder than the single-harp and the *crwth* and seem primarily to have been played to accompany dancing rather than as an accompaniment for the voice. Dancing became a dominant form of recreation in late Tudor Wales, displacing other forms of entertainment. The poet's livelihood was threatened by the enthusiasm for private and public dancing. 'This is not good', complained Siôn Mawddwy, observing dancers 'shaking their tails' at the fair. Edward Maelor (*ob.* about 1603), a poet and crowder, was quite explicit that poets were no longer respected and their craft had been displaced by the dance. He expressed his complaint in a poem addressed to a faithful patron. The poets, he says, no longer received invitations to perform and doors were closed against them. If the poet went to a playing-place ready to show his expertise, more often than not there would be a dance – 'a freewheel bounce' – at the expense of the muse and the carefully crafted poem.[100]

Professional dancers, as already noted, had a place among the entertainers of mid-sixteenth-century Wales but as virtuoso or solo performers. In the second half of the sixteenth century dancing in Wales was transformed by country dances that – a crucial development – eroded the distinctions between audiences and performers. Scattered references show that group dances, including the morris dance performed by troupes of amateurs rather than solo professionals, became popular in seventeenth-century Wales, especially at the alehouse and revel.[101]

In north-east Wales at the end of the sixteenth century there is evidence for the growth of a festive culture, especially in the towns, that gathered pace in the first half of the seventeenth century and was generalized into the countryside after the Restoration.[102] These summer feasts included large public gatherings at which music and dancing were important elements. At Gwersyllt, Denbighshire, in July 1633, for example, it was estimated that some 4,000 people had gathered for 'morris daunsinge, druminge, fidlinge and other idle sportes'. This was a recreational culture in which the poets had only a marginal presence and some turned their backs on the towns. Edward Maelor, poet and crowder, composed a satire on Llangollen specifically after he 'had not soe much as his dinner' at the town wakes.[103] Siôn Mawddwy, a professional poet, felt he had the status of a lowly servant (*gwas isel*) at the fair where his craft was disregarded. The poet described how he was surrounded by alien sounds ranging from the 'giggle-gaggle' of the English spoken word (rendered *ffrit ffrat, whit what, when*) to the inharmonious music of the pipes likened to the noise of wasps in a sack or the honking of a multitude of geese. The poet longed to be with his patron where his craft was respected.[104] However, the professional poets, harpers and crowders were losing the patronage of the gentry and at the same time had no real role as entertainers in the new festive culture where dancing was preferred to listening.

CONCLUSION

The dominant themes relating to minstrelsy in early modern Wales, especially as they emerge from the legal record, have as much to do with power and social control as with culture and performance. The mid-Tudor prosecutions of vagabond–minstrels not only provide a remarkable snapshot of minstrelsy in mid-sixteenth-century Wales but also an illustration of the capacity of the Tudor State for social control through the new legal system that had incorporated the Welsh gentry. Minstrels were an early casualty of the supervisory role of the new Welsh justices appointed after the Act of Union. The mid-sixteenth-century prosecutions coincided with a period of political tension, but the idea of the minstrel as a seditious vagabond had a long historical pedigree in the administration of Wales reaching back to the legislation enacted in the aftermath of Owain Glyndŵr's revolt.

The connections between vagabondage and minstrelsy were complex and manipulated. There were long-term pressures affecting minstrelsy. On the one hand, minstrels were vulnerable to the State's concern about loitering and idle persons; marginal and itinerant ways of life could be redefined as vagabondage and their income as begging or extortion. On the other hand, minstrels of high status tried to protect their position through a strategy of social closure that acknowledged and rewarded their skill and learning through a licensing system but excluded the unlicensed minstrels as rogues and beggars. This strategy was only partially successful. Low-status entertainers were prosecuted as vagabonds, rather than the bards and musicians of high status and the graduates of *eisteddfodau*, but the distinctions between different types of minstrel became blurred. In the long run social and cultural shifts devalued the cultural capital of the bards, especially the poetry that had helped legitimate the status of patrons regarded as leaders of their localities. The social system of clientage with strong vertical links that had favoured bardic patronage was steadily transformed into a class system in which feasting and entertainment as expressions of local patronage that enhanced the prestige of hosts became unimportant. More generally, there was a broad change in taste that favoured public and private dancing and its music at the expense of poetry and its characteristic musical accompaniment. The context of patronage changed as the locus of popular entertainment shifted from the household to the alehouse and the open-air fair and revel. Festive culture, dominated by dancing, favoured new types of entertainer but in the process the music and action of the dance silenced the spoken word of the professional poet.

NOTES

1 Peter Burke, *Popular Culture in Early Modern Europe* (London: Temple Smith, 1978), ch. 4, especially 94–102, for references and problems of definition. The literature on minstrels is extensive but, because of the nature of the sources, tends to deal with courtly musicians. Recent valuable case studies of entertainers include: Russell Zguta, *Russian Minstrels. A History of the Skomorokhi* (Oxford: Clarendon Press, 1978); John Southworth, *The English Medieval Minstrel* (Woodbridge: Boydell, 1989); Christopher Page, *The Owl and the Nightingale: Musical Life and Ideas in France 1100–1300* (London: Dent, 1989); Timothy J. McGee, 'The Fall of the Noble Minstrel: the Sixteenth-century Minstrel in a Musical Context', in Leeds Barroll (ed.), *Medieval and Renaissance Drama in England* (London and Toronto: Associated University Press, 1995), vol. 7 98–120. Ruth Finnegan, *Oral Poetry* (Cambridge: Cambridge University Press, 1977), is a comparative study of entertainers in verbal traditions. Bruce R. Smith, *The Acoustic World of Early Modern England* (Chicago, IL, and London: University Chicago Press, 1999), is an innovative discussion of the significance of the aural dimension in popular culture.

2 See generally, Thomas Parry, *A History of Welsh Literature* (Oxford: Clarendon Press, 1955); A.O.H. Jarman and Gwilym Rees Hughes (eds), *A Guide to Welsh*

Literature, vol II. *1282–c. 1550* (Swansea, Christopher Davies, 1979); R. Geraint Gruffydd (ed.), *A Guide to Welsh Literature*, vol. III. *c.* 1530–1700 (Cardiff: University of Wales Press, 1997); the studies by D. J. Bowen of poets and patrons in the fifteenth and sixteenth centuries are particularly relevant, especially the series 'Beirdd a Noddwyr y Bymthegfed Ganrif', parts I–III, *Llên Cymru*, 18 (1994–95), 53–89, 221–57; and 19 (1996), 1–28. The forthcoming *Records of Early English Drama: Wales* (in the REED series published by the University of Toronto Press), edited by David Klausner, will make available many primary sources. The manuscript tradition is discussed by Daniel Huws, *Medieval Welsh Manuscripts* (Cardiff: University of Wales Press and National Library of Wales, 2000) and Graham Thomas, 'From Manuscript to Print – I. Manuscript', *A Guide to Welsh Literature*, III. 241–62.

3 Enforcement of the pre-Elizabethan legislation is discussed by Marjorie K. McIntosh, 'Local Responses to the Poor in Late Medieval and Tudor England', *Continuity and Change*, 3 (1988), 209–45, and C. S. L. Davies, 'Slavery and Protector Somerset: the Vagrancy Act of 1547', *Economic History Review*, 2nd ser., 19 (1966), 533–49. Elizabethan and Stuart vagrancy is discussed by A. L. Beier, *Masterless Men. The Vagrancy Problem in England 1560–1640* (London: Methuen, 1985), and Paul A. Slack, 'Vagrants and Vagrancy in England, 1598–1664', *Economic History Review*, 2nd ser., 27 (1974), 360–79. The continental context is examined by Robert Jütte, *Poverty and Deviance in Early Modern Europe* (Cambridge: Cambridge University Press, 1994).

4 Peter Roberts, 'Elizabethan Players and Minstrels and the Legislation of 1572 Against Retainers and Vagabonds', in Anthony Fletcher and Peter Roberts (eds), *Religion, Culture and Society in Early Modern Britain. Essays in Honour of Patrick Collinson* (Cambridge: Cambridge University Press, 1994), 29–55.

5 For some examples, see: Beier, *Masterless Men*, 96–9; G. Salgādo, *The Elizabethan Underworld* (London: Dent, 1977), 138–50; Walter L. Woodfill, *Musicians in English Society from Elizabeth to Charles I* (Princeton, NJ: Princeton University Press, 1953), 125–31.

6 National Library of Wales (hereafter NLW), Great Sessions 4/966/6/174–5; 21/8/rex m. 2r; 24/9/rex mm. 3d–4r; 4/1/2/36; Public Record Office (hereafter PRO), CHES 24/92/12. Abstracts of these documents will be published elsewhere. It may be noted that Welsh minstrels escaped prosecution under the short-lived Edwardian 'slave' statute.

7 D. J. Bowen, 'Y Cywyddwyr a'r Dirywiad', *The Bulletin of the Board of Celtic Studies*, 29 (1981), 475–6 (no. 17): *Cywydd a Wnaed am Dditio Gwyr oddi wrth Gerdd Gwynedd*, 'a poem made about the indicting of the Gwynedd minstrels'. I am most grateful to Prof. Dafydd Bowen for discussing the text of this poem with me and for commenting on a draft of this chapter.

8 *Calendar of State Papers Domestic* ... *1547–80*, ed. Robert Lemon (London, 1856), 82 (no. 50); *The Chronicle and Political Papers of King Edward VI*, ed. W. K. Jordan (London: Allen & Unwin, 1966), 37 (searches in Sussex, June 1550); *Acts of the Privy Council* (London, 1892), V. 323 (arrest of minstrels by Sir Henry Tirrell, 1556); surviving English assize records are discussed by J. S. Cockburn, *A History of English Assizes 1558–1714* (Cambridge: Cambridge University Press, 1972), xi–xiii, 333–4.

9 See further pp. 153–5 of this chapter and the discussion of the Act of Union in ch. 2, this volume.

10 NLW, Great Sessions 7/4/July 2 Eliz. (14 vagabonds prosecuted); 7/4/April 19 Eliz. (11 vagrants, 9 of them women, prosecuted); 7/4/April 28 Eliz. (24 prosecuted). Gipsies: Eldra & A. O. H. Jarman, *The Welsh Gypsies: Children of Abram Wood* (Cardiff: University of Wales Press, 1991), ch. 3, esp. 33; NLW, Great Sessions 7/5/July 41 Eliz. (record of the indictment as gypsies of William Barsey of Milton, Devon, and William Lasey of Aberystwyth, both styled labourers).

11 NLW, Great Sessions 4/781/4/28r–v.

12 *Geiriadur Prifysgol Cymru: a Dictionary of the Welsh Language* (Cardiff: University of Wales Press, 1950–), *s.v.* 'clêr'. The term *clêr* has been much discussed; see generally Huw M. Edwards, *Dafydd ap Gwilym: Influences and Analogues* (Oxford: Clarendon Press, 1996), 1–4.

13 Thomas F. O'Rahilly, 'Irish Poets, Historians, and Judges in English Documents, 1538–1615', *Proceedings of the Royal Irish Academy*, 36 (1921–24), section c, 86–7: two thirds of these minstrels 'will never be more than mere names to us; their very names in most cases would be forever unknown were it not for their chance preservation in these English records'.

14 But for women as patrons and composers, see Ceridwen Lloyd-Morgan, 'Women and Their Poetry in Medieval Wales', in Carol M. Meale (ed.), *Women and Literature in Britain, 1150–1500* (Cambridge: Cambridge University Press, 1993), 183–201; Nia Powell, 'Women and Strict-Metre Poetry in Wales', in Michael Roberts and Simone Clarke (eds), *Women and Gender in Early Modern Wales* (Cardiff: University of Wales Press, 2000), 129–58.

15 NLW, Great Sessions 21/8/rex m. 2r; on official and unofficial names, see generally, Richard Suggett, 'The Welsh Language and the Court of Great Sessions', in Geraint H. Jenkins (ed.), *The Welsh Language Before the Industrial Revolution* (Cardiff: University of Wales Press, 1997), 160–1; poems attributed to Robin Hwd are listed in NLW, Index to Welsh Poetry in Manuscripts.

16 Examples drawn from the references in note 6; see generally on Welsh names, T. J. Morgan and Prys Morgan, *Welsh Surnames* (Cardiff: University of Wales Press, 1985).

17 NLW, Great Sessions 4/968/7/15 (Thomas Bedlem and John Goch Bedlem, 1568); Great Sessions 7/4/July 2 Eliz. (Howell Wylte, 1560). On Myrddin Wyllt, wildness, poetry and prophecy, see A. O. H. Jarman, *The Legend of Merlin* (Cardiff: University of Wales Press, 1960).

18 Siôn Dafydd Rhys's treatise on giants in Chris Grooms, *The Giants of Wales: Cewri Cymru* (Lampeter, Lewiston and Queenston: Edwin Mellen Press, 1993), 298–9.

19 Cf. the late seventeenth-century account of the sleeping shepherd who became the 'most famous Bard' in Brecknock after encountering the hunter whose hawk flew at him, getting 'into his mouth & inward parts'. He awoke possessed of such a poetic gift that 'he left the sheep & went about the Countrey, making songs upon all occasions': *The Works of Henry Vaughan*, ed. I. C. Martin (Oxford: Clarendon Press, 1957), 696.

20 Examples from the sources in note 6. See generally, Prys Morgan, 'The Place-name as Surname in Wales', *National Library of Wales Journal*, 29 (1995), 63–75.

21 On attitudes to towns, see Helen Fulton, 'Trading Places: Representations of Urban Culture in Medieval Welsh Poetry', *Studia Celtica*, 31 (1997), 219–30.

22 Dafydd Wyn Wiliam, *Traddodiad Cerdd Dant ym Môn* (Denbigh, privately

published, 1989), 21–2, citing Bangor MS 14918, f. 9b; NLW, Great Sessions 4/780/3/63d.

23 David Powel, *The historie of Cambria, now called Wales* (London, 1584), 191–2; John Aubrey, *Three Prose Works*, ed. John Buchanan-Brown (Fontwell: Centaur Press, 1972), 284; Gwyn Thomas, *Eisteddfodau Caerwys: the Caerwys Eisteddfodau* (Cardiff: University of Wales Press, 1968), 56–67. See ch. 2 of the present volume for further details of declaimers.

24 J. E Caerwyn Williams and Patrick K. Ford, *The Irish Literary Tradition* (Cardiff: University of Wales Press, 1992), ch. 4; John Aubrey, *Monumenta Brittanica*, ed. John Fowles and Rodney Legg (Boston, MA: Little Brown & Co, 1980–82), 170–3.

25 NLW, Great Sessions 4/966/6/175 (dancers); Great Sessions 4/966/175; 24/9/rex m.3d; 4/1/2/36 (John Hudol); cf. Edwards, *Dafydd ap Gwilym: Influences and Analogues*, 35, for late medieval references to magicians and acrobats.

26 PRO, CHES/24/92/12.

27 In addition several fiddlers are named in Welsh sources but the term is not without ambiguity and there may not have been a straightforward correspondence between contemporary Welsh and Cheshire fiddlers. In Wales the dominant meaning of fiddle may have been an inferior type of crowd. On Welsh Musical instruments, see the general survey by Iorwerth C. Peate, 'Welsh Musical Instruments', *Man*, 47 (1947), 21–5; Osian Ellis, *The Story of the Harp in Wales* (Cardiff: University of Wales Press, 1991); D. Roy Saer, *The Harp in Wales in Pictures* (Cardiff: Gomer Press and National Museum of Wales, 1991). Bethan Miles, 'Swyddogaeth a Chelfyddyd y Crythor' (MA thesis, University of Wales, Aberystwyth, 1983) is a comprehensive account of the *crwth* and crowders.

28 The intriguingly named 'The Good Robin', indicted in Flint in 1569, almost alone among vagabond–minstrels in Wales had an English name: NLW, Great Sessions 14/68/Feb. 11 Eliz.

29 Cf. the autobiographical poetic complaints of Iocyn Ddu, made to sit among inferior minstrels in a Cheshire hall, and Robin Clidro, unpaid after singing at dinner in Ludow: texts and translations in Dafydd Johnston, *Canu Maswedd yr Oesoedd Canol: Medieval Welsh Erotic Poetry* (Cardiff: Tafol, 1991), 86–9, and Evan D. Jones, 'The Brogyntyn Welsh Manuscripts VI', *The National Library of Wales Journal*, 6 (1949–50), 228 and 243. Some references to Welsh minstrels in England are noted in D. J. Bowen, 'Agweddau ar Ganu'r Unfed Ganrif are Bymtheg', *Trans. Hon. Soc. Cymmrodorion*, session 1969, part II (1970), 331, n. 242.

30 Andrew Borde (or Boorde), *The fyrst boke of the introduction of knowledge made by Andrew Borde, of physycke doctor* (1542), ed. F. J. Furnivall, *Early English Text Society*, extra ser., 10 (London, 1870), 126. On English perceptions of the aural otherness of the Welsh, see Smith, *The Acoustic World of Early Modern England*, 298–302.

31 See the nuanced portrait of Robin Clidro by Cennard Davies, 'Early Free-Metre Poetry', in *A Guide to Welsh Literature*, III. ch. 3, esp. 78–81. Indictments in NLW, Great Sessions 4/966/6/175 (Robin Clidro); Great Sessions 4/966/6/174–5 and 4/1/2/36 (Richard Brydydd Brith); Great Sessions 4/1/2/36 & 24/9/rex m. 3d–4r (Ieuan Brydydd).

32 NLW, Great Sessions 24/9/rex m. 3d–4r; Historical Manuscripts Commission (hereafter HMC), *Report on Manuscripts in the Welsh Language* (London, 1899), I part 2, 922.

33 Thomas, *Eisteddfodau Caerwys: Caerwys Eisteddfodau*, 66–71; E. D. Jones, 'Presidential Address', *Archaeologia Cambrensis*, 112 (1963), 9–10; 'The Storie of the Lower Burowes of Merthyrmawr', ed. H. J. Randall and William Rees, *South Wales and Monmouth Record Society*, I (1932), 70–1. The recitation of elegies is discussed in ch. 2 this volume.

34 J. E. Caerwyn Williams, 'Anglesey's Contribution to Welsh Literature', *Anglesey Antiquarian Society and Field Club Transactions* (1959), 17, citing NLW, Wynnstay MS. 92, f. 97v; Ifor Williams, 'Cerddorion a Cherddau yn Lleweni, Nadolig 1595', *Bulletin of the Board of Celtic Studies*, 8 (1935–37), 8–10; HMC, *Report on Manuscripts in the Welsh Language*, I, part 2 (London, 1899), 641; Wiliam, *Traddodiad Cerdd Dant ym Môn*, 21–2, citing Bangor MS. 14918, f. 9b.

35 NLW, Great Sessions 4/124/4/1; 4/139/1B/32 (reference kindly supplied by Murray Ll. Chapman). 'The Hunt's Up' was a popular sixteenth-century minstrel's tune, cf. *Ballads from Manuscripts*, ed. Frederick J. Furnivall, 2 vols (London: Ballad Society, 1868–72), I. 310–12. My thanks to Bethan Miles for this information.

36 NLW, Great Sessions 7/6/Sept. 38 Henry VIII; Great Sessions 7/8/June 4 Edw. VI; Nia Powell, 'Robert ap Huw: A Wanton Minstrel of Anglesey', *Welsh Music History*, 3 (1999), 5–29.

37 Davies, 'Slavery and Protector Somerset', 537–8; *Acts of the Privy Council*, II. 431.

38 See generally, Marjorie Keniston McIntosh, *Controlling Misbehavior in England, 1370–1600* (Cambridge: Cambridge University Press, 1998).

39 NLW, MS. 9051E, item 12, abstract in *Calendar of Wynn (of Gwydir) Papers 1515–1690* (Aberystwyth: National Library of Wales, 1926), 2–3. These undated orders presumably embodied the instructions given by the Privy Council to Sir William Herbert when appointed president of the Council in the Marches: *Chronicle and Political Papers of King Edward VI*, ed. Jordan, 24, 34–5.

40 NLW, Great Sessions 4/124/4/1; 4/124/5/72; 4/126/3/42. See generally, Peter Clark, *The English Alehouse: a social history 1200–1830* (London: Longman, 1983), 169–71, for the idea of the alehouse culture.

41 Penry Williams, *The Council in the Marches of Wales Under Elizabeth I* (Cardiff: University of Wales Press, 1958), xiv, 138.

42 PRO, CHES 24/92/12.

43 *A Calendar of the Register of the Queen's Majesty's Council in the Dominion and Principality of Wales and the Marches … [1535] 1569–1591*, Record Series, no. 8, ed. Ralph Flenley (London: Cymmrodorion, 1916), 145.

44 J. Gwynfor Jones, 'The Welsh Poets and their Patrons *c.* 1550–1640', *Welsh History Review*, 9 (1978–79), 245–77, esp. 274–7.

45 Dylan Foster Evans, '*Goganwr am Gig Ynyd': the Poet as Satirist in Medieval Wales*, no. 6 Research Papers (Aberystwyth: Centre for Advanced Welsh and Celtic Studies, 1996); Edwards, *Dafydd ap Gwilym: Influences and Analogues*, Ch. 2.

46 *A Collection of Highland Rites and Customes Copied by Edward Lhuyd from the Manuscript of the Rev. James Kirkwood (1650–1709) and Annotated by him with the Aid of the Rev. John Beaton*, ed. J. L. Campbell (Cambridge: D.S. Brewer for the Folklore Society, Mistletoe Series, 1975), 40.

47 Gruffydd Robert's *Gramadeg Cymraeg* (Milan, 1567) cited by Evans, *The Poet as Satirist*, 26; *Geiriadur Prifysgol Cymru*, *s.v.* 'cyff clêr'; Thomas Pennant, *Tours in*

Wales, ed. John Rhys, 3 vols (Caernarvon, 1883), II. 100–1; John David Rhys [Siôn Dafydd Rhys], *Cambrobrytannicae Cymraecaeve Linguae Institutiones* [etc.] (London, 1592), marginal note on p. 147.

48 Suggett, 'Slander in Early-Modern Wales', 126; *A Catalogue of Star Chamber Proceedings Relating to Wales*, ed. Ifan ab Owen Edwards (Cardiff: University of Wales Press, 1929), 43; NLW, Great Sessions 13/23/9/unnumbered presentment.

49 PRO, STAC 8 James I/205/21–22; G. Dyfnallt Owen, *Wales in the Reign of James I* (London: Royal Historical Soc. Studies in History 53, 1988), 5. Libels printed in *Records of Early English Drama: Shropshire*, ed. J. A. B. Somerset, 2 vols (Toronto: University of Toronto Press, 1994), I. 66–70; II. 546–8, 639–41.

50 Pauline Croft, 'Libels, popular literacy and public opinion in early modern England', *The Bulletin of the Institute of Historical Research*, 68 (1995), 266–85; Adam Fox, 'Ballads, Libels and Popular Ridicule in Jacobean England', *Past and Present*, 145 (1994), 47–83.

51 D. Aneurin Thomas, *The Welsh Elizabethan Catholic Martyrs* (Cardiff: University of Wales Press, 1971), 105; cf. Owen, *Wales in the Reign of James I*, 108, n. 95.

52 Glanmor Williams, *Wales and the Reformation* (Cardiff: University of Wales Press, 1997), passim.

53 Acts 4 Henry IV, c. 27; 25 Henry VI; Ivor Bowen, *The Statutes of Wales* (London: T. Fisher Unwin, 1908), 34, 45. The wording of the original statute is 'Westours, Rymours, Ministralx & autres vacabondes'; cf. the ordinances in the 'Record of Caernarvon', *Registrum Vulgariter Nuncupatum 'The Record of Caernarvon'*, ed. H. Ellis (London: Record Commission, 1838), 238 ('plusours Wastours Rymors Mynistralx & autres vacabundez') and 132 where an ordinance against 'les Westres Barthes & Rymors' is attributed to Edward I. The meaning of the Anglo-French word rendered 'waster' in the 1543 translation of the statute is not certain. The *OED*, following T. Gwynn Jones, explains 'westour' as a form of the Welsh *gwestwr*, 'a vagrant who went about exacting free board and lodging' or 'a bard on circuit': *Oxford English Dictionary* (Oxford: Clarendon Press, 1988), *s.v.* 'waster', sense I3. On the context of Henry IV's anti-Welsh legislation, see R. R. Davies, *The Revolt of Owain Glyn D r* (Oxford: Oxford University Press, 1995), 281–92.

54 See generally, R. Wallis Evans, 'Prophetic Poetry', in Jarman and Hughes (eds), *A Guide to Welsh Literature*, Vol II. ch. 13, and the citations in n. 60 below.

55 Cf. Art Cosgrove, 'The emergence of the Pale, 1399–1447', in A. Cosgrove (ed.), *A New History of Ireland*, vol. II. *Medieval Ireland 1169–1534* (Oxford: Clarendon Press, 1987), 555, for the order in 1435 to the 'marshal' of the faithful English minstrels to capture those Irish entertainers regarded as spies and guides; Brian Ó Cuív, 'The Irish Language in the Early Modern Period', in T.W. Moody, F.X. Martin and F.J. Byrne (eds), *A New History of Ireland*, vol. III: *Early Modern Ireland 1534–1691* (Oxford: Clarendon Press, 1976), 520–1; J. E. Caerwyn Williams & Patrick K. Ford, *The Irish Literary Tradition* (Cardiff: University of Wales Press, 1992), 176–7; Pádraig A. Breatnach, 'An Appeal for a Guarantor', *Celtica*, 21 (1990), 28–37.

56 Davies, *Revolt of Owain Glyn D r*, 34. Irish hill-top assemblies: Marc Caball, 'Aspects of Sixteenth-century Élite Gaelic Mentalities', *Études Celtiques*, 32 (1996), 208 (abolished 1572); Kenneth Nicholls, *Gaelic and Gaelicised Ireland in the Middle Ages* (Dublin: Gill & Macmillan, 1972), 30–1.

57 Text of British Library Lansdowne MS 111, f. 10, in Edward Owen, *A Catalogue*

of the Manuscripts Relating to Wales in the British Museum, Record Series, no. 4 (London: Cymmrodorion, 1900), part I, 72, with clarification of names by Ifor Williams, *Hen Chwedlau* (Cardiff: University of Wales Press, 1949), 1; R. R. Davies, 'The Peoples of Britain and Ireland, 1100–1400. IV: Language and Historical Mythology', *Trans. Royal Hist. Soc.*, 6th ser., 7 (1997), 23; Bowen, 'Y Cywyddwyr a'r Dirywiad', 455 and 476.

58 Richard Suggett, 'Festivals and Social Structure in Early-modern Wales', *Past and Present*, 152 (1996), 90–1, n. 38.

59 NLW, MS. 9051E, item 12.

60 Keith Thomas, *Religion and the Decline of Magic* (London: Weidenfeld & Nicolson, 1971), 397–404; Glanmor Williams, 'Prophecy, Poetry, and Politics in Medieval and Tudor Wales', in *British Government and Administration. Studies Presented to S. B. Chrimes*, ed. H. Hearder and H. R. Loyn (Cardiff: University of Wales Press, 1974), 104–16; Ralph Griffiths, *Sir Rhys ap Thomas and his Family: a Study in the Wars of the Roses and Early Tudor Politics* (Cardiff: University of Wales Press, 1993), 103–4; Peter Roberts, 'Tudor Wales, National Identity and the British Inheritance', in Brendan Bradshaw and Peter Roberts (eds), *British Consciousness and Identity: the Making of Britain* (Cambridge: Cambridge University Press, 1998), 35–7.

61 Thomas, *Religion and the Decline of Magic*, 420–1; Suggett, 'The Welsh Language and the Court of Great Sessions', in *The Welsh Language Before the Industrial Revolution*, ed. Jenkins, 174–6.

62 Williams, 'Prophecy, Poetry, and Politics in Medieval and Tudor Wales', 112–13. Cf. the list of manuscripts in Margaret Enid Griffiths, *Early Vaticination in Welsh with English Parallels* (Cardiff: University of Wales Press, 1937), 219–20.

63 NLW, MS. 3041B (formerly Mostyn MS. 133), 375–9; HMC, *Report on Manuscripts in the Welsh Language* (London, 1898) I, part 1, 109; NLW, Great Sessions 21/8/rex m. 2r.

64 Robert Recorde, *The Grovndes of Artes* [etc.] (London, 1552), dedication to Edward VI, sig. AVv-AVir; William Salesbury, *A briefe and a playne introduction* [etc.] (London, 1550), introduction, sig. Eiir–v; Sir John Wynn, *The History of the Gwydir Family and Memoirs*, ed. J. Gwynfor Jones (Llandysul: Gomer Press, 1990), 24.

65 Edwards, *Dafydd ap Gwilym: Influences and Analogues*, ch. 1, esp. 34–5; Glanmor Williams, *Recovery, Reorientation and Reformation: Wales, c. 1415–1642* (Oxford: Clarendon Press, 1987), 163.

66 Text and translation: 'Statud Gruffudd ap Cynan/The Statute of Gruffudd ap Cynan', ed. David Klausner, *Welsh Music History*, 3 (1999), 282–98. Discussion of different texts in T. Gwynn Jones, 'Bardism and Romance: a Study of the Welsh Literary Tradition', *Trans. Hon. Soc. Cymmrodorion*, Session 1913–14 [1915], 240–64; Thomas, 'From Manuscript to Print – I. Manuscript', in *A Guide to Welsh Literature* III. *250, discusses copies including those owned by poets.*

67 Thomas, *Eisteddfodau Caerwys: Caerwys Eisteddfodau*, 42–5. Not all versions state that the *eisteddfod* was to be held 'under the commission of the king'; D. J. Bowen, 'Graddegion *Eisteddfodau* Caerwys, 1523 a 1567/8', *Llên Cymru*, 2 (1952–53), 128–34.

68 Thomas, *Eisteddfodau Caerwys*, 43–4; D. J. Bowen, 'Graddau Barddol Tudur Aled', *Llên Cymru*, 18 (1994–95), 98–100.

69 Kay Brainerd Slocum, '*Confrérie, Bruderschaft* and Guild: the Formation of

Musicians' Fraternal Organizations in Thirteenth- and Fourteenth-century Europe', *Early Music History*, 14 (1995), 257–74; G. R. Rastall, 'The Minstrel Court in Medieval England', in *A Medieval Miscellany in Honour of Professor John Le Patourel, Proceedings of the Leeds Philosophical and Literary Society*, 18 (1992), 96–105; Woodfill, *Musicians in English Society*, 109–20; Bowen, 'Agweddau ar Ganu'r Unfed Ganrif ar Bymtheg', 327–30.

70 John David Rhys, *Cambrobrytannicae Cymraecaeve Lingvae Institvtiones* (London, 1592), 302; *Gramadegau'r Penceirddiaid*, ed. G. J. Williams and E. J. Jones (Cardiff: University of Wales Press, 1934), 136, 151.

71 The offices held by the patrons of the *eisteddfod* are given in the versions of the proclamation in NLW, MS. 6434D, f. 345v, and Peniarth MS. 75 (transcript in HMC, *Report on Manuscripts in the Welsh Language*, I, part 2 [London, 1899], 503); on the political context, see S. J. Gunn, 'The Regime of Charles, Duke of Suffolk, in North Wales and the Reform of Welsh Government, 1509–25', *Welsh History Review*, 12 (1984–85), 470–8.

72 Bowen, 'Graddegion *Eisteddfod* Caerwys, 1523 a 1567–68', 128–34. Not all the silver prizes are specifically mentioned until the 1594 petition for a third *eisteddfod*. The silver harp in the keeping of the Mostyn family has survived and is of 'simple workmanship', about six inches long with a loop for a chain: Iorweth C. Peate, *Diwylliant Gwerin Cymru* (Liverpool: Hugh Evans a'i Feibion, 1942), 76, and idem, *Tradition and Folk Life* (London: Faber & Faber, 1972), 90 and plate 42.

73 Susan Reynolds, *An Introduction to the History of Medieval Towns* (Oxford: Clarendon Press, 1977), 164–8; Heather Swanson, 'The Illusion of Economic Structure: Craft Guilds in Late Medieval English Towns', *Past and Present*, 121 (1988), 29–48.

74 Jones, 'Bardism and Romance', 259–9; Thomas, *Eisteddfodau Caerwys*, 70–3; Klausner, 'Statud Gruffudd ap Cynan', 295.

75 Acts 3 Henry VIII, c. 2; 6 Henry VIII, c. 3; 11 Henry VIII, c. 2; *Tudor Royal Proclamations*, vol. I: *The Early Tudors (1485–1553)*, ed. Paul L. Hughes and James F. Larkin (New Haven, CT, and London: Yale University Press, 1964), nos 63, 108, 118, 121; R. W. Heinze, *The Proclamations of the Tudor Kings* (Cambridge: Cambridge University Press, 1976), 89–94.

76 The term 'vagabond' had been used to designate suspect and wandering persons in the March in the last quarter of the fifteenth century; cf. *The Marcher Lordships of South Wales, 1415–1536. Select Documents*, ed. T. B. Pugh (Cardiff: University of Wales Press, 1963), 93.

77 Powell, *The historie of Cambria*, 192.

78 D. J. Bowen, *Gwaith Gruffudd Hiraethog* (Cardiff: University of Wales Press, 1990), xxvi–vii; HMC, *Report on Welsh Manuscripts* (London, 1905), I, part 3, 1021; *Tudor Royal Proclamations*, nos 250, 352.

79 NLW, Peniarth MS 194 described in HMC, *Report on Welsh Manuscripts*, I: 3, 1021–3.

80 Act 26 Henry VIII, c. 6; Ivor Bowen, *The Statutes of Wales*, 57; *Letters and Papers, Foreign and Domestic, of the Reign of Henry VIII*, ed. J. S. Brewer, IV, part 1 (1870), 1044 (no. 2331); *'The Record of Caernarvon'*, 296.

81 Act 4 Henry IV, c. 27 confirmed 25 Henry VI; Bowen, *Statutes of Wales*, 34, 45.

82 Instructions to Lord Compton, 1617, printed in Thomas Rymer, *Foedera* [etc.]

(London, 1727), XVII. 31–2; Caroline A. J. Skeel, 'The St Asaph Cathedral Library MS. of the Instructions to the Earl of Bridgewater, 1633', *Archaeologia Cambrensis*, 6th ser., 17 (1917), 200.

83 Text of the commission in HMC, *Report on Manuscripts in the Welsh Language*, I: 1, 291–2. David Powel, *The historie of Cambria*, 440–1, for Sidney's ancestry.

84 HMC, *Report on Manuscripts in the Welsh Language*, I: 1 , 291–2.

85 Bowen, 'Graddegion *Eisteddfodau* Caerwys, 1532 a 1567/8', 128–34; Evan D. Jones, 'Simwnt Fychan a Theulu Plas y Ward', *Bulletin of the Board of Celtic Studies*, 7 (1933–35), 141–2.

86 On the idea of social closure, see Frank Parkin, *Class, Inequality and Political Order* (London: MacGibbon & Kee, 1971).

87 NLW, Great Sessions 4/968/7/15; 14/68/Feb. 11 Eliz.; 4/5/2/20 and 47.

88 Text of the petition in HMC, *Report on Manuscripts in the Welsh Language*, I: 1, 293–5.

89 Ibid.; Bowen, 'Y Cywyddwyr a'r Dirywiad', 476.

90 On the decline of the poetic tradition, see especially Ceri W. Lewis, 'The Decline of Professional Poetry', in *A Guide to Welsh Literature* III. ch. 2; J. Gwynfor Jones, *Continuity and Change in Wales* c. *1500–1603. Essays and Studies* (Aberystwyth: University Centre for Educational Studies, 1999), ch. 6; Nia Powell, 'Robert ap Huw', 11–13.

91 See generally, W. Ogwen Williams, 'The Survival of the Welsh Language After the Union of England and Wales: the First Phase, 1536–1642', *Welsh History Review*, 2 (1964), 78–86.

92 Lewis, 'Decline of Professional Poetry', 60.

93 D. J. Bowen, 'Y Cywyddwyr a'r Dirywiad', 492 (no. 96).

94 NLW, Great Sessions 4/781/4/28.

95 Siôn Lewys Môn: NLW, Great Sessions 4/16/4/75.

96 Ann Rosser, *Telyn a Thelynor. Hanes y Delyn yng Nghymru 1700–1900* (Cardiff: National Museum of Wales, 1981).

97 Aubrey, *Three Prose Works*, 299; NLW, Great Sessions 4/781/4/28r–v; 4/884/4/8d; 4/17/5/34.

98 Siôn Mawddwy, *Cywydd Dychan i'r Ffair a Moliant Syr Sion Games o'r Drenewydd*, 'a poem in satire of the fair and in praise of Sir John Games of Newton': Bowen, 'Y Cywyddwyr a'r Dirywiad', 484; T. Gwynn Jones, *Llên Cymru, Detholiad o Ryddiaith a Phrydyddiaeth* (Aberystwyth, 1926), part III, 67–8. Cf. also the earlier satire on Flint and its piper in Thomas Roberts (ed.), *Gwaith Tudur Penllyn ac Ieuan ap Tudur Penllyn* (Cardiff: University of Wales Press, 1958), 51–2, with free translation in *Presenting Welsh Poetry*, ed. Gwyn Williams (London: Faber & Faber, 1959), 35–7.

99 D. J. Bowen, 'Detholiaid o Englynion', *Bulletin of the Board of Celtic Studies*, 15 (1954), 186–7.

100 H. C. Jones, *Gwaith Huw Ceiriog ac Edward Maelor* (Cardiff: University of Wales Press, 1990), xxxi–xxxii, 40–1. I am grateful to Huw Ceiriog Jones for discussing this passage with me.

101 NLW, Great Sessions 4/16/1/25; 4/27/1/53; 4/20/4/72–5. Cf. Brinley Rees, *Dulliau'r Canu Rhydd 1500–1650* (Cardiff: University of Wales Press, 1952), 18–19, for English terms for dancing in Welsh contexts. The subject needs further exploration.

102 Suggett, 'Festivals and Social Structure', 79–112.

103 Great Sessions 4/20/4/72–5; Suggett, 'Festivals and Social Structure', 92; Jones, *Gwaith Huw Ceiriog*, 136–7.
104 Bowen, 'Y Cywyddwyr a'r Dirywiad', 484; Jones, *Llên Cymru*, part III, 67–9, gives 'this, that, which, what, when' as the peremptory English monosyllables.

Chapter 6

Reformed folklore? Cautionary tales and oral tradition in early modern England

Alexandra Walsham

PROTESTANTISM AND PRINT have often been presented as inherently hostile to oral tradition. Historians have credited both with a leading role in marginalizing, fossilizing, and ultimately suffocating the vernacular culture of late medieval England. Still widely regarded as a movement whose success depended upon the spread of literacy and the advent of the press, the Reformation is commonly associated with attempts to eradicate the 'heathenish superstitions', 'popish fables' and 'old wives tales' which the populace had inherited orally from its 'benighted' Catholic ancestors.

This chapter reinforces recent suggestions that both aspects of this paradigm are in need of refinement. Important work by Keith Thomas, Daniel Woolf, Adam Fox and others has taught us that literacy and orality coexisted in sixteenth- and seventeenth-century society in a mutually enriching equilibrium. For all their 'imperialistic potential' print and writing never entirely displaced speech: on the contrary, their increasing diffusion served in the short term to enhance and rejuvenate oral culture and communication.[1] Here I want to argue that Protestantism's part in the eclipse and demise of the authority of the spoken word was similarly equivocal. Although it aligned itself powerfully with the authority of writing and print and developed a pronounced polemical bias against verbal transmission, in many respects the Reformation did more to sustain and stimulate the latter than it did to erode and extinguish it. As a study of the many pious anecdotes of providential punishment circulating in this period will reveal, Protestantism effectively forged an oral tradition of its own – albeit one deeply infected by literature and learning. Recycling older materials and incorporating new ingredients, it created a distinctive body of tales and stories which might legitimately be described as a corpus of Protestant legend and folklore.

I

Long before the Reformation, ecclesiastical leaders heralded literacy as a potent instrument of civilization and enlightenment and an efficient remedy for the evils of heresy and disbelief: 'W'ithout lytterature', wrote a Benedictine monk around 1513, the 'comyn people ... Ben lyke to Brute beestes'.[2] Echoed and elaborated after the invention of the mechanical press, this was a theme which the Protestant reformers commandeered as their own. Loudly condemning the Roman Catholic hierarchy for tyrannically withholding the vernacular Bible from the laity, they liked to depict themselves as liberators democratically dispersing the holy text of Scripture to a populace whose religion had hitherto consisted of the mindless performance of empty rituals.[3] In his *Acts and Monuments* John Foxe declared triumphantly that unless the Pope abolished printing it would 'at length ... root him out'.[4] Many an Elizabethan and Stuart preacher spoke of literacy as nothing less than an agent of salvation: 'how many for want of reading have lost their precious souls?' lamented George Swinnock in 1663.[5] Protestant confidence in the power of the written word to dispel the dark mists of popish idolatry and semi-pagan superstition persisted throughout the seventeenth century and can be detected in John Aubrey's 'Remaines of Gentilisme and Judaisme' (*c.* 1686–88) beneath a thin veneer of nostalgia: 'the many good Bookes, and variety of Turnes of Affaires, have put all the old Fables out of dores: and the divine art of Printing and Gunpowder have frighted away Robin-good-fellow and the Fayries'.[6]

The corollary of Protestantism's attempt to affiliate itself with the forces of rationality and knowledge was its characterization of Catholicism as a faith rooted in rural ignorance and unthinking traditionalism. Illiteracy came to be seen as a chief cause of the residual popery which plagued Puritan evangelists in the dark corners of the land.[7] Ministers repeatedly attributed the ungodliness of their congregations to the defects of their education and the incorrigible pelagianism of the figures who inhabit George Gifford's *Countrie Divinitie* (1581) and Arthur Dent's *Plaine Mans Path-way to Heaven* (1601) is in large part a function of their inability to read.[8] Over time the two became synonymous, the stigma of the one reinforcing the slur and taint of the other. As Alison Shell observes in a forthcoming monograph, Catholicism was thus inexorably conflated with orality.[9]

This tendency was closely linked with the reformers' assault on the blind devotion of popish lay-people to 'humane traditions' passed down to them by their forefathers.[10] Protestant propagandists launched a vehement attack upon the extra-biblical foundations of the old religion, denouncing the Church of Rome for elevating papal decretals, conciliar decrees and a miscellaneous collection of verbally transmitted doctrines to equal standing with Scripture, and for insisting that belief in them was necessary to ensure eternal life. To accord such importance to tenets which could not be found in the canonical books of the Bible was, in the eyes of the godly, to cast an outrageous slight on Scripture, to insinuate that it was both imperfect and incomplete. This theme was graphically embodied in an illustration in Foxe's *Acts and Monuments*: 'A lively picture describyng the weight and substaunce of Gods most blessed word, agaynst the doctrines and vanities of mans traditions' (Plate 1). In it, the single volume of *Verbum Dei* easily outweighs the messy jumble of flimsy authorities piled on by the pope and his minions, despite the desperate efforts of a friar and the devil to drag the scales of justice down on Antichrist's side. The opposition between Scripture and tradition was a constant refrain in anti-Catholic controversial works from the 1530s onwards, reflecting the issue's status as a crucial point of differentiation between the two faiths. For their part, committed Romanists continued to defend the Church's role as a faithful custodian of teachings derived from Christ and his disciples but never inscribed in holy writ.[11]

Protestant polemicists like William Perkins compared this body of precepts with the Hebrew *Cabbala* – a supplementary code delivered to Moses, which had also remained unrecorded for several generations. Giving expression to a tacit anti-semitism, they dismissed it as 'no better than a Jewish dotage'.[12] They scoffed at suggestions that the 'great chest of traditions which Saint Peter did not put in writing' was in any way an infallible guide to God's will. While they had to concede that the Old and New Testaments themselves had been preserved orally by the patriarchs, prophets and apostles for decades and centuries before being immortalized on paper, they were insistent that, once fixed in written form by the Lord's appointment, it alone became the fount and foundation of Christian faith and truth.[13] The Bible should be 'the sole anker of our hope', said the future Archbishop of Canterbury George Abbot; the very word Scripture itself expressed 'the manner of delivering' divine truths, declared the Yorkshire preacher Francis Bunny, 'namely by writing'.[14] In short, they came close to claiming that textuality was intrinsic to the sanctity of holy writ, that God's meaning resided in the actual letters arranged on the page. It was no wonder that their Catholic opponents accused them of 'inkie divinitie'.[15]

In tract after tract Protestant divines denigrated Catholicism's dependence on a set of tenets enshrined in the unstable spoken word. Unwritten verities, remarked Abbot, were the 'sandy foundation' on which 'all your rotten building doth rest'. The mere credit of men, maintained William Middleton, was 'a poor stay for a Christian conscience'. Meditating on the unreliability of information conveyed by the ephemeral mechanism of speech, Antony Wootton wondered how traditions could ever be kept 'without adding and altering, if they have no better guide then the memories of men ... which may often faile them'.[16] '[I]f entrance once be given to laws that pass by the

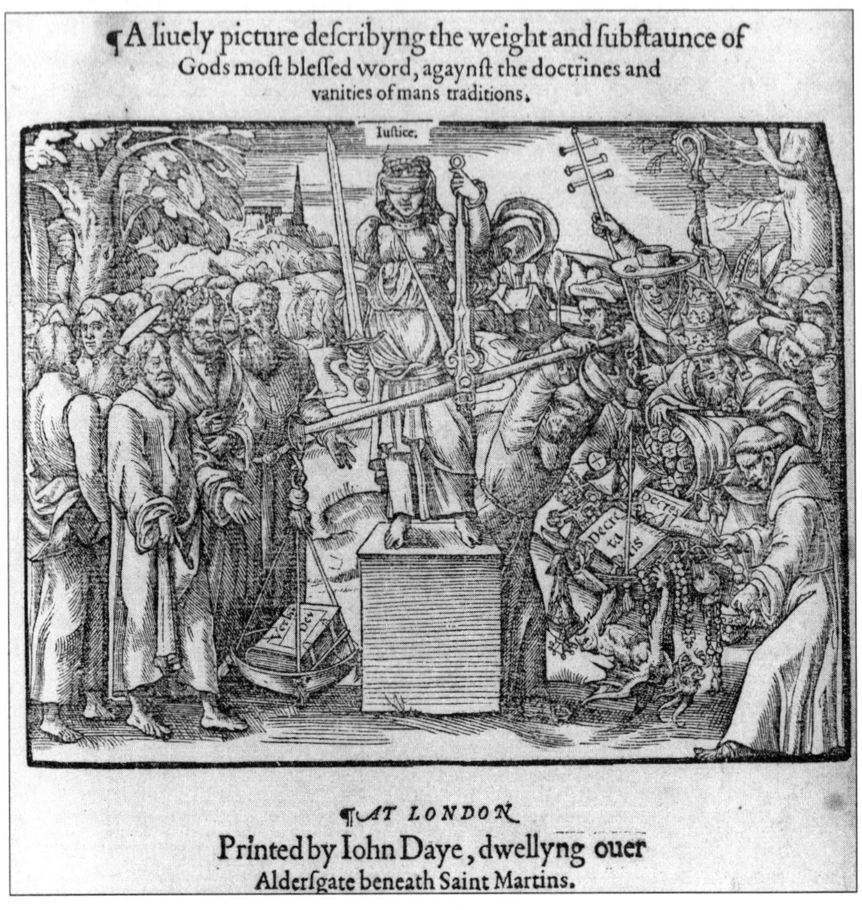

Plate 1. A lively picture describyng the weight and substaunce of Gods most blessed word, agaynst the doctrines and vanities of mans traditions. John Foxe, *Acts and Monuments* (London, 1576 edn), II. 771.
(By permission of the British Library, c.15, c.8.)

word of mouth', feared Edwin Sandys, anarchy and heresy would reign: 'the undoubted articles of our belief cannot choose but at the length become doubtful and uncertain, like a tale that passeth from man to man, and is told as many ways as there are men to tell it'. The primitive Christians, he added, 'never inquired what had been whispered in men's ears; that which they believed and taught, they read it out of the book'. Richard Hooker likewise observed in his *Lawes of Ecclesiastical Politie* (1595): 'What hazard the truth is in when it passes through the hands of report ... how maimed and deformed it becomes'. Writing thirty years later Bishop Joseph Hall of Exeter closely echoed these rhetorical complaints: 'As for orall Traditions, what certaintie can there be in them? What foundation of truth can be layd upon the breath of man? How doe wee see the reports varie, of those things, which our eyes have seene done? How doe they multiply in their passage, and either growe, or dye upon hazards?'[17]

An integral part of this sustained Protestant critique of unwritten traditions was the claim that many of them had been fabricated by the corrupt medieval priesthood to magnify their position and keep the laity in passive submission. In a tract which branded 'the pretensed religion of the Sea of Rome ... a false, bastard, new, upstart, hereticall and variable superstitious devise of man', Josias Nicholls accused the Catholic clergy of manufacturing 'verie fables' to legitimize their innovations and give themselves an air of 'antiquitie'.[18] Carrying forward the early reformers' contempt for miracle tales and the legends of the saints, the Jacobean minister Richard Sheldon was equally scathing about 'old Monkes fictions' and Romish 'legerdermaine': such false and lying wonders were 'always in hugger mugger, brought from farre off, and beleeved by hearesay'. Incorporated in the Golden Legend, they amounted to nothing less than a dunghill of lies. According to the Norfolk physician John Harvey, counterfeit prophecies and foolish tales of hobgoblin, Guy of Warwick, Robin Hood and Maid Marian were also the 'trim worke' of 'idle Cloistermen, mad merry Friers, and lustie Abbey-lubbers'. Designed 'to busie the minds of the vulgar sort' and deflect them from meddling with 'mysticall privities', they were a kind of popish opium of the people.[19] For Reginald Scot, the whole myth of witchcraft was also part of this Catholic conspiracy: silly nonsense dreamt up by 'masse preests', passed down by 'old doting women' and 'mothers maids', and eventually 'swallowed up through tract of time, or through their own timerous nature or ignorant conceipt'. In his *Perambulation of Kent* (1576) William Lambarde likewise devoted much space to exposing historical forgeries perpetrated by the 'Popes parasites', which had been absorbed into oral culture and 'common opinion'. Among the many examples of the 'grosse jugling that these slowe bellyed Syres used to delude the world' which he cited, were the legends about the miraculous moving eyes of the Holy Rood of Boxley, the wonders worked by Our Lady of Chatham, and the 'unwritten vanities' connected with St Thomas à Becket at Canterbury.[20] Curiously anticipating the insights of Eric Hobsbawm and Terence Ranger, such writers declared Roman Catholicism guilty of inventing 'traditions'.[21]

By this insidious, two-way process of association, then, popery came to be inextricably linked with verbal transmission. The equation of 'oral tradition' with 'superstition' was already a trope centuries old: in the twelfth century Guibert of Nogent was contrasting unimpeachable written evidence with inauthentic spoken report and using it to discredit facets of popular Breton belief about saints and relics of which he fiercely disapproved.[22] No doubt this polemical dichotomy has even earlier antecedents: it was a perennial product of moments of cultural contest, displacement and rupture rather than an exclusive legacy of the Lutheran and Calvinist religious revolutions.

In the context of the Reformation, however, it took on explicitly anti-Catholic overtones. Confessional prejudice converged with learned contempt of the illiterate to create an enduring nexus between the medium of the spoken word and the dissemination of ridiculous and improbable 'popish' fictions. In turn, it might be observed, this interconnection acquired a gender dimension: as preachers began to trace the causes of vestigial Catholicism to female credulity, so 'old wives' tales' became a form of shorthand for the 'lying vanities' which underpinned the 'Romish' religion. Thus Edwin Sandys deplored the way in which the 'dotages of silly women' were mingled with the 'divine scriptures' and Nicholas Udall complained about Catholic preachers who filled their sermons with apocryphal fables recounted by foolish dames instead of expounding the Gospel and Law.[23]

Protestant suspicion of 'uncertaine tradition' was but one strand in a wider body of contemporary discourse contributing to the devaluation of oral testimony and remembered information. In the sphere of the law, the shift from memory to written record gathered momentum as local custom and judicial precedent were fixed in printed texts.[24] Growing emphasis on the need for documentary evidence likewise led heralds, antiquaries and historians to disparage common report and hearsay as untrustworthy sources for understanding events in the past.[25] At the village level this manifested itself in the declining prestige of the elderly as the caretakers of ancestral wisdom.[26] Although in practice the marginalization of speech was more protracted and incomplete, by 1700 the unreliability of oral tradition was almost axiomatic in educated circles. Indeed, a year earlier it had been the subject of precise mathematical analysis by a member of the Royal Society. Such trends were also an index of the extent to which experimental discovery had begun to dislodge inherited learning as the basis of 'knowledge'.[27]

Daniel Woolf has seen these developments as symptomatic of an emerging cultural gulf between ordinary people and educated elites. He detects behind such trends the beginnings of 'a *social* – as distinct from a merely *intellectual* – bias' against verbally conveyed information, the result of which was to erect a permanent 'barrier between "proper" history and mere legend – what we would now call folklore'.[28] However, to interpret this split as an index of incipient class alienation is arguably to ignore the extent to which denigration of the oral had an ideological tincture. For, as the preceding paragraphs have shown, the whole concept of 'oral tradition' had its taproot in anti-Catholic propaganda, and before that in the conflicts between the late medieval papacy and the heretics and councils who challenged its authority. It was the controversialists who effectively forged the notion of 'folklore', though the term itself – a conscious Anglo-Saxon revival – was only coined in 1846, by the antiquary William Thoms in a letter printed in the weekly magazine *The Athenaeum*.[29] And whereas the origins of the movement to collect and classify 'popular antiquities' have often been located in the sense of estrangement eighteenth- and nineteenth-century intellectuals felt from the culture of the 'vulgar',[30] this was surely in part a consequence of the very processes we have been exploring. Two hundred years earlier reforming zeal was a powerful stimulus to quasi-anthropological investigation and analysis of the 'profane' customs and 'idle' traditions practised and believed by the semi-popish multitude. Both were depicted as residual categories brought about by resistance to the transformative forces of Protestantism and print, and in works like Thomas Becon's *The Reliques of Rome* (1563) and Philip Stubbes's *The Anatomie of Abuses* (1583) they were denounced as remnants of the heathen idolatry of pre-Christian England.[31] The same assumptions underlay Thomas Browne's celebrated *Pseudodoxia Epidemica* (1646), in which the errors of the common people were attributed to 'the Priests of Elder time [who] have put upon them many incredible conceits', while in 1725 the Newcastle vicar Henry Bourne would declare in his *Antiquitates Vulgares* that the opinions of the ignorant were 'generally either the produce of Heathenism; or the Inventions of indolent Monks' who carefully handed them down to posterity.[32] But it was John Brand, in a revised and expanded version of Bourne's tract dated 1777, who expressed the presumed link between superstition and verbal diffusion most lucidly: popular beliefs, 'consecrated to the fancies of the multitude by a usage from time immemorial, though erased by public authority from the written word, were committed as a venerable deposit to the keeping of oral tradition ... after having been snatched out of the smoking ruins of Popery'.[33] Forced out of the official mainstream, Catholicism, together with its precursor, paganism, persisted precisely because it remained impervious to the transfiguring influence of literacy and printing. Embedded within these statements was a religious theory of survivalism which social Darwinism and Victorian romanticism would transform into a scientific one – a scholarly quest to recover remaining traces of an intriguing primitive religion, remnants of a Celtic and Saxon rather than a Roman twilight. While earlier works were increasingly read less as diatribes against vulgar misconceptions than entertaining anthologies of customs and fables, the boundary between antiquarianism and polemic remained very blurred until well into the nineteenth century, and even beyond. In the mid-1820s, we can still find a reader congratulating the editor of one such collection for exposing 'with a masterly hand the superstitions and monkery of the olden time'.[34]

Such works and their successors explain why oral transmission was for so long an indispensable element of the definition of folklore. However, since the 1970s this set of presuppositions and polarities has been assaulted from all sides. Recent folklorists have not only thoroughly discredited the idea of archaic survivals, but rejected the misguided persuasion of their predecessors that folklore was a pure distillation of the untainted spring waters of continuous oral tradition. Concurring with a number of studies stressing the extent to which literacy penetrated pre-industrial popular culture,[35] they are becoming more alive to the role which print and writing played in the dissemination of all folk genres and to the frequency with which tales and stories handed down by word of mouth were contaminated by contact with literary sources, if not originally initiated by them. Often, as Stith Thompson has observed, 'the problem of priority is quite unsolvable'.[36] Few, moreover, have escaped the distorting effects of 'bourgeois filtering' by Georgian, Victorian and Edwardian editors.[37] Historians, on the other hand, are now less confident that Protestantism and print should be seen as inseparable twins. There is growing recognition that, in the guise of preaching, catechizing, psalm-singing and godly discussion of sermons and Scripture, the Reformation actually catalysed orality.[38] These insights provide an important backdrop for the second part of this chapter, which contends that English Calvinism also, rather ironically, generated a form of folklore of its own – a cluster of traditions no less vulnerable to the vagaries of oral transmission than those which had crystallized around medieval Catholicism.

II

Cautionary tales of the judgements God visited upon flagrant and incorrigible sinners circulated widely in sixteenth- and seventeenth-century England: stories of sabbath-breakers, swearers, drunkards, adulterers and other ungodly livers struck down suddenly by the avenging arm of the Almighty. A few examples must suffice to convey the flavour of this perennially popular genre: the case of Anne Averies, a London artisan who perjured herself after stealing a ball of twine in 1576 and died a ghastly death vomiting up her own excrements; the Lincolnshire youth who constantly swore by God's wounds and God's blood only to perish with his own pouring forth unstoppably from his ear, nose and throat in 1581; the impious nobleman who went out hunting on Sundays instead of attending divine service and was punished when his wife gave birth to a baby with a head resembling one of his beloved hounds; Dorothy Mattley, the Derbyshire washerwoman who dramatically sank into the earth in 1650 after denying that she had cheated a young lad of twopence; and John Duncalf, the Bible-stealer from Staffordshire whose hands and legs fell off after being attacked by gangrene in 1677.[39]

Gory stories of this kind were powerful vehicles for conventional Christian morality and for a peculiarly literal brand of providentialism. The notion that God actively intervened in human affairs to reward the good and discipline the wicked was by no means an innovation of the post-Reformation period, but such beliefs were bolstered by Calvinist theology. Part of the common outlook of Protestants of all persuasions, they belie Max Weber's influential thesis that the Reformation was an agent of the 'disenchantment of the world': on the contrary it appears to have strongly reinforced the idea of a 'moralised universe'.[40] Indeed, the collection of anecdotes of divine vengeance was nothing less than an industry in the Elizabethan and Stuart periods. Ministers like John Foxe, Henry Burton, Samuel Clarke, Thomas Taylor and William Turner published increasingly bulky anthologies of 'remarkable providences'. These fed off and into the private compilations of lay people such as Nehemiah Wallington and engendered inexpensive commercial imitations by Nathaniel Crouch and other entrepreneurial publishers. The Huntingdon schoolmaster Thomas Beard's *The Theatre of Gods Judgments* (1597) is the most famous of these pious encyclopedias: expanded and reissued three times before 1648, it became an indispensable work of reference for all future collectors.[41]

Directly or indirectly, these judgement books were heavily indebted to medieval compendia of sermon exempla – works which themselves bear the tell-tale marks of verbal transmission. In such texts as Caesarius of Heisterbach's *Dialogue on Miracles*, Johannes Herolt's *Promptuarium Exemplorum*, and the anonymous *Speculum Exemplorum*, Protestant preachers discovered many stories which underlined the lesson that sinners could not escape the searing wrath of God: stories of lecherers whose genitals are burnt to cinder, of girls who turn to stone after dancing on a holy day, and of usurers eaten by adders and toads. In appropriating them for their own purposes, they were carrying on a process of ecclesiastical colonisation of vernacular narratives that had its origins in the late twelfth and early thirteenth centuries. Didactic tales of this type represented a fusion between written doctrine and oral tradition.[42] Characterized by a telescoped time-frame between evil deed and heavenly revenge, by the systematic excision of superfluous circumstantial detail, and by a suspicious degree of correspondence between punishment and crime, such exempla continued to find a niche in Protestant collections and to be adapted to survive in the new theological environment. The canine-faced infant and Lincolnshire swearer are cases in point: a version of the latter story can be found in Richard Whitford's *Werke for Householders* (1531) and, like the monstrous child, almost certainly has even earlier antecedents.[43]

Post-Reformation anthologies of providences grew in the same way as their Catholic precursors, by being constantly augmented by topical examples. Many of these came from blackletter broadside ballads and pamphlets which functioned as forerunners of the newspaper, and from the popular chronicles and plays which were parasitic upon them. Edmund Bicknoll, author of *A Swoord against Swearers and Blasphemers* (1579) drew the tale of Anne Averies from a tract printed by John Alde in 1576, while Beard's source for the story was John Stow's *The Chronicles of England*.[44] Thomas Taylor's *Second Part of the Theatre of Gods Judgments* gave 'but a meere nomination' of some instances of divine ire against sexual lust 'because most of them have been Stag'd, Book'd, and Balleted, and disperst abroad through the Kingdome'.[45] The sad fates of Dorothy Mattley and John Duncalf had similarly been reported in cheap print before being immortalized in Samuel Clarke's *Mirror* and William Turner's *Compleat History*.[46] Combining factual accuracy with moralistic commentary, this ephemeral journalism was itself often based on gossip and rumour gleaned from travellers and carriers by the hack writers of the capital.[47]

Other examples were derived from direct eyewitness testimony: from letters describing divine judgements sent in by colleagues, friends and even complete strangers, and from accounts conveyed to the compilers of such encyclopedias by word of mouth. The collection of punishments visited upon Catholic persecutors which John Foxe appended to his *Acts and Monuments* contained many graphic tales of the gruesome deaths that had befallen the enemies and betrayers of the Marian Protestants which were communicated to him by people who claimed to have seen them with their own eyes. Thus the Bishop of Chester who slandered the recent martyr George Marsh in a sermon in the cathedral in 1555 soon afterwards 'turned up his heels and died', according to 'a report [which] went in all men's mouths', of a particularly ghastly form of venereal disease; thus the dire penalty dealt out to a Kentish priest by the name of Nightingale who preached 'the Popes blasphemous doctrine' and dropped dead in the pulpit was testified by Robert Austen of Chartham 'who both heard and saw the same, and it is witnessed also by the whole country round about'.[48] Samuel Ward similarly derived many of his cases of drunkards who came to untimely ends from verbal report. The case of three neighbours from Barnwell near Cambridge who drank a barrel of beer and expired within twenty-four hours had been substantiated by a local justice of the peace 'besides the common fame'.[49] Thomas Beard even included 'a common and vulgar storie which is almost in every childes mouth' of a convicted criminal who bit off his own mother's ear, blaming her for bringing him up so badly.[50] One prodigious occurrence which the Cheshire schoolmaster Edward Burghall included in a manuscript entitled 'Providence Improved' had been related to him by Mrs Crewe of Utkinton, who herself had it 'from a known and approved witness'.[51] Nehemiah Wallington's notebooks are also full of stories of sabbath-breakers overtaken by the hand of God which he had heard 'very creadably' or which were 'attested by severall parsons of Credit'. Nor did such collectors disdain tales which had entered into oral tradition. Wallington solemnly recorded the case of four alcoholics from Eyam in Derbyshire who read the service for the churching of women over a cow and were 'strangely and fearfully punished' for this 'wicked and horrible fact', noting that 'this was don neere thirtie yeeres agoe, but yet it is still fresh in memorie theire'.[52] More famously, the story of the bull which broke loose in Chipping Sodbury, headed straight for the chancellor of the diocese who had just presided over the burning of a Gloucestershire heretic, and gored him to death, had been passed down faithfully from father to son before being relayed to John Foxe half-a-century later.[53]

The very fact that so much of this providential material was verbally transmitted led to growing concern about its authenticity. Private letter writers and diarists like Joseph Mede and Walter Yonge carefully discriminated 'false' and 'flying rumours' from trustworthy relatings, remarking that 'vulgar report' was 'commonly corrupted in the telling'.[54] It became necessary for the authors, editors and publishers of cases of divine justice to pre-empt and deflect allegations that they were mere 'fables'. News pamphlets self-consciously entitled themselves 'true reports' and concluded with the names and addresses of eyewitnesses ready to ratify the truth to sceptical readers.[55] Henry Burton insisted that there were 'no fained miracles, nor fabulous stories, nor ould wives tales, for prophane scoffers to jeare at' in his *Divine Tragedie Lately Acted* (1636), but only examples confirmed by diligent enquiry and 'such, as will abide the triall and search of this present age'.[56] Both a symptom and a cause of the devaluation of oral testimony discussed above, earnest protestations of this kind did nothing to dispel the suspicions of one Puritan who wrote to John Winthrop, Governor of Massachusetts, in Boston: 'it is feared that there is a great fayling in many and chiefe circumstances in the Instances alleaged, if some few of them alsoe were not taken too suddenly on trust and heare-say without well looking after the truth'.[57]

These concerns were closely linked with the way in which supernatural news had become a highly lucrative sector of the seventeenth-century publishing industry. Unscrupulous stationers like John Trundle were not above updating cautionary tales which had lost their topical interest and reprinting them embellished with spurious details to deceive unwary buyers.[58] Doubts about the veracity of stories of sinners requited were also a response to their increasing exploitation for the ends of sectarian propaganda. Burton's *Divine Tragedie* was compiled in the wake of Charles I's re-proclamation in 1633 of the Book of Sports, to provide proof of the Lord's seething rage at this anti-sabbatarian legislation: Laudians quickly dismissed these cases as pieces of malicious gossip started by the self-styled godly. Some of the accounts of punished Catholic persecutors Foxe had incorporated in his *Acts and Monuments* can similarly be shown to have been ingenious tools of faction, and when the Welsh magistrate William Vaughan's wife was slain in her bed by a flash of lightning in 1611 his 'popish' enemies apparently 'made a taunting table talke of this heavenly visitation', claiming it was evidence of God's anger at his excessive moral severity.[59] After the outbreak of the Civil War these tendencies intensified and crudely partisan accounts of judgements upon Roundheads and Royalists proliferated in large numbers, further corroding the credibility of the genre.[60]

By the middle of the seventeenth century there were consequently calls for more rigorous, quasi-scientific methods of verification to be employed by those who compiled providential judgements for posterity. In the 1650s the Presbyterian minister Matthew Poole laid down detailed guidelines for the registration of 'illustrious providences'. These were designed to undo the damage done by the 'great mixture of false and foolish and unwitnessed fictions' published alongside properly documented accounts. It was not merely 'foule impostures' which fostered atheistical scoffing and undermined the majesty of God; as one commentator upon the project remarked, 'I have often observed that assone as the first wonder rebateth those that at first overspoke the truth, doe in the end by multiplications of falls surmisalls and devised causes eclipse and affront the truth'. Poole's elaborate plans for the setting up of a network of clerical investigators in each county never came to fruition, though they were revived twenty-five years later on an even more ambitious scale by Increase Mather in New England.[61]

Even in blueprint, these schemes bear a remarkable resemblance to the coordinated activities of the amateurs who lay behind the foundation of the Folklore Society in 1878. Inspired partly by anxiety about the intrinsic unreliablity of the spoken word, they also anticipated the problems that would be faced by modern theorists and practitioners of oral history.[62] As comments of the kind already quoted suggest, at least some contemporaries were beginning to find the highly stereotyped nature of stories of divine judgement somewhat unsettling. They were beginning to be conscious of the distortion created by recollecting events with the benefit of hindsight, of the errors introduced by faulty memory, and of the selective omissions typical of tales afflicted by 'structural amnesia'. They were already hazily aware of the manner in which chronology tended to become compressed, familiar formulae were interpolated in untidy reminiscences, and local history was gradually remodelled into edifying legends and myths. They also displayed an embryonic recognition of the way in which print and writing themselves served to fix but also to fundamentally transfigure oral tradition.[63] Indeed, cautionary tales are examples *par excellence* of the impulses to allegorize and moralize reality which postmodernists like Hayden White have argued lie at the heart of narrativity.[64] The satisfying poetic justice which is characteristic of such anecdotes may make them imperfect guides to what 'actually' occurred, but what it does highlight are the providential assumptions which were part of the mental furniture of early modern minds, together with the conventions and stereotypes which shaped verbal and written testimony in this period.[65]

Oral tradition, then, filtered into printed collections of God's judgements in a variety of ways. But cultural traffic did not travel in a single direction: just as rumour, gossip and remembrance infiltrated literature, so in turn did stories from cheap print and pious encyclopedias return to the realm of the spoken word. Sung at street corners and read aloud in private homes and alehouses, ballads and pamphlets could become part of the culture and experience of the unlettered. Recounted by preachers from their pulpits, rehearsed in conversation with one's neighbours and peers, stories of divine retribution sometimes achieved the status of notorious commonplaces. In 1635, for instance, the case of the 'lamenting lady', a barren thirteenth-century countess who gave birth to 365 mouse-sized babies after slandering a beggar woman blessed with twins, was said to be on the lips of every inhabitant of a small Devon village.[66] Assisted by their circulation in the press, some tales eventually entered into collective social memory. Registered in the copyright stock of specialist seventeenth-century booksellers, reprinted in small octavo formats, and revived in popular anthologies like Nathaniel Crouch's *Wonderful Prodigies* (1682), accounts of the providential deaths of many Elizabethan and Stuart evildoers were gradually transmuted into folklore. Shedding the journalistic detail which had originally recommended them to sensation-seeking readers, the stories of Anne Averies, John Duncalf, the Lincolnshire swearer and the sabbath-breaking nobleman became Protestant exempla, reappearing time and again in devotional tracts and didactic broadsides.[67] As for Dorothy Mattley, swallowed up by a gaping hole which opened beneath her, she achieved the ultimate apotheosis of novelization. Her sorry fate was the subject of a colourful vignette in John Bunyan's *Life and Death of Mr Badman* (1680).[68] Just as this tale contained echoes of the punishment which befell the biblical rebels Korah, Dathan and Abiram, so too did early modern judgement stories supply the template for subsequent narratives. For instance, Francis Spiera, the sixteenth-century Italian lawyer who suffered torment on his deathbed after denying and dissembling his faith, became the prototype for a whole dynasty of Stuart apostates.[69] Moreover, many works which followed in the footsteps of Beard's *Theatre of Gods Judgments* were the product of a process of uncritical accretion. Successive compilers simply lifted material from previous treatises and inserted it in their own volumes almost verbatim, giving off the misleading impression that they were recording direct oral testimony or an active tradition – in a manner all too reminiscent of the writings of the earliest folklorists.[70]

A few stories of divine chastisement even found their way into the collections of pioneering scholars in this field – figures like Thomas Percy and F. J. Child who supposed them to be 'reliques of ancient English poetry' and prose communally composed and uncontaminated by contact with writing.[71] In fact, R. S. Thomson has shown that the origins of some 80 per cent of ballads in such anthologies can be traced to printed broadsides dating from before 1700, and Margaret Spufford's analysis of Katherine Brigg's *Dictionary of British Folktales* (1970) reveals a smaller but still significant degree of overlap between stories told by word of mouth in the second half of the twentieth century and the ephemeral literature of early modern England.[72] *Young Bateman, or the Fair Maid of Clifton*, together with its variant *The Suffolk Miracle*, is one such cautionary tale which seems to have slipped into oral tradition. The story of a faithless maiden borne away by the ghost of the dead lover she had betrayed, a ballad on this theme was entered in the Stationers' Register at least as early as 1603. More than two centuries later it was dictated by a schoolmistress and printed in *Walks around Nottingham* (1835).[73] The Babes in the Wood is another familiar fairytale which can be traced back to a blackletter broadside. Entitled *The Norfolk Gentleman, his Last Will and Testament* and first published in 1595, this is the saga of a cruel uncle who contrives to kill his orphaned niece and nephew in order to inherit their wealth and then suffers a succession of disasters inflicted by the heavy hand of God. Left in the forest by one of the ruffians hired to murder them, the children die in each other's arms and are buried in leaves by sorrowful robins. The subject of a late Elizabethan play by Robert Yarrington and recycled in a slightly different guise in a chapbook of 1706, this story also appears to have passed into common currency before being captured once more in print and celebrated as a specimen of popular balladry.[74]

In both these cases the basic tale may well have predated the advent of Protestantism and the press. However, not so the legend of the supernatural curse associated with the execution of the Marian martyr George Marsh, which Christina Hole recorded in her *Traditions and Customs of Cheshire* in 1937. According to her source, his ghost had haunted the house in 1732 and his bloodstained footprint remained on the stones of Smithills Hall, oozing occasionally.[75] Examples such as this underline the difficulty and the futility of trying to disentangle oral and written tradition and reinforce recent suggestions that what should be stressed instead is their interdependence – their 'mutual infusion' and 'the constant process of osmosis' between the two media.[76] They also provide intriguing evidence of a curious syncretism between older cultural patterns and distinctively post-Reformation concerns and preoccupations.

How, then, should we interpret the stories of God's judgements which we have been exploring? Should we follow Ronald Hutton's lead and, in a candid re-application of the theory of survivals, see the traces of late medieval Catholic belief which can be detected in these tales as evidence of the adaptability with which English society responded to the challenges presented by the Protestant Reformation? Together with liturgical rituals which reproduced themselves as festive customs and pastimes after they had been driven out of formal religion, might they not provide us with insight into processes which helped to ease the ideological upheavals of the era – processes to which the clergy, displaying 'a canny sense of priorities', turned a blind eye? Hutton interprets the very existence of such stories and practices not as an index of rejection of and resistance to the religious revolution, but as a testament to its ultimate acceptance. But he may perhaps take too little account of the complex processes by which the folklore collections which are his quarry came about.[77]

Here the work of Bob Scribner provides a valuable corrective. For Scribner, such stories were all too often 'forms of downward mediation by educational and literate elites' – like German legends of incombustible Luther, the work of zealous pastors desperate to make an impression on a populace which had so far proved rather unreceptive to the Protestant Gospel. According to his anlaysis, these folktales were not Catholic survivals rooted in the ignorance of rural mentalities, but part of an ecclesiastical programme for the 'reform of popular culture'. Creatively assimilated to pre-existing narrative types, they represented a highly imaginative attempt to hijack pre-Reformation culture as a vehicle for confessional and evangelical propaganda, an ingenious weapon in the politics of religious confessionalization – but one which may only have had minimal impact. They were, in short, invented traditions.[78]

In the case of cautionary tales, it may be most fruitful to combine aspects of both these models – to recognize the element of conscious clerical appropriation and composition at work, but also to acknowledge the effects of a more organic process of 'recontextualization' by which central components of medieval culture were spontaneously rehabilitated in a reformed guise.[79] From whichever angle they are analysed, these anecdotes of providential justice shed light on the continuities which both mitigated and facilitated the cultural disjunctures which followed in the wake of the English Reformation. They also underline the role which oral communication, in conjunction with writing and print, played in the creation and consolidation of a collective Protestant outlook.

III

In conclusion, it is time that historians set aside the lingering assumption that the Reformation dealt a death blow to oral tradition and gave due credit to the ways in which, at least in the short term, it served to revitalize it, though not in an entirely pure or autonomous form. As we have seen, despite its polemical denigration of the 'unwritten verities' which underpropped the ramshackle edifice that was Roman Catholicism, Protestantism ended up begetting a kind of folklore of its own – a collection of edifying legends whose structure and character owed almost as much to verbal as they did to literary transmission, and whose circulation attests, directly and indirectly, to the vigour and vitality of oral culture in early modern England.

It might be added, by way of a coda, that the Reformation acted as a stimulus to orality in a second and somewhat paradoxical sense. Reduced to the status of a proscribed religious minority and deprived of access to the mainstream press, Catholicism made ingenious use of ephemeral speech as 'a supple and evasive means of popularising dissident ideas'. It proved, as Alison Shell compellingly argues, 'exceptionally willing to exploit orally transmissible media'.[80] Just as stories of the supernatural judgements visited upon popish persecutors had assisted in sustaining the morale of secret Protestant congregations in the mid-1550s, so did tales of the terrible punishments which overtook heretics help to strengthen the solidarity of the Elizabethan recusant community and foster a cohesive sense of confessional identity. Disseminated orally along the Catholic underground and subtly remoulded each time they were told, accounts of hangmen driven stark staring mad, of Protestant ministers consumed by disgusting diseases, and of presiding judges who suffered fatal heart attacks were eventually recorded in writing by secular and Jesuit priests and incorporated, sometimes only after several generations, in printed martyrologies.[81] But their initial diffusion by word of mouth surely only served to cement the paradigm with which we began. Denounced as 'godly frauds' and 'meere Canterburie tales' by Protestant propagandists, they too contributed to forging a damning and enduring link between the spoken word and 'popish superstition'.[82]

NOTES

I am grateful to Jonathan Barry, Patrick Collinson, Julia Crick, Alison Shell and the members of the Early Modern Research Seminar at the University of Leicester for their helpful comments on earlier versions of this essay.

1 See, among others, Walter J. Ong, *Orality and Literacy: the Technologizing of the Word* (London and New York: Methuen, 1982); Keith Thomas, 'The Meaning of Literacy in Early Modern England', in Gerd Baumann (ed.), *The Written Word: Literacy in Transition* (Oxford: Clarendon Press, 1986), 97–131 (quotation at p. 113); D. R. Woolf, 'Speech, Text, and Time: the Sense of Hearing and the Sense of the Past in Renaissance England', *Albion*, 18: 2 (1986), 159–93; Tessa Watt, *Cheap Print and Popular Piety, 1550–1640* (Cambridge: Cambridge University Press, 1991); Adam Fox, *Oral and Literate Culture in England 1500–1700* (Oxford: Oxford University Press, 2000).

2 Henry Bradshaw, *The Life of Saint Werburge of Chester*, ed. Carl Horstmann, Early English Text Society, OS, 88 (London: Trübner, 1887), 131.

3 For example, on the title page of the Great Bible (1539 and subsequent editions), and in an illustration contrasting 'The night of Popish superstition' with 'The returne of the Gospells light' included in Michael Sparke's *The crums of comfort* (London, 1628 edn), facing sig. A7r.

4 John Foxe, *Acts and Monuments*, ed. S. R. Cattley, 8 vols (London: Seeley, Burnside & Seeley, 1853–59), III. 720.

5 George Swinnock, *The Christian mans calling ... the second part* (London, 1663), 22.

6 John Aubrey, 'Remaines of Gentilisme and Judaisme', in *Three Prose Works*, ed. John Buchanan-Brown (Fontwell, Sussex: Centaur Press, 1972), 290.

7 See Christopher Hill, 'Puritans and "The Dark Corners of the Land"', *Transactions of the Royal Historical Society*, 5th series, 13 (1963), 77–102; Christopher Haigh, 'Puritan Evangelism in the Reign of Elizabeth I', *English Historical Review*, 92: 362 (1977), 30–58.

8 George Gifford, *A briefe discourse of certaine pointes of the religion, which is among*

the common sort of Christians, which may be termed the countrie divinitie (London, 1581); Arthur Dent, *The plaine mans path-way to heaven* (London, 1601).

9 I am grateful to Alison Shell for permitting me to read and cite parts of her forthcoming monograph for Cambridge University Press, which explores the interconnections between post-Reformation English Catholicism, anti-Catholicism and orality. This section is greatly indebted to her insights.

10 William Perkins, *A reformed Catholike: or, a declaration shewing how neere we may come to the present Church of Rome in sundrie points of religion* (Cambridge, 1604), 142.

11 See George H. Tavard, *Holy Writ or Holy Church: the Crisis of the Protestant Reformation* (London: Burns & Oates, 1959); Alister McGrath, *The Intellectual Origins of the European Reformation* (Oxford: Blackwell, 1987), ch. 5; Peter Marshall, 'The Debate over "Unwritten Verities" in Early Reformation England', in Bruce Gordon (ed.), *Protestant History and Identity in Sixteenth-century Europe* (Aldershot: Ashgate, 1996), I. 60–77. For key discussions, see Perkins, *Reformed Catholike*, 122–43; Antony Wootton, *A defence of M. Perkins booke, called A reformed Catholike* (London, 1606), 399–404; Francis Bunny, *Truth and falshood: or, a comparison betweene the truth now taught in England, and the doctrine of the Romish church* (London, 1595), fos 1r–3v. On the Catholic side, a notable contribution was the Jesuit James Gordon Huntley's *A treatise of the unwritten word of God, commonly called traditions* ([St Omer] 1614), which drew on Cardinal Robert Bellarmine's *Disputationum ... de controversis Christianae fidei* (Ingolstadt, 1601).

12 Perkins, *Reformed Catholike*, 140.

13 George Gifford, *A dialogue between a papist and a protestant, applied to the capacitie of the unlearned* (London, 1582), 13.

14 George Abbot, *The reasons which doctour Hill hath brought, for the upholding of papistry ... unmasked* (Oxford, 1604), 303; Bunny, *Truth and falshood*, fo. 2r.

15 As noted by Richard Bernard, *Rhemes against Rome* (London, 1626), 34.

16 Abbot, *Reasons*, 304; William Middleton, *Papisto-mastix, or the Protestants religion defended* (London, 1606), 40; Wootton, *Defence*, 428–9.

17 *The Sermons of Edwin Sandys*, ed. John Ayre, Parker Society (Cambridge: Cambridge University Press, 1842), 14–15 and 13 respectively; Richard Hooker, *The lawes of ecclesiastical politie* (London [1594]), bk I. ch. 13; Joseph Hall, *The olde religion: a treatise, wherin is laid downe the true state of the difference betwixt the reformed, and Roman church* (London, 1628), 167.

18 Josias Nicholls, *Abrahams faith: that is, the olde religion* (London, 1602), 208.

19 Richard Sheldon, *A survey of the miracles of the church of Rome, proving them to be antichristian* (London, 1616), 34, 316, and passim; J[ohn] H[arvey], *A discoursive probleme concerning prophesies* (London, 1588), 68–9.

20 Reginald Scot, *The discoverie of witchcraft* (London, 1584), bk IVI. ch. II; William Lambarde, *A perambulation of Kent* (Chatham, W. Burrill, 1826 edn; [1576]), quotations and citations at 276, 221, 281, 204–5, 324–6, 276 respectively.

21 Eric Hobsbawm and Terence Ranger (eds), *The Invention of Tradition* (Cambridge: Cambridge University Press, 1983).

22 For earlier manifestations of this theme, see Julia M. H. Smith, 'Oral and Written: Saints, Miracles and Relics in Brittany, *c.* 850–1250', *Speculum*, 65 (1990), 309 and 309–43, passim. I owe this reference to my colleague Julia Crick. In addition to the forthcoming work of Alison Shell (see n. 9), see also David Vincent, 'The Decline of the Oral Tradition in Popular Culture', in Robert D. Storch (ed.),

Popular Culture and Custom in Nineteenth-century England (London-Canberra, Croom Helm, 1982), 21–4; and idem, *Literacy and Popular Culture: England 1750–1914* (Cambridge: Cambridge University Press, 1989), 5–6.

23 Sandys, *Sermons*, 18; Udall quoted in Fox, *Oral and Literate Culture*, 175.

24 For subtle discussions of the complex nature and effects of these shifts, see Adam Fox, 'Custom, Memory and the Authority of Writing', in Paul Griffiths, Adam Fox and Steve Hindle (eds), *The Experience of Authority in Early Modern England* (Basingstoke: Macmillan, 1996), 89–116; Richard J. Ross, 'The Memorial Culture of Early Modern English Lawyers: Memory as Keyword, Shelter, and Identity, 1560–1640', *Yale Journal of Law and the Humanities*, 10 (1998), 229–326; Andy Wood, 'Custom and the Social Organisation of Writing in Early Modern England', *Transactions of the Royal Historical Society*, 6th series, 9 (1999), 257–69; idem, *The Politics of Social Conflict: the Peak Country*, 1520–1770 (Cambridge: Cambridge University Press, 1999), 150–62.

25 See Barbara Shapiro, *Probability and Certainty in Seventeenth-century England* (Princeton, NJ: Princeton University Press, 1985), ch. 5; D. R. Woolf, 'The "Common Voice": History, Folklore and Oral Tradition in Early Modern England', *Past and Present*, 120 (1988), 26–52; Adam Fox, 'Remembering the Past in Early Modern England', *Transactions of the Royal Historical Society*, 6th series, 9 (1999), 233–56.

26 See Keith Thomas, 'Age and Authority in Early Modern England', *Proceedings of the British Academy*, 62 (1976), 233–6, 246–8.

27 'The Credibility of Humane Testimony', in *The Philosophical Transactions and Collections [of the Royal Society] to the End of the Year MDCC. Abridged and Disposed under General Heads*, 4th edn (London, 1731), III. 662–5. For the displacement of 'traditional' by 'experimental knowledge', see Keith Thomas, *Religion and the Decline of Magic* (Harmondsworth: Penguin, 1973), 509–14, 771–2, 793–4, and Jonathan Barry, 'Introduction: Keith Thomas and the Problem of Witchcraft', in Jonathan Barry, Marianne Hester and Gareth Roberts (eds), *Witchcraft in Early Modern Europe: Studies in Culture and Belief* (Cambridge: Cambridge University Press, 1996), 28.

28 Woolf, '"Common Voice"', 47, 48.

29 W. J. Thoms in *The Athenaeum* (22 August 1846), 862–3.

30 For instance, Peter Burke, *Popular Culture in Early Modern England* (London: Wildwood House, 1978), esp. 281–3; Thomas, *Religion and the Decline of Magic*, 797–8.

31 Thomas Becon, *The reliques of Rome* (London, 1563); Phillip Stubbes, *The anatomie of abuses* (London, 1583).

32 Thomas Browne, *Pseudodoxia epidemica: or, enquiries into very many received tenets, and commonly presumed truths* (1646), in *The Major Works*, ed. C. A. Patrides (Harmondsworth: Penguin, 1977), 178; Henry Bourne, *Antiquitates Vulgares or the Antiquities of the Common People* (Newcastle, 1725), xii.

33 John Brand, *Observations on the Popular Antiquities of Great Britain*, ed. and enlarged by Henry Ellis, 3 vols (London: Bell, 1890 edn), I. xi.

34 For a useful survey, see Richard M. Dorson, *The British Folklorists: A History* (London: Routledge & Kegan Paul, 1968), quotation at p. 39.

35 See, for instance, Thomas Laqueur, 'The Cultural Origins of Popular Literacy in England 1500–1850', *Oxford Review of Education*, 2: 3 (1976), 255–75; Vincent, 'The Decline of the Oral Tradition'; Jonathan Barry, 'Literacy and Literature in

Popular Culture: Reading and Writing in Historical Perspective', in Tim Harris (ed.), *Popular Culture in England, c. 1500–1850* (Basingstoke: Macmillan, 1995), 69–94.

36 Stith Thompson, *The Folktale* (Berkeley, CA: University of California Press, 1977), 180.

37 For a helpful discussion of these trends, see Ruth B. Bottigheimer, 'Fairy Tales, Folk Narrative Research and History', *Social History*, 14: 3 (1989), 343–57.

38 See, in particular, R. W. Scribner, 'Oral Culture and the Diffusion of Reformation Ideas', reprinted in his *Popular Culture and Popular Movements in Reformation Germany* (London and Ronceverte: Hambledon Press, 1987), 47–69; Richard Gawthrop and Gerald Strauss, 'Protestantism and Literacy in Early Modern England', *Past and Present*, 104 (1984), 31–55; Patrick Collinson, 'Elizabethan and Jacobean Puritanism as Forms of Popular Religious Culture', in Christopher Durston and Jacqueline Eales (eds), *The Culture of English Puritanism, 1560–1700* (Basingstoke: Macmillan, 1996), 32–57. The other half of the equation – the link between Catholicism and hostility to print – has also been questioned: see my '"Domme Preachers"? Post-Reformation English Catholicism and the Culture of Print', *Past and Present*, 168 (2000), 72–123.

39 These stories were recited in numerous publications in the period, as cited below.

40 See Bob Scribner, 'The Reformation, Popular Magic and the "Disenchantment of the World"', *Journal of Interdisciplinary History*, 23: 3 (1993), 475–94; idem, 'Reformation and Desacralisation: From Sacramental World to Moralised Universe', in R. Po-Chia Hsia and R. W. Scribner (eds), *Problems in the Historical Anthropology of Early Modern Europe*, Wolfenbütteler Forschungen, 78 (Wiesbaden: Harrassowitz Verlag, 1997), 75–92; and my *Providence in Early Modern England* (Oxford: Oxford University Press, 1999), esp. ch. 2, which is a fuller discussion of the genre of judgement tales.

41 John Foxe, 'The severe punishment of God upon the persecutors of his people and enemies to his word', appended to *Acts and Monuments*, vol. VIII; [Henry Burton] *A divine tragedie lately acted, or, a collection of sundry memorable examples of Gods judgements upon sabbath breakers, and other like libertines* ([Amsterdam], 1636); Samuel Clarke, *A mirror or looking glasse both for saints and sinners* (London, 1656); William Turner, *A compleat history of the most remarkable providences, both of judgement and mercy* (London, 1697). Nehemiah Wallington's collections of judgements can be found in his notebooks: British Library, Sloane MS 1457 and Add. MS 21,935; Folger Shakespeare Library, Washington, DC, MS V.a.436. Edward Burghall, 'Providence Improved', printed in T. Worthington Barlow, *Cheshire: Its Historical and Literary Associations* (Manchester: Burge & Perrin, 1852), 150–89. Richard Burton [Nathaniel Crouch], *Admirable curiosities, rarities, and wonders, in England, Scotland, and Ireland* (London, 1682); idem, *Wonderful prodigies discovered in above three hundred memorable historys* (London, 1682). Thomas Beard, *The Theatre of Gods Judgments* (London, 1597; 1612; 1631). The 1648 edition was augmented with a *Second part* compiled by Thomas Taylor. All subsequent references are to the 1631 edition.

42 On exempla, see Frederic Tubach, *Index Exemplorum: a Handbook of Medieval Religious Tales* (Helsinki: Suomalainen Tiedeakatemia Akademia Scientiarum Fennica, 1969); Jean-Claude Schmitt (ed.), *Prêcher d'examples: récits de prédicateurs du moyen âge* (Paris, 1985); Claude Brémond, Jacques Le Goff and

Jean-Claude Schmitt, *L'Exemplum. Typologie des sources du moyen âge occidental* (Turnhaut, 1982); Aron Gurevich, *Medieval Popular Culture: Problems of Belief and Perception*, trans. J. M. Bak and P. A. Hollingsworth (Cambridge and Paris: Cambridge University Press and Editions de la Maison des Sciences de l' omme, 1988), ch. 1. For continental Protestant exempla collections, see the essays by E. H. Rehermann and H. Schade in Wolfgang Brückner (ed.), *Volkserzählung und Reformation* (Berlin: Erich Schmidt Verlag, 1974).

43 For the Lincolnshire swearer, see Phillip Stubbes, *Two wunderfull and rare examples* (London [1581]) and the variant in Richard Whitford, *A werke for housholders* (London [1531?]), sigs C3v–C4r. For the dog-headed baby, see Beard, *Theatre of Gods Judgments*, 210, who cited it from a Lutheran exempla collection. It can also be found in Tubach, *Index Exemplorum*, no. 646.

44 Edmund Bicknoll, *A swoord agaynst swearyng* (London, 1579), fo. 36r–v; Beard, *Theatre*, 178, citing John Stow, *The chronicles of England, from Brute unto this present yeare of Christ* (London, 1580), 1185.

45 Taylor, *Second part of the Theatre*, 94. I am grateful to the Burke Library of Union Theological Seminary, New York, for permitting me to read and cite its copy of this rare tract.

46 For the ballad and pamphlet versions, see *A most wonderful and sad judgement of God upon one Dorothy Mattley* (London [1661?]); J. C., *A warning for swearers. By the example of God's judgments upon a man born ... in Staffordshire, who had stolen a bible* (London [*c.* 1677–86?]); *Strange News from Stafford-shire; or, a dreadful example of divine justice* (London, [*c.* 1677]); *Strange and true news from Staffordshire* (London, 1677). The Duncalf case also generated a sermon published by the local rector, Simon Ford, *A discourse concerning God's judgments, which was published with a narrative by J. Illingworth, Concerning the man whose hands and legs lately rotted off* ... (London, 1678). These cases are cited in Clarke, *Mirror* (1671 edn), 510; Turner, *Compleat history*, pt I. ch. 104, 15–16.

47 For a discussion of this genre, see Walsham, *Providence*, 33–51.

48 Foxe, *Acts and Monuments*, vii. 53 and 38 respectively. Foxe's Victorian editor Cattley, replaced the original vivid description of the bishop's condition with the euphemism 'a disgraceful disease': see Warren W. Wooden, *John Foxe* (Boston, MA: Twayne Publishers, 1983), 117–19. On Foxe's sources, see also T. Freeman, 'Notes on a Source for John Foxe's Account of the Marian Persecution in Kent and Sussex', *Historical Research*, 67: 163 (1994), 203–11.

49 Samuel Ward, *Woe to drunkards* (London, 1622), 21.

50 Beard, *Theatre of Gods Judgment*, 208.

51 Burghall, 'Providence Improved', 153.

52 BL, Sloane MS 1457, fos 6r, 5v, 19v.

53 Foxe, *Acts and Monuments*, iv, 127–8.

54 For Mede, British Library, Harleian MS 389, fo. 239v, and cf. fos 188r, 243v, 266r. For Yonge, British Library, Add. MS 35, 331, fo. 59v, where he questions a report of a woman bitten by an adder after collecting foliage to decorate a maypole.

55 See, for example, *A true and most dreadfull discourse of a woman possessed with the devil* (London [1584]), sig. A3r, and T. I., *A miracle, of miracles. As fearefull as ever was seene or heard in the memorie of man ... sent by divers credible witnesses to be published in London* (London, 1614). The witnesses are listed on sig. B3r.

56 Burton, *Divine tragedie*, 3–4.

57 *The Winthrop Papers*, ed. W. C. Ford *et al.*, 6 vols (Boston, MA: Massachusetts Historical Society, 1929–92), III. 400.
58 Trundle's *A miracle, of miracles* is a case in point: it was an updated version of *A true and most dreadfull discourse of a woman possessed* (both cited n. 55).
59 See Thomas Freeman, 'Fate, Faction and Fiction in Foxe's Book of Martyrs', *Historical Journal*, 43: 3 (2000), 601–23. William Vaughan, *The spirit of detraction* (London, 1611), sig. *1v.
60 In such works as John Vicars, *A looking-glasse for malignants* (London, 1643).
61 Cambridge University Library, MS Dd. 3.64, fos 136r–v, 139v; Increase Mather, *An essay for the recording of illustrious providences* (Boston, 1684), Preface.
62 Notable discussions include Jan Vansina, *Oral Tradition: A Study in Historical Methodology*, trans. H. M. Wright (London: Routledge & Kegan Paul, 1961); Paul Thompson, *The Voice of the Past: Oral History* (Oxford: Oxford University Press, 1988 edn), esp. chs 4–5; David Henige, *Oral Historiography* (London: Longman, 1982); John Tosh, *The Pursuit of History: Aims, Methods and New Directions in the Study of Modern History* (London and New York: Longman, 1991), ch. 10; Gwyn Prins, 'Oral History', in Peter Burke (ed.), *New Perspectives on Historical Writing* (Cambridge: Polity Press, 1991), 114–39.
63 For the role of print in fixing and transforming oral tradition, see Ruth Finnegan, *Literacy and Orality: Studies in the Technology of Communication* (Oxford: Blackwell, 1988) and, on early modern England, Fox, 'Remembering the Past'.
64 Hayden White, 'The Value of Narrativity in the Representation of Reality', in W. J. T. Mitchell (ed.), *On Narrative* (Chicago, IL: University of Chicago Press, 1981), 13–14.
65 A number of scholars have recently analysed legal documents in this light: Natalie Zemon Davis, *Fiction in the Archives: Pardon Tales and their Tellers in Sixteenth-century France* (Cambridge: Polity Press with Basil Blackwell, 1988); Laura Gowing, *Domestic Dangers: Women, Words and Sex in Early Modern London* (Oxford: Clarendon Press, 1996), 52–8 and ch. 7; Tim Stretton, *Women Waging Law in Elizabethan England* (Cambridge: Cambridge University Press, 1998), 18–19 and ch. 8.
66 *The lamenting lady* (London [1620?]); T[homas] B[edford], *A true and certaine relation of a strange-birth* (London, 1635), 12.
67 For one pictorial broadside, which includes three of these four examples, see *The theatre of Gods judgements. Or, the vialls of wrath poured out upon obstinate and resolute sinners* (London, [1680?]). For ballads as the vehicles of post-Reformation tradition, see Watt, *Cheap Print*, 122–5.
68 John Bunyan, *The Life and Death of Mr Badman Presented to the World in a Familiar Dialogue between Mr Wiseman and Mr Attentive*, ed. James F. Forrest and Roger Sharrock (Oxford: Clarendon Press, 1988), 32–3.
69 There were two prose versions of Spira's death: Matteo Gribaldi, *A notable and marveilous epistle* (London, 1550 [and 1570?]) and Nathaniel Bacon, *A relation of the fearefull estate of Francis Spira* (London, 1638). A ballad was entered in the Stationers' Register on 15 June 1587; the story was also included in Beard, *Theatre of Gods Judgment*, 73–4, and referred to by numerous other writers. The second Spira appeared in 1693, followed by *Spira Respirans* (1695), *A true second Spira* (1697), and *The third Spira* (1724). See also Michael MacDonald, 'The Fearefull Estate of Francis Spira: Narrative, Identity, and Emotion in Early Modern England', *Journal of British Studies*, 31: 1 (1992), 32–61; idem and Terence

Murphy, *Sleepless Souls: Suicide in Early Modern England* (Oxford: Clarendon Press, 1990), 39–40, 67–9; M. A. Overell, 'The Exploitation of Francesco Spiera', *Sixteenth Century Journal*, 26: 3 (1995), 619–37.

70 See, e.g., Turner, *Compleat history*, pt I. ch. 107. Elisabeth van Houts has noticed a similar process at work in medieval histories: see 'Genre Aspects of the Use of Oral Information in Medieval Historiography', in B. Frank, T. Haye and D. Tophinke (eds), *Gattungen mittelalterlicher Schriftlichkeit* (Tübingen: Gunter Narr Verlag, 1998), 305.

71 Thomas Percy, *Reliques of Ancient English Poetry*, 3 vols (Edinburgh: Nichol, 1858 [1765]); F. J. Child, *English and Scottish Popular Ballads*, 5 vols (New York: Cooper Square, 1965 [1882–98]).

72 R. S. Thomson, 'The Development of the Broadside Ballad Trade and its Influence on the Transmission of English Folk-songs', unpublished PhD dissertation (Cambridge University, 1974); Margaret Spufford, 'The Pedlar, the Historian and the Folklorist: Seventeenth Century Communications', *Folklore*, 105 (1994), 20–1. Katharine M. Briggs, *A Dictionary of British Folk-tales in the English Language*, 4 vols (London: Routledge & Kegan Paul, 1970).

73 The ballad, entitled *A warning for fayre maides by thexample of Jarmans wyfe of Clifton*, was entered in the Stationers' Register on 8 June 1603, and reprinted consistently throughout the seventeenth century and beyond. See Briggs, *Dictionary*, pt B, I. 449–50 and 577–8, 586–7 for variants. 'The Suffolk Miracle' was printed in Child, *English and Scottish Popular Ballads*, V. 66 (no. 272).

74 *The Norfolk Gentleman, his last will and testament* appears to have been first published in 1595 and appeared repeatedly thereafter. Briggs, *Dictionary*, pt A, II. 390–1; and pt B, II. 162, for a Yorkshire variant based on a 1706 chapbook. Robert Yarrington, *Two Lamentable Tragedies* (London, 1601). The story appeared in Percy's *Reliques*, III. 140–7 and Joseph Jacobs, *More English Fairy Tales* (London: D. Nutt, 1894), 111.

75 Christina Hole, *Traditions and Customs of Cheshire* (London: Williams & Norgate, 1937), 206.

76 Fox, 'Remembering the Past', 233; Smith, 'Oral and Written', 311. See also P. R. Coss, 'Aspects of Cultural Diffusion in Medieval England: the Early Romances, Local Society and Robin Hood', *Past and Present*, 108 (1985), 35–79.

77 Ronald Hutton, 'The English Reformation and the Evidence of Folklore', *Past and Present*, 148 (1995), esp. 115–16.

78 Bob Scribner, 'Is a History of Popular Culture Possible?', *History of European Ideas*, 10: 2 (1989), 177, 179; idem, 'Luther Myth: A Popular Historiography of the Reformer' and 'Incombustible Luther: the Image of the Reformer in Early Modern Germany', both reprinted in idem, *Popular Culture and Popular Movements in Reformation Germany* (London and Ronceverte: Hambledon Press, 1987), esp. 320–2, 352–3.

79 For 'recontextualization', see James Fentress and Chris Wickham, *Social Memory* (Oxford: Blackwell, 1992), 83–4 and ch. 2, passim.

80 See n. 9 above.

81 One late sixteenth-century collection of judgements in manuscript can be found in John Morris, *The Troubles of Our Catholic Forefathers Related by Themselves*, 3 vols (London: Burns & Oates, 1872–77), III. 57–9. Others were transcribed by Christopher Grene in the late seventeenth century and fed into Richard Challoner's *Memoirs of Missionary Priests* (1741–42). See Anne Dillon, *The Construction*

of Martyrdom in the English Catholic Community, 1535–1603 (Aldershot, Ashgate, 2002), ch. 2, on this process in relation to narratives of martyrdom.

82 Quotations from George Hakewill, *An answere to a treatise written by Dr Carier* (London, 1616), 26.

Chapter 7

The genealogical histories of Gaelic Scotland

Martin MacGregor

INTRODUCTION: CONTEXTS FOR THE GENRE

'Gaelic' genealogical history is a convenient term to use to represent a genre of history writing which flourished between the seventeenth and nineteenth centuries in the Scottish *Gàidhealtachd*, or Gaelic-speaking area. The genre consists of the histories of the specific clans to which their authors belonged or were connected; it employs English as its normal language, even though the authors were invariably Gaelic speakers; and it draws upon a variety of sources, both written and oral. The corpus is substantial but neglected, and this dictates the scope of my ambition. What follows is a survey which seeks to define, describe and explain the existence of the genre and to open it up to the detailed discussion and analysis it requires and deserves.

Any discussion of these texts must begin by acknowledging that, although they all have something to say about the history of the *Gàidhealtachd* in the medieval or later medieval era, in the form we now possess them they were written down much later. It follows that their treatment of the past can only be evaluated once we have placed them in their own present, broaching questions of authorship, language of composition, approach, sources and motives. The potential worth of such an exercise can swiftly be appreciated if we remind ourselves that, if we exclude formal documents such as the charters of the lords of the Isles,[1] then the indigenous contemporary written sources for the history of the Scottish *Gàidhealtachd* in medieval and later medieval times are sparse, particularly if Gaelic Ireland is invoked as a point of comparison.[2] In the case of the Gaelic historical tracts we find in Ireland, particularly those prose texts which date from the fourteenth to the sixteenth centuries, and are concerned to glorify a particular kindred, Scotland has none at all.[3] In these circumstances the Scottish historian can find some consolation, not merely in the fact that many of these Irish sources contain Scottish material,[4] but also in the remarkable outpouring of historical tracts in Gaelic Scotland after the mid-seventeenth century, and in the sources these embody. Interestingly, for all the continued historiographical activity represented by the output of Séathrún Céitinn (Geoffrey Keating, d. 1644?), An Dubhaltach MacFirBhisigh (d. 1671), Dáibhídh Ó Duibhgeannáin (d. 1696), and the 'Four Masters', there seems to be no contemporary Irish parallel to the Scottish genealogical histories.[5] But comparisons can certainly be made with the earlier Irish prose tracts just mentioned, and not just in terms of a common objective of kindred-glorification. We find 'gross distortions of time-scale as well as the introduction of international folk-motifs' in both the Irish tracts and the Scottish histories.[6]

A central argument to be advanced is that the birth of the genealogical history genre was intimately linked to the death of what are commonly referred to as the learned orders or classes (Gaelic *aos dána*, literally 'folk of gifts') of Gaelic society. These were exclusively male castes dedicated to the pursuit of particular intellectual and artistic activities – poetry, history, law, music and medicine, as well as crafts such as metalwork, woodwork and monumental sculpture – on an hereditary and professional basis. From the thirteenth until the earlier eighteenth century, their patrons and paymasters were the Gaelic ruling elite in both Scotland and Ireland, and one of the benefits which this symbiotic relationship conferred upon the learned orders was the status of nobility. Of greatest social rank and influence were the poets, and we should note that poetry and history – here almost synonymous with genealogy – were very closely allied, to the extent that some learned lineages, and individual members thereof, espoused both disciplines. The poets were largely responsible for the creation of Classical Gaelic (also known as early Modern Irish), the artificial language used by the learned orders in general after *c.* 1200 as a vehicle for the 'classical tradition' of learning which they fostered.[7]

This classical tradition engendered a subtle and fluid interaction between orality and literacy in the spheres of preservation and transmission, composition and delivery, and education; but it could be argued that it was the spoken word that counted for most, particularly for public, aural consumption.[8] Pointers lie in the regular employment of dictation in the compilation of Classical Gaelic manuscripts, and in evidence that the act of writing down classical poetry was quite separate from, and subsequent to, the act of composition, so that we might wonder whether all poems had to achieve written status. This last is consistent with the fact that the primary function of the work of the classical poets and genealogists was its oral recitation before an elite audience at crucial points within the life-cycle of this society:

> Their work was to hand down to posterity the valorous actions, conquests, batles, skirmishes, marriages and relations of the predicessors by repeating and singing the same at births, baptisms, marriages, feasts and funeralls, so that no people since the curse of the Almighty dissipated the Jews took such care to keep their tribes, cadets and branches, so well and so distinctly separate.[9]

Gaelic high culture, propagated and regulated by the 'closed shop' of the learned orders, on behalf of a lay elite, in an artificial, non-vernacular language, must nevertheless have achieved a wider audience.[10] This may seem an unlikely claim, which moreover needs to be argued for theoretically rather than empirically, given our ignorance of popular culture within Gaelic Scotland in the late medieval era. However, pathways for transmission are easily identifiable. Downward social mobility was a hallmark of late medieval Gaelic society, and personnel within both learned and lay aristocratic lineages who lost status over time must have carried their cultural inheritance with them. The learned orders themselves were hierarchically organized, and the lower rungs of these ladders may have reached or penetrated the realms both of non-aristocratic society, and of vernacular speech. Highland Perthshire provides evidence for the mediating role of itinerants such as chapmen (*pacairean*), and the minstrel bands known as *Cliar Sheanchain*, 'as literary receptors and disseminators, operating between the spheres of high and popular culture, and across social classes'.[11]

Such brief contextualization may begin to explain the relevance of an analysis of a written genre to a book about the spoken word. The bond between the genealogical histories and a classical tradition which was both oral and literate, and which, although elite in origin, experienced wide social dispersal, makes these texts nodal points for the interaction of elite and popular culture, and of the spoken and written word. Deconstructing them can tell us much about the relationships among all these phenomena, and provides an object lesson in the potential complexities these relationships can engender. It will already be clear that classical material could have entered the histories via oral *and* written streams of transmission, and in fact we shall see that various springs may have fed the oral stream. However, we shall also see that classical learning did not constitute the sum total of the orally derived content of the histories, which also potentially embraced the traditions of non-classical groupings from different social levels, as well as fictional narratives. A crucial medium for all this oral information was the oral informant, sometimes named. Their identity and status, the chronological horizons of their knowledge, the likely origins of fictional narratives within the histories, the relationship between oral and written sources, and the question of cultural exchange, will all receive some preliminary attention in this chapter. It should be noted that the term 'lay' is used here to denote the non-classical (rather than non-clerical) component of Gaelic society. The same is true of 'vernacular', which is applied to both 'low' and 'high' non-classical culture and groupings. Our still severely limited knowledge of the social structure of the seventeenth-century Highlands dictates the employment in discussion of a very rudimentary distinction between aristocratic and non-aristocratic society.

Applying the criteria used below to define the genre, nearly fifty genealogical histories have so far been either securely or provisionally identified.[12] These texts rarely existed in isolation, but commonly spawned a number of variant recensions. This proliferation of manuscripts (for, whether original or variant, it is manuscripts we are dealing with) seems to be fundamental to the purpose and mechanics of the genre. The total number of histories and recensions which survive is at present unknown, but the scale seems impressive enough to suggest that there is a phenomenon at work here.[13]

Yet it is a phenomenon which has been severely unacknowledged and neglected, and this seems all the more curious given that the wider late seventeenth-century context into which it clearly fits, and the other elements which go to make up that context, have indeed been the subject of scholarly recognition and attention. The period saw a pronounced surge in antiquarian, collecting and publishing endeavours in the Scottish *Gàidhealtachd* in respect of literary, ethnographical and linguistic studies. The verse anthology known as the *Fernaig Manuscript* was compiled in Wester Ross *c.* 1688–93.[14] More significant for us are the fruits of collaboration emanating from a network whose existence is best revealed through the contact between Edward Lhuyd or Lhwyd and many of its members, notably Rev. Iain (John) Beaton. Lhwyd, the great Welsh polymath, Celtic scholar and keeper of the Ashmolean Museum, visited Scotland as part of his 'grand tour' of the Celtic countries undertaken between 1697 and 1701. Beaton, the minister–physician from the Isle of Mull, was his chief Scottish informant.[15] In Kintyre Lhwyd met Eoghan (Hugh) MacLean, schoolmaster at Kilchenzie, who between 1690 and 1698 wrote Gaelic manuscripts containing heroic and romantic tales, poetry and two metrical tracts.[16] Rev. Raibeart (Robert) Kirk saw Bedell's Gaelic Bible, as adapted to Scottish needs, through the press in 1689–90, and completed *The Secret Commonwealth of Elves, Faunes and Fairies* in 1691, and a Gaelic vocabulary in 1702.[17] Kirk was assisted with Bedell's Bible by his friend, Rev. James Kirkwood, who was the ultimate source of the manuscript called *A Collection of Highland Rites and Customes,* perhaps written by Kirk, which was copied by Lhwyd *c.* 1699.[18] Beaton commented extensively on this manuscript for Lhwyd,[19] who made his copy from a copy of Kirkwood's manuscript in the possession of Sir Robert Sibbald, president of the Edinburgh Royal College of Physicians, and the first professor of medicine at Edinburgh University. Sibbald corresponded with Beaton about Highland customs, and motivated Màrtainn (Martin) Martin to undertake fieldwork into the natural and human past and present of the Western Isles which he published in 1703.[20] Lhwyd's stimulus also galvanized the antiquarian Rev. Robert Wodrow to seek information from Beaton on Highland history, language and folklore in 1701.[21] Another to pay homage to Beaton's learning was Rev. Daniel Campbell, who was appointed His Majesty's Historiographer in Scotland in 1700.[22]

Since this loose collaborative nexus clearly counted the history of the *Gàidhealtachd* among its preoccupations, we would naturally expect that its activities, and the birth and development of the genealogical history genre, were connected in terms both of root causes and personnel. Such an expectation is enhanced by the fact that some of the genealogical historians had Gaelic literary and linguistic interests. Rev. Seumas (James) Fraser, author of two histories, and a pivotal figure in the evolution of the genre, was also the author of 'Hibernilogia a volum of Irish [i.e. Gaelic] verse', and 'An Irish Dictionary'.[23] Dr Eachann (Hector) MacLean, who wrote a history of his own kindred *c.* 1734, also made a verse compilation.[24] Fraser was tapped by Lhwyd as a potential informant,[25] and further research may allow us to draw other genealogical historians into the wider web.

That the genealogical histories should be so neglected within the broader canvas of which they form so integral and conspicuous a part seems doubly odd given that Donald Gregory's *History of the Western Highlands and Islands of Scotland from* AD *1493 to* AD *1625*, first published in 1836, and arguably the *fons et origo* of modern scholarly historical writing on the late medieval *Gàidhealtachd*, drew extensively upon them.[26] Two explanations can be offered. Since Gregory wrote, a strong prejudice against these texts has surfaced occasionally within local and mainstream Scottish historical writing.[27] Superficially this is easy to understand, for their late date is only the most obvious problem these histories present as sources for the medieval and late medieval *Gàidhealtachd*. Secondly, the sheer scale of the phenomenon, and the consequent labour required to analyse it thoroughly, presents real difficulties. William Matheson's comment, relating to one particular kindred, is generally applicable:

> A thoroughgoing criticism of [MacKenzie] traditions should be based upon a detailed study of the various family histories and their recensions, showing how they are related to one another, and possibly to other similar works such as Sir Robert Gordon's *Genealogical History of the Earldom of Sutherland*. This would be a difficult undertaking, not only on account of the great number of MSS., but also because some of the more important of them, believed to be in private hands, would require to be traced.[28]

The scale of the undertaking is probably the prime reason why usage of the genealogical histories in our era has been restricted to the study of specific texts for specific purposes. Such piecemeal activity has had an impact nevertheless: one senses that the stock of the genealogical histories is now on the rise, thereby enhancing the need for a general appraisal. The key figure in the process of rehabilitation has been the late William Matheson. His groundbreaking series of studies demonstrates an acute awareness both of the pitfalls these works present to the unwary, and of the folly of ignoring them altogether. In discussing Alexander MacKenzie's *History of the MacKenzies*, essentially a conflation of various MacKenzie genealogical histories, Matheson comments: 'The resulting account of early clan history fails to carry conviction, but it does not follow that the traditions themselves are to be discarded. The need is for a new and more critical approach to them.'[29] Noting that these MacKenzie accounts are often in conflict with one another, he adds: 'Contradictions there are, but in a sense they inspire confidence – the confidence that we are dealing with genuine traditions, though considerably distorted and confused. We are thus left with the problem of trying to unravel this tangled skein of traditions with the help of such other sources of information as may be available'.[30]

Others who have followed in Matheson's footsteps are David Sellar, a feature of whose valuable series of studies of kindred origins has been the fruitful interplay between the genealogical content of genealogical histories and earlier genealogical sources, demonstrating in the process that the former do often contain a reliable genealogical core;[31] and John Bannerman, whose extensive use of genealogical histories in his contributions to *Late Medieval Monumental Sculpture in the West Highlands*[32] forms the basis of his following summation: 'it is surprising how often the narrative of the Clan Donald historians of the seventeenth century is confirmed by [late medieval] documentary evidence, and this despite the bias inherent in the fact that Hugh MacDonald, the Sleat *seanchaidh*, and the MacMhuirich authors of the *Book of Clanranald* were in the employ of the MacDonalds'.[33] More recently, Steve Boardman has demonstrated that traditional accounts of the Campbell acquisition of Lorn in 1470, preserved in part in manuscript histories of the Stewarts of Appin, and perhaps also the MacLarens of Balquhidder, are correct in asserting that that takeover was a much murkier affair than the bland character of the contemporary legal documents recording the conveyancing of this lordship would have us believe.[34]

DEFINING THE GENRE: DATE, AUTHORSHIP, LANGUAGE, SOURCES

I commence an overview of the genre by seeking to define it. 'Gaelic' genealogical histories are works of narrative prose composed in manuscript, typically in English, between the mid-seventeenth and mid-nineteenth centuries. Usually they take as their subject the history of a particular kindred, and are written by a member of that kindred, or an affiliate, of high social rank. As Gaels and aristocrats, our authors have certain access to oral, and likely access to written material in Gaelic. The multilingual competence of our authors enables them to draw upon, and to some degree to seek to synthesise, a range of sources which may include historical works originating in Lowland Scotland, England, continental Europe or the ancient world; documentary evidence, both published and unpublished; oral history in vernacular Gaelic; and material derived from the Classical Gaelic tradition.

Strict application of these criteria entails the exclusion of some works which fail to meet them all, although they are clearly related to the genre. I suggest, tentatively, that those texts which fail in part because they were all composed before the mid-seventeenth century can be divided into two broad types. The first are 'remotely related' precursors, which are sometimes exploited as sources by genealogical histories, but which differ from them on grounds of authorship and/or purpose as well as date. The *Ewill Troubles of the Lewes* is concerned with one specific episode, rather than the full span of kindred history.[35] *Ane Breve Cronicle of the Earlis of Ross,* the bulk of which predates 1615, has strong ecclesiastical concerns, which probably reflect its authorship, or a phase thereof.[36] Sir Robert Gordon's *Genealogical History of the Earldom of Sutherland* also falls on the grounds of date and authorship, and is in any case a work with its own distinctive approach and agenda.[37] The second are 'closely related' precursors, which I would subdivide into texts concerning the Campbells, and those concerning other clans. None of these last is known to have survived independently, and hence we know nothing of their sources, but they seem to have been genealogically-based histories of a specific kindred, normally written by a kindred member or affiliate. To this extent they have much in common with the genealogical histories, some of which use them as a ground or source type.[38]

The Campbell texts are particularly interesting. The *Black Book of Taymouth,* a eulogistic history of the Campbells of Glen Orchy, was commenced in 1598 by William Bowie, a Lowland servitor of that kindred.[39] 'Colvin's Genealogy of the Campbells', produced between 1650 and 1660, is not known to have survived independently, but was very influential, acting as a ground for several of the Campbell genealogical histories.[40] Its author, Alexander Colville, justice depute in Edinburgh from 1607 until 1664, may have completed the first draft of this text *c.* 1638; and may also be the author of *Information anent the Pedigree of the Noble and Antient House of Lochow* (1634).[41] These works differ from the genealogical histories in their Lowland authorship, but, for the 'Colville texts' at least, access to the Classical Gaelic tradition in its decline, and a willingness to put it in the same frame as documentary and chronicle evidence, provide crucial points of contact which may justify describing them as 'proto-genealogical histories'.[42]

Moving beyond the mid-seventeenth century, Màrtainn Martin's famous *Description of the Western Islands* is atypical in its subject matter, and is a published work.[43] The eighteenth century apparently saw the rise of a Scottish family history-writing industry, moulded by quasi-professional antiquarians such as George Crawfurd, William Buchanan of Auchmar and Walter MacFarlane. The texts relating to Highland lineages generated by this movement can be difficult to demarcate from the genealogical histories.[44] The former tend to be 'scholarly', almost wholly genealogical exercises, reliant upon printed histories and documentary evidence. They lack the genealogical histories' partisan and ideological edge, and the indigenous dimension created by the use of Gaelic classical and vernacular sources. I suspect that their authors usually have no close bond with the lineage concerned.

Vernacular history, or oral tradition in its unadulterated form, whether written down since the eighteenth century or tape-recorded in the twentieth century, fails primarily on the grounds not so much of date as of lack of variety or synthesis of source; it is a constituent of the genealogical histories, and not to be confused with them.[45] In like manner, there is a clutch of clan histories which we can rule out, partly because they are published works mainly of the later nineteenth century, and partly because their contents do not represent one 'pure' genealogical history, but syntheses of several such accounts, along with other material, such as fresh injections of oral tradition or documentary evidence.[46]

I now propose to comment in more detail on the main criteria of date, authorship, language, content and sources, before exploring the reasons for the birth of the genre. It should be borne in mind that the conclusions which follow may be subject to modification as further genealogical histories are uncovered. In terms of date, the main surge in the writing of these histories is between the mid-seventeenth century and *c.* 1720; and of this cohort, the bulge is before *c.* 1705.[47] Moreover, there is one example of a history written down between 1717 and 1722, but only after a prolonged gestation whose first phase consisted of the absorption and assimilation of oral sources. Alasdair (Alexander) Campbell, the author of the *Craignish History*, was born *c.* 1670, and 'when but a boy ... listened with a greedy ear to all the traditions, and poems of my countrymen', while one of his key oral informants died in the later 1680s.[48] Thus, Gaelic genealogical history is more a phenomenon of the later seventeenth than of the earlier eighteenth century; it virtually dies out between 1750 and 1800, undergoes a revival in the 1820s and 1830s, and produces two outlying instances in the 1860s, by the one author.

Under the social dispensation which was breaking down in the *Gàidhealtachd* by the seventeenth century, we can define the status of our authors, virtually to a man, as that of *daoin' uaisle* (noblemen) or higher. A number of them belonged to the ruling families of kindreds, or of branches of kindreds.[49] They also form a reasonably representative cross-section of the indigenous elite. Non-professional men – members of the ruling grades, and tacksmen – are the largest single grouping. They are closely followed by clergymen and lawyers, who dominate a professional sector which also includes representatives of the military and medicine. The MacMhuirichs provide the only clear-cut instance of authorship by members of the learned orders.[50]

Overwhelmingly, the histories are written in English or Scoto-English. A version of one specimen is in Latin,[51] and another is in the Classical Gaelic utilized primarily by the learned orders. Yet it is usually clear that the author was familiar with vernacular Gaelic at least, and sometimes we have specific statements to that effect. Seumas Fraser refers to 'our Irish [Gaelic] language',[52] and Alasdair Campbell to his 'knowledge ... of our country language, viz. the Irish as it is spoke in Argyleshire'.[53] Hence the substantial amount of Gaelic which these texts embody, and, since without exception it is rendered phonetically into an English-based orthography, it may constitute a valuable and untapped source for the study of Scottish Gaelic dialects in the early modern era.

This Gaelic matter can be classified under four headings. That of nomenclature embraces personal names – including *far-ainmean* (by-names) and *sloinnidhean* (pedigrees) – and place-names. The by-names and place-names are frequently tied to narratives of the events which supposedly gave rise to them. Nomenclature also embraces a healthy smattering of technical vocabulary, naturally resorted to where a ready English equivalent did not exist, which again could profitably be siphoned off for study in its own right. A term such as *léine-chrios* ('bodyguard') – used for example to describe the nature of the dependency of the MacRaes upon the MacKenzies[54] – is well enough known; but what of 'the artery called in Galic *strurossach*', also called 'the master vein in the foot', mentioned in connection with the death of MacDonald of Sleat at the siege of Eilean Donnain *c.* 1539;[55] or *airgiod cagainn*, a military levy being claimed in 1649?[56]

Secondly, where the histories contain reported speech, whether it be the statement of an individual, or conversations or exchanges involving more than one party, it is sometimes clear that our authors are following a Gaelic source, probably an oral informant. Often they simply translate or paraphrase this into English,[57] but on occasion the original is imported in part or in whole directly into the narrative. This is how the *Craignish History* describes the decision taken *c.* 1400 by Iain Anfhann, 'Weak John', to resign the whole lordship of Lochawe to his brother in exchange for other lands: 'It is told of this John when he declared his choice in presence of a great convention of friends, who were dividing the lands and disputing about the interest of the two brothers said *Togive dur skiggarick ... dar skaggarik bii an laggan beg sho agy fen*, i.e. end your jangling and wrangling I'll content myself with this little valley'.[58]

Thirdly, and clearly linked to our second category, the histories are liberally peppered with sayings or pieces of extempore verse which seem to have lodged themselves with proverbial force within the collective memory.[59] Here we remember Màrtainn Martin's observation on the Western Isles that 'the natives are generally ingenious and quick of apprehension ... several of both sexes have a gift of poesy, and are able to form a satire or panegyric *ex tempore*'.[60] Alasdair Campbell also alludes to 'extemporary rhymeing, a thing much in use among the Highlanders',[61] and provides representative instances of rhymes and proverbs in his *Craignish History*. One concerns the early fifteenth century, and a stratagem adopted by Raghnall mac Mhaol-Coluim (Ronald son of Malcolm) of the Craignish lineage to put an end to excessively heavy harvest obligations being imposed upon his tenants by the 'Baron MacIgeill':

> which gave rise to a byword well known among all the highlanders to this day which they commonly upbraid the reapers with, when they doe not bind as they cut down,
>
> Buan Ronill vic voal-Callum din Varon Macigeil
> Buan un Diu, agus ceangil a marich.
>
> That is to say, You give me such shearing as Ronald the son of Malcolm gave the Baron Mac Igeill, to witt shearing to day, and binding to morrow.[62]

Lastly, there is more formal Gaelic poetry.[63] A bridge between this and the extempore verse found within the last category perhaps exists in the form of the two quatrains which the *Sleat History* represents as having been composed spontaneously by the Earl of Mar in the aftermath of the battle of Inverlochy in 1431.[64] A number of fragments of classical verse are caught in the amber of the histories. The *MacLean History* gives 'The Beginning of Mac Vurich's Panegyrick on the MacLeans ...';[65] the *Sleat History* preserves a quatrain supposedly sung by the Irish harpist Diarmaid Ó Cairbre, in advance of his assassination of his patron Aonghas (Angus) Óg in 1490;[66] the *MacRae History* has a quatrain from an elegy on the death of MacDonald of Sleat *c.* 1539;[67] and, with respect to the death of Raghnall mac Mhaol-Coluim *c.* 1447/48, Alasdair Campbell comments:

> I heard ane elegant epitaph made upon him in the Irish language, they say compozd by his own harper, the last stanza of which being all I remember and is in English much to this purpose,
>
> Many a mournful, or sorrowful, white keirchieft matron is to be seen this day at Killmolrie, tearing their hair, bewailing the fall of the great Ronald in the bottom of deep water.[68]

The linguistic flavour, if not the language, of these texts is one factor which justifies our describing them as 'Gaelic'. Another is their content and structure. These are kin-based histories, according a primacy to genealogy which is usually manifest in the titles they bear, even in the case of more ambitious projects such as Seumas Fraser's 'Polichronicon seu Policratica Temporum; many Histories In One, or nearer, The True Genealogy of the

Frasers', whose preface begins, 'Genealogy and antiquity is the glory of a name or nation.'[69] Another work which alludes to a wider agenda, the *Craignish History*, commences as follows:

> As it is naturall for all men to have a byass or propensity chiefly to that which most nearly concerns themselves, and must own the same if they confess the truth, so I frankly acknowledge that my first desire to look into the abstruse secrets of antiquity, was principally founded on the desire I had of setting the storie of this branch of which I myself am a son in a true light, being a debt I think I indispensibly owe to posterity, which without arrogance or vanity I presume to say, there is not any of the present generation so well instructed to pay.[70]

Another mission statement to centre upon genealogy, although according it a role ostensibly counter to that avowed by Fraser, is that of Lachlann Macintosh of Kinrara, at the outset of his *Macintosh History*: 'For I have not set this task to myself by any means in order to parade the antiquity of the Mackintosh family, or of the honourable lineage from which it has sprung ... [but] that I may make clear to all Mackintoshes and Chattans, ignorant of their origin, the true knowledge of their descent'.[71] Even snippets such as these demonstrate a connection between genealogy and motive, and complexities in the conception of the role of the former, to which we shall return.

Besides content, genealogy also dictates structure. We see this in the pan-Gaelic grand design of the first part of the history in the *Red Book of Clanranald*, which begins with the coming of the Gaels to Ireland in the person of the sons of Míl, *c.* 1700 BC, and thereafter systematically narrows its focus from the stock which gave rise to Somerled or Somhairle (d. 1164) in Scotland, via the most important division of Somhairle's descendants, Clann Domhnaill, to the branch of the latter, Clann Raghnaill (the Clanranald), which employed those responsible for writing this history. In like manner, the *Sleat History* moves from Somhairle to Clann Domhnaill to the branch of the latter of most concern to the writer, namely Clann Uisdein (the MacDonalds of Sleat). The so-called *Invereshie Book Genealogy* has been dubbed 'virtually a manual on the anatomy of Clan MacPherson', devoting a section apiece to the descendants of the three brothers cited in its title, and within each section dealing first with the ruling lineage, and next with the various branches in the order of their coming into being.[72] The author of the *MacRae History* takes another approach: 'And here I am to begin the method I mean to follow, in the rest of this Genealogy, which is to treat of all the younger branches of the family first, and then of the eldest, as the root of another generation.'[73]

Classical Gaelic genealogists used the term *craobhsgaoileadh* 'tree-branching', to describe the depiction of a kindred through the methodical reconstruction of its descent lines, and this is an apt enough visual metaphor for the genealogical histories. To employ another, genealogy provides the skeleton upon which the histories are hung, and the vertebrae, joints and sinews by which they are articulated; in some cases they consist of little more than the skeleton itself. There are implications to be drawn as to how our historians conceive of history and approach its writing. The stages in a pedigree become the stepping stones by which the past is entered, and from which it is surveyed. By the same token, the kin imperative means that the dead remain embodied in the living; that the past is foreshortened, and made present. Hence the instinctive feeling for kin-based continuity which pervades the *mentalité* of our authors, and their texts. The *Sleat History* concludes its explanation as to how the twelfth century Maurice MacNeill earned the sobriquet *Mac an t-saoir*, 'From that time the posterity of Maurice are called MacIntyres (or Wright's sons) to this day'; treating of the later fourteenth century, it describes how Domhnall, son of Lachlann MacLean, 'got himself possessed of Ardgour, which his posterity enjoy to this day'; in connection with the Battle of Inverlochy in 1431 it mentions Alasdair Carach who 'held the lands of Lochabber, east of Lochy, and whose posterity are yet there'.[74] Of Gill-Adhamhnain, grandfather of Somhairle (d. 1164), the *Red Book of Clanranald* says, 'it was Gill-Adhamhnain who erected the monastery of Screen in Tireragh in County Sligo in the province of Connachht; and his name is commemorated there'.[75] Writing in the early eighteenth century of an offshoot of the Campbells of Craignish called Sliochd Thearlaich Dhuibh, who settled at Ardeonaig on south Loch Tayside, and whose origins he puts in the thirteenth century, Alasdair Campbell comments: 'A black and bloody head strong race they were, I have seen some of them, and are yet to be seen in that countrey ... the last famous chieftain ... before he dyed ... had time to send ... his beloved gun, as his last legacie to the house of Craiginsh ... which gun I saw, and had often in my hands ...'.[76]

I come now to consider sources, the use of a range of which I have made fundamental to my definition of the genre of genealogical history. In fact, the range and number of sources drawn upon is on occasion impressive, and there is also some evidence of sophistication with regard to awareness of their comparative value. Both Alasdair Campbell and Seumas Fraser include discussion of sources among their prefatory material, the latter's summation being as follows: 'For me to give in the particulars whence I have derived my information, knowing full well *quantus author tanta fides*, these may be referred to four heads. 1. Manuscripts and charters in our possession. 2. Church records and Records in publick offices. 3. Printed history. 4. Instructions receaved from the Bards, and nearest neighbours and allyes'.[77]

Fraser's analysis is reasonably representative of the genre as a whole, but I would extend it to six source types. The first, corresponding to Fraser's third, consists of printed works – historical, literary, philosophical or religious in substance, often synthetic in approach, and emanating from Lowland

Scotland, England, continental Europe or the ancient world. Staples are the sixteenth-century Scottish historians Hector Boece (*c.* 1470–1536) and George Buchanan (1506–82),[78] and the Bible, but it is clear that were a list of all such works to be compiled, it would be extensive. The topic clearly demands investigation in its own right.[79] For now I simply note that these works are used by our authors as means of contextualization, and this implies an intent to integrate their histories with Scottish and British history. A significant exception, at least as far as its pre-seventeenth-century content is concerned, is the *Red Book of Clanranald*, whose template is primarily pan-Gaelic.

Contextualisation of a more localized variety stems from the use our authors make of each other. At least as far as the pronounced surge of activity in the later seventeenth century is concerned, we appear to be dealing with a literary scene whose networks, friendships and rivalries engendered a hothouse, slightly incestuous atmosphere within which genealogical histories were bred almost as a self-perpetuating craze. Alexander Colville's lost 'Genealogy of the Campbells' formed the ground for *Ane Accompt of the Genealogie of the Campbells*; *Ane Accompt* was a source for both the *Craignish History* (which had independent access to Colville) and the *Auchinbreck History*.[80] Iain MacRae and Seumas Fraser, each the author of two histories, were the ministers of neighbouring parishes – Kirkhill and Dingwall – and close personal friends; Fraser dedicated his history of the Bissets and Frasers of Lovat 'to the Reverend his beloved Brother Master John MacRay parson of Dingwall'.[81] MacRae, or one of those who added to his *MacRae History*, had access to the MacKenzie history by Dr Seòras MacKenzie: Dr Seòras claims to have had six earlier MacKenzie histories available to him.[82] There was also a MacKenzie–Macintosh connection: Lachlann Macintosh of Kinrara and Murchadh MacKenzie of Ardross, both authors of Macintosh histories, each possessed copies of the *Applecross MS*, by Iain MacKenzie of Applecross.[83]

Thirdly, there is widespread use of published and unpublished documentary record. Unpublished material, usually deriving from the archive of the kindred to which the author is affiliated, is on occasion inserted more or less verbatim into the text.[84] The author of the *Sleat History* clearly had access to the charter chest of the MacDonalds of Sleat,[85] while Alasdair Campbell informs us: 'after my return to Scotland from studying the Laws abroad in the year 1706, the illustrious hero John present Duke of Argyll ordered me to sett in order and review his archives and charters, and the year following 1707, George Campbell of Craignish my brother now deceast put the same task in my hand as to his papers'.[86]

Some of the histories claim to rely on documentary sources no longer extant. The Matheson history written in 1838 made use of family papers of seventeenth-century provenance apparently now lost.[87] Seumas Fraser had access to records, including an annalistic compilation, maintained at the Valliscaulian Priory of Beauly,[88] and another chronicle, *Scriptum Bunchriviae*, 'bearing the exact date of the death of all our lords and gentlemen for 200 yeares, for by tradition among us there was a cell at Bunchrive [Bunchrew, near the church of Fernua, near Inverness] of heremits ... which book is now miscarried; the old Cumings at Inverness had it'.[89] Their preservation of such material clearly adds potential value to the histories concerned, but we need look no further than the alleged forging proclivities of Sir Seòras MacKenzie to be reminded that some records may be lost because they never existed in the first place.[90]

Fourthly, some of our authors draw upon those earlier manuscript works which I have suggested have affinities with the genealogical histories proper. Of the 'distantly related' category of precursor, *The Ewill Trowbles of the Lewes* is used by Iain MacKenzie of Applecross,[91] and Sir Robert Gordon's history was known to Seumas Fraser.[92] Of the 'closely related' category, the *Red Book of Clanranald* relies heavily upon a presumably earlier text for its pre-Civil Wars content, while both earlier MacKenzie histories are mentioned by Rev. Iain MacRae in the *Ardintoul MS*.[93] Lachlann Macintosh made use of 'three old manuscripts', by which 'the antiquity of the [Macintosh] family and their pedigree is testifyed'. That of Fearchar Macintosh, supposedly to be identified with the chief who was incarcerated in the castles of Edinburgh and Dunbar from 1495 to 1513, covered events down to *c.* 1496. That of 'a parson of Croy, called sir Andrew MacPhail', came down to *c.* 1550, and that of 'George Monro of Davachgartie [Davochcartie], who sometime dwelt in Connadge [Connage]', dealt more narrowly with four chiefships spanning *c.* 1496–*c.* 1550. Lachlann Macintosh goes out of his way to demonstrate that these works 'ought not to be look'd upon as fabulous and untrue', citing instances where their accuracy surpasses that of the late medieval Scottish historians John Mair (*c.* 1467–1550) and Hector Boece.[94] Fearchar's narrative was also available to Murchadh MacKenzie of Ardross, author of another of the Macintosh genealogical histories, the *Ardross MS*.[95]

Fifthly, and of particular interest from the perspective of this book, a number of our historians indicate their reliance upon oral sources. Sometimes this is a straightforward tapping of an individual for information concerning a specific episode occurring up to a century before,[96] but other informants provide a more profound and pervasive input. The brief, but consistent, general descriptions applied to them – 'several sensible old men of the last generation'; 'the most intelligent and best informed men yet alive'; 'the oldest and wisest, not only of my own, but of all our neighbours' families' – suggest that we are dealing with individuals whose reputation as oral historians derived from age and acumen.[97] Further deductions can be made from the more detailed information fortunately provided by two of our authors. In another of his many works, Sir Aeneas MacPherson of Invereshie, born *c.* 1644,[98] and writer of the *Invereshie Book Genealogy*, lists

> a few of those I hade at divers times the honour to discourse with of the rise and origine of most of the Highland families, as for instance, John Grant of Ballindalloch ... John Grant of Gartinmore, Grigor Grant of Achachiernach, and Sweine Grant of Gartinbeg, amongst the Grants. William McIntoshe of Kyllachie, Hector McIntosh of Connadge, and John McIntosh of Forter ... amongst the McIntoshes. Alexander Fraser, alias McKutcher, among the Frasers, and John McDonald (alias Lame) among the McDonalds, two of the greatest poets and genealogues in the Highlands. Mcpherson of Brecochie, Mcpherson of Phoyness, Thomas Mcpherson of Eterish, and James Mcpherson, grand-uncle to the deceast John Mcpherson of Invereshie, amongst the Mcphersons. John Robertson of Inverchroskie (alias the barron Reid), John Robertson of Faules ... Robertson of Fouet, amongst the Robertsons. Donald Shaw of Dalnafert, John Shaw of Geuslich, and Robert Shaw the Drover, amongst the Shaws. Robert Farquharson of Invercauld and Wardes, William Farquharson of Inverey, and James Farquharson of Camdell, amongst the Farquharsons.[99]

Insofar as individuals among these twenty-two informants have been identified, they are lay-aristocrats, members of the ruling lineages, or of the ruling families of cadet branches, of prominent kindreds in the eastern Highlands; and seem to belong to the first or second generations above Aeneas MacPherson, with dates of birth taking us back at least as far as the last quarter of the sixteenth century.[100]

Alasdair Campbell used five principal oral informants for his history of the Campbells of Craignish. Four of these were his own kin, their common ancestor being Alasdair's great-grandfather Raghnall Ruadh, *Am Baran Ruadh* of Barrichbeyan, said to have been born in 1555 and died in 1639. It was in Raghnall Ruadh's time, apparently, that his lineage succeeded to the chiefship of the Campbells of Craignish, the last three representatives of the previous ruling lineage all having died between 1537 and 1546.[101] As Alasdair Campbell points out, Raghnall Ruadh's father, Iain, 'who lived to a great age, even untill the said Ronald [Raghnall] was fourty years old, did overtake alive, and having lived within a mile of them after he came to mans age and estate might have conversed as certainly he did with the three last McDugalls of Craiginsh ...'.[102] Alasdair Campbell's fifth informant was a great-great-grandson of the last of this trio.

The typical oral informant of Alasdair Campbell and Aeneas MacPherson is thus revealed as a layman of noble status, whose knowledge of the history of a particular aristocratic lineage stemmed in part from his belonging to it. He is clearly distinct from the *seanchaidh* in its original and technical sense of a historian-cum-genealogist within the professional learned orders,[103] although his knowledge could well have benefited from the opportunities for contact with such historians which his status would have afforded him, and he – along with the authors of the genealogical histories – might be considered as their successor.[104] He is also distinct from the *seanchaidh* in its more modern sense of demotic storyteller, although he might be considered the forerunner, and perhaps in some cases was even the actual blood ancestor, of such storytellers.

Aeneas MacPherson and, particularly, Alasdair Campbell, are at pains to emphasize the reliability of these informants, and the reasons for it. MacPherson refers to his twenty-two informants as 'all of them men of sense and reputation, and most of them so very old that if they were not acquainted with Finlay More [Fionnlagh Mór, head of the Farquharsons, and said to have died at the battle of Pinkie in 1547[105]] himself, they were at least personally known to all his children, from whose account (which could not so properly be called tradition as a certain knowledge) ...'.[106] There may be some chronological exaggeration here but, as already noted, some of his informants gave MacPherson access to the oral memory as it existed *c.* 1600. The information supplied by Alasdair Campbell about the origins of his own informants enables him to demonstrate that he can tap into that memory even further back, in the early sixteenth century, and the era of the previous ruling lineage of the Campbells of Craignish, which had held that position from the early fifteenth century. So it is that his oral evidence can meet the test of the documentary record also available to him, leaving him bullish about the prospects for his history of his use of the two combined:

> Parchments are the best genealogists; yet I must say I have been often surprised to find how exactly, what these men abovementioned delivered agreed to a trifle with the records herein cited, and proves what I so justly asserted in the beginning of this introduction that no people have their history so exactly keept by tradition as the Highlanders ... it can be no surprize that as certain an account of their transactions and proceedings might be transmitted by tradition as by wryteing. But I have the last to fortify and support the first, which may make this account next to a demonstration.[107]

My sixth source type, material derived from the classical tradition of the learned orders, is also of special relevance, given its reliance upon both the written and the spoken word. Furthermore, it can be argued that access to this tradition, and the extent of dependence upon it, are benchmarks which we can use to define divisions and subdivisions within the overall genre of genealogical history.[108] From a classical perspective, the purest specimen is of course the history in the *Red Book of Clanranald*, the only example produced entirely under the aegis of the learned orders, and hence written in Classical Gaelic. For the MacMhuirich authors, purity extended naturally to their sources. The earlier part of the history, covering events prior to the Wars of the Three Kingdoms in the mid-seventeenth century,[109] draws upon annalistic compilations (relating to the lordship of the Isles and Clann Raghnaill, for the compilation of the latter of which at least the MacMhuirichs were presumably responsible[110]), classical poetry, genealogy, and material drawn from the synthetic history of the Gaels. There is no evidence of the use of formal documentary record, and the only trace of an external non-classical source is a measured and apostrophic dismissal of Buchanan.[111]

Possible classical authorship for the *Sleat History* has recently been mooted by John Bannerman, who has suggested that the 'Hugh MacDonald' sometimes associated with the text may have been one and the same as Aodh Beaton, a member of the North Uist branch of a professional kindred primarily associated with the practice of medicine.[112] It certainly looks as if the author had access to the classical tradition, for his views on the origins of the Beatons are identical with those given learned expression by this North Uist lineage,[113] while one of his sources is clearly an indigenous chronicle, albeit one whose chronology may mark it out as distinct from that of the MacMhuirichs.[114] Nevertheless, these two texts are very different animals. In its broad range of sources, haphazard organization, racy polemicism and unabashed partisanship, the *Sleat History* is much closer to, for example, the *Craignish History*. This points to the authorship of a committed amateur rather than a professional, and Captain Uisdean MacDonald of Paiblesgarry in North Uist, who has also been advanced as a candidate, and who belonged to the ruling lineage of the MacDonalds of Sleat and North Uist (*Clann Uisdein*) whose cause this text so conspicuously champions, surely fits the mould.[115]

The two major Campbell histories, *Ane Accompt of the Genealogie of the Campbells*, and *The Genealogical and Historicall Account of the Family of Craignish*, make explicit their reliance upon a genealogical core provided by the MacEwen professional lineage. They claim to have had access to this both in its original form, and via Alexander Colville, who 'revised these Genealogies as the McEunes [MacEwens] left them betwixt the years 1650 and 1660 and his Second Edition of them is it that goes by the name of Colvin's Genealogy of the Campbells'.[116] *Ane Accompt* was written between 1670 and 1676 by Raibeart Duncanson, minister of Campbeltown, 'assisted by several other good shenachies', and the ninth earl of Argyll.[117] If *seanchaidh* here bears its original technical meaning of professional historian,[118] then those involved cannot have been members of the by now defunct MacEwen lineage; likely candidates would include members of the MacLachlan learned kindred serving in the ministry in Argyll.[119]

The most cryptic allusion to the likely use of classical material is Seumas Fraser's citation of 'Instructions receaved from the Bards' as one of his source categories.[120] These 'bards' could be from his own locale in the eastern Highlands. But another possibility stems from his friendship with Iain MacRae. In his *MacRae History*, the latter says of the origins of that kindred:

> A more particular account might be had from such as conversed with and have known those historians and genealogists, such as Fergus MacRourie, Mildonich MacLean, etc., who were good scholars and acquainted with the manuscripts and records of Ireland, kept for giving an account of the tribes who came from Ireland to Scotland and became heads of families and chiefs of clans ...[121]

'Mildonich MacLean' we can identify as Maol-Domhnaich Ó Muirgheasáin,[122] who died *c.* 1662 as the head of the prominent lineage of poets and historians which served the MacLeans of Duart and the MacLeods of Dunvegan.[123] Iain MacRae also cites him as a source in his MacKenzie history, the *Ardintoul MS.*[124] 'Fergus MacRourie' is as yet unidentified.[125] It would appear that Iain MacRae did not have access to the knowledge of these men first-hand, but rather via intermediaries such as 'Sir Allan MacLean of Doward [Duart], who was curious and taught in these things, being at Dingwall in the year 1663 ...'.[126] MacRae's friend Seumas Fraser could also have profited thereby, and specific evidence to this effect may lie in his knowledge that in his final illness in 1558, Alasdair Fraser of Lovat was attended by Seumas Beaton, of the Beatons of Dervaig.[127]

Whatever use others may have made of their learning, we would expect the Ó Muirgheasáins, perhaps the Beatons, and the lineage (if lineage it is, and distinct from the two just mentioned) represented by 'Fergus MacRourie' and 'Fergus Mackenzie', to be the source of classical material in those genealogical histories which treat of their own patrons. They are doubtless the subject of the following comment in the *MacLean History*:

> This family had their shenachies and bards as every family of distinction in the Highlands had. Yet they were so ungratefull to their benefactors or so ignorant as to have left nothing upon record worth noticing preceeding the family's settlement in the island of Mull, or, if they did committ any thing of this kind to writ, it has been lost by the injuries of the times. All that remains is a bare catalogue of names from Gillean upwards to Inighisteurteamher ... This catalogue was in the custody of Mr John Beaton the last of the shenachies a man pretty well skilled in Irish antiquities. There was also another catalogue agreeing with this exactly in an old genealogical manuscript preserved for a long time in the Laird of Coll's family which is now lost.[128]

Unsympathetic though he was, the author drew upon these genealogies, along with another classical source in the form of a eulogy of the MacLeans by a MacMhuirich.[129] Finally, the *Bannatyne MS*, dealing with the MacLeods of Dunvegan and Harris, even though apparently written down as late as *c.*1830, nevertheless 'contains material said to be derived from the classical tradition'.[130]

We can now offer a summative but provisional model of the written and oral pathways by which classical material came into the genealogical histories. Indebtedness to specific written classical sources is manifest in the

Red Book of Clanranald, the *Sleat History*, Campbell histories and the *MacLean History*; but we should also allow for the possibility that some chains of oral transmission had their origins in written classical exemplars. Identification of oral pathways *per se* is complicated considerably by the probability, broached at the outset, of elements of classical knowledge having undergone widespread social dissemination, presumably by primarily oral means, by the time the genealogical histories came to be written. Hence it may be useful to distinguish between 'historical' and 'immediate' oral routes. The former would consist of long-standing transmission within learned lineages such as the MacMhuirichs (which Niall MacMhuirich could have drawn upon alongside written sources in the *Red Book of Clanranald*);[131] and classical permeation of vernacular historical traditions, both elite and popular. The latter would refer to specific points of oral interchange in the era of the making of the histories, whether direct – Uisdean MacDonald and the North Uist Beatons – or indirect, via aristocratic intermediaries such as Ailean MacLean of Duart.

The difficulties inherent in seeking to separate classical 'high' vernacular from 'low' vernacular elements within the genealogical histories are exemplified if we turn finally to a type of material whose influence and presence is highly visible within them. This is fictional or quasi-fictional narrative; put most simply, story. Serious study of this material would be a considerable undertaking in its own right, and cannot be attempted here.[132] In terms of potential range, it spans both the learned and vernacular, and written and oral, worlds of late medieval Gaeldom, and embraces overlapping and related categories such as historical legend, supernatural legend (including migratory legend, explaining the origin of a particular local [place] name or feature), international tales, hero tales based on the cycles of early Gaelic literature, and the romantic hero tales created in the medieval and early modern eras in Ireland and Scotland.[133] A scholar versed in these fields, and suitably armed with the Aarne–Thompson classification of international tales, and Stith Thompson's *Motif-Index of Folk Literature*, would undoubtedly reap a rich harvest from the genealogical histories, the fruits of which could profitably be compared to the corpus of written Gaelic medieval and early modern tales, to the late medieval Irish historical tracts already mentioned,[134] and to Gaelic oral tradition recorded in the modern era.[135]

Research of this order would certainly benefit folklore studies, but without necessarily pinpointing precisely for us how such material came into the genealogical histories. Was its origin classical or vernacular, or both? If there was a vernacular contribution, did it come from social strata below the aristocratic? These are two questions worth asking, even if answering them all too rapidly becomes an exercise in trapping quicksilver. With regard to the first, non-classical informants might seem the most likely avenue, and apparently in favour of this is the fact that fictional narrative plays a negligible role in the history in the *Red Book of Clanranald*.[136] But to conclude that the more classically oriented a history, the weaker the influence of fictional narrative, and that the latter thus goes hand in hand with vernacular input, would be premature.[137] The responsibilities of professional historians were not confined to the recording of the 'hard' history of their patrons' lineages in genealogy, annal or prose, but also included the preservation, creation and telling of tales, for the purposes of courtly entertainment. To judge by the intermingling of such material within classical manuscripts, and indeed within classical poetry, no rigid line of demarcation seems to have been observed between the two functions, or, presumably, the personnel who fulfilled them.[138] Heroic narratives were a resource to be quarried in order to provide role models for the lineage, and cast a virtuous light upon its deeds. In any case, given the likely wider dissemination of such narratives, it becomes very difficult to seek to assign instances of them in the histories to either a 'vernacular' or 'classical' origin. As hinted at in the *MacRae History*, the informants known to have been tapped by the authors of the genealogical histories were probably as well versed in the classical tradition, including its fictional narrative component, as they were in the inherited histories of their own noble lineages.[139]

With regard to the second question, does the role of these same informants make it unnecessary to posit a distinct, non-aristocratic source of vernacular input? Yet we have already noted the influence of what we dubbed the 'collective memory' on the Gaelic linguistic dimension of these texts.[140] Moreover, it is difficult to conceive that historical and quasi-historical tales concerning the ruling lineages were *not* circulating at lower social levels in medieval and late medieval times; these could be regarded as the precursors of what have been called the 'historical legends' relating to the sixteenth and seventeenth centuries which constitute a prominent strand in modern Scottish Gaelic oral tradition as collected from the eighteenth century onwards.[141] In fact, the histories provide clear pointers both to the circulation of such tales, and their own use of them. Iain MacRae relates two 'vulgar tradition[s]', concerning early MacRae history, both of which he is at pains to reject.[142] In treating of Gill-Adhamhnain, grandfather of Somhairle, in the *Red Book of Clanranald*, Niall MacMhuirich interjects: 'if it were to my purpose I could recall when I was in that territory [Co. Sligo]; and the tradition of the local people is kept alive, especially amongst the descendants of Gill-Adhamhnain, in those parts'.[143] Seventeenth-century Sligo oral tradition may thus explain the folktale-influenced treatment of Gille-Brighde and Somhairle, son and grandson of Gill-Adhamhnain, in the *Red Book of Clanranald*.[144]

Nevertheless, the authors of the histories may have accessed 'popular' material of this order not only first-hand, but also via the mediating role of their aristocratic oral informants. Thus, the latter could have acted as vital points of contact and exchange, not only between the classical and the vernacular, and literate and oral, worlds, but also between 'high' and 'low' vernacular tradition. They were well placed to receive, say, the fictional narrative component of the classical tradition, through the written or spoken word; to transmit this orally, along with the histories of their own lineages, to lower vernacular levels; and either to recycle this material once it had been the subject of popular treatment or to pick up original material of this type which was circulating independently, in its own right, at the popular level. In terms of our conception of how the genealogical histories were made, such an hypothesis would mean that the credit for assimilating the different elements of native tradition, and then synthesizing this with printed and documentary sources, need not automatically lie with the authors. Oral informants could have played a dynamic role in the first stage of this process, with some 'authors' cast as the passive reporters or 'collectors' of the indigenous tradition of late medieval Gaelic Scotland.[145]

CAUSATION: COMMON FACTORS

We come now to the motives for writing these histories. While acknowledging that these must have varied over the two centuries of the genre's existence, the primary issue for us is what gave it birth in the second half of the seventeenth century, given that this also proved to be the most active phase in its life-cycle.

Our perspective must be European. The valuable parallel researches of David Allan, focusing mainly on Lowland Scotland, reveal that there, as in England, France and the Dutch Republic, there was a seventeenth-century craze for lineage-centred genealogical history. In France, for example, two printed and two manuscript works of this kind were produced in the 1550s: the respective figures for the 1630s are 27 and 14. A pan-European explanation for this surge in activity would see such texts as defence mechanisms by which the traditional aristocracy sought to stave off the dangers rising up around it. The first of these was biological. Significantly accelerating extinction rates have been detected among, for example, England's noble families in the seventeenth century. In these circumstances, detailed genealogical tracts could function as quasi-legal texts, as 'entails writ large', by which succession could be ensured even if the main line failed. Allied to this, if a family's right to a particular title or estate had been controversially acquired, leaving open the possibility of a legal challenge at a later date, the genealogical tract could be used to legitimize retrospectively the act of acquisition. A second danger was economic pressure, leading to endemic debt or bankruptcy. In these circumstances, the role of the genealogical tract would be consolatory, providing 'an honourable fig-leaf in times of advancing financial nakedness'.[146]

Lack of research means that we cannot say whether the biological imperative applied to the Lowland Scottish scenario. But economic pressure certainly did, and to this we can add other, peculiarly local, factors. One was the changing nature of the Lowland Scottish elite, because of the 'rise of the middling sort' and the significant growth of the Scottish peerage in the first half of the seventeenth century.[147] Genealogy was a way for the old aristocracy to assert that it was still there, the new aristocracy to assert that it had arrived. After the Union of the Crowns in 1603, monarchical absenteeism and the loss of the Scottish court doubtless magnified these internal insecurities and rivalries, as the Scottish elite was pitched into competition for places and preference with the English nobility. The genealogical tract, like architecture and horticulture, may have become a means of competitive display, of impressing an English audience, of cutting a dash on a British stage.[148] Finally, Michael Lynch has pointed to these texts as one manifestation of a 'cult of honour' in seventeenth-century Scotland. This was inspired partly by the scramble for status among nobles old and new, and partly by a 'new patriotism' which, after 1660, found expression in the desire of nobility and the middling sort to forget their Covenanting pasts, and focus their loyalty anew on the crown.[149]

Several of these trends are visible in the contemporary Scottish *Gàidhealtachd*, and form likely reasons for the birth of the genealogical history genre there. Most obviously, a clutch of factors – legislation tying punitive financial sanctions to the heads of clans which failed to keep the peace, requiring annual appearances by chiefs before the Privy Council, and the education of the children of the Hebridean elite in the Lowlands; the concomitant rise of absenteeism in the south, and of conspicuous consumption on the southern model; and the fiscal demands and physical destruction which flowed from military action during the Covenanting, Cromwellian and Restoration eras – combined to induce a state of widespread and chronic indebtedness among the upper echelons of many kindreds.[150] Again, in Gaelic Scotland a pre-existing means of expressing a 'new patriotism' centred on the crown was *rìoghalachd*, the literary topos rehearsing loyalty to the true line of the kings of Scots, and which operated irrespective of the vicissitudes of current political circumstance.[151] *Rìoghalachd*, primarily associated with poetry, saturates the genealogical histories. For Covenanting kindreds like the Campbells and the Frasers; for the MacKenzies, whose Civil War record was one of vacillation, and for the Macintoshes, who had remained neutral,[152] the need to re-emphasize loyalty to the crown after 1660 was especially acute, and may explain both the prominence of the theme within the texts produced on their behalf between the Restoration and 1680, and the distortion of earlier events to suit.[153] Yet the fact that a text like the *Sleat History*, emanating from a

Royalist kindred, is nevertheless absolutely fixated upon demonstrating historical MacDonald loyalty to the Scottish crown, suggests that a stimulus other than the immediate political past, and to be discussed shortly, was also at work.

As with Lowland Scotland, lack of research means we cannot advance accelerating extinction rates as a spur to the writing of the genealogical histories. Even so, there is no doubting their quasi-legal status and function; and this we can link to the prominence of lawyers among our authors, which is in turn symptomatic of the extent to which members of the Highland aristocracy embraced the law as a profession in the seventeenth century.[154] The key here is the significantly more powerful grip which Scots law came to exert over the Highlands during that century, squeezing out the distinctive, indigenous legal and customary practices with which it had previously co-existed.[155] For us, the most important shifts concerned the related issues of land-tenure and marriage practice. Relevant expertise was provided by Edinburgh-based lawyers, often of indigenous origin, who also acted as the agents of the Gaelic elite in its dealings with the government.[156] Within this increasingly pervasive legal climate, engendered in part by state *diktat*, the elite found itself under pressure, first articulated by Parliament in 1597, to demonstrate acceptable title to its lands.[157] If such title did not exist,[158] there was a role for the genealogical histories as 'surrogate charters'. More than this, and whether independent evidence of title existed or not, history could conveniently be rewritten within these texts in order to make them compatible with the principles of Scots law.

Thus, nothing said in the genealogical histories concerning the occupation of, and succession to, land, can be taken at face value.[159] They commonly assert that the right of a ruling lineage to its territories is based upon continuous possession from time immemorial, in one direct and unbroken descent in the male line, governed by primogeniture. According to Seumas Fraser in the Preface to his Fraser history, 'we have a *vitum dominium*, a right conveyed to us by our ancesters, for 400 yeares preceeding anno 1650 bypast, and, *jure prisco*, now ancient posesors here in the North of Scotland, and tearmed Frasers of Lovat, by an uninterrupted succesion from father to sone, never falling to a daughter or collaterall line dureing the aforsaid space ...'.[160] MacKenzie tracts similarly claim that the clan was rooted in Kintail virtually from birth, whereas William Matheson has shown that it was probably displaced between the mid-fourteenth and later fifteenth centuries.[161]

The emphasis upon primogeniture must derive from the fact that, as John Bannerman has demonstrated, the system of tanistry, which allowed for succession by collateral males, survived in the west Highlands among territorial kindreds until at least the mid-sixteenth century.[162] Even if we assume that it had ceased to be operative elsewhere in the *Gàidhealtachd* by this point, it was presumably once in more general or universal use. Bannerman noted the failure of the genealogical historians to acknowledge occurrences of tanistry for what they were, and ascribed this to later generations' ignorance of it.[163] This may be true for some histories, particularly those written towards the end of the lifetime of the genre. But given that tanistry definitely survived into the seventeenth century among professional kindreds,[164] it could equally be that, in some of our earlier texts at least, genealogical historians were responding to their own age by seeking to elide tanistry from the record, in order to elevate primogeniture as the historical norm.[165] Whether acting knowingly or not, they could resort to various stratagems to do so.[166] They could simply overlook cases of collateral succession, or incorporate them into the direct line, whose length and antiquity would thereby conveniently be extended.[167] Between the earlier fifteenth and the mid-sixteenth century it is clear that tanistry was active in determining the succession to the chiefship of the MacLeods of Dunvegan.[168] The *Bannatyne MS* presents the period as an aberration, commencing with the usurpation of the chiefship by an ambitious uncle, and ending with the restoration of the 'rightful' lineage – of which the author happened to be a descendant – by general acclamation following two clan assemblies. Particularly interesting is the *Sleat History*'s claim that Iain MacIain of Ardnamurchan, who succeeded his uncle, cheated his uncle's sons out of their patrimony. What was probably an unexceptional case of tanistry becomes another cudgel with which to beat an individual whom the Sleat historian is concerned to portray in the worst light possible.[169] Finally, let us note that the genealogical histories' desire to turn primogeniture into a Holy Grail assumed forms other than the expunging of tanistry. Primogeniture could act as a facade concealing disputes over the chiefship among different lineages within a kindred; and as a reason for splicing together the potentially very different traditions of the origin of a kindred without seeking to reconcile them. *Ane Accompt of the Genealogie of the Campbells* 'valiantly attempt[s] to incorporate the British, the Gaelic and the Norman tradition of ancestry into one direct male line descent',[170] significantly lengthening the Campbell pedigree in the process.

CAUSATION: LOCAL FACTORS

The topos of *rìoghalachd*, and the issue of succession, are indications that, as we would expect, Scottish Gaelic participation in what was a European phenomenon assumed its own distinctive form and flavour. This extends to causation *per se*. The fact that the genealogical histories come on stream later than genealogical activity elsewhere might be explained in terms of simple time-lag, yet the relatively clear-cut manner in which they do so in the mid-seventeenth century, and notably after *c.* 1660, suggests that a specific trigger is at work. I believe this to have been not so much the Restoration, as the demise of the pursuit of history and genealogy by the learned professional classes. In a development which paralleled the emergence of vernacular from the shadow of classical verse, the new historiography rose from the rubble of the learned tradition, as another manifestation of the tectonic shift from medievalism to modernism taking place in the Scottish *Gàidhealtachd* in the seventeenth century.

The learned orders in Scotland took a long time to die, between *c.* 1600 and *c.* 1750, and various milestones could be pointed out along the way.[171] But there is clear evidence linking the extinction of specific learned lineages with the birth of the genealogical history genre in the central decades of the seventeenth century.[172] The interface is at its clearest with the hereditary poets and historians to the Campbells, the MacEwens, who were squeezed into oblivion between 1627 and 1656.[173] As we have seen, the same time frame saw the production of what we have referred to as the Campbell proto-genealogical histories. The author of the earliest of these, the *Information* of 1634, clearly had access to manuscripts maintained by the MacEwens, but lacked the linguistic expertise to exploit them.[174] If the author were Alexander Colville, then by the 1650s he had found a means of circumventing this difficulty, for we have already noted the indebtedness of 'Colvin's Genealogy of the Campbells' to the MacEwens' written legacy.[175] The title of *Ollamh Muileach*, held by both the supreme poet and the supreme physician to the head of the MacLeans of Duart, fell into disuse on the death of Maol-Dòmhnaich Ó Muirgheasáin *c.* 1662; as we have seen, it was in 1663 that Iain MacRae, author of two histories, tapped into Ó Muirgheasáin's knowledge as relayed to him by Sir Ailean MacLean of Duart.[176] Iain Beaton, last incumbent of the office of principal physician, died in 1657.[177] It was between 1660 and 1670 that Gille-Críost Beaton set down a group of Beaton pedigrees, partly in order to assert the orthodox classical view of the origin of his kindred.[178] Here, as with the history in the *Red Book of Clanranald*,[179] there is a real sense of representatives of the learned orders setting down their knowledge as a legacy, with deliberation, finality, and, perhaps, an almost millenarian urgency.[180]

There was, and perhaps still is, a tendency to see the withering of the classical tradition as inseparable from the death of a Gaelic polity, and to mourn it accordingly.[181] But in terms of cultural organization and expression, and notwithstanding the obvious indebtedness of vernacular to classical forms, the waning of the hegemony of the learned orders possessed a 'democratising', liberating and energising dimension. This was true for historiography as for poetry, and most obviously manifest in the sheer level of activity in these genres in the later seventeenth and early eighteenth centuries.[182] Moreover, the accumulated knowledge of the classical tradition was now ripe for reinterpretation and manipulation according to new criteria and desires. In the case of the Beaton pedigrees, the *Red Book of Clanranald*, and the *Black Book of Clanranald*, classical literati retained control of their legacy long enough to set it down as it stood, and on their own terms. In the case of the collaboration between Iain Beaton, and Edward Lhwyd and his 'circle', we see the interface of the classical tradition and the world of post-Renaissance scholarship.[183] The genealogical histories represent an indigenous 'spin' on the classical tradition, but are innovative in their use of other languages and sources, including vernacular oral historians who now, perhaps for the first time, achieve formal prominence and credibility.

However, innovation was not necessarily synonymous with respect for historical truth. Granted, objective accuracy had hardly been a *sine qua non* for the classical historians, who had developed the manufacture and manipulation of pedigrees in particular into a fine art. Nevertheless, the genealogical histories give centre stage to beliefs which went beyond the boundaries of acceptability as these were understood by practitioners of the classical tradition. Thus, and interestingly, they help to demarcate what these boundaries were.

I give two examples which both relate to kindred origins.[184] Early seventeenth-century evidence already cited suggests that classical literati explicitly rejected a Geraldine descent for the MacKenzies.[185] It follows that this myth was not created by the first earl of Cromartie or any of the other post-1660 MacKenzie genealogical historians, as has hitherto been assumed; but to a man they accept it, and present Colin (Fitz)Gerald, the wholly fictitious Norman–Irish saviour of King Alexander III, as the starting-point of the lineage.[186] We saw that genealogical histories of the Campbells assert that they are Britons (i.e. Welsh, descending from King Arthur) *and* Norman *and* Gaelic (via the Fenian hero, Diarmaid Ó Duibhne). Classical sources, whether poetic or genealogical, and whether the products of a Campbell milieu or not, are virtually unanimous in ignoring the last two theories in favour of the first.[187] Given that some of these sources must emanate from the MacEwens, I see no reason to believe that the 'ancient books of the learned' maintained by them (which have not survived independently) would have departed from the classical orthodoxy. I suggest, then, that it was at a stage during, or subsequent to, the demise of the MacEwens that the 'Norman' and 'Gaelic' strands were grafted on to a MacEwen, 'British', core.[188] Indeed, the accretions can readily be stripped away to reveal that core, which proves to be perfectly consistent with older, classical genealogical tradition.[189] Hence, to speak of a 'MacEwen–Colville' account of Campbell origins runs the risk of eliding the real gap which may exist between these two elements.[190]

The waning of the learned orders stemmed from their loss of patronage during the seventeenth century, as the elite of Gaelic Scotland became steadily assimilated into the Scottish and British aristocracy. This latter phenomenon demanded fresh expression and validation, in an appropriate idiom and language. Thus, it could be argued that the genealogical history genre, a cultural tool already well established in Lowland Scotland and England, was adapted within Gaelic Scotland to fill a cultural vacuum created by the reorientation of the elite, and to meet ideological needs flowing therefrom. We can bolster this argument in two ways. First, there is the intimacy of the bond sometimes evident between these works and the heads of the lineages concerned. The authors were often reasonably close blood relations of the chief.[191] In some instances they dedicate their histories to him, broaching the possibility that these were commissioned.[192] Gilleasbuig, ninth earl of Argyll, played an active part in the production of the first major Campbell history.[193] Secondly, there are the linked questions of language, audience and purpose. The overwhelming choice of English or Scoto-English, rather than Gaelic, as the medium for the histories, makes sense if the target audience embraced points south. To this we must conjoin comments David Allan makes in his analysis of the broader genre of family history concerning 'the enthusiastic multiplication of existing texts ... [and the] circulation of manuscripts, possibly to an interested elite audience'.[194] The Gaelic genealogical histories regularly exist in multiple copies, although further work would be required to show how many of these were of an early date, and how wide a circulation they achieved.[195] Extended circulation would be absolutely consistent with the need to validate membership of a Scottish and British aristocracy through the assertion of 'Norman' or 'British' origins, as Campbell and MacKenzie histories do; or through the assertion of a common origin with a kin-group of southern Scotland, as the *Macintosh History* does.[196]

The genealogical histories did not address this wider world in a spirit of unequivocal amity and brotherhood. For some authors, the existence of a potential southern audience meant an opportunity to settle old historiographical scores. This was very much a minority voice, located predictably at that end of the genealogical history spectrum most heavily influenced by the classical tradition. It may be invidious to cite the *Red Book of Clanranald* as a case in point, since Niall MacMhuirich did not forsake the classical language to which he was born and bred, implying a different primary audience, and distinctive motives.[197] Even so, his stated aim in writing the 'Civil Wars' section of this history may suggest the hope that knowledge of it would be carried beyond the Gaelic world: 'what induced me to write even this much was, when I saw that those who treated of the affairs of the time have made no mention at all of the Gael, the men who did all the service'.[198] No such ambiguities attach to the *Sleat History*, which constantly berates Boece, Buchanan, and other 'partial pickers of Scottish chronology and history', for their negative portrayal of the Gaels, particularly the accusation of disloyalty to the crown.[199] Although nowhere else do we find this reactive and corrective reflex so explicitly paraded, it very likely underpinned the emphasis on *rìoghalachd* so prevalent across all the genealogical histories.

A final distinctive cause needs discussion, and again its roots lie in the key seventeenth-century theme of assimilation of the indigenous elite. A strain of kin-competitiveness – genealogy as an assertion of the superiority of one lineage *vis-à-vis* others – runs through the genre. There was nothing new about the mechanism within or without the Gaelic world, but now it probably gained in urgency and influence for two reasons. One was the wider Scottish and British stage upon which the elite wished to preen its plumage. The other was the fading of other mechanisms, including military ones, by which superiority had traditionally been asserted, during a century which saw the eclipse of inter-clan warfare and increasing recourse to Scots law as a means of fomenting, pursuing and resolving disputes.[200]

The best exemplar is again the *Sleat History*, which deals pejoratively with the MacDougalls, MacRuairics (both of whom shared a common origin with the MacDonalds; the MacRuairies are ignored entirely) and the MacLeans; and with other MacDonald branches such as those of Ardnamurchan and Glen Garry, this last because it had the temerity to dispute the right of the Sleat branch to the headship of Clann Domhnaill as a whole come the late-seventeenth century.[201] The author of the *Craignish History* describes his branch of the Campbells as 'the oldest of all the Legittimat cadets now extant of that ancient Stock the Knights of Lochow, now Dukes of Argyll'.[202] The *MacLean History* deals at length with the rival claims of the branches of Duart and Lochbuie to headship of the clan.[203] Fierce kin-competitiveness, coupled with authorial animosities, fuelled the clutch of histories from the eastern Highlands relating to the Clan Chattan confederation, and to the Farquharsons.[204] Such activity bears the distinct odour of something stronger and less connected to reality than mere antiquarianism, and foreshadows the historiographical dead-end which is the popular clan history of modern times.[205]

CONCLUSIONS

This chapter has sought to demonstrate the inappropriateness of models which regard orality and literacy as invariable opposites, and synonymous with 'popular' and 'elite' respectively, to understanding the culture of late medieval and early modern Gaelic Scotland in general, and the genealogical histories in particular. Consider the web of sources and pathways at whose centre these texts lie. Material from the classical, 'high' vernacular and 'low' vernacular traditions, which provided the bulk of the indigenous content, could all have reached the histories by a range of oral routes, both 'historical' and 'immediate'. The 'historical' interconnectedness of these traditions makes it very difficult to say with which of them some of the material in the histories originated: all three, as we saw, could have contributed to the fictional narrative component of these texts. On the written side of the equation, the classical tradition was again available to the genealogical histories, either through direct use of manuscripts or through oral chains of transmission which began with manuscripts. To this we can add the use of documentary record, of printed works, and of each other. The resultant amalgam was overwhelmingly given written expression in languages other than Gaelic. At those points in the narrative where oral or written Gaelic sources were drawn upon, the governing language was used either to represent them phonetically (this applies whether the source was in classical or vernacular Gaelic), sometimes with accompanying translation; or to translate or paraphrase them. Gaelic oral narrative is preserved, not merely in written form, but in another language.

The mechanics of composition are revealed most clearly in the *Craignish History*. Alasdair Campbell began with a Gaelic oral infrastructure, assimilated from boyhood onwards: rhymes and proverbs, exemplifying the 'collective memory'; the traditions of a clutch of elite vernacular historians whom he was actively seeking out by the 1680s at least; a classical elegy, heard and barely remembered. Onto this he grafted the fruits of his labours in the Argyll and Craignish charter chests in 1706 and 1707, a sprinkling of printed works, and the written classical tradition of the MacEwens, both first-hand and as mediated by Colville and Duncanson. The whole, written up in English between 1717 and 1722, was in part for Campbell a means of demonstrating the equal legitimacy of his oral and written evidence.

The process of cultural exchange within late medieval and early modern Gaelic Scotland should not be envisaged as a straightforward circle linking all relevant parties. We can readily argue for transmission outwards and downwards from the classical tradition; but we have encountered evidence suggesting that wherever and as long as that tradition remained active and healthy, it resisted penetration by views originating outwith itself which it considered erroneous or unorthodox. The dynamos who powered the cycle that did exist, and who linked it to the classical tradition, were, we have argued, elite vernacular historians. In them the three indigenous historical traditions met; among them were the aristocratic oral informants utilized by authors of the genealogical histories, and most of the authors themselves; and the descriptor *seanchaidh* came to be applied to them individually, in recognition of their risen status, as the professional historians previously so styled died out along with the classical tradition.[206]

Did the genealogical histories represent a 'new historiography', articulated by the 'new *seanchaidh*'? The logic of our argument insists that they are not automatically entitled to be viewed as the most thoroughgoing commixture thus far of the elite and popular cultures of Gaelic Scotland. Just such a commixture may have constituted the oral repertoires of generations of elite vernacular historians prior to the mid-seventeenth century. Whether this had taken written form before then is a question fraught with imponderables. Even if, as is possible, future research were to demonstrate that the apparent catalyst for the genealogical histories, the demise of the classical tradition, had taken place in some areas of Gaelic Scotland prior to *c.* 1600, we are still faced with the almost complete absence of written histories from this period, including the known 'close precursors' to the genealogical histories. But if we allow that these precursors may have given written expression to these oral repertoires, then any definition of the newness of the genealogical histories must narrow still further. There are four relevant aspects: status, scale, scope and purpose. The general collapse of the classical tradition in the seventeenth century left the grouping to which our authors and their oral informants belonged high and dry as the *de facto* new historical elite of Gaelic Scotland. In their authorship and content and profusion – the genealogical histories were formal written confirmation of this new reality. Almost certainly, their synthesizing of the indigenous historical traditions with particular categories of written material – notably printed works of external origin – resulted in a new fusion which is consistent with the primary purpose of the genre, the need of the ruling elite of Gaelic Scotland for new history.

A future research agenda would begin with the identification and publication of more genealogical histories. Of those already known, a number remain unpublished. Existing editions do not always satisfactorily take into account the 'multi-manuscript' phenomenon referred to above, or the integrity of their primary text.[207]

Once authoritative texts have been established, they can be sifted to isolate the sources they embody. Our preliminary discussion of these gives some sense of the fruits they would yield. Enough has already been said concerning the potential benefits to be derived by scholars of Gaelic lexicography, linguistics, poetry and folklore. A definitive listing of the printed works which the genealogical histories draw upon would help to delineate the intellectual horizons of post-Renaissance Gaelic Scotland, and thus its cultural 'modernity' or 'conservatism' in a European context. Study of these works might also reveal whether they acted as models as well as sources for the genre.

Source analysis of the histories faces its most vital challenge in seeking to separate out the respective contributions of the three indigenous historical traditions. The problem is least pronounced with elements of classical content such as genealogy, classical poetry and annalistic evidence. The annalistic component of the *Red Book of Clanranald* and the *Sleat History* is clearly visible, for example, and needs to be investigated in the light of other evidence, from within and without the genealogical history genre, for the existence of such a source or sources, with Iona as one likely place of compilation.[208] The 'low' vernacular tradition reveals itself in the 'vulgar tradition' twice invoked in the *MacRae History*; perhaps also in the seam of rhymes and proverbial sayings, and in non-classical theories of clan origins. The 'high' vernacular tradition is likely to prove hardest of all to isolate in its own terms, given its central recycling role, but this is a task well worth taking seriously given the indications that it embodies the oral memory of aristocratic lineages as it existed at least as far back as *c.* 1500.

Sources are inseparable from reliability. Although this issue requires separate and detailed examination, the degree to which the genealogical histories do seem to be dependent on earlier historiographical strata bolsters the interim assessment of their value offered at the outset. Likewise, the preliminary discussion of the identity and motives of their authors offered here means that we can make due compensation for the biases inherent in their treatment of relations with the crown and with other kindreds, of land tenure and succession, and of marriage and legitimacy. Self-evidently, the histories' employment of the written word conferred no magic veracity upon their sources, oral or otherwise, but instead laid them open to fresh or further manipulation.

Further investigation of the authors is needed before we can fully appreciate the nature of their relationships with each other (especially the 'circle' which seems to have existed in the vital first phase of the genre's existence), with the indigenous ruling elite, with the origins of modern Gaelic scholarship and antiquarianism, and with broader intellectual currents such as post-Restoration Episcopalian culture, and Scots law. A more considered understanding of their *mentalité* will enable us to refine the explanation of their motives offered here.

Yet I would submit that the core motive may remain the desire for homogeneity. The broader geographical resonance of the genre was entirely appropriate, for the chosen medium matched the message. However distinctive the flavour imparted to the genealogical histories by features such as their use of indigenous (especially classical) sources, they are ultimately pleas on the part of the elite of Gaelic Scotland to be regarded as indistinguishable from their Lowland Scottish and English counterparts in matters such as origins, antiquity, landholding and loyalism.[209] As such, they take their place beside all the other proofs of the fundamental shift in the identity of that elite taking place in the course of the seventeenth century, a process arguably instigated and certainly encouraged by state action, but which developed its own dynamic and momentum.

NOTES

My grateful thanks to the editors, and to David Allan, Steve Boardman, Maureen Byers, William Gillies, Colin Kidd, Iain MacIver, Jean Munro, David Sellar and Domhnall Uilleam Stiùbhart, for their very kind assistance and advice.

1 *Acts of the Lords of the Isles, 1336–1493*, ed. J. Munro and R. W. Munro (Edinburgh: Scottish History Society [hereafter SHS], 1986).

2 The source categories are four. The first is poetry. If we confine ourselves to compositions in the literary dialect, Classical Common Gaelic, rather than in the vernacular, then Katherine Simms has estimated a surviving corpus for Ireland of 2,000 plus, of which perhaps 1,000 predate 1566: K. Simms, *From Kings to Warlords: the Changing Political Structure of Gaelic Ireland in the Later Middle Ages* (Bury St Edmonds: Boydell Press, 1987), 4. For Scotland Derick Thomson estimates around 160 items in total, of which roughly 86 can be dated between *c.* 1450 and *c.* 1550: D. S. Thomson, *An Introduction to Gaelic Poetry* (Edinburgh: Edinburgh University Press, 1989), 20. In terms of genealogy, the main elements in the Scottish corpus are MS 1467 (National Library of Scotland, *Advocates' MS* 72.1.1; Martin MacGregor, 'Genealogies of the Clans: Contributions to the Study of MS 1467', *Innes Review*, 51 (2000), 131–46); Archdeacon Domhnall (Donald) Munro's MacDonald pedigrees, in *Monro's Western Isles of Scotland and Genealogies of the Clans 1549*, ed. R. W. Munro (Edinburgh: Oliver & Boyd, 1961), 89–94; the 'Kilbride' MS, in *Collectanea de Rebus Albanicis* (Edinburgh: Iona Club, 1847), 360–1; the collection of Beaton pedigrees written down between 1660 and 1670, in J. W. M. Bannerman, *The Beatons: a Medical Kindred in the Classical Gaelic Tradition* (Edinburgh: John Donald, 1986), 5–44; and material in the *Black Book of Clanranald*, in A. Cameron, *Reliquiae Celticae*, ed. A. MacBain and J. Kennedy, 2 vols (Inverness: Northern Chronicle Office, 1892–94), II. 145, 300–4, 307–9. This is dwarfed by the great late medieval Irish compilations – the Ó Cianáin manuscript of the mid-fourteenth century, and the later Books of Uí Mhaine, Ballymote and Lecan; see Simms, *From Kings to Warlords*, 6–7. If we focus upon the non-poetic and non-genealogical component of the contents of Classical Gaelic manuscripts – religious and medical material, for example – then Scotland is better off, see D. MacKinnon, *A Descriptive Catalogue of Gaelic Manuscripts* (Edinburgh: Constable, 1912); but the disparity reasserts itself with annalistic compilations, for Gaelic Scotland has only crumbs to set against works like the *Annals of Ulster*: Simms, *From Kings to Warlords*, 3. Known survivors are a text emanating from Easter Ross (*The Calendar of Fearn*, ed. R. J. Adam (Edinburgh: SHS, 1991); and two related texts from western Perthshire, the Chronicle of the Book of the Dean of Lismore and the Chronicle of Fortingall, for discussion of which see M. D. W. MacGregor, 'A Political History of the MacGregors before 1571', unpublished PhD dissertation (University of Edinburgh, 1989), 15–17. None of these is in Gaelic.

3 Simms, *From Kings to Warlords*, 7–8; and see ibid., 2–3, for her comments on the statements of the 'rights' of kings, another source-type lacking in Scotland.

4 Cf. Nollaig Ó Muraíle, 'Irish Genealogical Collections: the Scottish Dimension', in Ronald Black, William Gillies and Roibeard Ó Maolalaigh (eds), *Celtic*

Connections: Proceedings of the Tenth International Congress of Celtic Studies, 2 vols (East Linton: Tuckwell Press, 1999), I. 251–64.

5 Brian Ó Cuív, 'The Irish Language in the Early Modern Period', in T. W. Moody, F. X. Martin and F. J. Byrne (eds), *A New History of Ireland*, 9 vols (Oxford: Clarendon Press, 1976–) III. 509–45, esp. 531–2, 534–5, 538–9. The corrective tone, range of native sources and knowledge of foreign authors displayed in Keating's *Fora feasa ar Éirinn*, along with the wide circulation the work achieved in manuscript form, are characteristics it shares with the Scottish genealogical histories; see ibid., 531. One history surviving only in part concerns that branch of the Scottish MacDonalds which came to possess the Glens of Antrim, and spawned the MacDonalds of Antrim. It seems to fit the Scottish rather than the Irish historiographical context: Archibald MacDonald, 'A Fragment of an Irish MS. History of the MacDonalds of Antrim', *Transactions of the Gaelic Society of Inverness* [hereafter TGST], 37 (1934–36), 262–84.

6 Simms, *From Kings to Warlords*, 8.

7 See in general Derick S. Thomson, 'Gaelic Learned Orders and Literati in Medieval Scotland', *Scottish Studies*, 12 (1968), 57–78.

8 Katharine Simms, 'Literacy and the Irish Bards', in H. Pryce (ed.), *Literacy in Medieval Celtic Societies* (Cambridge: Cambridge University Press, 1998), 238–58, at pp. 248–52; W. Gillies, 'Gaelic: the Classical Tradition', in Cairns Craig (general ed.), *The History of Scottish Literature*, 4 vols (Aberdeen: Aberdeen University Press, 1987–88) I. 245–61, at 250–1.

9 'The Genealogical and Historicall Account of the Family of Craignish', ed. Herbert Campbell, in *Miscellany of the Scottish History Society* (Edinburgh: SHS, 1893–), IV. 190.

10 See also John MacInnes, 'Gaelic Poetry and Historical Tradition', in *The Middle Ages in the Highlands* (Inverness: Inverness Field Club, 1981), 142–63, at p. 146, 156; John MacInnes, 'The Panegyric Code in Gaelic Poetry and its Historical Background', *Transactions of the Gaelic Society of Inverness*, 50 (1976–78), 435–98, at pp. 444–5, 461; Derick S. Thomson (ed.), *The Companion to Gaelic Scotland* (Oxford: Basil Blackwell, 1983), 280; Dòmhnall Eairrdsidh Dòmhnallach, 'Trì ginealaichean de sgeulachd', in William Gillies (ed.), *Gaelic and Scotland: Alba agus a' Ghàidhlig* (Edinburgh: Edinburgh University Press, 1989), 185–221, at pp. 185–7.

11 Martin MacGregor, '"Surely One of the Greatest Poems Ever Made in Britain": the Lament for Griogair Ruadh MacGregor of Glen Strae and its Historical Background', in Edward J. Cowan and Douglas Gifford (eds), *The Polar Twins* (Edinburgh: John Donald, 1999), 114–53, at p. 136.

12 I intend to publish a provisional checklist of these texts in a forthcoming article in *Scottish Gaelic Studies*. This article is referred to below as MacGregor, 'Provisional Checklist'.

13 William Matheson, 'Traditions of the MacKenzies', *TGSI*, 39–40 (1942–50), 193–228, at p. 224, n. 4; see below, p. 222.

14 *Companion to Gaelic Scotland*, 71–2.

15 Ibid., 149–50; Bannerman, *Beatons*, 130–3. Another to whom Lhwyd appealed for information was Cailean (Colin) Campbell, minister of Ardchattan in Argyll: *A Collection of Highland Rites and Customes*, ed. J. L. Campbell (Cambridge: The Folklore Society, 1975), 1. Cf. Colm Ó Baoill, 'Gaelic Manuscripts in the Colin Campbell Collection', *Scottish Gaelic Studies*, 14 (1983–86), 83–99.

16 J. L. Campbell and Derick Thomson, *Edward Lhuyd in the Scottish Highlands 1699–1700* (Oxford: Clarendon Press, 1963), xvii–xviii, 10.
17 *Companion to Gaelic Scotland*, 145; *Highland Rites and Customes*, 5.
18 Highland Rites and Customes, 3–6.
19 Ibid., 7–8.
20 Ibid., 3; Bannerman, *Beatons*, 132–3; Martin Martin, *A Description of the Western Islands of Scotland circa 1695* (Edinburgh: Birlinn, 1994), 13.
21 Bannerman, *Beatons*, 132–3; *Highland Rites and Customes*, 1–2.
22 Bannerman, *Beatons*, 132.
23 *Chronicles of the Frasers: the Wardlaw Manuscript, 916–1674*, ed. W. MacKay (Edinburgh: SHS, 1905), xliv–xlv.
24 *Bàrdachd Chloinn Ghill-Eathain: Eachann Bacach and Other Maclean Poets*, ed. Colm Ó Baoill (Edinburgh: Scottish Gaelic Texts Society [hereafter SGTS], 1979), xviii–xix, xxx; Nicholas Maclean-Bristol, *Warriors and Priests: the History of the Clan MacLean, 1300 1570* (East Linton: Tuckwell Press, 1995), 158–9.
25 *Highland Rites and Customes*, 1, 11–13.
26 D. Gregory, *The History of the Western Highlands and Islands of Scotland from AD 1493 to AD 1625* (Glasgow: Thomas D. Morison, 1881).
27 *Misc. Scot. Hist. Soc.*, IV. 177, 185; A. A. M. Duncan and A. L. Brown, 'Argyll and the Isles in the Earlier Middle Ages', *Proceedings of the Society of Antiquaries of Scotland*, 90 (1956–57), 192–220, at p. 195 and n. 1.
28 Matheson, 'MacKenzies', 224, n. 4.
29 Ibid., 193.
30 Ibid., 195.
31 See especially W. D. H. Sellar, 'The Earliest Campbells – Norman, Briton or Gael?', *Scottish Studies*, 17 (1973), 109–25.
32 K. A. Steer and J. W. M. Bannerman, *Late Medieval Monumental Sculpture in the West Highlands* (Edinburgh: HMSO, 1977), 97–163, 201–13, 215.
33 J. W. M. Bannerman, 'The Lordship of the Isles', in J.M. Brown (ed.), *Scottish Society in the Fifteenth Century* (London: Edward Arnold, 1977), 209–40, at 210. See p. 212, this volume, for reservations about Hugh MacDonald's status as a MacDonald 'employee'.
34 Steve Boardman, 'The Tale of Leper John and the Campbell Acquisition of Lorn', in E. J. Cowan and R. Andrew McDonald (eds), *Alba: Celtic Scotland in the Middle Ages* (East Linton: Tuckwell Press, 2000), 219–47. For other recent or ongoing studies of particular genealogical histories, see Alan G. Macpherson, 'An Old Highland Genealogy and the Evolution of a Scottish Clan', *Scottish Studies*, 10 (1966), 1–43; W. Gillies, 'The Clanranald Histories: Authorship and Purpose', in G. Evans, B. Martin and J. Wooding (eds), *Proceedings of the First Australian Conference of Celtic Studies* (forthcoming) my thanks to Prof. Gillies for giving me access to this article; W. Gillies, 'Oral and Written Sources and Effects in the Clanranald Histories', in D. Scheunemann (ed.), *Orality, Literacy and Modern Media* (Columbia, SC: Camden House, 1996), 27–43; W. Gillies, 'Sources of the Books of Clanranald', *Études celtiques*, 29 (1992), part 2, 459–60 (abstract).
35 See MacGregor, 'Provisional Checklist', section Ic(3).
36 Ibid., section Ic(1).
37 Ibid., section Ic(2); David Allan, '"What's in a Name?": Pedigree and Propaganda in Seventeenth-century Scotland', in E.J. Cowan and R.J. Finlay (eds), *Scottish*

History: the Power of the Past (Edinburgh: Edinburgh University Press, 2002), 147–67. My thanks to Dr Allan for allowing me to consult this article prior to its publication.

38 See p. 209, this volume, and MacGregor, 'Provisial Checklist', sections Ia and III.

39 MacGregor, 'Provisional Checklist', section Ib(1); MacGregor, 'MacGregors', 255.

40 MacGregor, 'Provisional Checklist', section Ib(3).

41 Ibid., section Ib(2). I owe these points to David Sellar.

42 See also pp. 212, 220f., this volume. Note in particular the remarks by the author of the *Information* on the sources available to him, commencing with Classical Gaelic genealogies: 'But because the names before [the Middle Ages] are so Irish like, and hard to be both written and pronounced, and are more fit to be read in conference then committed to write, I shall content myself to inform your Lo[rdship] of the last and surest actions of that house, which may be proven by either evidents or chronicles': Archibald Campbell, *Records of Argyll* (Edinburgh: Blackwood, 1885), 4. He makes use of George Buchanan, Hector Boece and Henricus Stephanus; various documents, one of them at least from the charter chest of the earls of Argyll (ibid., 7); and, perhaps, oral evidence.

43 Martin's book might more naturally belong with works of topographical reportage of the *Gàidhealtachd* such as Archdeacon Domhnall Munro's famous account of 1549 (above, n. 2), *Ane Descriptione of Certaine Pairts of the Highlands of Scotland*, apparently composed *c.* 1644; see *Geographical Collections relating to Scotland made by Walter MacFarlane*, ed. Arthur Mitchell, 3 vols [Edinburgh: SHS, 1906–8] II. 144–92; for the date see ibid., xxxi, xlv; and the *Description of the Lewis* written by Iain Morison of Bragar between 1678 and 1688 in ibid., 210–15; *An Clàrsair Dall: the Songs of Roderick Morison and his Music*, ed. William Matheson (Edinburgh: SGTS, 1970), 207.

44 Examples of texts of this type which I have excluded are 'MacNaughtan of that Ilk', in *Highland Papers*, ed. J. R. N. MacPhail, 4 vols (Edinburgh: SHS, 1914–34) I. 104–13, and 'Memoirs or a Memorial of the Antient and Honourable Family of Robertson of Strowan', in *Genealogical Collections Concerning Families in Scotland Made by Walter MacFarlane*, ed. James Toshach Clark, 2 vols (Edinburgh: SHS, 1900), II. 311–15. Some texts which I have included, notably MacGregor, 'Provisional Checklist', section II (19, 21), are very marginal cases, and should perhaps be excluded also.

45 Although the sources of the *Morison MS* (MacGregor, 'Provisional Checklist', section II (22)) require further analysis, its reliance upon oral tradition may be such as to render its categorization as a genealogical history, as defined here, doubtful.

46 See for example the comments on the late nineteenth-century history of the Stewarts of Appin in Boardman, 'The Tale of Leper John', 219–20. We might describe these works as 'phase two' genealogical histories; at least two texts which I have classified as genealogical histories (MacGregor, 'Provisional Checklist', section II(24, 26)), have potential affinities with them, and may be transitional. The earliest of these 'phase two' histories may be 'a Seneachie', *An Historical and Genealogical Account of the Clan MacLean* (London and Edinburgh: Smith, Elder & Co., 1838). For other later nineteenth-century MacLean histories, see Nicholas Maclean-Bristol, 'The Macleans from 1560–1707: a Reappraisal', in *The Seventeenth Century in the Highlands* (Inverness: Inverness

Field Club, 1986), 70–88, at p. 70. See also John H. J. Stewart and Duncan Stewart, *The Stewarts of Appin* (Edinburgh, 1880); A. & A. MacDonald, *The Clan Donald*, 3 vols (Inverness: Northern Counties Publishing Company, 1896–1904); Angus MacKay, *The Book of MacKay* (Edinburgh: Norman Macleod, 1906); Alexander MacKenzie, *History of the Clan Mackenzie with Genealogies of the Principal Families* (Inverness: A. and W. MacKenzie, 1879); *History of the Mathesons: with Genealogies of the Various Families*, 2nd edn, edited, largely re-written and added to by Alexander MacBain (Stirling: Eneas MacKay, 1900). Between 1881 and 1898, MacKenzie also published histories of the Camerons, Chisolms, Frasers, MacLeods, MacDonalds and lords of the Isles, MacDonalds of Glengarry, MacDonalds of Clanranald, and Munros.

47 MacGregor, 'Provisional Checklist', section II, within which the histories are listed in approximate chronological order.

48 *Misc. Scot. Hist. Soc.*, IV. 179, 183–4, 187, 191.

49 Three MacKenzie authors of MacKenzie histories – Iain Molach of Applecross, Sir Seòras (George) of Rosehaugh, and Sir Seòras, first earl of Cromartie – were all great-grandsons of Cailean, the chief of the kindred who died in 1594, while Cromartie was also brother-in-law of the contemporary chief: *The Scots Peerage*, ed. J. Balfour Paul, 9 vols (Edinburgh: David Douglas, 1904–14), III. 69–75; VII. 500–5; MacFarlane, *Gen. Coll.*, I. 98–100; *Highland Papers*, II. 68. Lachlann Macintosh of Kinrara was uncle and tutor of the contemporary Macintosh chief (Macpherson, 'Genealogy', 41, n. 31). Captain Uisdean (Hugh) MacDonald, the likely author of the *Sleat History*, was nephew of the head of his kindred, Sir Seumas MacDonald of Sleat (see above p. 212); and William Matheson, 'Notes on North Uist Families', *TGSI*, 52 (1980–82), 318–72, at pp. 323–4 and n. 29.

50 The compiler of MacGregor, 'Provisional Checklist', section II (22), Domhnall Morison, a teacher and latterly a cooper, may have descended from the MacGille-Mhoire lineage of lawmen in Lewis. His Gaelic sobriquet, Domhnall Bàn Sgoileir (Fair Donald, the scholar), confirms his erudition: F. W. L. Thomas, 'Traditions of the MacAulays of Lewis', *Proceedings of the Society of Antiquaries of Scotland* [hereafter *PSAS*], 14 (1879–80), 363–431, at pp. 385–6; *An Clàrsair Dall*, xxxiii.

51 MacGregor, 'Provisional Checklist', section II (9).

52 *Chronicles of the Frasers*, 2.

53 *Misc. Scot. Hist. Soc.*, IV. 187–8.

54 Ibid., 214: 'Lena Chreash vic Kennich' (*léine-chrios MhicCoinnich*).

55 *Highland Papers*, I. 215–16.

56 *Chronicles of the Frasers*, 339: '*argid cagging*, cheawing mony'. Cf. William Matheson, 'Traditions of the Mathesons', *TGSI*, 42 (1953–59), 153–81, at p. 163, and 177, n. 35; William Fraser, *The Earls of Cromartie*, 2 vols (Edinburgh: T. and A. Constable, 1876), II. 468: '*creach vachtin* [? *mhacaoimh*], the young mans hership'.

57 E.g. *Misc. Scot. Hist. Soc.*, IV. 243.

58 Ibid., 220–1; cf. *Chronicles of the Frasers*, 112.

59 Ibid., 113, 138, 175, 222.

60 Martin, *Western Islands*, 95; cf. ibid., 241.

61 *Misc. Scot. Hist. Soc.*, IV. 217.

62 Ibid., 227–8; cf. ibid., 217. For an impromptu verse preserved in the *Bannatyne*

MS, see William Matheson, 'Aonghus nan Aoir: a Case of Mistaken Identity', *Scottish Studies*, 21 (1977), 105–8, at pp. 106–7.

63 See also *Chronicles of the Frasers*, 40, 41.

64 *Highland Papers*, I. 42–3. Derick Thomson has suggested that these are 'the earliest surviving example we have in Scottish Gaelic of a strophic metre which is probably to be linked to the *ochtfhoclach* metre which has a much more ancient origin' ('The McLagan MSS in Glasgow University Library: a Survey', *TGSI*, 58 (1992–94), 406–24, at 417–18, 424, n. 26). It should be noted that the versions in the McLagan MSS, on which he bases his text and analysis, could be as much as a century later than those in the *Sleat History*, and lack the contextualization afforded by the latter.

65 MacFarlane, *Gen. Coll.*, I. 119, 142; *Scottish Gaelic Studies*, 9 (1961), 90–1.

66 *Highland Papers*, I. 52, where the harpist's forename is *Art*.

67 Ibid., I. 216, 239.

68 *Misc. Scot. Hist. Soc.*, IV. 228.

69 *Chronicles of the Frasers*, 1.

70 *Misc. Scot. Hist. Soc.*, IV. 187.

71 MacFarlane, *Gen. Coll.*, I. 145.

72 Macpherson, 'Genealogy', 6–7.

73 *Highland Papers*, I. 210.

74 Ibid., I. 7, 27, 40.

75 *Reliquiae Celticae*, II. 152–3; Gillies, 'The Clanranald Histories'.

76 *Misc. Scot. Hist. Soc.*, IV. 208. Cf. ibid., 205, 215; Macpherson, 'Genealogy', 13.

77 *Chronicles of the Frasers*, II. xx–xxi; *Misc. Scot. Hist. Soc.*, IV. 187–93.

78 *Highland Papers*, I. 10; II. 73, 75.

79 See p. 225 this volume.

80 *Misc. Scot. Hist. Soc.*, IV. 190–1; *Highland Papers*, IV. 59.

81 *Highland Papers*, I. 196.

82 Ibid., II. 199; *West Highland Notes and Queries*, series 2, no. 16 (April 1997), 26. MacRae died in 1704 and MacKenzie in 1725, the year given in the dedication of his history. If the attribution of the *MacRae History* to Iain MacRae is correct, then either he had access to an early version of MacKenzie's history, or a redactor of MacRae's original text (which has not survived) made use of MacKenzie post *c.* 1725. The version printed in *Highland Papers*, I. 198–239, comes down to *c.* 1785 (ibid., 203, n. 1, 230, 236).

83 *Highland Papers*, II. 2–3.

84 See MacFarlane, *Gen. Coll.*, I. 198–200; *Highland Papers*, I. 206–8; *Chronicles of the Frasers*, 98–9, 108–9, 130–1, 144, 151–5, 193–6, 197–9.

85 *Highland Papers*, I. 59, 63–4 and cf. ibid., 31.

86 *Misc. Scot. Hist. Soc.*, IV. 191.

87 Matheson, 'Mathesons', 153.

88 *Chronicles of the Frasers*, xx, 3, 79, 115.

89 Ibid., xvi, xx, 3, 128. Presumably *Scriptum Bunchriviae* is distinct from the 'manuscript of Fern' and the 'Abbacy book of Fern' also mentioned by Fraser (ibid., 115, 120). The former may correspond to the extant *Calendar of Fearn* (*Calendar of Fearn*, 24, 92). The latter may correspond, or be related to, a text on the abbots of Fearn, apparently lost and apparently written by Master Thomas Ross in the later sixteenth century: ibid., 22, n. 20.

90 *Highland Papers*, II. 3; Matheson, 'MacKenzies', 200. See above pp. 212, 225

and nn. 110, 208, for other lost annalistic compilations of which traces survive in the genealogical histories.

91 *Highland Papers*, II. 264.

92 *Chronicles of the Frasers*, xx.

93 Gillies, 'The Clanranald Histories'; Matheson, 'MacKenzies', 226, n. 51.

94 My thanks to Jean Munro for giving me access to her forthcoming edition of the English, and apparently original, text of Macintosh of Kinrara's history, from which these phrases are taken. Cf. MacFarlane, *Gen. Coll.*, I. 148–50.

95 Macpherson, 'Genealogy', 34.

96 *Misc. Scot. Hist. Soc.*, IV. 243. Cf. Archibald MacDonald, 'Fragment of a MacKenzie MS.', *TGSI*, 36 (1931–33), 187–212, at 205.

97 *Misc. Scot. Hist. Soc.*, IV. 191; Maclean-Bristol, 'The Macleans', 70; *The Loyall Dissuasive and other papers concerning the affairs of Clan Chattan: by Sir Aeneas Macpherson, Knight of Invereshie 1691–1705*, ed. A. D. Murdoch (Edinburgh: SHS, 1902), 219.

98 Ibid., 4, and n. 1.

99 Ibid., 219–21. MacPherson's intention, revealed in this same passage, to use these oral sources as the basis of a 'larger tractat of more use and value', may refer to the *Invereshie Book Genealogy*.

100 Ibid., editor's notes; Macpherson, 'Genealogy', 4.

101 *Misc. Scot. Hist. Soc.*, IV. 191–3, 240–2; *Collectanea de Rebus Albanicis*, 197–8.

102 *Misc. Scot. Hist. Soc.*, IV. 193. The Campbells of Craignish used the subsidiary surname *MacDubhghaill*, 'MacDougall'.

103 The surnames of the informants described by MacPherson as 'two of the greatest poets and genealogues in the Highlands', suggest they were of non-professional origin. The editor's equation of 'John McDonald (alias Lame)' with the well-known poet Iain Lom is questionable.

104 See n. 118.

105 *Loyall Dissuasive*, 231.

106 Ibid., 221.

107 *Misc. Scot. Hist. Soc.*, IV. 193.

108 See pp. 221f.

109 *Reliquiae Celticae*, II. 148–75. Cf. p. 209.

110 For evidence of the existence of these chronicles, see ibid., 155–63 (the 'Lordship' or 'Iona' Chronicle', for which see also p. 225 and n. 208); ibid., 166–73, esp. 166–9 (the 'Clann Raghnaill Chronicle').

111 Ibid., 170–1. For valuable discussion of the authorship, sources and – from a Classical Gaelic perspective – innovative approach of the *Red Book of Clanranald*, see Gillies, 'The Clanranald Histories'.

112 Bannerman, *Beatons*, 17–20.

113 See MacGregor, 'Provisional Checklist'.

114 See *Highland Papers*, I. 14, 17, 23, 27, 28, 34, 49, 63. But see Gillies, 'The Clanranald Histories', for the suggestion that dates given in the earlier sections of the *Red Book of Clanranald* may be based on erroneous interpretations of roman numerals.

115 See n. 49; Matheson, 'North Uist Families', 323–4, and 363, n. 29; William Matheson, 'Hugh MacDonald's Manuscript', *Notes and Queries of the Society of West Highland and Island Historical Research*, 21 (August 1983), 16–17. He was known to Màrtainn Martin, with whom the identification of the author of the

Sleat History as someone named Hugh MacDonald apparently began; Martin, *Western Islands*, 17–18, 250.

116 See n. 42; MacGregor, 'Provisional Checklist' *Highland Papers*, II. 74; *Misc. Scot. Hist. Soc.*, IV. 190–1. On Alexander Colville or Colvin, see Sellar, 'Campbells', 112.

117 *Misc. Scot. Hist. Soc.*, IV. 191; Sellar, 'Campbells', 113.

118 Genealogical histories of the late seventeenth and early eighteenth centuries continue to use the word in this sense (*Highland Papers*, II. 73; MacFarlane, *Gen. Coll.*, I. 118; *Misc. Scot. Hist. Soc.*, IV. 190). But for the argument that in the later seventeenth century we see *seanchaidh* developing the new meaning of 'aristocratic lay-historian', see p. 224, and MacGregor, 'Provisional Checklist'.

119 J. W. M. Bannerman, 'The MacLachlans of Kilbride and Their Manuscripts', *Scottish Studies*, 21 (1977), 1–34, at p. 13. These MacLachlan clergymen must have been well known to Duncanson, who was himself a prominent minister within the Synod of Argyll from 1658 until 1661. For his career, see *Minutes of the Synod of Argyll, 1639–1661*, ed. Duncan C. MacTavish, 2 vols (Edinburgh: SHS, 1943–44), I. vii–viii; for his own competence in Gaelic, and his role in the Synod's projects to publish religious material in the language, which also involved these MacLachlans, see ibid., II. 177, 198, 224.

120 See p. 207.

121 *Highland Papers*, I. 198–9.

122 Bannerman, *Beatons*, 19, gives this as an instance of a servitor being identified by the surname of his employer; Matheson, 'MacKenzies', 227, n. 68, noting that elsewhere MacRae calls Maol-Domhnaich *MacEoin* (i.e. *mac Eoin*, his patronymic), suggests that *MacLean* 'may be a copyist's error for MacEan'.

123 Ibid; Bannerman, *Beatons*, 34–5; 50, n. 296.

124 Matheson, 'MacKenzies', 227, n. 68.

125 *Bàrdachd Chloinn Ghill-Eathain*, 171–3. It has been suggested (Matheson, 'MacKenzies', 226–7, n. 68) that he may have been a Beaton. If so, he may have belonged to the branch based at Dervaig in Mull, among whom *Ruairi* recurs as a forename (Bannerman, *Beatons*, 49–54, esp. 52–3). For the demonstrably close links of the head of these Beatons with contemporary Ó Muirgheasáins and MacMhuirichs in the early seventeenth century, see ibid., 50–1. One key piece of evidence, the implications of which cannot be discussed here, has hitherto been overlooked. The *Ardintoul MS*, describing the visit of the MacKenzie Chief Coinneach to the court of MacLean of Duart in the early seventeenth century, mentions 'Fergus Mackenzie McLean's genealogist who told them that they were not descended of the Geralds but of the Kings of Ireland, as the most of the clans of the west and south west parts of Scotland were ...' ('Fragment of a MacKenzie MS', 204–5).

126 *Highland Papers*, I. 199.

127 *Chronicles of the Frasers*, 145–6.

128 MacFarlane, *Gen. Coll.*, I. 118–19.

129 Ibid., 119–21, 142; *Scottish Gaelic Studies*, 9 (1961), 90–1.

130 *An Clàrsair Dall*, xxxiv–xxxv; Matheson, 'Aonghus nan Aoir', 106; Bannerman, 'Lordship', 225, n. 64. It has been suggested that the *Bannatyne MS* is in part based on earlier written sources: William Matheson, 'The Morrisons of Ness', *TGSI*, 50 (1976–78), 60–80, at p. 75, perhaps including an annalistic compilation (cf. Steer and Bannerman, *Monumental Sculpture*, 97–100), but the matter requires more detailed investigation.

131 On another aspect of orality in the *Red Book of Clanranald*, Niall MacMhuirich's use of eyewitness testimony from aristocrats involved in the Montrose campaigns during the Civil Wars, see Gillies, 'The Clanranald Histories'.

132 See for example n. 135; the narratives in the *Bannatyne MS* concerning Coinneach Odhar, and the 'Fairy Cup' and *Bratach Shìth* or 'Fairy Flag' linked to the MacLeods of Dunvegan; Matheson, 'MacKenzies', 220–3; *Highland Papers*, I. 58; *Chronicles of the Frasers*, 233. Cf. Juliette Wood, 'Folkloric Patterns in Scottish Chronicles', in Sally Mapstone and Juliette Wood (eds), *The Rose and the Thistle: Essays on the Culture of Late Medieval and Renaissance Scotland* (East Linton: Tuckwell Press, 1998), 116–35; R. Dorson, 'Introduction: Folklore and Traditional History' and 'Sources for the Traditional History of the Scottish Highlands and Western Islands', *Journal of the Folklore Institute*, 8 (1971–72), 79–81, 145–84; A. J. Bruford, 'Problems in Cataloguing Scottish Supernatural and Historical Legends', *Journal of the Folklore Institute*, 16 (1979), 155–66; John MacInnes, 'Clan Sagas and Historical Legends', *TGSI*, 57 (1990–92), 377–94.

133 *Companion to Gaelic Scotland*, 148–9, 280–2, 283–5.

134 See pp. 196–7, this volume.

135 Thus, what the *Sleat History* has to say about the origins of the Macintyres (*Clann an t-Saoir*), the earl of Mar and the battle of Inverlochy in 1431, and fratricidal conflict within the ruling MacDonald lineage in North Uist, *c.* 1500–1600, could all be compared with recordings made this century: *Highland Papers* I. 7, 39–43, 65–72; School of Scottish Studies, University of Edinburgh Sound Archive 1952/125/4; 1971/175 B11; A. J. Bruford and D. A. MacDonald (eds), *Scottish Traditional Tales* (Edinburgh: Polygon, 1994), 422–6, 484–5.

136 The exception is the treatment of Gille-Brighde and his son Somerled (*Somhairle*), on which see above p. 215.

137 Note the influence of folktale upon the late medieval Irish historical tracts, produced under classical auspices (p. 197).

138 This may be more true of Scotland than of Ireland: Gillies, 'The Clanranald Histories'.

139 See the passage quoted here at p. 213.

140 See p. 204.

141 *Companion to Gaelic Scotland*, 148.

142 *Highland Papers*, I. 203–4, 204–5.

143 *Reliquiae Celticae*, II. 659; translated in Gillies, 'The Clanranald Histories'.

144 *Reliquiae Celticae*, II. 154–5.

145 This is not to deny an active role to authors such as Aeneas MacPherson and Alasdair Campbell, who were clearly assiduous in their pursuit of oral informants, and active assimilators of native tradition; see pp. 209–11.

146 Allan, '"What's in A Name?"'.

147 Michael Lynch, *Scotland: A New History* (London: Century, 1991), 247–56.

148 Ibid., 257 ff.; Allan, '"What's in A Name?"'.

149 Lynch, *Scotland*, 261–2.

150 Allan I. Macinnes, *Clanship, Commerce and the House of Stuart* (East Linton: Tuckwell Press, 1996), 72–4, and chs 4 and 5, esp. 91–2, 96–7, 104–8, 110–12, 126–8; Jean Munro, 'When Island Chiefs came to Town', *Notes and Queries of the Society of West Highland and Island Historical Research*, 19 (December 1982), 11–19.

151 MacInnes, 'Gaelic Poetry', 147; MacInnes, 'Panegyric Code', 437.

152 Macinnes, *Clanship*, 94–8.
153 For the MacKenzie historians' 'concerted effort to conceal the fact that the early record of the clan was one of rebellion against the Crown', see Matheson, 'MacKenzies', 193–5, 201, 212, 214.
154 Douglas A. Watt, 'Chiefs, Lawyers and Debt: a Sudy of the Relationship between Highland Elite and Legal Profession in Scotland *c.* 1550 to 1700', unpublished PhD dissertation (University of Edinburgh, 1998); Alick Morrison, 'The Accounts of a Doer: Alexander MacLeod the "Advocat"', *TGSI*, 50 (1976–78), 97–172, at pp. 97–8. It is particularly striking that the Campbell ruling lineage should have turned first to Alexander Colville (above, p. 202) to revise the genealogies of the MacEwens.
155 Note particularly the demise of the active practice of Gaelic law by the indigenous lawmen, or *britheamhain*, a process complete by *c.* 1600 at the very latest: *An Clàrsair Dall*, 187; Matheson, 'Morrisons of Ness', 60–80; John Bannerman, 'The Scots Language and the Kin-based Society', in Derick S. Thomson (ed.), *Gaelic and Scots in Harmony* (Glasgow: Department of Celtic, University of Glasgow, 1989), 1–19, at pp. 12–14; and the adoption of primogeniture alone as the system of succession among territorial kindreds after 1600: Bannerman, *Beatons*, 86–7.
156 Munro, 'Island Chiefs', 11–19; Macinnes, *Clanship*, 71, 73.
157 *The Acts of the Parliaments of Scotland*, ed. T. Thomson and C. Innes, 12 vols (Edinburgh: HMSO, 1814–75), IV (1593–1625): 138–9.
158 For instances of the destruction of Highland charter-chests before *c.* 1600, see *Acts of the Lords of the Isles*, lxxix.
159 For reasons of space, the discussion which follows deals solely with land tenure. The histories' response to the distinctive nature of marriage custom in the late medieval *Gàidhealtachd* – secular marriage and divorce, concubinage, and the lack of distinction between legitimate and illegitimate offspring which flowed from these – requires separate and detailed analysis. I merely note here the use of illegitimacy as a device to explain away the failure of an individual to succeed to the chiefship, when primogeniture apparently entitled him to do so (Matheson, 'MacKenzies', 210); or to stigmatize certain lineages and individuals, notably Dubhghall, progenitor of the MacDougalls of Lorn, and Iain MacIain of Ardnamurchan; see pp. 219, 223 and *Highland Papers*, I. 11–13, 15–16, 60; Macpherson, 'Genealogy', 35–6. Cf. also *Misc. Scot. Hist. Soc.*, IV. 218–19, 231–2.
160 *Chronicles of the Frasers*, 1.
161 Matheson, 'MacKenzies', 200–1, 208–14.
162 Steer and Bannerman, *Monumental Sculpture*, 99–100, 113, 114, 127, 132–3, 148.
163 Ibid., 99–100, 127.
164 Bannerman, *Beatons*, 86–7.
165 For a very likely eighteenth-century instance of the deliberate misrepresentation of tanistry for legal motives, occurring outwith the genealogical history genre, see ibid., 31–2. For evidence that the succession to the chiefship of the MacKenzies in the later middle ages 'was not as regular as the seventeenth-century historians would have us believe', see Matheson, 'Mathesons', 160, 178–9, and Matheson, 'MacKenzies', 210–13. The succession to the chiefship of the MacKenzies and the Mathesons would bear re-examination in the light of what we now know of the survival of tanistry in the late medieval *Gàidhealtachd*.
166 See also n. 159.

167 For a possible instance of the latter tactic, see Matheson, 'Mathesons', 164–6.
168 Steer and Bannerman, *Monumental Sculpture*, 99–100.
169 Ibid., 113, and cf. 127. For a very similar use of the misrepresentation of tanistry as an offensive weapon in one of the 'Campbell precursors' to the genealogical histories, see *The Black Book of Taymouth*, ed. Cosmo Innes (Edinburgh: Bannatyne Club, 1855), 12, 64.
170 Sellar, 'Campbells', 115.
171 Bannerman, *Beatons*, 120–33; D. S. Thomson, 'The MacMhuirich Bardic Family', *TGSI*, 43 (1963), 276–304, at p. 301; Thomson, *Introduction to Gaelic Poetry*, 20; W. Gillies, 'Some Aspects of Campbell History', *TGSI*, 50 (1976–78), 256–95, at pp. 261, 280.
172 Note also Watson's perceptive observation that 'the poet selected to be honoured by Charles II at his Restoration in 1660 as his Gaelic poet laureate was not MacMhuirich nor any trained professional bard, but the self-trained poet John MacDonald [Iain Lom]': W. J. Watson, 'Classic Gaelic Poetry of Panegyric in Scotland', *TGSI*, 29 (1914–19), 194–217, at p. 216. Màrtainn Martin, writing between *c.* 1695 and 1703, dates the decline in the status of the classical poets to 'within these forty years': Martin, *Western Islands*, 176.
173 Bannerman, 'MacLachlans of Kilbride', 17; *Argyll Synod*, II. 15, 141; W. J. Watson, 'Unpublished Gaelic Poetry – IV., V.', *Scottish Gaelic Studies*, 3 (1931), 139–59, at pp. 152–9.
174 Campbell, *Records of Argyll*, 3–4; above, n. 42.
175 See 212.
176 See p. 213, and cf. *Companion to Gaelic Scotland*, 4.
177 Bannerman, *Beatons*, 35, 121. For the demise of the Ó Conchobhair medical lineage which served the MacDougalls of Dunollie *c.* 1672, see ibid., 148.
178 Ibid., 3–5, 7–11, 18–20. For parallel instances of conscious Beaton antiquarianism, both associated with Iain Beaton (d. 1657), see ibid., 29, 111.
179 Niall MacMhuirich brings this history down to 1686, although he copied the pre-Montrose Wars sections from another source or sources: Gillies, 'The Clanranald Histories'.
180 See ibid.
181 Osborn Bergin, *Irish Bardic Poetry* (Dublin: Dublin Institute for Advanced Studies, 1970), 22; Gillies, 'Gaelic: the Classical Tradition', 260.
182 For the apparent blossoming of vernacular poetry between *c.* 1645 and *c.* 1725, see A. Maclean Sinclair, 'The Gaelic Bards and the Collectors of their Works', *TGSI*, 24 (1899–1901), 259–77, at 264–5.
183 See pp. 199–200. Note also 'the herbal garden established in Edinburgh *c.* 1670 by Dr later Sir Robert Sibbald and Dr Andrew Balfour, founders of the Royal College of Physicians in 1681', and modelled on that maintained by the lineage of Beaton physicians based at Pennycross, Isle of Mull (Bannerman, *Beatons*, 92).
184 See also W. F. Skene, *Celtic Scotland: A History of Ancient Albyn*, 3 vols (Edinburgh: David Douglas, 1886–90), III. 346–59.
185 See n. 125, where the same descent for the MacLeans is also rejected. For the (late?) classical belief that these clans had a common, but non-Geraldine, origin, see Matheson, 'MacKenzies', 217.
186 Ibid., 193, 195, 205–6, 212, 214; Skene, *Celtic Scotland*, III. 351–4; Jean Munro, 'Mackenzie Manuscript Histories', *West Highland Notes and Queries*, series 2, no. 19 (March 1999), 12–17, at p. 12.

187 Gillies, 'Campbell History', 279–81; Sellar, 'Campbells', 118. Further evidence for the 'integrity' of the classical tradition *vis-à-vis* the genealogical histories lies in its reservations concerning the persona of King Arthur; see MacGregor, 'Provisional Checklist'.

188 Ibid. As with the notion of a Geraldine origin for the MacKenzies and MacLeans, belief in 'Norman' and 'Gaelic' origins for the Campbells probably both pre-existed the genealogical histories, but only achieved mainstream acceptance within them: Steer and Bannerman, *Monumental Sculpture*, 140, 211; William Gillies, 'Heroes and Ancestors', in Bo Almqvist, Séamas Ó Catháin and Pádraig Ó Héalaí (eds), *The Heroic Process: Form, Function and Fantasy in Folk Epic* (Dublin: Glendale Press, 1987), 57–74, at pp. 61–3.

189 Sellar, 'Campbells', 119.

190 Ibid., 113, 117–19; MacGregor, 'Provisional Checklist'.

191 See n. 49.

192 *Chronicles of the Frasers*, xliv, 24–8; *West Highland Notes and Queries*, series 2, no. 16 (April 1997), 26; MacFarlane, *Gen. Coll*, I. 144–6; cf. Macpherson, 'Genealogy', 41, n. 31. One of the Campbell 'precursors' to the genealogical histories, *The Black Book of Taymouth*, was dedicated by William Bowie to his patron Donnchadh Dubh, Chief of the Glen Orchy Campbells, in 1598. In the 1630s these same Campbells commissioned a series of paintings of the kings and queens of Scotland, and of their own ancestors, as well as a great genealogy board: *Black Book of Taymouth*, 253–4; xxviii, 75, 77–8.

193 Cf. p. 213, for the involvement of Sir Ailean MacLean of Duart, although not, apparently, with respect to the history of his own kindred.

194 Allan, '"What's in A Name?"'.

195 One copy of *Ane Accompt of the Genealogie of the Campbells* was 'given by the ... late Earl Archibald [Campbell, d. 1685] to his daughter Lady Anne the present Countes of Murray' (*Misc. Scot. Hist. Soc.*, IV. 191). Perhaps marriage was one occasion for the copying and circulation of genealogical histories. See also MacFarlane, *Gen. Coll.*, I. vii–viii, 145; Macpherson, 'Genealogy', 5, 41, n. 32; *West Highland Notes and Queries*, series 2, no. 16 (April 1997), 26; *Highland Papers*, I. 197 and II. 3, 70–1; Graeme M. MacKenzie, 'The Rarest Decision Recorded in History: the Battle of the Clans in 1396', *TGSI*, 59 (1994–96), 420–87, at pp. 429–31.

196 For the Macintosh claim to descend from the earls of Fife, see MacFarlane, *Gen. Coll.*, I. 148, 150–2, 153 ff., and Skene, *Celtic Scotland*, III. 356–9. On the seventeenth-century fashion for claiming common ancestry for kindreds on either side of the Highland line, see Bannerman, *Beatons*, 3–5.

197 For discussion see Gillies, 'The Clanranald Histories'. There is no evidence that Niall's work was translated into English.

198 *Reliquiae Celticae*, II. 202–3.

199 *Highland Papers*, I. 10–11, and passim. Note also the *Sleat History*'s rejection of new-fangled ideas on Beaton origins: MacGregor, 'Provisional Checklist' .

200 Macinnes, *Clanship*, 37–46.

201 *Highland Papers*, I. 11–13, 15, 23, 59–60, 63–5; Steer and Bannerman, *Monumental Sculpture*, 113.

202 *Misc. Scot. Hist. Soc.*, IV. 191.

203 MacFarlane, *Gen. Coll.*, I. 122–5.

204 Macpherson, 'Genealogy', 3, 7, 30–1; *Loyall Dissuasive*, 218–41.

205 For the same motive at work in the nineteenth-century *Bannatyne MS*, see p. 219.
206 See pp. 210–12; MacGregor, 'Provisional Checklist'.
207 The editor of the *Chronicles of the Frasers* omits all sections dealing with 'England, the Popes, France, Germany, and almost every Continental state ... and many pages have thus been discarded' p. xx.
208 See pp. 211–12, and n. 110; Matheson, 'MacKenzies', 208, 217, and 226–7, n. 68. Iona was of course the customary place of burial for the ruling grades of kindreds within the MacDonald lordship of the Isles down to *c.* 1500.
209 Cf. pp. 207–8 for the integrating intent behind the genealogical historians' use of printed works such as Hector Boece, George Buchanan and William Camden.

Chapter 8

Constructing oral tradition: the origins of the concept in Enlightenment intellectual culture

Nicholas Hudson

> [M]any circumstances of those times we call barbarous are favourable to the poetical spirit. That state, in which human nature shoots wild and free, though unfit for other improvements, certainly encourages the high exertions of fancy and passion ... An American chief, at this day, harangues at the head of his tribe, in a more bold and metaphorical style, than a modern European would adventure to use in an epic poem.[1]

This statement from Hugh Blair's *A Critical Dissertation on the Poems of Ossian* (1763) reflects an important reassessment of oral tradition among scholars during the middle decades of the eighteenth century. It was during this period that scholars began to acknowledge that a society without writing could, as Blair indicates, function as an organized political culture with a tradition of common values and practices. Such a culture, it was thought, could also nourish a 'poetical spirit' that equalled and even excelled the literary resources of European nations in their modern, developed state. These views marked a radical departure from the generally negative opinion of pre-literate cultures that prevailed in the Renaissance and the seventeenth century. In *Purchas his Pilgrimes* (1625), a major source of information about non- European peoples in the early century, Samuel Purchas echoed the conventional view that alphabetical writing marked the main distinction between civilized peopled and 'barbarians': 'amongst Men, some are accounted Ciuill, and more both Sociable and Religious, by the Vse of *letters* and Writing, which others wanting are esteemed British, Sauage, Barabarous.'[2] According to Purchas and his contemporaries, illiterate 'savages' lacked history, government, poetry or really 'society' of any kind.

Between the Renaissance and the Enlightenment, in short, Western attitudes to non-literate cultures transformed fundamentally, paving the way for our modern appreciation of oral tradition as a legitimate basis for poetical expression and social organization. What were the historical factors that instigated this change? Elsewhere, I have traced the concept of oral tradition to theological debates between Catholics and Protestants concerning the authority of customary or 'unwritten' practices and doctrines.[3] In this chapter, I will argue that the emergence of this concept in the Enlightenment was linked to a much wider revolution of ideas about language, history and culture. Increasingly, scholars began to recognize the predominant and, in some respects, damaging influence of writing over their conceptions of language and society. They began to recognize more clearly the special powers of speech not possessed by written language, a development that led to a deeper appreciation of so-called 'primitive' language in non-literate societies.

Readers will recognize the irony of this development: as European society became *more* literate, it gained an ever sharper awareness of oral cultures and their special characteristics. Despite being surrounded by a predominantly oral culture, medieval authors were virtually unconscious of 'orality' as a special state of either language or society. They failed to distinguish between oral and literate societies, for they did not conceive of speech and writing as inherently dissimilar forms of language. Relying on Aristotle's *De interpretatione* (largely as explained in the late Roman tradition of Porphyry and Boethius), they regarded writing as an 'image' of spoken language, which in turn was an 'image' of 'mental experience'. Aristotle's definition implied no deficiency in the power of writing to convey either words or thoughts. Consider, for example, the following paraphrase of Aristotle's model (as presented by Boethius) by William of Ockham, the great nominalist philosopher of the early fourteenth century:

> According to Boethius in the first book of *De interpretatione*, language is threefold: written, spoken and conceptual ... A written term [*terminus scriptus*] is part of a proposition written on some material, and is or can be seen with the bodily eye. A spoken term is part of a proposition uttered with the mouth and able to be heard with the bodily ear. A conceptual term is a mental content or impression which naturally possesses signification or consignification, and which is suited to be part of a mental proposition and to stand for what it signifies.[4]

According to Ockham, the difference between mental, verbal and written discourse consisted merely in the *medium* of transmission. This understanding of language justified the medieval practice of treating the propositions of written logic as the key to understanding the structure of reality itself. They assumed that language, written or spoken, mirrored the world, and that the syntax of written Latin revealed mysteries of predication immanent in the very things of nature.

Hence, contrary to what might be assumed, the failure to distinguish clearly between oral and written language is especially characteristic of European scholarship *before* the advent of print culture. It was, indeed, only after Gutenberg that scholars gained a strong awareness of the special characteristics of oral and written language. With the new humanist concern for popular education (leading, as Lawrence Stone argued, to an educational 'revolution'), scholars began to worry about the predominance of illiteracy and the alleged deficiency of oral language and its associated habits of thought.[5] For example, the Spanish humanist Juan Luis Vives lamented the wandering of minds undisciplined by the practice of writing:

> [T]here are some people who do not understand how to write down what they would be well able to speak; this happens, as far as I can discover, because a wandering and unsettled mind is capable of sufficient attention for speech, but not for understanding what is written; it cannot support the strain of collecting and, as it were, compelling itself.[6]

Vives's conviction in the value of literacy, highly typical of humanist educators,[7] was further promoted in Northern Europe by Protestantism, with its demand for the individual reading of Scripture and its decreased value for the oral transmission of Christian practice. The steep, even meteoric, rise in literacy in Britain and other parts of Northern Europe during the sixteenth century arose from both these sources.[8] The expanding middle-classes sent their boys to new grammar schools; universities entered an era of flourishing expansion. Everywhere educated people began to associate illiteracy with ignorance, superstition and social inferiority.

Influenced by the same movement of ideas, Renaissance authors began to differentiate more clearly between societies with writing and those without. Their conception of language gained a temporal dimension virtually absent from medieval thought: because humanists thought that the invention of writing had inaugurated progress towards reason, civil order and religious enlightenment, they characterized non-literate people as embodying an *original* state of pre-literate barbarity. Accounts of the New World often included references to the childish amazement of native peoples at the writing of the Europeans, for the alphabet seemed to exemplify, more than other inventions, the technical superiority of the conquering culture. As Roger Williams wrote in his *Key to the Language of America* (1643), 'when they talke amongst themselves of the *English* ships, and great buildings, of the plowing of their Fields, and especially of Bookes and Letters, they will end thus: *Manittôwock*. They are Gods.'[9] The ignorance of oral people with writing was a source of self-congratulatory humour: in a popular story, rehearsed by several authors, an 'Indian slave' steals a gift of figs that he is carrying to a neighbour, along with a letter explaining the gift. When his theft is exposed by the letter, the lesson is not lost on the slave. The next time, he is careful to hide his master's 'talking paper' under a rock so that it will not see him eating the figs.[10]

Yet neither Williams nor the authors who told this story had a full or sophisticated concept of an 'oral tradition': they viewed non-literate peoples simply in contrast to the rationality and order that they closely associated with literacy. In the view of Charles de Rochefort, for example, the peoples of Carribean had no 'tradition' whatsoever: 'indeed these Savages themselves speak not thereof but at adventure, and as people tell stories of what they had seen in dreams, so careless have they been in preserving the tradition of their Origine; and they palpably contradict and confute one the other by the difference of their Relations'.[11] Johan de Laet observed similarly of the native people of Newfoundland that they are 'rude & sans civilité, n'ayant nulle religion ou cognoissance de Dieu, nul regime Politique entr'eux'.[12] They 'se gouuernent pour la plupart sans loix, sans institutions Politiques à la façon des bestes'.[13] Travel writers showed some awareness that American and Carribean peoples used songs and dance to preserve the memory of victories and other great events. Moreover, the Aztecs and Incas were widely regarded as being far ahead of other American peoples in possessing at least some form of visual records – 'hieroglyphics' in Mexico and *quippos* in Peru.[14] Nevertheless, most authors stressed, like Francisco Lopez de Gómora, that people without letters were like 'beasts'.[15] Particularly as humans and beasts shared the capacity to make significant sounds, speech was not regarded as the distinctive mark of rationality or even humanness. It was instead writing that marked the line between *animal rationale* and the condition of brutes.

Given the prevailing aesthetic outlook of the Renaissance, there could be little 'poetic' about the language of beasts and savages. Influenced by humanism, with its profound reverence for the *written* traditions of language, authors of the Renaissance regarded poetical language as the last product of linguistic refinement, the highest achievement of an advanced and literate culture. As Walter J. Ong observed, humanists set out to 'to make the measure of all speech a fixed *written* tradition'.[16] It was, for example, the *written* tradition that Italian humanists like Dante, Biondi and Veronese made the model of correct and eloquent Latin, for they denied that the illiterate masses of ancient Rome even knew Latin: they spoke instead some barbarous vernacular.[17] These attitudes continued to shape perceptions of non-literate peoples and cultures in the early eighteenth century. As Jean Terrasson wrote in 1715, 'Language never improves among a savage and barbarous people, who make no other us of it but only to express the Necessities of the Animal Life.'[18] In 1741, John Oldmixon was still referring to the American languages as 'dreadful' and 'barbarous'.[19] Even authors who studied and understood native tongues, like John Williams, had nothing complimentary to say about native poetry or oratory. While acknowledging that native oratory was 'copious and patheticall',[20] Williams regarded books and letters as an important sign of Europeans uperiority to Americans in all areas of life.

Obviously, such an understanding of language differed profoundly from the praise of native oratory found in the work of Enlightenment authors like Hugh Blair. During the late eighteenth century, authors increasingly departed in significant ways from a humanist tradition that regarded written tradition as the foundation of literary excellence. But how and when did new ways of conceiving language emerge?

A major development in linguistic thought from the Renaissance to the Enlightenment was increasing awareness of the differing natures and functions of writing and speech. This is a historical development that I have described in detail elsewhere:[21] for my purposes here, I will review some of the main features of the scholarly process that led to a clearer recognition of the special features of spoken language. As I have contended, grammarians and other scholars before the eighteenth century made no clear distinction between the nature of writing and speech. They tended, indeed, to understand language largely as it was *written,* and placed little significance on those features of language exclusive to speech. This tendency to imagine language entirely through the medium of writing was exemplified by two major branches of sixteenth- and seventeenth-century linguistics. The first was the vigorous campaign to rationalize the orthography of vernacular languages to make writing a more faithful 'copy' of speech. In the works of Sir Thomas Smith, James Hart, Charles Butler, Robert Robinson and others, discrepancies between writing and speech were decried as failures correctable by the reform of spelling. The aim of these authors was to create a script in which 'each simple sound hauing a proper mark appointed to it selfe, may by the same be as apparently scene to the eye, as the sound it selfe is sensibly discerned by the eares'.[22] A second branch of early modern linguistics was the invention of a 'real character' or written language to replace speech for the purposes of international communication and science. The many projects of seventeenth-century scholars – including Francis Lodwick, Cave Beck, George Dalgarno and John Wilkins – envisioned a visual language that mirrored the nature of things more accurately than any existing form of speech.[23]

Common among these trends was the assumption that writing can replace speech, for the two media differ essentially in their *means of transmission,* not in their natures. It is significant, therefore, that both these areas of linguistic study became more-or-less defunct after 1700, particularly in Britain. Even some earlier authors had strongly questioned the capacity of any writing to replace speech entirely. The sixteenth-century grammarian Richard Mulcalster, for example, denied that orthography could mirror speech in the way envisaged by contemporaries like Smith and Hart. These objections became more common towards the end of the seventeenth century: in *A Dissertation on Speech* (1700), Conrad Amman elucidated some of the objections to the wide-spread belief in the adequacy of writing to duplicate the nature and function of spoken language. Amman was a teacher of deaf–mute people, and this experience convinced him that any purely visual form of communication was inherently inadequate. First, the sound of speech was far richer and more various than any alphabet: 'many letters have their own compass and peculiar modifications; and the same character, even the same language, is not always pronounced in one and the same manner'.[24] Second, speech is the only 'natural' way for human beings to express their thoughts. 'Besides that certain signs, not uttered by the living voice, are liable to deceive', wrote Amman, 'every sincere mind, giving attention to itself when about to converse with another on a serious subject, feels a desire to declare the hidden thoughts of his heart ... by the use of Speech'.[25]

Readers of Jacques Derrida will remark that Amman's preference for speech over writing was hardly novel, but stems from a tradition at least as ancient as Plato's *Phaedrus*. Indeed, according to Derrida's thesis, 'phonocentricism' and the denigration of writing, represent twin pillars of the entire Western philosophical tradition.[26] This claim, despite what is sometimes pretended, relies on much more than an abstract analysis of the structure of signification; it derives much of its supposed authority from a generalized *history* of Western culture, a history that views the Western intellectual tradition as uniformly prejudiced against written language. For defenders of deconstruction, therefore, it is surely a problem that 'phonocentrism' by no means characterized Renaissance and seventeenth-century studies of language: Amman was challenging a very general confidence in written language exhibited, as we have considered, by projects for orthographic reform and a 'real character'. But these attitudes were also in the process of change. By the middle of the eighteenth century, Samuel Johnson both ignored projects for a 'real character' to replace speech and declared that projects to reform alphabetical writing were the defunct preoccupation of a previous age.[27] Johnson complained in the Preface to his *Dictionary* (1754) that 'penmen' had vitiated language by attempting to duplicate 'the boundless chaos of living speech' in their spellings. These reformers, he argued, forgot that all pronunciations reflect only the temporary habits of a particular time and place, and cannot be preserved as an absolute standard.[28] Hence, Johnson's own modest reforms of spelling in his *Dictionary* attempted to strengthen the internal analogies of written English rather than mirror speech. He viewed writing not as a 'copy' of speech, but rather as essentially distinct form of discourse with its own rules and standards.

What Johnson exemplified, in short, was a heightened appreciation that writing and speech were inherently *distinct* modes of communication. Writing and speech certainly influenced each other: indeed, Johnson was among the first to consider how literacy changes and (he believed) improves spoken language, making it available for study and improvement by 'poets', grammarians and lexicographers.[29] Such a position is correctly seen as reflecting Johnson's personal linguistic preference for print over the 'boundless chaos of living speech'.[30] Yet Johnson was saying something more interesting: he was challenging the ancient Aristotlean model of writing as an 'image' of speech – a challenge undertaken by many other writers of his generation. Even an author who did not, on the whole, agree with Johnson on linguistic issues, the elocutionist Thomas Sheridan, stressed the essential difference of writing and speech:

> These two kinds of language [writing and speech] are so early in life associated, that it is difficult ever after to separate them; or not to suppose that there is some kind of natural connection between them. And yet it is a matter of importance to us, always to bear in mind, that there is no sort of affinity between them, but what arises from habitual association of ideas. Tho' we cannot so easily separate them in our own minds, yet when we come to separate them in relation to others, we see clearly enough their utter independence of each other.[31]

The point made by Johnson and Sheridan was very modern, anticipating the argument of modern linguists such as Josef Vachek and Roy Harris:[32] writing cannot even potentially duplicate the functions of speech, for the two media operate according to different principles. Johnson stressed the inherently fluid and adaptable nature of speech, as opposed to the relative fixity of writing; Sheridan found a major deficiency in the incapacity of writing to express the passions through the oral resources of intonation and gesture. Johnson and Sheridan reflect an important shift in the understanding of the writing and speech: in an age increasingly dominated by writing and print, European scholars were beginning to acknowledge the inherent limitations of what could be achieved by visual language.

This is the crux of my thesis. With this separation of writing and speech in theories of language, European scholars also began to imagine oral and literate cultures as quite separate and dissimilar. Societies without writing, it was thought, retained a language that exhibited all the special powers of speech in their purest form, unchanged by writing. It was even proposed that the language of oral cultures might be *better* for lacking the pervasive influence of writing. This was a controversial point. Many scholars of language, such as Samuel Johnson, stressed that only writing and print could give language stability, coherence and elegance: the speech of oral cultures was unstable, vague and indistinct. But another school of thought contended that the propagation of literacy and print culture had destroyed the expressive force of speech, rendering it toneless and cold. This critique was made in France by Rousseau and in Britain, within a different context, by Thomas Sheridan. In his influential *Course of Lectures on Elocution* (1762), Sheridan complained that 'some of our greatest men have been trying to do that with the pen, which can only be performed by the tongue; to produce effects by the dead letter, which can never be produced but by the living voice, with its accompaniments'.[33] Sheridan's goal was to promote a more passionate oratory – the kind of persuasive elocution needed to promote Christianity and political freedom. This kind of oratory could only be achieved if speakers cultivated 'tones' and 'accents'. These qualities were the very 'life, blood, and soul' of language, yet they were 'utterly unnoticed in writing'.[34]

It was this general disdain for the stultifying influence of literacy, as exemplified by Sheridan, that led to the important reassessment of native oratory that we have already noted in Hugh Blair. Blair's tendency to 'classicize' native Americans, whose style of oratory he compared with the epic, echoed the view of previous authors like Cadwallader Colden, surveyor-general of New York. In *The History of the Five Indian Nations of Canada* (1747), Colden portrayed a chief named 'Dacanesora' who 'had a great Fluency in speaking, and a graceful Elocution, that would have pleased in any Part of the World'.[35] Danesora reminded Colden of Cicero: with his noble nose and patrician bearing, he even 'looked' like that Roman orator. Another historian of the Scottish Enlightenment, Adam Ferguson, shared Blair's opinion on the 'magnificent beauty' of Indian speech which 'no change of language can improve, and no refinements of the critics reform'.[36]

These passages reflect an important re-evaluation of oral language and culture in the mid-eighteenth century – a re-evaluation connected with the increasing tendency of linguists and grammarians to separate the functions of writing and speech. Enlightenment authors were contending, in particular, that writing lacked the resources of intonation that gave speech its special passionate force. But this new attention to intonation was not the only factor leading to a new interest in oral language and culture. A greater appreciation for oral cultures was connected as well with the critique of European society that was, indeed, a major characteristic of Enlightenment ideology. In the work of Adam Ferguson and Jean-Jacques Rousseau, the willingness to acknowledge the advantages of oral societies formed part of a challenge to the injustice and inequality of modern civilization, which both authors regarded as overrun with books and bookish speculation. But similar suspicions with literate society can be found in previous works such as the Baron de Lahontan's *Voyages* (1703), where the fictional Huron chief Adario questions whether ''twere better for the *French* that they were Strangers to Reading and Writing'.[37] What has writing done for Europeans, he asks, besides hatch vain disputes and scandals? A similar satire on European literacy is found in Jonathan Swift's *Gulliver's Travels* (1726). In Part 4, where Gulliver visits the land of the Houyhnhnms, Swift presents an early vision of an oral tradition: the rational horses in this country 'have no Letters, and consquently, their Knowledge is all traditional'.[38] Nevertheless, they remember their history entirely, for their harmonious society has remained uncluttered by the wars, feuds and other corruptions that fill the history-books of Europe.

Neither Lahontan nor Swift intended to present a serious vision of oral culture. Their purpose was satirical, not anthropological. Nonetheless, their work signals the rise of new perception of non-literate countries as embodying what had been allegedly lost in Europe – innocence, passion and naturalness. Sentimentalized Indians, almost invariably lamenting or dying, became stock figures in poetry. This poetry reflected the supposed virtues of native oratory, simple and passionate, yet filled with bold metaphors redolent of pagan myth and the natural world. Here was how Thomas Warton imagined the language of a native chief in *The Dying Indian* (1747):

> The dart of Izdabel prevails! 'twas dipt
> In double poison. – I shall soon arrive
> At the blest island, where no tygers spring
> On heedless hunters; where ananas bloom
> Thrice in each moon; where rivers smootly glide,
> Nor thund'ring torrents whirl the light canoe
> Down to the sea.[39]

Warton's poem reflects two significant trends in eighteenth-century poetics. The first was a heightened emphasis on the powerful expression of passion as the major characteristic of poetry. In contrast with neo-classical poets like Boileau or Pope, who described poetry as the 'painting' or 'dress' of thought, the English critic John Dennis maintained that the primary characteristic of poetry was the expression of strong emotions. 'Poetry is Poetry', he wrote, 'because it is more passionate and sensual than Prose.'[40] This heightened passion inspired the 'bold and figurative' language of poetry: Dennis and other authors of the 'Age of Sensibility' anticipated Wordsworth and the romantics in regarding metaphor as a natural response to states of heightened passion. In this way, we will note, new fashions in poetry and poetics dovetailed with trends in linguistics during the same period: non-literate language was deemed more 'poetic' because, as the grammarians were insisting, only speech could express the sentiments with full force.

A further, closely related, trend exemplified by Warton's poem was 'primitivism' – for 'primitive' people, in the supposed 'childhood' of human development, were surely more inclined to strong passions than civilized people. As Enlightenment philosophers were concluding, these strong passions, and not reason, inspired the first languages.[41] 'Primitive' language was therefore inherently more 'poetic' than modern European languages, which had lost in passion what they had gained in clarity and logic.[42] This way of understanding the history of language inspired works such as Robert Lowth's *Lectures on the Sacred Poetry of the Hebrews* (1749), which re-interpreted the Psalms and other lyrical parts of the Old Testament as the impassioned and spontaneous effusions of a primitive people. Moreover, the bold metaphorical style of the Old Testament reflected an essentially *oral* culture where poetic declamation, not writing, was the primary vehicle for cultural authority and memory. As Lowth wrote, 'Poetry was of singular utility, since before any characters expressive of words were invented, at least before they were commonly received, and applied to general use, it seems to have afforded the only means of preserving the rude experience of early times.'[43]

The significance of Lowth's comments is clear. Most obviously, he was beginning to identify a specifically oral kind of poetry, which he connected with a particularly passionate and metaphorical kind language. More daringly, he was claiming that one of the central texts of the Western tradition, the Old Testament, emerged from this very well of oral eloquence. The Enlightenment had opened the door to a reinterpretation of even sacred texts in the light of contemporary developments in linguistics, philosophy and poetics. And if the Bible could be interpreted as exhibiting traits of oral tradition, it was a short step to re-evaluating the great pagan texts of classical literature in the same way.

At the fountainhead of this pagan tradition was, of course, Homer. Ancient critics of Greek culture, such as the Jewish historian Josephus, had raised the heretical possibility that Homer was illiterate.[44] This possibility was revived during the *querelle des anciens et modernes* of the late seventeenth and early eighteenth centuries. Scholars who advocated the claims for modern literature over ancient literature – Claude Perrault, Jean Terrasson, Richard Bentley and others – portrayed Homer as an early and therefore primitive poet in a literary tradition that was essentially progressive. Paradoxically, this originally critical view of Homer as 'primitive' (and therefore inferior to modern authors) later became the inspiration for praising the peculiar beauties of ancient epic poetry. A key work in this re-evaluation was Thomas Blackwell's *An Enquiry into the Life and Times of Homer* (1735), which rehearsed many of the new ideas about the history of language. The first languages, Blackwell conjectured, were emitted in states of strong passion typical of primitive people. They were therefore highly intoned, song-like and figurative, for Homer belonged to an age still influenced by the first verse. He was not utterly barbaric, for his work shows the literary polish gained only by some degree of civilization or 'policy'. Nevertheless, the special power of the Homeric epic, its '*Original, amazing, metaphorical* Tincture', reflects the unique energy of language in its earliest state.[45]

Significantly, Blackwell did not try to argue that Homer was illiterate or belonged to an entirely oral culture: such a proposal still strained the credulity of scholars raised on the belief that only writing could preserve a substantial body of knowledge with any fidelity. Even in Blackwell's Scotland, where new ideas of the Enlightenment were accepted more readily than in England, scholars developed the concept of oral tradition with slowness and caution.

An important text in this development was *The Poems of Ossian* (1762–63) by the Highland scholar James Macpherson, who may well have trained under Blackwell at Marischal College in Aberdeen. Macpherson claimed that he had reconstructed the work of a great Highland bard, Ossian, from fragments preserved in the memories of ordinary people around Scotland. That such a substantial body of poetry – including two epics and other poems – could survive merely by oral transmission was indeed a claim of arresting novelty and interest. Influenced by prevailing notions of 'primitive' verse, Macpherson attempted to capture the flavour of oral recitation, its vivid metaphors, epithets and song-like cadences. Anticipating the modern discoveries of Milman Parry, Macpherson maintained that the very form of Ossianic verse had a mnemonic function that aided its survival in unwritten tradition.[46]

Yet even Macpherson began recede from these strong claims when they came under fire from sceptical contemporaries. The most belligerent of these critics was Samuel Johnson, whose famous accusation that Macpherson had forged the Ossian poems was based, in part, on his utter disbelief that such poetry could have been composed or transmitted without 'letters'.[47] A friendlier sceptic was David Hume, who reluctantly agreed with Johnson, a man from whom he was divided in religion and politics. Like Johnson, Hume concluded that the oral transmission of long poems contradicted that great arbiter of his empirical philosophy, experience. Consult experience, he urged: do we find presently that substantial compositions preserved without writing? This was a strong indication, Hume reasoned, that such a feat was impossible. Contrary to what is usually thought, acceptance of 'oral tradition' was undermined less by Johnson's anti-Scotticism than by a sceptical empirical philosophy developed by Hume in Scotland. He, not Johnson, was the most devastating critic of the authenticity of Macpherson's Ossian poems.

As this survey suggests, many of the authors who led the way in theorizing on the poetic potential of oral and 'primitive' cultures came from the periphery of English civilization – Scotland (Blair, Blackwell, Macpherson), Ireland (Swift, Sheridan), America (Colden). It was, that is, at the *periphery* that disillusionment with modern, literate culture was felt most keenly. Mostly here, it seems, authors were willing to experiment with the idea that non-literate peoples could be, in certain respects, superior. Nevertheless, as I have also considered, 'oral traditions' do not readily recognize their own predominant orality: it is a society emerging from orality into literacy which is positioned to perceive this difference most distinctly, for such a society has experienced this transition within living memory and will still retain a large body of oral culture in its midst. In mid-century England, we might note, about half the adult population remained so illiterate that they could not sign a marriage register (though, somewhat more probably, they read a little, a skill that usually precedes writing). Yet literacy had been the norm for generations in the gentry and upper–merchant classes, and had made important inroads into the class of small merchants and tradespeople.[48] The difference between orality and literacy, that is, was visible (and audible) all around, and this experience shaped the understanding of literate people towards non-alphabetic societies elsewhere in the world. Orality and literacy, moreover, became temporalized: histories of language, such as Warburton's influential history of scripts in *The Divine Legation of Moses* (1738), strengthened the assumption that writing developed long after speech, and that this event represented a pivotal stage in the progress towards modern civilization.[49] In looking to their own past, therefore, Europeans increasingly expected to find evidence of 'oral' culture.

That eighteenth-century England was precisely at that point of emerging as a 'literate' society perhaps explains why an Englishman advanced the first sustained argument that Homer belonged to an 'oral tradition'. Almost unnoticed amid the noise of the Ossian controversy, Robert Wood made this case in *An Essay on the Original Genius and Writings of Homer*, written in 1767 and published in 1769. Wood represents a crescendo in the intellectual developments that I have traced from the Renaissance. For he had absorbed the intellectual conditions of his time – a time of increased interest in the sound of language, along with a new interest in 'primitive' speech and culture. His case for the oral sources of Homeric verse was grounded not in historical evidence, but rather in the conjecture that only a tradition without letters could have produced poetry of this kind. The very 'genius' of Homer, the 'musical' quality of his language and his direct knowledge of nature, derived from a primitive age when speech, unrestrained by writing, was passionate and spontaneous. In contrast with the 'cold and languid circumlocution' of modern 'artificial language', the language of Homer exemplifies the 'passionate expression of Nature, which, incapable of misrepresentation, appeals directly to our feelings, and finds the shortest road to the heart'.[50] The faithful *mimesis* that Wood found in Homeric verse showed the advantages of an 'unlettered' time when nature was known though direct experience rather than books. In contrast with scholars of the Renaissance and the seventeenth century, therefore, Wood portrayed the peculiar beauties of Homer not as the fruits of literate refinement but of untrammelled nature. He suggested that Homer exemplified the same virtues found in the orators of the New World. If scholars like Blair and Ferguson were classicizing the American native, Wood and others compared Homer to the 'primitive' peoples of the New World.

Wood's thesis does not, of course, represent the fully developed theory of oral tradition as delineated in our time by Milman Parry. In the last years of the eighteenth century, the German scholar F. A. Wolf buttressed Wood's case for Homer's orality with a historical investigation of language and poetry in ancient Greece. Wolf even dared to challenge belief in the existence of a single individual named 'Homer', paving the way for nineteenth-century discussions of the bardic tradition that composed and transmitted the epics under that name.[51] From this nineteenth-century scholarship sprang Parry's investigation of oral tradition as a source for Serbo-Croat heroic verse. The general thesis nonetheless stands: as society grows in literacy, it also becomes more aware of 'orality' as a separate mode of expression and being. Orality is a fundamentally *literate* concept.

Yet the groundwork forathese developments had already been laid in the Enlightenment. During that age, intellectual culture nourished a new understanding of non-literate language and culture. The old view that both literature and society had benefited from literacy was challenged by a more complicated view celebrating the supposed beauties of 'primitive' speech. Authors of this era increasingly acknowledged that pre-literate peoples could have a continuous tradition of history, government and poetry. This acknowledgment arose from a number of interrelated intellectual factors – doubts concerning the adequacy of writing, a connected revival of prosody, satire of European manners and society, a new aesthetic and moral taste for sentiment, the *querelle des anciens et modernes*. These factors led scholars to reassess not only non-European cultures but *themselves*. The 'Other' of oral culture became ambivalent and complicated. For a new generation, the Other was no longer just a negative, a mere absence of all order and knowledge, as it was for authors of the Renaissance and the seventeenth century. When Enlightenment scholars measured Europe against the pre-literate cultures of the New World, they generally found both gain and loss – a gain of clarity, sophistication and reason, but also a loss of passion and the expressive energy. In these ways, the difference between orality and literacy became a site for exploring a range of philosophical, linguistic and historical divisions at the centre of Europe's perception of itself and the world.

NOTES

1 Hugh Blair, *A Critical Dissertation on the Poems of Ossian* (London, 1763), 2.
2 Samuel Purchas, *Purchas his Pilgrimes*, 4 vols (London, 1625), I. 176.
3 See Nicholas Hudson, '"Oral Tradition": the Evolution of an Eighteenth-century Concept', in Alvaro Ribiero, SJ, and James G. Basker (eds), *Tradition in Transition: Woman Writers, Marginal Texts, and the Eighteenth-century Canon* (Oxford: Clarendon Press, 1996), 161–76.
4 William of Ockham, *Philosophical Writings*, trans. Philotheus Boehner, rev. Stephen F. Brown (Indianapolis, IN and Cambridge: Hackett Publishing Co., 1990), 47.
5 See Lawrence Stone, 'The Educational Revolution in England, 1560–1640', *Past and Present* 28 (1964), 41–80. Stone's views are expanded and refined in Rosemary O'Day's *Education and Society 1500–1800: the Social Foundations of Education in Early Modern Britain* (London and New York: Longman, 1982).
6 Juan Luis Vives, *Vives: On Education. A Translation of the 'De Tradendis Disciplinis'*, trans. Foster Watson (Cambridge: Cambridge University Press, 1913), 114.
7 See Richard Mulcaster, *The First Part of the Elementarie* (London, 1582; facsimile

reprint, Menston: Scolar Press, 1970), 24–5. See also Lawrence Stone, 'Literacy and Education in England 1640–1900', *Past and Present* 42 (1969): 69–139; Joan Simon, *Education and Society in Tudor England* (Cambridge: Cambridge University Press, 1966).

8 See David Cressy, *Literacy and the Social Order: Reading and Writing in Tudor and Stuart England* (Cambridge: Cambridge University Press, 1980).

9 Roger Williams, *A Key to the Language of America* (London, 1643), 118.

10 See Francisco Lopez de Gómara, *Histoire généralle des indies occidentales & terres neuues* (1554), trans. M. Fumée (Paris, 1569), ch. 28, sig. D5v; Geraldus Vossius, *Quatuor artibus popularibus* (Amsterdam, 1650), 14–15; John Wilkins, *Mercury: or the secret and swift messenger* (1641), 3rd edn (London, 1707; facsimile reprint, Amsterdam and Philadelphia: John Benjamins, 1984), 3–4.

11 Charles de Rochefort, *The History of Carriby-Islands* (1658), trans. John Davies (London, 1666), 116.

12 Johan de Laet, *L'Histoire du Nouveau Monde, ou Description des Indes Occidentales* (Leiden, 1640), 36.

13 Ibid., 50.

14 See Gómara, *Histoire généralle*, 238–9; Purchas, *His Pilgrimes*, 1: 178–9.

15 Gómara, *Histoire généralle*, sig. Kk2v (p. 254).

16 Walter J. Ong, *Ramus, Method, and the Decay of Dialogue* (Cambridge, MA: Harvard University Press, 1958), 122.

17 See Angelo Mazocco, *Linguistic Theories in Dante and the Humanists* (Leiden, New York and Cologne: E. J. Brill, 1993), 13–23.

18 Jean Terrrasson, *A Critical Dissertation upon Homer's* Iliad (1715), 2 vols (London, 1722), 2, 526.

19 John Oldmixon, *The British Empire in America*, 2 vols, 2nd edn (London, 1741), 1. 276.

20 Williams, *A Key to the Language of America*, 177.

21 See Nicholas Hudson, *Writing and European Thought, 1600–1830* (Cambridge: Cambridge University Press, 1994).

22 Robert Robinson, 'The Art of Pronunciation' in E. J. Dobson (ed.), *Phonetic Writings* (London, New York and Toronto: Oxford University Press, 1957), 19–20. On the rationalization of orthography in the Renaissance, see D. G. Scragg, *A History of English Spelling* (Manchester: Manchester University Press; New York: Barnes & Noble, 1974); F. H. Brengelman, 'Orthoepists, Printers, and the Rationalization of English Spelling', *Journal of English and Germanic Philology*, 79 (1980), 332–54; Hudson, *Writing and European Thought*, 92–9.

23 There are now numerous good discussions of the projects for a new universal or philosophical script that proliferated in the seventeenth-century. Especially useful studies include Vivian Salmon's Introduction to *The Works of Francis Lodwick* (London: Longman's, 1972), James Knowlson's *Universal Languge Schemes in England and France 1600–1800* (Toronto and Buffalo, NJ: University of Toronto Press, 1975), and M. M. Slaughter's *Universal Languages and Scientific Taxonomy in the Seventeenth Century* (Cambridge: Cambridge University Press, 1982).

24 John Conrad Amman, *A Dissertation on Speech* (London: Sampson Low, Marston Low & Searle, 1873), 60.

25 Amman, *A Dissertation on Speech*, 8.

26 While Derrida refers to the history of writing in several of his works, this subject

is especially prominent in *Of Grammatology* and *Dissemination*, the latter book containing a discussion of the *Phaedrus*. For a summary of Derrida's thesis on writing and its significance in Western philosophy, see Christopher Norris, *Deconstruction: Theory and Practice* (London and New York: Methuen, 1982), 24–41.

27 Samuel Johnson, *Grammar of the English Tongue*, in *A Dictionary of the English Language* (London, 1755; facsimile reprint, New York: AMS, 1967), sig. a2v.

28 Johnson, Preface to *Dictionary*, sig. a2r.

29 See Samuel Johnson, *A Journey to the Western Isles of Scotland*, ed. Mary Lascelles, vol. 9 of *The Yale Edition of the Works of Samuel Johnson* (New Haven, CT: Yale University Press, 1971), 114–15. This discussion of the influence of literate culture on language occurs as part of Johnson's case against the authenticity of Macpherson's *Poems of Ossian*, discussed below.

30 Johnson, Preface to *Dictionary*, sig. a2r.

31 Thomas Sheridan, *A Course of Lectures on Elocution, Together with Two Dissertations on Language* (London, 1762), p 7. On Sheridan's views concerning writing and speech, see Michael Shortland, 'Moving Speeches: Language and Elocution in Eighteenth-century Britain', *History of European Ideas*, 8 (1987), 639–53; Peter de Bolla, *The Discourse of the Sublime: Readings in History, Aesthetics and the Subject* (Oxford and New York: Blackwell, 1989), 163–82.

32 The papers of Josef Vachek, who has written extensively on the special nature and function of written language, are collected in *Written Language Revisited*, ed. Philip A. Luelsdorff (Amsterdam and Philadelphia: John Benjamins, 1989). See also Roy Harris, *The Origin of Writing* (London: Duckworth, 1986).

33 Sheridan, *Course of Lectures*, xii.

34 Ibid., 71.

35 Cadwallader Colden, *The History of the Five Indian Nations of Canada* (London, 1747), 156.

36 Adam Ferguson, *A History of Civil Society* (Edinburgh, 1767), p. 265.

37 Louis Armand de Lom d'Acre, Baron de Lahontan, *Voyages*, ed. Stephen Leacock (Ottawa: Graphic Publishers, 1932), 318.

38 Jonathan Swift, *Gulliver's Travels* (Oxford: Clarendon Press, 1965), part 4, ch. 9, p. 273.

39 In *The Three Wartons: a Choice of Their Verse*, ed. Eric Partridge (London: Scholartis Press, 1927), 92.

40 John Dennis, *The Advancement and Reformation of Modern Poetry* (London, 1721), 24.

41 The thesis that language began with 'cries of passion' derives from classical philosophy, particularly Lucretius's discussion of primitive speech in Book 5 of *De rerum naturae*. This argument was widely revived in the 'conjectural histories' of language by Enlightenment philosophers such as Bernard Mandeville and Etienne Bonnot, Abbé de Condillac. For a good discussion of Mandeville's theories on the origin of language, see E. J. Hundert, 'The Thread of Language and the Web of Dominion: Mandeville to Rousseau and Back', *Eighteenth-century Studies*, 21 (1987), 169–91. The major modern scholar on the linguistic thought of Condillac is Hans Aarsleff. See Aarsleff's 'The Tradition of Condillac: the Problem of the Origin of Language in the Eighteenth Century and the Debate in the Berlin Academy Before Herder', in *From Locke to Saussure: Essays on the Study of Language and Intellectual History* (Minneapolis: University of Minnesota Press, 1983), 149–209.

42 For discussion of this theory on how languages develop, see Nicholas Hudson, 'Theories of Language', in H. B. Nisbet and Claude Rawson (eds), *The Cambridge History of Literary Criticism* (Cambridge: Cambridge University Press, 1997), 4. 335–47. 'Primivitism' is discussed in the same volume by Maximilian E. Novak, 456–69.

43 Robert Lowth, *Lectures on the Sacred Poetry of the Hebrews.*

44 Flavius Josephus, 'Against Apion', in *Works*, trans. William Whiston (Baltimore, MD: Armstrong & Berry, 1839), part 1, section 2. 580.

45 Thomas Blackwell, *An Inquiry into the Life and Time of Homer* (London, 1735), 46.

46 James Macpherson, *Fingal, an Ancient Epic Poem in Six Books: together with several Other Poems, composed by Ossian the Son of Fingal* (London, 1762). See Hudson, 'Oral Tradition'.

47 See Johnson, *Journey to the Western Isles of Scotland*, 114–15.

48 On rates of literacy in eighteenth-century England, see Roger S. Schofield, 'Dimensions of Illiteracy in England, 1750–1850', in Harvey Graff (ed.), *Literacy and Social Development in the West* (Cambridge: Cambridge University Press, 1981), 201–13; idem, *The Legacies of Literacy* (Bloomington and Indianapolis: University of Indiana Press, 1987), 230–3.

49 Warburton's dissertation on writing comprises book 4, section 4, of the second volume of *The Divine Legation of Moses* (London, 1738–41). It was later translated into French and published separately by Marc-Antoine Léonard des Malpeines as *Essai sur les hieroglyphs des egyptiens* (Paris, 1744), a version that became the basis for the French Enlightenment's understanding of the history of writing, including the article 'Écriture' in the *Encyclopédie.*

50 Robert Wood, *An Essay on the Original Genius and Writings of Homer* (London: John Richardson, 1824), 176.

51 See F. A. Wolf, *Prolegomena to Homer* (1798), trans. James E. G. Zetzel (Princeton, NJ: Princeton University Press, 1985). Wolf praises the 'brilliant audacity' of Robert Wood (p. 71). A good summary of these developments leading to Milman Parry's discoveries can be found in Adam Parry's Introduction to his edition of *The Making of Homeric Verse: the Collected Papers of Milman Parry* (Oxford: Clarendon Press, 1971).

Chapter 9

'Things said or sung a thousand times': customary society and oral culture in rural England, 1700–1900

Bob Bushaway

Things cleared away then down she sits
And tells her tales by starts and fits
Not willing to lose time or toil
She knits or sews and talks the while [1]

John Clare's long poem sequence *The Shepherd's Calendar* celebrates English rural popular culture or, at least, that part of it represented by the local customs of his own village of Helpston in Northamptonshire in the late eighteenth century. Rural popular culture was most often despised and derided by contemporaries whose judgements have been shared by some later commentators alike as merely a degraded reflection of urban civilization or as an irredeemably backward product of social and economic structures rooted in ignorance and folly and most usually thought of as surviving from earlier times. Historians have, in general, noted the decline of oral tradition in the English countryside as an early stage on the road to spreading popular literacy. One writes: 'If the oral tradition largely defined the pre-industrial popular culture, the significance of its decline revolved around the question of superstition. The world of those whose horizons were limited by the oral tradition was suffused with the supernatural.' [2] In eighteenth- and early nineteenth-century England, as in earlier periods, rural popular culture was the subject for humour or condemnation by elite culture or was treated as the object of crusade by reformers and radicals in the name of reason. Rural popular culture was also subjected to attack by the propertied who regarded customary ways of life in the countryside and their cultural expression as an obstacle to improvement and to progress through economic liberalism.[3] Rural popular culture was vulnerable to such attack not least because it was an oral culture rather than a written or document-based culture. As Clare's reminiscences show, however, orality provided a richness of discourse to Helpston's popular culture which never left him and which for many English rural communities sustained the rural labourer's world until well into the twentieth century.[4] Far from declining, oral tradition retained cultural vitality and injected vibrancy which differentiated rural popular culture by locality, by region or by agricultural area in the form of accent, dialect and local knowledge.

John Clare's work illustrates how village culture embraced both written and printed forms but remained essentially an oral world. *The Shepherd's Calendar* is paradoxically the printed record of an oral culture, a literary description of a customary world, an expression of popular cultural life for an elite readership. Although Clare's original intentions were compromised by his editor, John Taylor, who insisted on correcting Clare's grammar and punctuation and in deleting his dialect terms, Taylor's unsympathetic editing did not entirely destroy the chronicle of English village culture and the extent to which its customary framework was maintained by the evidence of the spoken word or the rhythm of song. From *January*'s description of the tavern where the printed word of newspaper or *Old Moore's Almanac* 'a theme for talk supplys' to *December*'s account of a visit from the seasonal wassail singer who 'oft for pence and spicy ale ... tells her tale', Clare's poem reveals that the rural popular culture of which he was a product was largely an oral one – notwithstanding the co-existence and close relationship between orality and various forms of popular literature derived from and reinforced by the popular oral world. Literacy levels were not the key determinant of the extent of oral culture in eighteenth- and nineteenth-century rural Britain, although these rose considerably through the period as work by David Vincent and others has shown. Rather, oral culture in the countryside was a composite framework binding human experience and perception, and combining oral and popular literature together to form a diversity of rural popular cultures; defined by region, type of agriculture work, gender, and age.[5]

In Clare's world, word and song accompany work and leisure; chant and verse describe seasonal rituals and customs; narratives and tales fill the domestic interior; gossip and news disseminate the conversation between neighbours; knowledge is passed on and lessons learned; and the pace of village life and culture is measured by what Clare refers to as 'things said or sung a thousand times' when recalling cottage storytelling.[6]

Historians have tended to collude with the views of contemporary critics of rural popular culture, because the very lack of documentary sources and the difficult nature of remaining records have obscured the richness and importance of village life and labour or rendered it problematical to recover. Charting the decline of aspects of rural popular culture is a familiar process from John Aubrey's writing in the seventeenth century to the prose and poetry of Thomas Hardy and Edward Thomas at the beginning of the twentieth century.[7] The flight of the oral tradition in face of rising popular literacy through the nineteenth century is the orthodox explanation for the disappearance of customary society.[8] Similarly, 'traveller's tales' have suggested to recent historians that all was mired in superstition and ignorance steadily dispelled by the advance of literacy and reason, a view which accords with that of many contemporaries. There are exceptions. Some historians – notably the late Edward Thompson and Raphael Samuel – have attempted to redefine the nature of English rural popular culture, and rural society in general, in more vibrant ways.[9] Samuel has written of the historian's vocation as placing him 'far above the madding crowd; he surveys them [popular rural society], retrospectively, from a height, as objects of reform rather than as the active agents – or subjects – of change'.[10] Thompson used the term 'customary consciousness' to describe the relationship between successive generations and the contest between elite and popular groups.[11] Thompson argued that even the growing impact of popular literacy in rural England can be related to the overall importance of oral culture: 'Traditions', he wrote, 'are perpetuated largely through oral transmission, with its repertoire of anecdote and of narrative example; where oral tradition is supplemented by growing literacy, the most widely circulated printed products, such as chapbooks, almanacs, broadsides, "last dying speeches" and anecdotal accounts of crime, tend to be subdued to the expectations of the oral culture rather than challenging it with alternatives'.[12] This is exactly the world recorded by Clare in the late eighteenth and early-nineteenth centuries in *The Shepherd's Calendar*. In support of this idea, Barry Reay has written compellingly of the 'orality of print'.[13] Far from subverting or displacing oral culture, popular printing tended to draw from its forms and to reinforce its idioms. Literacy and orality in rural England were mutually supporting during the eighteenth and nineteenth centuries.

Comprehended within these terms is the notion that the relationship between social groups in town or village, workplace or place of worship, leisure venue or customary space, ritual location or realm of memory, was a reciprocal one in which rights and responsibilities were defined, disputed, defended, exercised or contested by oral, dramatic or ritual discourse.[14] Whether this relationship was based upon consensus or conflict, social groups in the English village confronted one another across a landscape defined by reference to past and future but enacted in the present through orally transmitted customs and rituals in which roles, social positions and obligations were closely delineated by oral tradition. This discourse, termed 'folklore' by some in the nineteenth century who claimed proprietorial rights in its 'collection', in preference to the cumbersome but more expressive earlier term 'popular antiquities', used in the eighteenth and early nineteenth centuries, provided the immediate context for village life.[15] Popular voices in the village were the most important instrument for the defence of custom, whether raised in defiance, used in song, softened in storytelling, made solemn in oath-taking, given legal force in court testimony, passing on wisdom, describing the local environment, defaming a neighbour, claiming a right, demanding a ritual dole, pointing out a significant feature of the landscape, declaiming the part of 'King George' in the local Christmas mummers' play, singing in the local west gallery band or seasonal ritual, crying out the injustice of food market manipulations, or 'hallooing largesse' in harvest to celebrate abundance and supplement harvest wages.

Customary consciousness relied for its formation and transmission on an oral culture. Indeed, it might even be suggested that it was the existence of a vibrant oral popular culture which provided the basis for customary society in the English countryside for much of the eighteenth and nineteenth centuries until those popular voices were drowned out by the noise of agricultural machinery and the sonorous prohibition of statute law, to be replaced by new forms of printed discourse and the clamour of changing patterns of rural work and leisure.

Oral culture has at least three aspects. Firstly, it provides a generalized environmental context in which social groups work out their relationships and transact their social, economic and political affairs; secondly, oral culture is itself the medium of expression for those relationships and transactions; and, thirdly, it is the product of those same processes, providing definitive and enduring outcomes in the form of a legacy for the future. As Thompson has suggested, oral culture can be the single dominant characteristic of a society or it can co-exist with literacy in all its forms.[16]

For an oral culture to sustain itself certain features are required to be present. Discourse between individuals and groups takes place by word of mouth. Social venues and occasions exist for the expression and transmission of oral culture.[17] The social environment is conducive to forming and using memory tools such as formulaic songs and rituals. Clare wrote: 'I heard my mother's memory tell' as if memory itself was empowered with the possibility of speech. 'In simple prose or simpler rhymes' he recounts that she retold stories from her own experience, or from local tales, or from popular stories common in chapbook or ballad literature.[18] Modes of work and leisure in the English countryside provided proximity and opportunity for oral discourse or depended upon oral forms for learning or practical demonstration. Oral culture operated most successfully at the local level or in the small-scale community where it was based upon a shared language of values, customs, ideas, songs, symbols, rituals and ceremonies within a common experience. In these circumstances, popular culture was most usually transmitted by observed practice, by repetition and accumulation based upon memory and word of mouth. These characteristics have been well described by social anthropologists and historians for certain kinds of societies where different identities, languages and historical records can be described in opposition to the dominant hegemonic culture. The experience of Wales, Scotland and Ireland within the hegemonic construction of a Britain dominated by English culture provides an historical example although, upon investigation, a complex emerges in which social, institutional and cultural contexts operated to form and reform relationships not necessarily resulting in the sudden death of orality.[19] The situation in rural England differed only in the extent to which it was dialect and regional form rather than language which formed the medium of discourse. The importance of oral culture within English rural society during the eighteenth and nineteenth centuries and especially its significance for customary consciousness or the ideology of custom, are often overlooked by historians frustrated by a fragmentary or partial record or where inspired to document a radical or rationalist triumph.[20]

Custom required an appeal to the legitimation of the past in the form of repeated annual or regular testimony in ritual discourse in the present which made an unambiguous, oral or vocal affirmation and declaration of 'witness' for the future by the participants. Custom took the form of personal and collective testimony legitimated by deed. These testimonies consisted of oral and visual signifiers which gave form and meaning to the participants' actions, and which emphasized that such behaviour was in accordance with custom or *lex loci* and that due response was required. An orally communicated consensus was proclaimed to the local community in the form of customary collective action through word and deed. In rural England in the eighteenth and nineteenth centuries, the local community was a spatial and temporal construction delineated by shouts, songs, chants, tellings and re-tellings, through a range of annual perambulatory rituals which provided a memory tool to access the mental map of the village sanctioned by its members and, sometimes, legitimated by reference to Church and State. Popular culture in the village shaped a circle of customary consciousness based upon oral discourse, which can be marked out and represented in diagrammatic form as shown below:

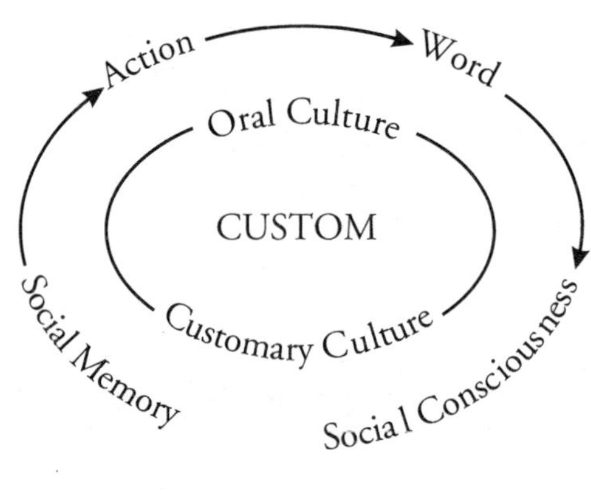

Custom was therefore reinforced and bound by a systematic and regular structure of oral witness and ritual performance. Most accounts of rural society in England during the eighteenth and nineteenth centuries omit any notion of popular culture or customary consciousness or relegate it to the margins in accounts of pastimes or leisure pursuits or quaint superstitions and picturesque survivals. The relevant volume of *The Agrarian History of England and Wales* describes a social structure, social institutions and social activities in terms of formal institutions and official culture. There are separate accounts of the rural labourer, as a rank in the table of social status, and of the labourer's pleasures alongside similar pieces on the country house and hunting, which gloss over the existence of an orally transmitted rural popular culture still vibrant at the time of the Great Exhibition,[21] and still distinctive at the beginning of the Great War.

More sympathetic writers, whilst admitting the fact of rural popular culture, describe it as being in decline and decaying under the pressure of rural depopulation. One account concludes that, 'following the geographical and social intermixing engendered by the Great War, the year 1918 ... finally and symbolically clanged shut, like a blood-stained cast-iron gate, on an already dwindling cultural tradition that had existed in one form or another over more than a thousand years'.[22] These words concur with the steady witness of the late Laurie Lee who was born at the beginning of the Great War.[23]

It was the attack on customary consciousness through the late eighteenth and nineteenth centuries which undermined the English rural oral tradition, and led to the final decline of the labourer's cultural world. Historians who are deaf to those customary voices do not hear a distinctive rural popular culture at all. Concerning village benefit club processions and festivals at Whitsuntide, Alfred Williams might have been describing the general aspects of much popular culture, when he concluded: 'The village fair and church festival were condemned because simple people assembled together to indulge in simple amusements ... they [elite culture] said it was hateful and abominable, pure barbarism, it was time it was put a stop to; they could see all manner of evil in it, it was nothing but a 'drunken, rowdy show; a public pest and a nuisance.'[24] Unsympathetic accounts are written entirely from the perspective of formal institutions and official culture and are constructed from the records of the elites for whom the destruction of custom was a necessary step in the progress towards an all-consuming ideology of possessive individualism.[25]

Some anthropologists define the term 'oral tradition' as a set of cultural processes and products which are passed down through time in an unwritten form.[26] One cultural anthropologist has written: 'In its most general sense, oral tradition comprises any established custom, set of beliefs, or repeated routine that exhibits some continuity from the past (or is believed to do so) and is transmitted not through writing but by word of mouth.'[27]

In English rural society the relationship between custom and oral culture reached a crucial stage during the period from the late eighteenth to the end of the nineteenth centuries when rapid population growth, economic and industrial change, new moral imperatives and the attack on customary consciousness produced crisis in the rural community. During this period, oral culture reinforced customary consciousness and allowed the statement of new and vibrant customary forms which, far from being backward or primitive, were progressive and dynamic. The village benefit club walking at Whitsun is one example of such innovative creation. The historians of these new forms of customary consciousness are rare but one annalist, drawn from the world of oral rural culture itself, wrote that, until the coming of the National Health Insurance Act in 1910, village benefit clubs offered the only protection to rural labourers and their families from the uncertainties of sickness of injury.[28]

From these voluntary associations, grew other kinds of democratic co-operative societies. The great event of the customary calendar in the latter half of the nineteenth century, was the benefit club day at Whitsun and the procession through the village of club members, the annual dinner and the various exhibitions of garden produce and music bands from the associated clubs and societies. Benefit clubs required an organizational structure of committees, elected representatives, minute books, secretaries and treasurers and were, occasionally, presided over by the local clergyman or publican, but the annual Whitsun procession with its club banners, medals and sashes, local band and club staffs with ornate brass heads or willow wands, followed by dinner and dancing, links it firmly to the oral tradition in which previous rural festivals had been rooted such as the parish Whitsun ale. A description of a Cotswold ale in the late eighteenth century could be matched by the photographs of late nineteenth-century benefit club days in Cotswold villages such as Ebrington. An observer of the former wrote:

> These sports are resorted to by great numbers of young people of both sexes, are conducted in the following manner. Two persons are chosen, previous to the meeting, to be Lord and Lady ... A large empty barn, or some such building, is provided for the Lord's hall, and fitted up with seats to accommodate the company. Here they assemble to dance and to regale in the best manner their circumstances and the place will afford, and each young fellow treats his girl with a ribbon, or favour. The Lord and Lady honour the hall with their presence, attended by the steward, sword-bearer, purse-bearer and mace-bearer, with their sacred badges or ensigns of office. They have likewise a page, or train-bearer, and a jester dressed in a parti coloured jacket, whose ribaldry and gesticulation contribute not a little to the entertainment.[29]

The Ebrington photograph, dated 1903, is not completely removed from this much earlier description. The benefit club procession was accompanied by a village band consisting of brass players and a bass drum; members of the entertainment committee rode on an open cart, sitting on chairs; women and girls, although marching on a separate day, were accompanied by a banjo player; the procession was proceeded by the Ebrington club banner. Earlier versions of the banner, dating from 1856, depicted the associative nature of the club with the phrases 'Unity is Strength' and 'Let Brotherly Love Continue'. The central image of the banner showed five farm workers combining to pull up a stump of a tree, at their feet, a sickle, pick, shovel and rake. As with so many of these banners, similar to trades union banners, the maker was G. Tutil of the City Road, London.[30] On death, benefit club staffs were broken and the brass heads were either interred with the deceased member or kept by relatives as a memento. Rather than interpreting new customary forms in the latter half of the nineteenth-century, as degraded or controlled versions of the older popular calendar festivals, it should, perhaps, be noted that the connection between them was stronger and more continuous and linked them together within the framework of oral culture. Far from the degenerate survivalism of traditional culture, or from the world we have lost, beloved of popular antiquaries and early folklore alike, a revitalized customary consciousness underpinned a distinctive rural popular culture in which orality remained the medium of expression and transmission from the late eighteenth century until the years after the First World War.

Oral culture in rural England was linked closely to popular memory. Within customary society, memory provided the continuity for both individual and collective action by those in the local community. Oral culture, however, also had a close relationship to printed forms. There was no dichotomy between popular oral culture and popular literacy. Indeed, the rise of cheap printed materials such as ballad sheets and chapbooks, available throughout rural England at local fairs and markets and distributed by 'higglers' and other itinerant traders, both reinforced and was underpinned by oral culture. John Clare wrote:

> Both my parents was illiterate to the last degree, my mother knew not a single letter, and superstition went so far with her that she believed the higher parts of learning was the blackest arts of witchcraft, and that no other means could attain them; my father, could read a little in a bible or testament, and was very fond of the superstitious tales that are hawked about a sheet for a penny, such as old Nixons Prophecies, Mother Bunches Fairy Tales and Mother Shiptons legacy etc, etc, he was likewise fond of Ballads and I have heard him make a boast of it over his horn of ale with his merry companions at the Blue Bell public house which was next door that he could sing or recite above a hundred; he had a tolerable good voice, and was often called to sing at those convivials of bacchanalian merry makings ...[31]

In the 1890s, Henry Burstow of Horsham in Sussex stated that his father could sing nearly 200 songs and Henry himself could list some 420 songs from 'Boney's Farewell to Paris' to 'Turnips Are Round'. He recollected: 'In learning and retaining all my songs my memory had seemed to work quite spontaneously, in much the same way as the faculties of seeing and hearing; many of the songs I learnt at first time of hearing, others, longer ones, I have learnt upon hearing them twice through; none, not even '*Tom Cladpole's Trip to London*', nor '*Jan Cladpole's Trip to 'Merricur*', each of which has 155 verses, has ever given me any trouble to acquire'. Henry Burstow learned his songs from his father and mother, his brother-in-law and a network of friends, neighbours and fellow workers, and in public houses in nearby towns and villages; and '... the remainder I learnt from ballad sheets I bought as they were being hawked about at the fairs, and at other times from other printed material'.[32] Burstow was clearly remarkable but not entirely unusual. His world was exactly that of John Clare's father 100 years earlier insofar as the nexus of orality within rural popular culture was concerned. Popular memory was the medium for the transfer of oral culture and was decisive, as can be demonstrated by a consideration of four areas in which oral culture provided both a general context and the particular mechanism of transmission. These are: ritual and ceremony; law and custom; knowledge and wisdom; and environment and community.

The first area for consideration is annual ritual and ceremony, defined by custom, conveyed by oral discourse and operated as a local chronology for experience in the English village. Clare's village of Helpston is typical in this respect and Clare provides a calendar of customary events which linked social groups and offered opportunities for rituals of social cohesion and social disunity alike. In 1825, Clare recorded the Helpston customary calendar in a letter to William Hone, the radical printer. He noted the following customs: St Mark Eve's divination practised by young men and women, Whitsun good luck wishing at the Eastwell spring with the drinking of sugar and water, processing on Holy Thursday, May Day sports and garlanding, mumming at Christmas (which Clare refers to as the 'Morris Dance'), St Thomas's Eve divination and Plough Monday 'plough bullocks'.[33] This chronology which Clare recorded and amplified in his other work linked a variety of activities from midwinter perambulations to spring collective rituals around Easter, Rogationtide, May and Whitsun, to work-based secular events concerning the pattern of agricultural labour culminating in harvest and Michaelmas, to autumn perambulation customs. The common elements in all these forms were: firstly, the reliance upon popular memory for the purpose, route, meaning, structure and form of the particular ritual or ceremony; secondly, the collection of community largesse; thirdly, the provision of an opportunity for social disruption as well as the renewal of ideas of social cohesion; and fourthly, the use of set oral forms such as songs, rhymes, greetings, verses, challenges, incantations, chants, slogans, exchanges, ritual texts, collective labels. Whilst these are not unique to Clare's Helpston, their local specificity is emphasized by dialect, song form, play form and rhyme form in a way which identified then as a part of Helpston's oral culture.

The text of the Mayer's song from another English village, Swinton, illustrates, for example, many of these elements. The two versions of the May song which were recorded by chance in the mid-nineteenth century both aimed at the collection of largesse and were examples of 'doling customs'. Their joint existence indicated change although the correspondent who noted down the 'May songs' stated that his informant told him that they '*must* be sung before the first of May'.[34] Acceptance of the legitimacy of such behaviour by mid-century was not universal in Victorian England. Support for such activities was increasingly withdrawn by middle-class patrons or only given on the strict understanding that events were to be orderly and seemly, controlled by established institutions such as the local school or church. Maying, May carolling and garlanding or green boughing on the first of May were common to many places in England during the eighteenth and nineteenth centuries. Local variation was indicated in the form and structure of the calendar custom prevalent in a specific area or region, the shape and construction of the garland and the form of the carol. At Swinton, in Lancashire, the custom was recorded in 1861. The leader of the band of Mayers was Job Knight who, attesting to the legitimacy of the custom, stated that their visits usually began in mid-April and ended on the evening of 30 April and was within memory from the last thirty years. Two songs were used, the old May song and the new May song, the first of which brought luck to the household and concluded with a clear reference to the custom's orality. May was 'sung' in Swinton.

> So now we're going to leave you, in peace and plenty here,
> for the Summer springs so fresh, green and gay;
> we shall not sing you May again until another year,
> for to draw you these cold winters away.[35]

The form of 'May garlanding' which had been once common in the eighteenth century – a youth festival centred on a tall May pole taken from the woodland with distinctive features of social disruption – was widely condemned and failed to continue to command support in the Victorian age. At either end of the process of the application of social control to Maying stand Samuel Bamford and Flora Thompson. Bamford, recalling his village of Middleton at the end of the eighteenth century, wrote that May-eve was 'Mischief neet' when a complex symbolic code was invoked by use of greenery of different types or natural materials to indicate social criticism of the inhabitants of each dwelling. The deposit of greenery before the door was accompanied with general disruptive acts such as setting cattle astray, treading down of gardens or taking gates off hinges.[36] These symbols were interpreted by reference to mnemonic rhymes such as those used in Lancashire. For example,

> Wicken [mountain Ash], sweet chicken
> Oak, for a joke
> Ash, for trash.[37]

Flora Thompson wrote of 'May garlanding' in her Oxfordshire childhood in the 1870s as a children's calendar custom, organized around the schoolroom, where the May garland was carried in procession from door to door beginning with the rectory and the squire's house, on a seven-mile tour of the village and its surrounding farms.[38]

Doling customs, defined by reference to an oral declaration that the particular visit was sanctioned by the legitimation of the customary calendar, occurred at various set times of the year, principally, Christmas and New Year, Easter, Maytide, Whitsun, Rogationtide, sheep shearing, haymaking and harvest, and the 'doling days' of autumn and early winter which preceded Christmas and which coincided with certain saints' days such as those of St Catherine, St Clement and St Thomas.[39]

The oral declaration of the visitant set out the elements underpinning the specific form of customary collective action. The visitant entered into a ritual discourse with the householder which proclaimed purpose, identity, local affiliation, legitimation, saluted the household, claimed a specified dole or other customary right and affirmed that this was an annual visit rather than a random occurrence of begging. Such songs or rhymes were ritual calling-cards for the visitants. Cheshire 'soul caking', also common throughout the north midlands in the late eighteenth and nineteenth centuries, was begun with verses of salute:

> You gentlemen of England, pray you now draw near
> To these few lines, and you shall soon hear
> Sweet melody of music all on this evening clear
> For we are come a-souling for apples and strong beer.[40]

The attack on customary ideology between 1750 and 1850, associated with demographic, economic and industrial change, and the transformation of English rural society, illustrated that oral culture provided an affirming and a defining framework for the remaking of custom and customary consciousness in the second half of the nineteenth century. This process was both dynamic and progressive. A renewed and vibrant rural plebeian culture emerged as a result. Far from being an example of degenerate survivalism or traditional culture in disintegration, oral culture in English rural society provided a cohesive element to customary consciousness.

The second area where oral tradition continued to have a significant role was the interaction between law and custom and between literate and oral cultures. Illustrations of the relationship can be found in the first twenty-eight reports of the Charities' Commissioners from 1819 to 1835. Some examples from Buckinghamshire suffice to show how oral culture transmitted vital evidence of rights and benefits for the village poor which were then recorded in the reports of the Charities' Commissioners and, without which, such rights and benefits might have been extinguished. At Wingrave, for example, a 'small piece of land ... was given in exchange at the Enclosure in 1798, for land "left for the purpose of furnishing rushes for the church on the feast Sunday" ... The rent of this land is received by the parish clerk, who provides grass to straw the church on the village feast day.'[41] The customary practice of church rushbearing became, in this example, the symbolic legitimation for the social calendrial rites which established the feast Sunday as a continuing village convivial festival.

At Horton, it was recorded: 'The Reverend William Brown, Rector of Horton from 1796 to 1851, bequeathed £500, to be given in bread to the poor who shall attend morning service in the church.' Brown's charity, preserved in local customary consciousness and recorded by the Charities' Commissioners, reaffirmed a dole right for the poor of Horton parish.[42] A further example from Bledlow will suffice to indicate the importance of oral testimony to customary consciousness. Under the Bledlow Enclosure Act 'A piece of land called the scrubbs, containing about 20 acres, was allotted to the poor in lieu of common rights.'[43] This provision was drawn to the attention of the commissioners and was duly noted. In these Buckinghamshire examples, oral testimony preserved the 'mental map' of the local community, aided social memory in place of documentary records and archives, provided an interpretation of the local topography and its history, underlined local customary leisure patterns and calendar events and protected the legal memory of doles and benefits for the local poor.

All these features are present in the account of Gang Monday land in the parish of Edgcott, Buckinghamshire, recorded by the Charities' Commissioners:

> There is about an acre of land in the parish so-called, in respect of which Robert Markham, esq., pays the overseers about 3l yearly. This used formerly to be distributed in cakes and beer to the tenants, two cakes each and as much beer as they chose to drink at the time; the residue was distributed to all poor persons who came for it, whether parishioners or not. Since the inclosure of the parish about 30 years ago, this sum has been distributed about Christmas in coals, to all poor householders, parishioners, who came for it, in equal shares. Before the inclosure the poor people had a right to get fuel on the common ... No accounts have been kept. We recommend that they should be kept in future.[44]

This is an oral record of an elaborate set of entitlements and social occasions, captured and transferred into a documentary record at the time of the commissioners' enquiry.

An entire history is here preserved by oral testimony. Ganging days were the dates of the Rogationtide parish perambulations or processions – communal calendar customs designed to preserve not only the memory of the parish boundaries but also common rights including those of the poor. The cakes and ale dole was to provide for those who accompanied the procession. At Edgcott the memory of the custom, extinguished at enclosure, was preserved in oral culture along with the memory of the fuel rights of the poor by that date commuted to a Christmas dole of coal. All would have been extinguished without the oral transmission of these memories as an accurate historical record of events in the parish.

Buckinghamshire calendrical rights of commensality were also defined by oral testimony as was the case in the Buckinghamshire village of Cuddington where 'one sack of wheat and two sacks of barley are given to the poor on St Thomas's Day'.[45] The date of this pre-Christmas dole right was 21 December and customary practices of collecting money, food and drink were widespread on this date. At Cuddington, an elaboration of the right was preserved in oral culture and annual collective action was duly reported to the Charities' Commissioners. Similarly, fuel rights were underpinned. At Ellesborough at enclosure 'an allotment of about 50 acres of scrub and underwood was awarded to the poor of the parish for fuel, which they cut for themselves during the winter when they have occasion for it'.[46] Customary consciousness, reinforced by word and deed, defined fuel rights and gave poor people access to be used at their discretion.

That poor people might take action 'for themselves' was increasingly denied them after 1834. At Great Wishford in Wiltshire, such fuel rights were defended by annual ritual and the oral declamation: 'Grovely, Grovely, and all Grovely!' The shout, made round the village before dawn on Oak Apple Day, 29 May, and before the altar at Salisbury Cathedral, remains the most striking example of the oral defence of custom in the eighteenth and nineteenth centuries.[47]

As R. J. Olney wrote of attitudes towards literacy in nineteenth-century rural Lincolnshire: 'Why should the poor need to write? The labourers were not expected to play any part in parish affairs.' Oral culture forced the poor to the attention of their parish governors in a way which could not be ignored. Olney, referring to customary consciousness as the 'old culture', pointed out that 'The old culture was slow to die, for it was not lacking in strength and suppleness to adapt itself to changing conditions.'[48] Orality was the means by which customary consciousness was transmitted, adapted and reinforced throughout most of the eighteenth and nineteenth centuries in rural England.

Calendrical rights, related to dole or fuel customs, such as Guy Fawkes or 'Bonfire Day' as it was known in nineteenth-century rural England, used oral testimony and ritual to proclaim their legitimacy. 'Remembering the fifth [of] November', in the words of the chant of visitants or collectors of largesse in the streets, was simplified to 'memb'ring' in the popular tongue and, with blackened faces and in costume, householders and passers-by were told that 'memb'ring' was the purpose and that the dole was a legitimate accompaniment to the custom itself.[49] In Lancashire, the popular voice called the date 'Plot Night'.[50] In an example from late Victorian rural Hertfordshire, the verses of the song used on the occasion proclaimed loyal intent by the shout 'God Save the Queen' even though Queen Victoria herself had decided by royal proclamation to drop the '[f]orm of Prayer of thanksgiving to be used yearly upon the fifth day of November, for the happy deliverance of King James I and the Estates of England etc.' from the *Book of Common Prayer* in 1859.[51] The response of plebeian village society was, in part, the evolution of bonfire clubs, especially in the southern counties of England but 'memb'ring' in most cases continued up to and beyond the First World War, with village societies collecting subscriptions, organizing winter carnivals and donning disguise in the form of clowns, Zulus and Red Indians, in order to maintain the social basis of this key pre-Christmas calendrical festival appropriated by popular culture from its original political and state framework, in order to affirm local community loyalties and links against all-comers.[52]

Edwin Grey wrote of his recollections of rural life in Hertfordshire in the 1860s and 1870s. He recalled that 'many of the children left [British and National schools] at 10 years of age to go to work, and as they had then little or no occasion for writing and 'summing, these two accomplishments were commonly lost though the reading of the Bible still remained'. The acquired skills of literacy were not put to use as the world in which they moved was essentially an oral one as was reflected in the richness of life in the hamlets of 'Chapel Row', 'Pimlico', 'Hatching Green' and the 'Bowling Alley' in the southern part of the parish of Harpenden in Grey's childhood.[53]

The oral world to which the railway did not come until 1867 was still one in which gleaners threshed their gleaned wheat in an old barn by flail; where benefits continued such as cherry-gathering, gathering dead wood for fuel, or 'wooding' as it was referred to in the popular tongue, and where the annual Hiring Fair occurred around Michaelmas with labourers wearing the 'badges' of their trades, whipcord for the ploughmen and a wisp of cow hair for the cowmen; ten o'clock provided the opportunity of a short break from labour for 'beever', a word which would have been familiar to John Clare, and the harvest brought with it the extra wages and allowance in beer which made up what the labourers referred to as 'their month' and where gleaners returned to the hamlets with the shout of acclamation which concluded the in-gathering of the crop:

> Wheat, wheat, harvest home
> see what great bundles we bring home.[54]

The oral transmission of knowledge and wisdom held Grey's childhood world together even though his community was entering the late Victorian period. Men were known locally by their nicknames such as 'Clipper Weston', 'Slappy Twidell', 'Wacky Russell' and 'Slenderman Heath'. Words were shortened and pronunciations omitted unnecessary syllables such as the diminutive form most commonly used in speech.[55] The Statute Fair was known locally as 'The Statty Fair'.[56] Alternative wisdom and belief was widespread and 'rough music' was still occasionally to be heard in the hamlets.

Place names also went through a transformation brought about by the popular tongue. Grey recalled that 'The name "Bowling Alley" was hardly ever, amongst this agricultural community, pronounced properly as written. Until then it was spoken as Bow'n' Alley, or more often still as Bow'n' olly, for the labourers would never use long words (if they could possibly avoid it), but would always shorten them'.[57]

Grey's childhood world was a richly oral one in which accent mingled with dialect words and shortened terms to produce a highly local but deeply coloured discourse. In referring to the old word 'flack' meaning to comb, he gives the example of 'A mother would say to her little girl: "come 'ere an' let me flack yer' air out, it's all of a tangle".' But this was distinguished from 'flacking' for quick, sharp movements as in the example of a mother saying to her child 'keep still; don't keep flacking about'.[58] Grey's was a village community in which the village crier, one Tom Lovett, still announced notice of meetings and other important local events.[59] News was still passed by word of mouth rather than through the medium of the local press and the ballad seller was a regular visitor to the village, carrying sensationalist accounts of murders or trials, exactly as would have been recognized by John Clare. Grey remembered that the ballad seller '... would pass slowly along the roadway by the front of houses, singing some harrowing verses made up specially for the occasion, the singer fitting some sort of a drawling tune to the words, the more harrowing and bloodcurdling he could make the sordid theme appear the better in all probability would be the sale of his papers, for many of the people would buy whether they could read it or not; the verses would be there for anybody to read who wished. These verses were printed on single sheets of cheap paper and sold at one penny or halfpenny per sheet.' Grey could even recall the last such ballad seller he encountered, a man 'singing and selling verses relating to the murder of Miss Harriet Lane by Henry Wainright whose terrible murder took place in 1875'.[60]

Information, news, knowledge, the passing of wisdom between generations or of gossip among neighbours was essentially an oral transaction in rural England well towards the end of the nineteenth century. It was not literacy itself but cheap printed alternatives to ballads which ultimately saw their demise.[61] The currency of knowledge in the English village community until the 1920s was the spoken word. Conversation was the natural medium of social intercourse in which local lore and practical wisdom was transferred effortlessly from inhabitant to stranger, parent to child, old labourer to young, neighbour to neighbour and wife to husband. Those outside the nexus of local discourse mistook silence for ignorance or miscomprehended dialect and lore for simplicity. Those who took the trouble to comprehend the meaning could share in the world of oral communication. At the end of the nineteenth century, some mediators such as Alfred Williams and George Sturt attempted to present this world for a middle-class urban readership. The former recorded the comments of the Surrey farmworker Fred Grover, called Bettesworth in Sturt's accounts, at the beginning of the twentieth century: 'Queer anecdotes came from him as plentiful as ever, and shrewd observations. Now it would be of his harvesting in Sussex that he told; now, of an adventure with a troublesome horse, or an experience on the scaffolding of a building, and again he would gossip of his garden, or of his neighbours, or of the old village life, or would discuss some scrap of news picked up at the public-house.'[62] Sturt recorded these conversations for an urban public titillated by rural ways before the First World War. His purpose was clear but this cannot disguise the accuracy of the oral world he described. In one conversation, Sturt noted:

> He touched on scythes for a moment, and then glanced off to name a distant village ... and to tell of a family of blacksmiths who once lived there. 'They used to make purty well all sorts o'edge-tools. And they earned a name fo't, too, didn't they? I've seen as many as four of 'em over there at a axe ... There was one part of making an axe,' said Bettesworth, 'as they'd never let anybody see 'em at.'[63]

Local knowledge was combined with anecdote, observation, practical experience and reflection, in a stream of orally transmitted wisdom. Alfred Williams made no apology to his readership for introducing his untutored voices. 'I am proud of every single one of them', he wrote; 'some of the dialect and narrative may appear a little barbarous to those of refined tastes, but I can assure them it is all accurate and characteristic, typical of the countryside still ... I have found the villagers industrious, sturdy in principle, breezily optimistic, cheerful, philosophic, and exceedingly kind-hearted, but poor ...'.[64] Williams recorded an account of Henry Brusden of Coate who knew Richard Jefferies in the latter's boyhood. 'His memory', wrote Williams, 'is remarkable; he can quote poems and recite rhymes innumerable, and compose them himself, too ...'.[65]

The practice of gleaning was maintained in the hamlets in which Edwin Grey grew up and his recollections of the custom indicate the extent to which this essentially collective activity was organized, maintained and continued within an oral environment. The gleaning gang of the Bowling Alley was organized by Mrs Day '[S]he it was who decided as to our route; to which farm and to which field we should go; the other women told of information obtained from their husbands as to the progress of the harvesting at the respective farms on which they worked, when such and such a field would probably be cleared and so on. This information was discussed and the final decision as to our destination rested upon Mrs Day, and to whichever farm she decided upon, all agreed and so started off.' The timing of gleaning depended critically upon oral information and the accurate judgment of the leader. If too early, the gleaning gang had to wait about before beginning because 'it was an unwritten law that gleaning should not commence until the last shock was carried'. If too late, other gleaning parties would have occupied the field already.[66]

The fourth area where the orality of rural popular culture can be examined concerns the network of community and local lore, 'folk' tales and narratives, histories, explanations and descriptions for the physical environment surrounding the village.[67] Oral culture operated as a form of binding structure in which local lore was a shared resource from which were constructed identities, memories and histories. Orality in rural England in the eighteenth and nineteenth centuries was the medium for the formation and transmission of social memory in which were located the individual, his or her relatives and their neighbours and the local community as a whole. This structure might look like the hierarchy of social strata with which historians of the Victorian countryside are familiar but the common framework was horizontally-organized within an immediate environment whose past, present and future were expressed orally. The oral transmission of local customary culture described the village community in both temporal and spatial terms, and although this structure could be regarded with indifference by those whose social positions led them to withdraw from all but contractual relations with the labouring poor and their families, its manifestations presented themselves regularly in an interconnected world of oral discourse, beliefs and rituals. The naming of the locality, its features, fields, farms, parts and places was fixed in oral culture and the mental map of the community was affirmed in customary consciousness through oral discourse.

Edward Thomas's long evocation of the continuity of rural culture embodied in the universal country figure 'Lob', points to the interconnection of local lore and narrative and the 'naming' of the community's surroundings as the oral fixitive of that culture. He writes:

> Yet Lob has thirteen hundred names for a fool,
> And though he never could spare time for school
> To unteach what the fox so well expressed,
> On biting the cock's head off, – Quietness is best, –
> He can talk quite as well as anyone
> After his thinking is forgot and done.[68]

Thomas's idea that there was an enduring continuity in rural popular culture at the beginning of the twentieth century is a corrective to those who see its demise as entirely brought about before the First World War. The world of John Clare's village of Helpston would not have been unfamiliar to Edwin Grey and Grey's Bowling Alley would have retained both the temporal and spatial ordering, through a vigorous oral popular culture, with which Clare would have been acquainted. Both men shared a customary consciousness which was expressed in oral terms. The customary calendar in rural Hertfordshire in the 1870s, while different in content, was similar in form to Clare's Northamptonshire in the 1790s, having some customary events in common such as May garlanding and the annual fair day when travelling ballad sellers 'hawked' their news. The houses and farms of the hamlets of rural Hertfordshire in the 1870s were visited by midwinter parties of carollers and handbell ringers, Thomasers on 21 December (St Thomas's Day); Christmas boxes were collected, 'memb'rers' went round in disguise on Bonfire Day; and harvest-home feasts took place at the end of the harvest. With the exception of 'memb'ring', these highlights in customary consciousness would not have been out of place in Clare's *Shepherd's Calendar.*

Customary consciousness was maintained and extended by oral culture in eighteenth and nineteenth century rural England, carrying it forward to the First World War. One Lancashire exile, in temporary khaki on the Gallipoli peninsula remembered it was 'plot night' on 5 November 1915 but that there were no fireworks – at least not of the kind he remembered at home.[69] Soldiers recruited from rural England, whether volunteers from 1914 or conscripts from 1916, took with them to war a sophisticated oral culture which provided a coping mechanism for the conditions which they faced in the environment of trench warfare. The alien landscape of the forward area and the front line was 'named' in a detailed way, drawn from memories of localities in England, and Scotland, Ireland and Wales, it should be noted, known to the soldiers themselves. Solidarity was maintained by word and song and alternative beliefs circulated widely.[70] Soldiers whose duties in their rural peacetime occupations had included management of horses, now managed horses for the British Expeditionary Force and, as Ivor Gurney recorded in one of his letters, those who sang and danced at Whitsun and the benefit cub walking, took their songs and dances into the army.

'In this band of ours', Gurney wrote of his service in B Company, 2nd/5th

Gloucestershire Regiment: 'I have discovered a delightful creature. A great broadchested heavy chap who has been a Morris dancer and whose father and grandfathers, uncles and other relations knew all the folk songs imaginable. High Germanie, High Barbary, O no John, I'm seventeen come Sunday – whole piles of 'em. He is a very good player too and a kind of uncle to the band he whistled 'Constant Billy' which I had never before heard.'[71] Gurney calls him 'the Morris dancer of old time, who is alternatively telling stories or answering questions in broad Gloucestershire, and playing cadenzas and hymn-tunes on his trombone'. He was one Fred Bennett, and Gurney recorded a snatch of his music, the lyrics to which might serve as an appropriate testimony to English rural culture before 1914:

> Here's luck to the world as sound as a wheel
> Death is a thing we all must feel.
> If life were a thing that money could buy,
> The rich would live, and the poor would die.[72]

NOTES

1 John Clare, *The Shepherd's Calendar*, ed. Eric Robinson and Geoffrey Summerfield (Oxford: Oxford University Press, 1973), 12.
2 David Vincent, 'The Decline of the Oral Tradition in Popular Culture', in Robert D. Storch (ed.), *Popular Culture and Custom in Nineteenth-century England* (London: Croom Helm, 1982), 31.
3 See Bob Bushaway, *By Rite: Custom, Ceremony and Community in England 1700–1880* (London: Junction Books, 1982).
4 See George Deacon, *John Clare and the Folk Tradition* (London: Sinclair Brown, 1983) and *John Clare's Autobiographical Writings*, ed. Eric Robinson (Oxford: Oxford University Press, 1983). Cf. Claire Lamont '"The Essence and Simplicity of True Poetry: John Clare and Folk-song', in *John Clare Society Journal*, 16 (July 1997), 19–33.
5 Clare, *The Shepherd's Calendar*, 2, 127.
6 Ibid., 18.
7 See *John Aubrey: Three Prose Works*, ed. John Buchanan-Brown (Fontwell: Centaur Press, 1972). Aubrey entitled one of his works 'Remains of Gentilism and Judaism'.
8 Vincent, 'Decline of the Oral Tradition', 36. See also idem, *Literacy and Popular Culture: England 1750–1914* (Cambridge: Cambridge University Press, 1989).
9 See E. P. Thompson, *Customs in Common* (London: Merlin Press, 1991) and Raphael Samuel (ed.), *Village Life and Labour* (London: Routledge & Kegan Paul, 1975).
10 Samuel, *Village Life*, p. xvi.
11 Thompson, *Customs in Common*, 15.
12 Ibid., 8.
13 Barry Reay, *Popular Cultures in England 1550–1750* (London: Longman, 1998), 48.

14 See Bushaway, *By Rite*, for a further discussion; cf. idem, 'Rite, Legitimation and Community in Southern England 1700–1850: the Ideology of Custom', in Barry Stapleton (ed.), *Conflict and Community in Southern England: Essays in the Social History of Rural and Urban Labour from Medieval to Modern Times* (Stroud: Alan Sutton, 1992).

15 See Richard M. Dorson, *The British Folklorists: a History* (London: Routledge & Kegan Paul, 1968).

16 Thompson, *Customs in Common*, 8. See also Andy Wood *The Politics of Social Conflict: the Peak Country 1520–1770* (Cambridge: Cambridge University Press, 1999); idem, 'The Place of Customs in Plebeian Political Cultural: England 1550–1800', *Social History*, 22 (1997), 46–60.

17 For discussions on the nature of oral culture see Jack Goody, *The Interface between the Written and the Oral* (Cambridge: Cambridge University Press, 1987); George Ewart Evans, *Where Beards Wag All: the Relevance of the Oral Tradition* (London: Faber, 1970).

18 Clare, *The Shepherd's Calendar*, 18.

19 See, for example, Penny Fielding, *Writing and Orality: Nationality, Culture and Nineteenth-century Scottish* (Oxford: Clarendon Press, 1996). See also the chapters by Eryn White and Richard Suggett, Donald Meek and Martin MacGregor in this volume.

20 See Jonathan Barry 'Literacy and Literature in Popular Culture: Reading and Writing in Historical Perspective', in Tim Harris (ed.) *Popular Culture in England c. 1500–1850* (London: Macmillan, 1995).

21 J.H. Porter, 'The Development of Rural Society', in G.E. Mingay (ed.), *The Agrarian History of England and Wales* (Cambridge: Cambridge University Press), vol. 6: *1750–1850*, 836–937.

22 Charles Phythian-Adams 'Rural Culture', in G. E. Mingay (ed.), *The Victorian Countryside* (London: Routledge & Kegan Paul, 1981), 2. 624.

23 Laurie Lee, *Cider with Rosie* (London, Penguin Books, 1962), 216: 'the last days of my childhood were also the last days of the village. I belonged to that generation which saw, by chance, the end of a thousand years life. The change came late to our Cotswold village, didn't really show itself till the late 1920s; I was twelve by then, but during that handful of years I witnessed the whole thing happen.'

24 Alfred Williams, *A Wiltshire Village* (London: Duckworth, 1920), 234.

25 Mingay, *Agrarian History*, passim.

26 See Ruth Finnegan, 'Oral Tradition', in D. Levinson and M. Ember (eds), 4 vols *Encyclopaedia of Cultural Anthropology* (New York: Henry Holt, 1996), 3. 887.

27 Ibid., 887–8.

28 Arthur A. Ashby, 'Village Clubs and Associations', in *Journal of the Royal Agricultural Society of England*, 75 (1914), 1–20.

29 Samuel Rudder, *A New History of Gloucestershire* (Cirencester: privately published, 1779), 23–4.

30 Edith Brill, *Life and Tradition on the Cotswolds* (London: Dent, 1973), photograph numbers 234, 235, 238, 243, between pp. 144–5.

31 Clare, *Autobiographical Writings*, ed. Robinson, 2. Adam Fox has shown a similar pattern for early modern England in his book *Oral and Literate Culture in England 1500–1700* (Oxford: Clarendon Press, 2000).

32 Roy Palmer first drew my attention to the prodigious Henry Burstow, for which

information I now record my gratitude. Henry Burstow, *Reminiscences of Horsham: Recollections of Henry Burstow* (Horsham: Bells, 1911), 107–8.

33 Deacon, *John Clare and the Folk Tradition*, 287–90. See also Bob Bushaway, 'Review of John Wardroper (ed.), *The World of William Hone*', in *John Clare Society Journal*, 17 (July 1998), 89–91.

34 For texts and full account see R. Chambers (ed.) *The Book of Days: a Miscellany of Popular Antiquities*, I. (London and Edinburgh: W. and R. Chambers, 1888), 546–9.

35 Ibid. For an account of earlier attitudes to maying see Ronald Hutton, *The Rise and Fall of Merry England: the Ritual Year, 1400–1700* (Oxford: Oxford University Press, 1994).

36 Samuel Bamford, *The Autobiography of Samuel Bamford*, ed. W. H. Chaloner (London: Frank Cass, 1967), vol. 1: *Early Days*, 144.

37 G. F. Northall, *English Folk-rhymes* (London: Kegan Paul, Trench, Trübner, 1892), 239.

38 Flora Thompson, *Lark Rise to Candleford* (Oxford: Oxford University Press, 1945), 196–204.

39 For a detailed description and discussion see Bushaway, *By Rite*: 'The Rituals of Privation and Protest', 167–206.

40 Northall, *English Folk-rhymes*, 216.

41 James Joseph Sheaham, *History and Topography of Buckinghamshire* (London: Longman, Green, Longman & Roberts, 1862), 12.

42 Ibid., 86–7.

43 Ibid., 108.

44 *Parliamentary Papers, 27th Report of the Commissioners Appointed to Inquire into Charities 1834*, 21 April, vol. 225, section xxi, p. 71

45 Sheaham, *History and Topography of Buckinghamshire*, 112.

46 Ibid., 129.

47 See R. W. Bushaway, '"Grovely, Grovely, Grovely and All Grovely": Custom, Crime and Conflict in the English Woodland' *History Today*, 31 (May 1981), 37–45.

48 R. J. Olney, *Rural Society and County Government in Nineteenth-century Lincolnshire* (Lincoln: History of Lincolnshire Committee, 1979), 83, 91.

49 Edwin Grey, *Cottage Life in a Hertfordshire Village* (St Albans: Fisher, Knight, [1935]), 214–15.

50 For Lancashire in the late eighteenth century see Bamford, *Early Days*, 159–60.

51 Grey, *Cottage Life*, 215. See also various rhymes in different parts of England in Northall, *English Folk-rhymes*, 244–50.

52 On 'Bonfire Clubs' see Chris Hare, 'The Skeleton Army and the Bonfire Boys, Worthing, 1884' *Folklore*, 99, 2 (1988), 221–31. James E. Etherington, 'The Community Origin of the Lewes Guy Fawkes Night Celebrations', *Sussex Archaeological Collection*, 128 (1990), 195–224. Gavin Morgan, 'The Guildford Guy Riots (1842–1865)', *Surrey Archaeological Collections*, 76 (1985), 61–8. Robert D. Storch '"Please to Remember the Fifth of November": Conflict, Solidarity and Public Order in Southern England, 1815–1900', in Storch (ed.), *Popular Culture*, 71–99.

53 Grey, *Cottage Life*, 11–12.

54 Ibid., 60–3, 123.

55 Ibid., 25, 40.

56 Ibid., 160, 209, 215.
57 Ibid., 40.
58 Ibid., 41.
59 Ibid., 43.
60 Ibid., 43–4.
61 See Leslie Shephard, *The History of Street Literature* (Newton Abbot: David & Charles, 1973), for a full discussion.
62 George Sturt, *Memoirs of a Surrey Labourer* (London: Duckworth, 1907), iv–v.
63 Ibid., 183.
64 Alfred Williams, *Villages of the White Horse* (London: Duckworth, 1918), vii.
65 Ibid., 124.
66 Grey, *Cottage Life*, 120–1.
67 For folk-tales, the definitive collection is Katherine M. Briggs, *A Dictionary of British Folk Tales in the English Language*, 2 vols (London: Routledge & Kegan Paul, 1971).
68 Edward Thomas, *Poems and Last Poems*, ed. Edna Longley (Plymouth, Macdonald and Evans, 1978), 70.
69 Susan Elandye, 'A Gallipoli Diary', *Lancashire Family History Society*, May (2000), 37. I am indebted to Frank Walmsley for this reference.
70 See John Brophy and Eric Partridge, *The Long Trail: Soldiers' Songs and Slang 1914–18* (London: Sphere Books, 1969).
71 *Ivor Gurney: War Letters*, ed. R. K. R. Thornton (Ashington, Northumberland and Manchester: Mid-Northumberland Arts Group–Carcanet, 1983), 38.
72 Ibid., 44. The particular significance of these words is their source. They comprise the final verse of a well-known folksong, *Death and the Lady*, having origins in the seventeenth century, when it was first published as a broadside by J. Deacon, sometime between 1683 and 1700. It was a regular item in the oral tradition and was collected in many places in the last decade of the nineteenth century. Known in another version as *Lord Lovel* it is to be found in Francis Child's *The English and Scottish Popular Ballads* (New York: Dover, 1965), II, no. 75, at 204–13. Another version is to be found in Cecil J. Sharp *English Folk Songs* (London: Novello, 1920), 96. The note given on p. xxvi cites information on other versions. Thus, these words have moved between printed and oral versions across more than three centuries in order for Gurney to encounter them from Fred Bennett, the Morris dancer in 1915.

Index